RICHARD BAXTER AND THE MILLENNIUM

CROOM HELM SOCIAL HISTORY SERIES

General Editors

PROFESSOR J.F.C. HARRISON and STEPHEN YEO
University of Sussex

CLASS AND RELIGION IN THE
LATE VICTORIAN CITY
Hugh McLaod

THE INDUSTRIAL MUSE
Martha Vicinus

CHRISTIAN SOCIALISM AND
CO-OPERATION IN VICTORIAN
ENGLAND
Philip N. Backstrom

CONQUEST OF MIND
David de Giustino

THE ORIGINS OF BRITISH
INDUSTRIAL RELATIONS
Keith Burgess

THE VOLUNTEER FORCE
Hugh Cunningham

RELIGION AND VOLUNTARY
ORGANISATIONS IN CRISIS
Stephen Yeo

CHOLERA 1832
R.J. Morris

WORKING-CLASS RADICALISM
IN MID-VICTORIAN ENGLAND
Trygve Tholfsen

THE COLLIERS' RANT
Robert Colls

YOUTH EMPIRE AND SOCIETY
John Springhall

THE ORIGINS OF BRITISH
BOLSHEVISM
Raymond Challinor

THE MERTHYR RISING
Gwyn A. Williams

KEIR HARDIE: THE MAKING OF
A SOCIALIST
Fred Reid

SEPARATE SPHERES: THE
OPPOSITION TO WOMEN'S
SUFFRAGE IN BRITAIN
Brian Harrison

THE RISE OF THE VICTORIAN
ACTOR
Michael Baker

AN ARTISAN ELITE IN
VICTORIAN SOCIETY
Geoffrey Crossick

THE PEOPLE'S HEALTH,
1830-1910
F.B. Smith

INDUSTRIAL CONFLICT IN
MODERN BRITAIN
James E. Cronin

RICHARD BAXTER AND THE MILLENNIUM

PROTESTANT IMPERIALISM AND
THE ENGLISH REVOLUTION

WILLIAM M. LAMONT

CROOM HELM LONDON
ROWMAN AND LITTLEFIELD TOTOWA N.J.

© 1979 William M. Lamont
Croom Helm Ltd, 2-10 St John's Road, London SW11

LAMONT, WILLIAM MONTGOMERY
    Richard Baxter and the Millennium
1. Baxter,R, b.1615
2. Millennium − History of Doctrines
I. Title
236'. 3'0924   BX5207.B3
ISBN 0-85664-999-6

First published in the United States 1979 by
Rowman and Littlefield
81 Adams Drive
Totowa, New Jersey

ISBN 0-8476-6189-X

Printed in Great Britain by
Biddles Ltd, Guildford, Surrey

CONTENTS

For LINDA
    Catriona, Ailsa and Tara

How much he hath benefited in these studies he hath endeavoured to give the World an account in a multitude of books, which he voides continually. Joachimus Fortius, who was resolved to write a booke every yeare while he lived, was but a slight pretender in comparison to Mr. Baxter's works — Henry Stubbe, *Malice Rebuked* . . . (London, 1659), p. 13.

To Matthew Sylvester: 'You tell us some of his Papers cannot be found. Good news!' — Samuel Young, *Vindiciae Anti-Baxterianae* (London, 1696), dedicatory epistle.

INTRODUCTION

This book concludes a trilogy on English Puritanism. *Marginal Prynne* (1963) studied the writings of a Puritan lawyer, William Prynne. *Godly Rule* (1969) explored the influence of ideas of Christ's Second Coming and the destruction of Rome upon English Protestants in the seventeenth century. *Richard Baxter and the Millennium* combines both the biographical and the apocalyptic: it studies the writings of another Puritan, the minister Richard Baxter, in the light of his interest in the Book of Revelation.

There is a symmetry about the process — biography, essay on millennium, biography plus essay on millennium — which would have been more pleasing if it had been planned. This was not the case. When I wrote about Prynne I had no idea of the power that images from the Book of Revelation could exercise over men as fuddy-duddy and hierarchical as he was. I was at something of a loss to explain his mood on the brink of the Civil War. The words I used were revealing: 'ethical craving', 'expectant rejoicing', 'radical', 'messianic recklessness'. The word which I avoided like the plague was 'millenarian'. Why? Because I then shared the common belief of the time that men who awaited Christ's Second Coming, and who took the prophetic books seriously, must belong to the lunatic fringe of society. By the time I wrote *Godly Rule* I was wanting to argue quite differently: not merely that it was possible for conservative gentlemen like Prynne to be moved by the Apocalypse, but that it was impossible to understand how the great English Revolution had happened without such a recognition. Since the study which now follows is based upon the recovery of Richard Baxter's apocalyptic papers, it would at least appear that *Richard Baxter and the Millennium* is the logical extension of themes which had been discussed in *Godly Rule*. But the progression is no more logical than that between *Marginal Prynne* and *Godly Rule*. Baxter was an exception to my *Godly Rule*: he was described in that book as a sceptic of millenarian ideas. This was how he appeared in Christopher Hill's *Antichrist in Seventeenth-Century England*: another work which cast the millenarian net wide, but not wide enough to include Baxter. In both *Godly Rule* and *Antichrist in Seventeenth-Century England* there is also the assumption that interest in the millennium tailed off after the Restoration; yet we shall see that the bulk of Baxter's writing on the Book of Revelation dates from 1686.

Not only are there contradictions between the three works, and places where I have radically changed my mind; the problems posed by each were quite different. There have been few biographies of Prynne; there was little in the way of personal unpublished material although much in the way of printed pamphlets. With Baxter almost the opposite is true. There is no shortage of biographies, even of good ones. There is a wealth of personal manuscript material, much of it curiously untapped. Baxter had written almost as much as Prynne in the way of pamphlets, but it is possible to test this record against his private correspondence in a way which was not possible for Prynne. Stereotypes, however, condition the historian's response as much as source material. With Prynne I had to get behind the image of the fanatic. Not that his career was untinged with fanaticism, but when I sought to explain his attitude to Civil War, regicide, Commonwealth and Restoration I found it in the confused responses of a moderate, conservative, royalist Anglican. With Baxter I have tried to escape the oppression of his sainthood. Not that there are not saintly passages in his career, but they do not explain why he reacted in the way that *he* did to Civil War, regicide, Commonwealth and Restoration. Thus I had to penetrate behind the 'fanatical' Prynne and the 'saintly' Baxter to what they had in common, while at the same time I had to recognise that neither description was itself illusory, only that it was irrelevant as an explanation of why they had adopted critical attitudes at different stages in the English Revolution.

The book which follows is no more a conventional biography of Baxter than my first book was of Prynne. What I have done in both books — and in the intervening *Godly Rule* — is to try to understand the English Revolution through its Puritan protagonists. No protagonist was more celebrated than Baxter. He was at the heart of great events: the seemingly cool observer and commentator on the Civil War; the man who blew cold and hot during the Commonwealth years of experiment; the victim of Restoration bigotry; the embodiment of what Weber and Tawney understood as the Protestant Ethic. To read him afresh is to read the English Revolution afresh; or that at least is the claim which the rest of this book will try to make good. And the inquiry begins at the end of Baxter's career, in a prison cell.

This book is about an improbable union. In 1686 Richard Baxter and the millennium came together. The Puritan minister was then aged seventy. He had been in prison for more than a year. He was visited by Matthew Henry who pronounced him, in a letter to his father, as 'alive

and one would think that were all'.[1] He was not to be released for a
further eight months after Henry's visit. In these conditions Baxter
nevertheless managed to read and write more than in any other comparable period of an exceptionally strenuous life. That was the judgement of his biographer, F.J. Powicke, who may even so have underrated his achievement. For a study of a number of his published works
in 1690 and 1691 – the last two years of his life – shows how much he
drew upon the capital of those prison years. The main focus of his
inquiries was the Book of Revelation. The last years of his life were
spent in resolving the question whether Jesus Christ would return on
Earth to inaugurate a thousand-year reign of His Saints in the imminent future. On two counts this union of Baxter with the millennium is
improbable. It comes at a time when the conventional wisdom is that
millenarianism had become 'a harmless hobby for cranky country parsons'.[2] It challenges Baxter's self-portrait – lovingly endorsed in a
number of carefully researched biographies – of a man who had largely
overcome by the end of his life the wounding combativeness of his
earlier years of controversy, and whose intellectual development could
be paraphrased, in the words of the foremost student of religious toleration, as a 'progess towards latitudinarianism'.[3] Neither of these judgements is borne out by a close study of the material of his declining
years. And behind both judgements lie false preconceptions about both
the millennium and the man.

First, the myth about the millennium. Traditionally, interest in the
Second Coming of Christ was linked with radical subversive groups.
Orthodox Christianity offered the Kingdom of God in the hereafter:
the poor would get their reward in heaven. The Digger, Gerrard Winstanley, commented:

> And yet they tell the poor people that they must be content with
> their poverty, and they shall have the heaven hereafter. But why
> may not we have our heaven here (that is, a comfortable livelihood
> in the earth) and heaven hereafter too, as well as you.[4]

Norman Cohn's study, *The Pursuit of the Millennium*, shows how
throughout the Middle Ages earlier Winstanleys had asked that same
question and found their answer in the Apocalypse: in visions of a perfect society in which the poor would come into their own.[5] There were
other ways of making sense of the mysterious allusions in the prophetic
books, which defused such revolutionary implications. One way was to
claim that the major prophecies referred back to the first century or

two of the Christian era. This preterist interpretation was put forward by the Jesuit, Alcasar, and accepted by Grotius. Another way was to say, as the Catholic writer Bellarmine did, that the prophecies referred exclusively to the very end of history. This futurist interpretation had Antichrist reigning for three-and-a-half years in the Last Days. Neither reading was attractive to Protestants, especially the latter one. The futurist interpretation offered an escape clause to the Pope, which was why a Protestant like James Durham dismissed it as a dream invented by the Roman Catholics 'to keep the Pope from being apprehended as the true Antichrist'.[6]

But there was a third Protestant way of reading prophecy which avoided either Catholic error and yet stamped on simplistic solutions of 'a world turned upside down'. This historicist interpretation of prophecy was embodied in the earliest defences of the English Reformation: that the prophecies of Daniel in the Old Testament and Revelation in the New Testament, when opened by skilled commentators, revealed a continuous historical process. At its heart was the struggle of Pope and Emperor. It was possible, by reading the symbols right, to trace throughout English history the nature of that conflict and to find, in the English Reformation, the supreme expression of the concept of Christian Empire.

A number of gifted Tudor propagandists developed this apocalyptic defence of the claims of the civil magistrate against the Papacy. The earliest may have been John Bale, but the greatest was incontestably John Foxe. Baxter, poring over the Apocalypse in 1686, is a less eccentric figure when we see him – as he saw himself – as a pupil of Foxe, and not as a secret Fifth Monarchist or Anabaptist.

Only in recent years has full justice begun to be done to the reputation of Foxe.[7] We have had to recover him from the nineteenth-century idolatry of the man who had given them their *Book of Martyrs*. Their *Book of Martyrs* was not his *Acts and Monuments*: it was the story of the Marian martyrs largely, with the boring bits left out. But the boring bits provided the eschatological reading of history which men in the sixteenth and seventeenth centuries were unable to ignore. The third English edition in 1576 ran to 2,008 folios, yet it was not until the 1583 version that Foxe included full details of the Marian persecution. This was the last edition to appear in his lifetime, and in the next hundred years was to be reprinted five times.

Foxe had begun his record of the sufferings of the persecuted from the origins of Christianity, when he himself was a Marian exile in Strasbourg in 1554. In other words, the first volume largely antedated the

Marian persecutions, and the title page makes clear his intention to deal
with the whole of Europe, and not merely England. The 1554 edition
of the first volume took the story of persecution in England from
Wycliffe to about 1500. Five years later Foxe was able to continue
events to 1547 in the Basle edition. Thus Foxe did not construct a
philosophy to provide a decorative framework for the narrative of
sufferings; the Marian martyrs' sufferings are fitted in — almost as an
afterthought — to substantiate the philosophy. This is not to deny the
appeal of the work at a simple popular level of anti-Catholicism; reinforced by the crudely effective woodcuts. But it was not for its assault
on Popery that Queen Elizabeth I ordered it to be one of the four
chained books in every parish church in England. It was, quite simply,
the best monarchist propaganda that a Protestant Englishman had ever
written.

Foxe traced five periods of Church history which had been foretold
in the Book of Revelation. The first was the time of persecution of
Christians under the heathen Emperors; then came the time of glory
under the first Christian Emperor, Constantine; next, decline under the
Roman Church; fourth, Antichristian enormities under the Hildebran-
dine Papacy. Foxe believed that he was writing in the fifth period, of
the last struggle between Christ and Antichrist. Henry VIII was the rein-
carnation of Constantine. The dark Marian interlude was Antichrist's
reply. But another Constantine, Queen Elizabeth, had come in answer
to Latimer's prayers. For all its detailed horrors, it is this imperial
comfort which is the book's lasting message.

Very swiftly man and myth became intertwined. At the end of the
seventeenth century Baxter was no more successful than his peers in
disentangling some of the complexities of Foxe's legacy. Perhaps his
two greatest influences on English Protestants were in inspiring generations after him to re-read the Books of Daniel and Revelation for prophetic insights and for detestation of Popery. But he himself was neither
intolerant nor, in the technical sense, a millenarian. His tolerance was
well in advance of his age: the opponent at different times of the Puritan bigots at Magdalene College, of the Calvinist Inquisitors who burned
Servetus, and of the destroyers of the Jesuit martyr, Edmund Campion,
and one of the few men to have a good word to say for the Dutch
Anabaptists in London in 1575. And his millennium was located in the
past. It had begun with the accession of the Emperor Constantine, and
ended around AD 1300. He is conscious certainly of writing in the Last
Days, and the pattern appears to lead directly to the Last Judgement.
There is no culminating vision of a New Jerusalem. But that is not the

whole story. Dr Marjorie Reeves has demonstrated the debt of Bale, Foxe and other sixteenth-century Protestants to a medieval Catholic source: the prophetic writings of Joachim of Fiore. Of Foxe she says that, although not a millenarian, 'he used the prophetic tradition to read the signs of the new age dawning.' And she notes how 'he gives a sense of history rising to a positive climax before the end, rather than of dissolving into failure'.[8] It is Foxe's amillennial historicism which would exercise so profound an appeal upon Baxter in the next century.

Other men of the seventeenth century learned other lessons from Foxe, not always correctly. They drew from him the conviction of England's special destiny in God's Plan as His Elect Nation, although we have seen the intended European dimension of the original work. Ralph Josselin never sounds more Foxeian than when he writes this entry into his diary on 17 November 1650, Queen Elizabeth's accession day: 'my thoughts much that God was beginning to ruine the kingdome of the earth, and bringing Christs kingdome in, and wee English should bee very instrumentall therein.'[9] Yet Josselin, like Foxe himself and Baxter too, had no time for the vulgar peddlers of millenarian dreams, who even dared to name the year of Christ's Second Coming. Men of the seventeenth century also credited Foxe with having unmasked Rome as Antichrist. But even this is not wholly true. Foxe thought that Rome was *an* Antichrist, but that the Turk was *the* Antichrist. This was the insight which Baxter would recover with telling effect in his revisionist studies of 1686.

Not all these ironies and complexities could be ignored by Protestant commentators who followed Foxe. There were at least three embarrassing legacies. He had located the millennium in the past; he had identified reform over-closely with the civil magistrate (tolerable perhaps in the reign of Elizabeth, less so in the reigns of James I and Charles I); many of the prophecies within the Books of Daniel and Revelation were left by him uncorrelated and seemingly self-contradictory. The two most important revisionists of Foxe were Thomas Brightman and Joseph Mede. Brightman offered a double millennium. He grafted on to Foxe's past millennium a second, stretching from AD 1300 to AD 2300. If some of the years of the second millennium were located in the past, the bulk still lay in the future. And Brightman, with his notable reassessment of the figure of Constantine, began the process of detaching the Apocalypse from its imperial associations. Milton's tutor at Cambridge, Mede, performed the outstanding intellectual feat of tying up the loose ends in apocalyptic prophecy, and correlating symbols, times and events within each prophecy. In the first half of the seventeenth century Mede had the stature of Newton in the second half. And Newton, when engaged in similar researches into the Apocalypse, was profoundly reverential of Mede's achievement.[10] It is not easy to think of many other instances when Newton was so magnanimous to a fellow scholar.

Newton could respect Mede, because their common pursuit of the millennium seemed to him a sober pursuit for the highest minds of the age. Bale, Foxe, Brightman and Mede had between them made the millennium respectable. To uncover the mysteries of the Apocalypse was not the necessary preliminary step to turning the world upside down.

This rapid summary of mainstream Protestant involvement with the millennium puts Baxter's researches in proper perspective. If he chose to study Revelation in prison in 1686 he did so in good seventeenth-century company. If he also wished to keep these studies secret, this also was perfectly intelligible. Nobody who studied the Apocalypse, however sober, conservative and proper they were, could fail to be aware of the damaging effect upon less tutored minds of such speculations. Munster, in the early sixteenth century, was the classic horror story for all cautious persons of the violence and rapine that could be unleashed when peasants read Revelation. And that horror story was reinforced by the Fifth Monarchist risings in 1657 and 1661 in England. What has sometimes been taken to be a diminution of interest in the Apocalypse after the Restoration may simply have been a more effective concealment of interests which had perforce to be driven underground. Newton himself kept his studies into Revelation secret; the fate of Fatio, his surrogate son, who ended up on the stocks at the beginning of the eighteenth century for a rash commitment to the wild millenarianism of the Cévennes prophets, was sufficient warning.

But it was not fear of being lumped with the wild men in a witch-hunt which caused Baxter to keep secret his studies into the Apocalypse. In Revelation, Protestants had found their identification of Rome with Antichrist. In 1686 a Roman Catholic ruled England, and Protestant opponents were being subjected to harassment. The imprisonment of Baxter was a warning to all enemies of Catholicism. Baxter was not the only student of Revelation who was prepared for combat with Rome at this time. Newton was simultaneously engaged in a courageous venture in university politics against Catholicism and his biographer tells us that Henry More, with whom he had discussed the prophetic books in 1680, also feared Papist retribution: 'Once Richard Baxter was imprisoned, the author of *A Modest Enquiry into the Mystery of Ini-*

quity and *The Antidote against Idolatry* could not rest secure.'[11] This comment obscures what is really most puzzling about Baxter's prison researches. Henry More, fellow student of the Apocalypse, did not see him as a fellow victim of Popery. On the contrary, More attacked Baxter for the comfort which he gave to Papists. This was not how Baxter saw his contribution, and his prison manuscripts are largely devoted to refuting More's charges. To understand how two such different views could be held about Baxter's researches it is necessary to turn from myths about the millennium to myths about Baxter.

The main biographical details can be swiftly recounted. He was born in 1615 in the village of Rowton in Shropshire. This was the parental home of his mother, Beatrice Adeney, and it was there that he spent the first ten years of his life. It was not until 1626 that he moved to his parents' home at Eaton Constantine, some ten miles from Rowton. In 1634 his mother died. Two years later his father, also named Richard, married Mary Huncks. His father died in 1663, but his stepmother lived on until 1680 and was a decisive influence on his life.

Baxter described his father as 'a mean Freeholder' with an estate 'entangled by Debts'. Although he had wanted to go to university, his father was persuaded by his schoolmaster John Owen that the route to advancement was through the patronage of Richard Wickstead, Chaplain to the Council of the Welsh Marches at Ludlow. The move was a bad one, as was a brief period at Court in the service of Sir Henry Herbert, Minister of the Revels. His personal piety alienated him from both Ludlow and Whitehall; his spiritual home was found in the company of fellow zealous Nonconformists in Shrewsbury between 1634 and 1638. In December 1638 he was ordained a deacon and became headmaster of a school at Dudley. In the autumn of 1640 he became assistant master at Bridgnorth in Shropshire, where he led the opposition to the new requirement of clergy that they should swear an oath never to attempt alteration in the contemporary diocesan Episcopal government. In April 1641 he became lecturer at Kidderminster in Worcestershire, and shocked many people there by rejecting infant baptism. He sided with Parliament when the Civil War broke out and retired first to Gloucester (where he began his life-long friendship with John Corbet) and then to Coventry (where he encountered a mad millenarian, Major Wilkie, and an equally mad Anabaptist, Abiezer Coppe). It was to combat such sectarian influences, which were robbing the Parliamentary cause of its moral status, that Baxter became chaplain in 1645 in his friend Edward Whalley's regiment. The breakdown of his health led to convalescence at Rous-Lench in Worcestershire. There he began writing *The Saints Ever-*

lasting Rest, only to break off to write a separate work, his *Aphorismes of Justification*. This was published in 1649: the first of over 140 pamphlets.

Much of the history of his years before 1649 has to be culled from his own retrospective memoirs or second-hand sources. After that date not only do we have a constant flow of printed works from Baxter, but also a voluminous personal correspondence and private papers in manuscript form. During the Commonwealth period he attacked Papists, Baptists and Quakers but worked for a more ecumenical spirit through the Association of Ministers which he began in Worcestershire. He was not among the 'reconciling' ministers, however, who went to the Netherlands to accompany Charles II back into England. But he became a Chaplain to the King in June 1660, and was offered a Bishopric, which he declined. He prepared the 'Reformed Liturgy' for the Savoy Conference in 1661, but was deprived of his ministry at Kidderminster when the 'Laudian' counter-revolution was successfully executed. He had stopped preaching before the St Bartholomew's Day ejection of ministers who would not conform to the Bill for Uniformity. Two weeks later he married Margaret Charlton, 21 years his junior. The depth of their relationship is movingly recalled in his memoir of her, written after her death in 1681. Equally revealing are the frequent but oblique allusions to her in letters by him to correspondents, who shared her curse of a melancholic nature. Retirement to Acton was softened by the friendship of Sir Matthew Hale there, whose influence probably lay behind his release from arrest in 1669 for violating the provisions of the Five Mile Act when he held 'conventicles' at Acton. A year later, Baxter and his wife moved to Totteridge to join his Gloucester friend, John Corbet, and his wife. In 1673, following the Declaration of Indulgence, the Baxters returned to London when the Corbets moved to Chichester. The Test Act followed on the Declaration of Indulgence, and warrants for Baxter's arrest were issued in 1675. In the erratic politics of the 1670s, Anglican attempts to silence him, which were often thwarted by his wife's resourcefulness, alternated with efforts to reach an accommodation, in which sympathetic Anglicans like Wilkins and Tillotson played key roles. Nevertheless by the time of the Popish Plot and Exclusion Crisis, Baxter had become disenchanted with the Church of England to the point when — for the first time in his life — he could seriously project a sectarian future for himself and his Protestant colleagues. At this dark point in his life — with his wife, stepmother, Corbet and Hale all dead — he found that old indiscretions were being raked up against him by his enemies. The greatest of these indiscretions was his *Holy Commonwealth* of 1659, not only for its flowery dedication to Richard Cromwell, but for its hostility to Charles I in a book written ostensibly against democracy. These 'Political Aphorismes' (its alternative title) were ordered to be burned, along with writings of Milton and Hobbes, in a decree of Oxford University in 1683. But it was a new work, his *Paraphrase on the New Testament* of 1684, which ultimately secured his trial and imprisonment in 1685. In his news-sheet, *The Observator*, Roger L'Estrange attacked it as a covert incitement to rebellion. This was the interpretation which Judge Jeffreys endorsed at his trial. Of his life after the sentence had been served, little need be said. He took a house in Finsbury in February 1687 and assisted Matthew Sylvester (his friend and later official biographer) with occasional sermons. He maintained a determinedly low political profile until the Glorious Revolution, but welcomed the accession of William III and Mary. He died on 6 December 1691 and was buried, alongside his wife, in Christ Church, Newgate.

What difference does it make to an understanding of Baxter to know that a large part of his declining years was spent in restating John Foxe? The first point to make is how little attention has been given in previous studies of Baxter to this prison material. We have seen one exception in F.J. Powicke who devoted four pages to itemising the main manuscript collection in 1686 (including his inquiries into the Apocalypse). But four pages in a two-volume biography is far from prodigality. Even then he added: 'There is not space to enlarge on his achievements, else a very interesting chapter could be added to the history of Books written in prison.' What clearly interested Powicke was not *what* he wrote, but *how much* he wrote. To produce in such quantities in such conditions was a tribute to the resilience of the human spirit; the content was of secondary importance. Something of Powicke's prejudice against the use of manuscript materials for his biography of Baxter comes out in the words:

> The existence of these has been no secret. They have long been known and to some small extent have been used. But thirteen folio volumes of close writing, often not easy to decipher, and quite as often concerned with things utterly dead and done with, may well have seemed rather a forbidding task, nor do I pretend to have had either the time or the will to explore the whole mass. I have simply looked it through with more or less care.[12]

Probably the legibility of Baxter's hand had less to do with the neglect of the manuscript material than the conviction that they were 'concerned with things utterly dead and done with'. Even the most recent scholar to draw attention to the apocalyptic material, Mr Roger Thomas, simultaneously plays down its significance. He commented:

> Much of the material Baxter must have intended to publish; that he never did so is of interest; indeed an interesting study could be made of the books Baxter did not publish and of the reasons why he did not publish them.

His explanation for the failure of Baxter to publish his apocalyptic material is that 'age probably prevented his publishing this sobering challenge to the wild men of his day.'[13] This will not do on a number of counts. Age did not prevent *some* of the material from being published in his pamphlets of 1691, *The Glorious Kingdom of Christ*, and *A Reply to Mr. Thomas Beverley's Answer*. He did not *want* his challenge to be published as a whole; there are strict instructions to his literary executors to keep the material secret. He was not attacking 'the wild men of his day'. He was attacking men whom he called 'Conformists', in particular the Cambridge Platonist Henry More, whom he respected, and his fellow Nonconformist prisoner, Thomas Beverley, whom he loved (and who was far from happy at being bracketed with More as a 'Conformist' by Baxter).[14]

There is a more interesting way of domesticating Baxter's interest in the Apocalypse than by claiming it to be a defence against fanaticism. The tone was set by Coleridge, who saw Baxter as a good man who had fallen into the seventeenth century. He alternated between praising Baxter for rising above his age and chiding him for being part of it. That tone of baffled geniality comes out well in his comments on Baxter's fascination with the occult:

> Hence the good man was ever craving for some morsel out of the almsbasket of all external events, in order to prove to himself his own immortality; and with grief and shame, I tell it, became evidence and authority in Irish stories of ghosts, and apparitions, and witches.[15]

Something of the same balance is struck by the best recent studies of Baxter. His millennial interests are not ignored in these works (as they would be in mere hagiography) any more than his interests in witchcraft, dreams, ghosts and strange noises in the night. But they are accommodated within a portrait of a clergyman accessible to nine-teenth-century Nonconformists: 'a representative of Puritanism at its central, modest best'; one who 'from the beginning displayed a remark-able liberalism and breadth of mind'; 'a Pen in God's Hand'; one who chose consistently 'the "mixed" species of government'; one whose compelling singleness of purpose is to be found in his dedication 'to the cause of Christian unity'.[16] Not all of his contemporaries would have recognised this irenic figure: certainly not the contemporary critic who summed up Baxter's career as 'The Saints Everlasting Contention'. Nor for that matter Bishop Stillingfleet, once Baxter's ally and then his enemy, who noted that, while peace and concord figured prominently on the title page of Baxter's works, the inside pages invariably breathed war and disharmony.[17]

But there is a sense in which the later biographers of Baxter see further than his contemporary opponents. It was easier to be Olympian if one was not the recipient of Baxter's barbs, of course, but there is also a real sense in which later critics could see how much that was generous in Baxter was falsified only by the conventions of the age. R.B. Schlatter and F.J. Powicke lamented Baxter's lapses into anti-Popish vulgarity, although Powicke detected a mellowing of spirit in his refusal to call the Pope Antichrist in 1684. W.K. Jordan qualified his general picture of Baxter's evolution towards eighteenth-century Lati-tudinarianism by remarking on his cruelty towards Catholics, but he put even that into the context of his age: 'England cannot yet afford the luxury of Roman Catholic toleration.'[18] To discard the seventeenth-century dross — the prejudices and contentiousness of that age, the love of bad puns, credulity about witches, dabbling in the occult, identifying Antichrist in prophecy — and to extract the residual gold — the piety which has moved Christians throughout the next three hundred years — does not seem a very discreditable exercise. It is what Professor Collin-son has described as the 'vertical' approach favoured by the 'religious, denominationally committed historians'.[19] I know no better demonstra-tion of the effectiveness of the 'vertical' approach to Baxter than a small lecture of 1951 by Geoffrey Nuttall entitled *Richard Baxter and Philip Doddridge*. Significantly subtitled 'A Study in a Tradition', it explores in a moving way Baxter's influence on eighteenth-century followers and hails him as 'a pioneer, before his time'.[20] And not only upon followers in the eighteenth century. In the Barbican House library in Lewes is lodged the diary of James Nye. He was a self-educated gard-ener, born at Chiltington, who spent most of his working life at Ash-combe House in Kingston, near Lewes, in Sussex (now the official

residence of the Vice-Chancellor of the University of Sussex). About
1852 he underwent a crisis of faith. His diary records how Baxter's
A Call to the Unconverted became one of the two books which 'set
me to work for life with all my might'.[21] This was how Baxter's teachings worked upon Nye two hundred years later. The strength of the
'vertical' approach is in recognising the force of this influence. Dr
Nuttall's lecture reinforces Professor Collinson's comment that 'those
who write from within the tradition with theological awareness and
spiritual sensitivity, have much the better chance of getting it right.'

But there is another way of looking at Baxter, and it is this way
which is followed in the rest of this book. The 'horizontal' approach is
an attempt to set Baxter in his contemporary context; not to emphasise
the special qualities of the man, which made his writings precious to a
nineteenth-century gardener faced with a spiritual crisis, but rather to
emphasise the qualities which he had in common with other men of his
time. The very readiness of the nineteenth-century Nonconformist to
see affinities with the experiences of the seventeenth-century Puritan
is, from this angle of vision, a delusion. It can be argued that the analogy of Victorian Nonconformity with Stuart Puritanism has done more
to cloud our understanding of the English Revolution than any other
single factor. Twentieth-century historians who show the falsity of
treating the Great Rebellion as S.R. Gardiner's 'Puritan Revolution'[22]
are demonstrating not that religion counted for less than their Victorian
predecessors had assumed but that it was not the religion of constitu-
tionally-minded nineteenth-century evangelicals which made men tick
in the seventeenth century. At its worst the 'horizontal' approach can
be a reductionist game: Baxter's sameness with his contemporaries is
seen as a diminishing trait. But Baxter's sameness with those who came
after him may also demean in a more subtle way. The very accessibility
of Baxter to later generations may represent a failure of the historical
imagination. The historian's loss may be the sociologist's gain. At the
heart of the Tawney/Weber thesis of the relationship between capitalism and the Protestant Ethic is the assumption that Baxter spoke for a
later age. Literary re-creations accentuate this effect. When Robert
Graves writes *Wife to Mr. Milton* he thinks that he has recalled the
seventeenth century for us when he has, in fact, restored the intellectual
and emotional milieu of *The Way of all Flesh*. The paradox is that the
'horizontal' approach can serve best by restoring *a sense of inaccessibil-
ity*. The world where the King is equated with God and the Pope with
Antichrist; where witches fly in the night and women give birth to
monsters; where Jesuits peddle lies and the Apocalypse conveys truths

– this was not what S.R. Gardiner had in mind when he wrote of the 'Puritan Revolution'. But this is the world of Richard Baxter. Weber and Tawney did not use Baxter crudely as a football in a sociological polemic; we shall see how sympathetic their portraits of him are. If ultimately they get him wrong it is because of an imaginative failure to enter his world. They both rely too much on a single source, his *Christian Directory*, and ignore other writings by him. More damaging still, Tawney thought that interest in the millennium ended for most English Protestants with Oliver Cromwell's short-lived experiment in rule by Saints, the Barebone's Parliament. That his son's Protectorate could inspire similar hopes in the cautious Baxter, and that these hopes could be revived so dramatically for him in prison in 1686, were left out of Tawney's calculations when he sought to characterise the response of Protestantism in the later seventeenth century to the rise of capitalism.

The book which follows is, therefore, a 'horizontal' view of Richard Baxter. It is not a biography. Its analysis is limited to four themes. These are the subjects of the first four chapters of the book. I want now to outline each of these themes in turn.

The first chapter discusses Baxter's involvement with the Apocalypse in 1686 and is based upon his manuscripts in prison. I begin with Baxter's quarrel with Henry More, because this was the inspiration for his researches on the millennium. The curiosity about the quarrel is that it began with Baxter's public denial in 1684 that the Pope was Antichrist. Powicke had thought that this showed a weakening of anti-Catholic bigotry; Henry More thought that it revealed a dangerous scepticism about the value of prophecy to Protestant Englishmen. Both judgements were wrong, but in order to prove the last charge wrong, Baxter dug deeper into apocalyptic speculation than he had ever done before. This involved no major departure for him any more than it did for More, however: the imagery of the Apocalypse was as legitimate a challenge to the scientific spirit as the apparitions, haunted houses and strange sounds in the night which had been an earlier common interest of both men. More's failure to recognise this common ground was a particular grievance to Baxter. He had admired More's early works on apparitions and on Antichrist. Because Baxter had given up believing in the Pope as Antichrist it did not follow – as More seemed to think – that he had given up believing in witches or ghosts or in the value of apocalyptic study itself. Both Baxter and More knew how such studies could be abused by the credulous: hence their insistence on a scientific approach to the investigation of 'strange providences'. Science could expose the charlatan, but the millennium posed other dangers which

Baxter indicated in his prison manuscripts. The greatest of these dangers was, paradoxically, to men who were good. It was good men and women who were afflicted with 'melancholia' who could be imposed upon. That is why a study of his correspondence with Mrs Gell is so revealing in this context. With so much in common More and Baxter nevertheless divided on the identification of Antichrist. To More an abyss had opened between them. Baxter did not take it so seriously, because his commitment to what others besides More had seen as a Protestant article of faith had never been absolute. This is shown by the variety of approaches which Baxter adopts, in public pamphlets and in private correspondence between the years 1653 and 1684, to the question of whether or not Rome is Antichrist. Baxter corresponds in prison with three Protestant millenarians, Thomas Beverley, Drue Cressener and Increase Mather. All three side with More against Baxter on the identification of the Pope as Antichrist, and seek to change Baxter's mind. Unlike More, however, they treat the difference as one not serious enough to constitute a permanent rift between them. Mather even urges Baxter to publish his writings, faults and all, as a contribution to a scholarly understanding of the millennium; as late as 1690 and 1691, Thomas Beverley and Baxter are engaged in a three-way correspondence with Edward Harley on the interpretation of the Apocalypse.[23] In the last section of the first chapter a summary is given of the positive insights which Baxter has derived from studying Revelation. The two most critical of these are his revaluation of 'National Churches' and his renewed understanding of what John Foxe had meant by 'Christian Empire'.

The second chapter takes up a second theme: Baxter's explanation of the origins of the English Civil War. The transition seems more abrupt and illogical than is the case. Ostensibly we have moved back in time and are now concerned with civil rather than ecclesiastical matters. Both impressions are delusive. Even his earliest analyses of the Civil War are written long after the event; the earliest full one is in 1659. He continues to worry away at the issues which it raises throughout his life, and some of the most revealing of these comments are contained in printed and unprinted material which are written *after* his 1686 researches. More important, the connection between these apocalyptic studies and his thoughts on the Civil War is not a tenuous one. His memoirs suggest the opposite: that the Civil War began as a squabble about the constitution and only subsequently (as late as 1643) degenerated into a war about religion. But these were memoirs written after the event and were not innocent of editorial influence. In an article in 1914

Alexander Gordon discussed Calamy's shortcomings as an editor. He was referring not only to Calamy's notorious liberties with Baxter's manuscript when he produced his own edition, but also to the readiness he showed to tamper with it earlier when he was assistant to Matthew Sylvester.[24] Sylvester emerges from Gordon's essay as the incorruptible editor, but in my second chapter harsher light is thrown on Sylvester and kinder light on Calamy. The key issue here is the omission of material in Baxter about Charles I's alleged warrant to the Earl of Antrim, and Sylvester rather than Calamy is shown to be the culpable party. How important the Antrim warrant was to Baxter is shown by its relationship to the very problems about Christian Empire and loyalty to Papist sovereigns which we now know to have been exercising his mind in prison in 1686. The analogy of 1641 with 1688 was to be the theme of his printed and unprinted arguments in 1690 and 1691. His interest in Popish responsibility for the Civil War bobbed just below the surface in earlier discussions, although important clues are provided by his references to the rival contributions made by the political theories of Thomas Bilson and Richard Hooker in precipitating the Civil War. There were good reasons, especially after the Restoration, why Baxter should play up constitutional factors and play down religious ones in the genesis of the English Revolution. But the truth was the opposite: like many Protestant Englishmen he was more concerned about Popery than about the Petition of Right, and it was by reading Revelation right that the Popish Plot could be defeated. His unpublished treatise, written shortly before his death, *A Political Catechise*, is the most illuminating exposure of Baxter's secret self.

The third chapter concentrates on Baxter's relationship with both Oliver and Richard Cromwell. The picture is muddied by Baxter's efforts to cover his trail at the Restoration. Baxter began the Commonwealth period as the opponent of Oliver Cromwell. He refused to take the Engagement Oath. He had opposed the regicide. He recognised the authority of the exiled Charles II. But this was not how he ended the Commonwealth period. He ended it as a committed supporter of Richard Cromwell. His *Holy Commonwealth* purports to be an attack on Harrington's *Oceana*. But it is not. It is a millennial document, embodying his hopes in Richard Cromwell as a Foxeian Christian Emperor. This is a remarkable *volte-face*, and because this period is well documented it is possible to trace Baxter's changing attitude between 1649 and 1659 on a number of issues. At first they seem unrelated to the quest for a 'Holy Commonwealth', and yet Baxter's rejection of rigid Calvinist doctrine, his efforts to find a middle way in disputes about the

Lord's Supper and his establishment of Ministerial Associations all play their part in a significant change of heart.

The fourth chapter discusses Baxter's leadership of Protestant Non-conformity after the Restoration. Between 1660 and 1676 Baxter remains committed to the idea of a National Church; his negotiations with Anglicans like Tillotson and Wilkins or with Independents like Owen do not differ in that respect. Between 1676 and 1684 a significant change occurs. Baxter moves towards a separatist alternative for English Nonconformists. This shift in his thinking is first halted, and then reversed, by his encounter with the Apocalypse from 1684. Baxter becomes convinced of the apocalyptic case for non-separatism: his new definition of 'National Churches' is the decisive watershed. His last posthumous treatise, *The Poor Husbandman's Advocate*, shows how the Apocalypse colours his social teachings as much as it does his views on church government and on the rights of magistrates. Paradoxically it is Calamy's lack of such intimations which enables him to give the emancipating leadership to Restoration Dissent in 1704 which Baxter might have given before 1684. The fifth and concluding chapter attempts to show how this 'horizontal' view of Baxter may help us towards a new interpretation of the English Revolution.

Notes

1. (Dr Williams's Library, henceforth DWL) *19 Henry MSS* 90.5.1, f.22v.

2. Christopher Hill, 'John Mason and the End of the World', *Puritanism and Revolution* (London, 1958), p. 336. But this view is heavily qualified in his later *Antichrist in Seventeenth-Century England* (Oxford, 1971), *passim*.

3. W.K. Jordan, *The Development of Religious Toleration in England* (Harvard, 1965), iii, p. 343.

4. Quoted in Christopher Hill, *Winstanley: The Law of Freedom and Other Writings* (Pelican, 1973), p. 44.

5. Norman Cohn, *The Pursuit of the Millennium* (London, 1957), *passim*.

6. B.W. Ball, *A Great Expectation* (Leiden, 1975), p. 75.

7. Most notably William Haller, *Foxe's Book of Martyrs and the Elect Nation* (London, 1963); V.N. Olsen, *John Foxe and the Elizabethan Church* (California, 1973).

8. Marjorie Reeves, 'History and Eschatology: Medieval and Early Protestant Thought in Some English and Scottish Writings' in P.M. Clogan (ed.), *Medievalia et Humanistica*, New Series 4 1973, pp. 107-8.

9. Alan Macfarlane (ed.), *The Diary of Ralph Josselin* (Oxford, 1976), p. 2.

10. Frank Manuel, *The Religion of Isaac Newton* (Oxford, 1974), p. 91.

11. Frank Manuel, *A Portrait of Isaac Newton* (Cambridge, Mass., 1968), p. 110.

12. F.J. Powicke, *A Life of the Reverend Richard Baxter . . .* (London, 1924), preface.

13. Roger Thomas, *The Baxter Treatises* (Dr Williams's Library, Occasional Papers 8, 1959), p. 2.

14. Thomas Beverley, *The Thousand Years Kingdom of Christ* (London, 1691), p. 5.

15. S.T. Coleridge, *Notes on English Divines* . . . , ed. D. Coleridge (London, 1853), i, p. 250.

16. Hugh Martin, *Puritanism and Richard Baxter* (London, 1954), p. 8; Jordan, *Development of Religious Toleration* iii, p. 332; G.F. Nuttall, *Richard Baxter* (London, 1965), pp. 114-32; N.H. Keeble (ed.), *The Autobiography of Richard Baxter* (Everyman, 1974), p. xxviii; F.J. Powicke, *The Reverend Richard Baxter Under the Cross* (London, 1927), p. 266.

17. Samuel Young, *Vindiciae Anti-Baxterianae* (London, 1696), pp. 62, 105.

18. Powicke, *A Life of the Reverend Richard Baxter*, pp. 258-61; Jordan, *Development of Religious Toleration*, iii, p. 343.

19. Patrick Collinson, 'Towards a Broader Understanding of the Early Dissenting Tradition' in R.C. Cole and M.E. Moody (eds.), *The Dissenting Tradition: Essays for Leland H. Carlson* (Ohio, 1975), p. 26.

20. G.F. Nuttall, *Richard Baxter and Philip Doddridge* (Oxford, 1951), p. 2.

21. I am grateful to my student, Vic Gammon, for the reference to Nye.

22. J.P. Kenyon, *The Stuart Constitution* (Cambridge, 1966), p. 7.

23. (British Library) Harley/Portland MSS Loan 29/73/2; 29/73/3. I am grateful to my colleague, Dr Colin Brooks, for drawing my attention to this source.

24. Alexander Gordon, 'Calamy as Biographer', *Congregational Historical Society Transactions*, August 1914, p. 235.

1   BAXTER AND THE MILLENNIUM

Baxter had not wanted his thoughts on the millennium to be published. He had written a voluminous amount in manuscript form in prison in 1686. But he did not aim at a wider audience. Of that there can be no doubt. One section of these notes is prefaced by this stern warning: 'some generall thoughts on the Revelations undigestedly and disorderly set down for my owne memory and not for the sight of any other'.

The words 'undigestedly' and 'disorderly' are significant. They suggest a horror of premature publication. As he goes on to express a sense of ignorance in a specialist field to which he has come late in the day, his awareness of the notorious proliferation of disagreements between expert authorities and his own reverence for 'the harder and digested studyes of those that differ', his words may be taken as a statement of diffidence. This view is reinforced by another section of the 1686 papers, in which he asks readers to ignore what he had earlier said on the Book of Revelation 'because it is too crude and hasty, and satisfyeth not myselfe as well as I am now satisfied'.

The work to which he was referring was the only printed pamphlet in which he had, up to that point in time, commented on the millennium: his *Paraphrase on the New Testament* of 1684. But although the comment supports the idea of a man ridden by scholarly caution, in another sense it works against this explanation of his reticence in 1686. For what he is clearly saying is that, however crude and hasty his first forays into the Apocalypse had been, he was now satisfied that he *had* attained an understanding. And what the papers excitedly communicate is precisely this sense of confidence. He believes that his prison researches have given him access to truths which were vital for his fellow Christians. It is true that the first part of the instructions which he gives to his literary executors about these papers is in line with the spirit of scholarly modesty:

I am still suspicious that I may be mistaken, and therefore I desire and charge my executors and friends that shall have this writing 1. That they communicate it on promise of secrecy to some impartiall Godly Divine that is well studied in the Revelations: And if he soundly confute it in the judgment of able impartiall men, he burne it.[1]

If the instructions had stopped there, Baxter's desire for secrecy about his apocalyptic material would cease to have been a mystery. But he went on to an unexpected formula. Not: if false, burn it; if true, publish it. Rather: if false, burn it; if true, conceal it:

> if not, that they will keep it utterly secret, till the Designe of papall prevalency be blasted by the providence of God; for even Great Truths may be silenced when they will do more hurt than good. I would not burden Papists by an unseasonable Truth.[2]

What truths were 'unseasonable', could 'do more hurt than good', and which lurked in Revelation for the comfort of Papists — until the 'providence of God' would blast Papal designs? A fellow student of the Apocalypse, Henry More, knew the answer. He made it the burden of his attacks on Baxter's *Paraphrase on the New Testament*: that Baxter had cruelly revealed in that work the divergence among Protestant interpreters of the Apocalypse; worse, he had argued against the conventional Protestant wisdom that the Antichrist in the prophetic texts was the Pope. Baxter does acknowledge in his notes the harmful effect of both findings. But his contrition takes an odd form. He recognises that his printed thoughts had been 'crude and hasty', but his later private thoughts are not the retraction on either point that More had hoped for. What is clear from reading this secret material in bulk for the first time is how disappointingly consonant it is with what he had published in 1684 already. He enlarges on his proofs for the belief that the Pope is not the Antichrist, and he exposes more Protestant squabbles over the way to interpret prophecy. Such negative findings — both of comfort to Papists — were best concealed in 1686 when a Papist King was strengthening his control over Protestant subjects.

But, compared to 1684, Baxter is an excited man in 1686. The excitement certainly does not come from the discovery of more negative evidence. His findings are positive: his researches convince him that the Apocalypse has truths to convey to his fellow Protestants. The two most important of these are that God rules through Christian Emperors and that He works by means of National Churches. When he is in a position to publish his writings in 1690 and 1691 these become the dominant themes of his pamphlets and not what, to him, were clearly minor questions of the identity of Antichrist or of the status of rival Protestant interpretations of signs and symbols in the prophetic texts.

But in 1686 both of these truths are 'unseasonable' to Protestants. Why? Ostensibly because both arguments support the existing Catholic ruler. James II was wanting his subjects to obey the authority of the civil magistrate; Nonconformists were being dragooned into a 'National Church'. In the climate of 1686 the publication of Baxter's material could only strengthen the forces of reaction. This judgement was an illusion (which Baxter freely exposed as such in his last pamphlets of 1690 and 1691): a 'National Church' headed by a Papist sovereign was a contradiction in terms; a true understanding of imperial political theory *encouraged resistance of, not submission to, a Christian Emperor who served Rome*. But the freedom to expose such illusions was possible only in 1690 and 1691 when a Protestant King was on the throne: then the apocalyptic intimations of 'National Churches' could be brought out, and the loyalist, not rebellious, implications of Christian Empire could be sustained.

When Baxter was discovering these truths in 1686 more disturbing questions were raised. What did the Apocalypse teach about the rights of Protestant subjects, the limits to the authority of Catholic Princes? These questions had been raised, and answered, by the great Tudor exponent of imperial political theory, Thomas Bilson, Bishop of Winchester. His influence on Baxter will be fully discussed in the next chapter, but at this stage it is worth noting that Baxter did not come fresh to these questions in 1686. On the contrary, ever since the Civil War had begun, Baxter had asked himself these questions. They had been forced on him by the suspicion that Charles I had issued warrants to Irish Papists to carry out the massacre of Irish Protestant subjects which had precipitated the English Civil War. This suspicion was publicly voiced by Baxter in 1659, but for obvious reasons it remained submerged in private papers and correspondence after the Restoration. It revived in acute form with the controversy after the Restoration over the nature of Charles I's specific instructions to one Irish Catholic rebel, the Earl of Antrim, and it was strengthened by Charles II's behaviour in the latter part of his reign. The accession of James II, and his subsequent actions, were for Baxter a vindication of his worst fears. Throughout these years of doubt Bilson's arguments for Protestant resistance to the Papist Prince were an invaluable prop to Baxter. But they were hypotheses which required a higher authentication. Baxter found this in the Apocalypse in 1686. In 1690 and 1691 Baxter was able to develop a justification – not only for deposing James II in 1688 but for opposing Charles I in 1642 – which was rooted in the Book of Revelation. These were the thoughts on the millennium which he had not wanted to publish in 1686.

How he had come to this study in the first place was seemingly accidental. From his own account the first inspiration had come from a fellow Nonconformist minister, John Humfrey. In 1684 Humfrey had persuaded him to write a paraphrase on the Epistle to the Romans. Baxter said that he found the work so 'pleasant' that he 'went over the New Testament to the Apocalypse'. Until then he had 'superficially read' a number of apocalyptic commentators without being over-impressed by any of them. Yet he had felt himself inferior to them and was willing to defer to their greater experience. The more he studied the Apocalypse, the less ready he was to be deferential. He became convinced that the Pope was not Antichrist and decided to publish his belief.[3]

The moment that he did so he crossed swords with Henry More. There was rich irony in this development. Baxter had been one of More's most fervent supporters. He had admired More's writings on apparitions and ghosts. He had admired his arguments from the Apocalypse to show that the Pope was Antichrist. The fact that his own researches on the same texts produced an opposite conclusion should not blind us to the extent of that debt. Baxter used More's *approach* to the identification of Antichrist to prove him wrong. Indeed both men came to the millennium from a shared interest in the occult.

The links between the two were obvious. As one recent writer has put it: 'was not the Book of Revelation almost wholly written in terms of "great wonders" and "great, marvellous" signs in heaven, and full of references to fire and blood and war and death?'[4] It was natural for both More and Baxter that an interest in signs and providences, witches and ghosts should anticipate an interest in the millennium. When Baxter, along with fellow Puritan William Prynne, would alert Protestants to the Jesuits' skill in metamorphosing themselves into every shape or size he was making a literal point. As early as 1655 Thomas White had written to him, asking him to use the contacts he had already made in his Worcestershire Association of Ministers, to elicit from ministers records of 'Providences' and 'Spiritual Experiences'. He knew the common pitfall: 'many pious persons are somewhat too credulous.' He thought, however, that Baxter, with the aid of fellow ministers of the calibre of Calamy and Vines, could judge 'the prudence as well as the piety of the Ministers'.[5] Matthew Poole's vision of 1657 soared higher still: of a co-operative venture for 'registring of Illustrious Providences', with a secretary in every county reporting material to Poole.[6] Baxter responded enthusiastically:

Your designe about gatheringe extraordinary Providences, I thinke to be very noble and excellent, and lament that every age had not some to doe it: you can hardly conceive the good that may be done by it in time, if rightly managed.

Baxter was scrupulous in informing Poole that White had been first in the field: 'I thinke it not fitt to meddle in it, without giving him notice.' Baxter borrowed from White the suggestion that Calamy and two or three ministers should join Poole in vetting the information when the venture did get under way. He confided to Poole his desire to project it beyond national frontiers: 'Pray get some Merchants to procure you the certaine narrative of the many hundreds said to be possessed of late in Germany.' In the meantime a rainfall of wheat in Surrey sounded promising.[7] Poole's project collapsed with the Commonwealth, but Increase Mather used Poole's manuscript as the basis for his organisation of Massachusetts ministers in 1681.[8] Baxter again was involved. In December 1690 he wrote to Mather:

I am so much taken with your history of prodigies that I propose to put my scraps into your hands (as much as is not lost) and not only so, but to furnish you with some from a friend, if you will reprint your booke while you stay here and adde them as a supplement: for I see you have great skille in selecting and contracting. I pray tell me whether you have any to tell (and when).[9]

Cheats were a problem. Henry Jessey's three-volume record of strange occurrences in England between 1660 and 1662 did for the study of prodigies what John of Leyden did for the Apocalypse: set the serious study of it back for several decades.[10] But Baxter's assumption is not that the study must be abandoned, but that it must be carried out with greater scientific thoroughness. He said of Jessey's works:

But the crafty enemy (who useth most to wrong Christ and his Cause, by his most passionate, injudicious followers), prevailed with some over-forward Minister of this strain, to publish them in many volumes, with the mixture of so many falsehoods, and mistaken circumstances, as turned them to the advantage of the Devil and ungodliness, and made the very mention of Prodigies to become a scorn.[11]

Baxter had criteria to test frauds: three 'sensible evidences' to be studied in conjunction with Scripture. They were apparitions, witches and

satanical possessions or diseases. Baxter had 'manifold and proved instances' of all three. Witchcraft had grown from a cottage industry of
silly old women to a flourishing coeducational enterprise:

> Sure it were strange, if in an Age of so much knowledge and confi-
> dence, there should so many score of poor Creatures be put to death
> as Witches, if it were not clearly manifest that they were such. We
> have too many examples lately among us, to leave any doubt of the
> truth of this.[12]

Baxter's belief in witchcraft was compatible with a keen sceptical
approach to the identification of individual cases. This approach flowed
from consciousness of his own powers. His medical skill had resulted in
cures within a few days for many of his parishioners. Had he 'the design
and conscience of a Papist' he knew how easy it would be to make the
common people believe 'that I had cast out a Devil'. Therefore caution
was essential: 'At this very time while I am writing this, I am put to
dissuade a man from accusing one of his neighbours of witchcraft,
because his daughter hath this disease, and cryeth out of her.'[13]
  Baxter was fascinated with the case of a fifteen-year-old bewitched
girl from Evesham. She 'daily voided' a considerable amount of flint
stones, 'as plaine flint as any was in the fielde, till they had large measures full of them'. To the case Baxter brought the vigilance recognised
by White, Poole and Mather, in their correspondence with him, as vital
if Papal deceptions and credulity were not to rule:

> lest there should be any deceit (partly at my desire but principally
> for his owne satisfaction) the learned godly prudent Minister of the
> towne, Mr. George Hopkins, my speciall beloved friend now with
> God took care that they might search her and be sure there was no
> deceit. And the witch was judged and she delivered.[14]

Baxter, White and Poole had stressed the need for teams of trained
investigators to work together to scrutinise supernatural claims. Calamy
had been one of the recommended investigators. It comforted Baxter
that he was also one of the ministers who had authenticated earlier
witch identifications.
  Against such a professional approach, a European figure of the
stature of Comenius seemed diminished. To Baxter his approach to
verification of supernatural claims was altogether too simple: 'when he
abjured the prophet to speak truth, and got him to swear as before the

Lord that it was truth; this seemed enough to confirm his belief of him.'[15] There was a double failure. There was a failure of technique. Comenius worked on his own. In Baxter's reproach is heard the authentic voice of the 1650s — all that optimism and energy revolving around the concept of a pooled application of resources. It was this voice which spoke in the contrary insistence of both White and Baxter that ministers co-ordinate their data and work through established institutions like the Worcestershire Association of Ministers. But there was also a failure of imagination. Comenius could only think of deception in terms of *conscious* motivation. Not so, said Baxter, drawing upon a fund of casuist experience: 'it is no wonder if that person swear that his words are true, who is first deceived himself before he deceives others.' Comenius had not made that imaginative leap. He had not come to terms with 'the Nature of Melancholy'.

On this subject Baxter was an expert. He contributed to its alleviation on two fronts. He published generalised comfort in moral treatises. He gave specific advice to individuals in distress, and his correspondence overflows with such material. In giving such comfort Baxter drew upon knowledge of his wife's temptations to despair, but above all from insight into his own self-destructive morbidity. In his memoirs there is a revealing comparison between two good ministers whom he loved. Simeon Ashe was a merry figure but the lugubrious James Nalton, 'the Weeping Prophet', wept his way to a premature grave. Baxter wanted to be an Ashe and fought continually against those impulses in his nature which drew him to Nalton. It was what Clarendon had in mind when he remonstrated with Baxter at the Savoy Conference on his failure to match the fatness of Thomas Manton. When Baxter protested that he did not know the secret, Clarendon dropped his jesting manner and chided him for being 'severe and strict, like a Melancholy Man, and made those things *sin* which others did not'.[16] Nothing was more prone to cast Baxter into gloom than thoughts about his health.[17] Critics were slow to respond with the proper amount of sympathy. Samuel Young ridiculed the 'long, tedious, pitiful, intolerable Impertinencies, as the telling when he fell ill, what Physician cured him, by what Medicines. When he had the Measles, when the Small Pox, when a Loosness, and how Cured'. John Owen drily commented: 'I do not think the World so much concerned in me, that I must tell them when I am sick, and when I am well; how old I am.'[18] Baxter wrote to a correspondent in September 1649 about his health:

If I have any ease one day, I am sicke another: nay I scarce remem-

ber that two houres together, for those two yeares I have bin free
from paine in one part, or another, except sleeping. My body is able
to study but two or three houres in a day when I am at best . . . I
hope none of this is your case. I can easily conjecture by your coun-
tenance and voice, that you are better able to study right on ten
houres, than I those two . . . And yet most of all being soo neare to
death, as in all likelyhood I am, soo that I never go up into the Pulpit, but I have cause to doubt much, whether it may not be my last.[19]

This was the man who in his *Saints Everlasting Rest* memorably conveyed at least one aspect of Heaven: 'There will be then no crying out
Oh my Head, Oh my Stomach, Oh my Sides, or Oh my Bowels.'[20] Baxter's first published writings in 1649 were dying thoughts. He did not
find it easy to be an Ashe, but at least his temptations to melancholia
made him an acute and sympathetic judge of that condition in other
people. Nobody taxed his casuistic genius more severely than the
sorrowful Mrs Katherine Gell.

Her correspondence with Baxter opens innocuously enough. She
writes of her concern to him in April 1657 that his *Saints Everlasting
Rest* had not driven out her melancholic impulses. She followed his
advice then to look after her family and children to correct despair. The
rub was that such activities cancelled out good thoughts as well as morbid ones — 'I had rather locke my selfe up in a roome alone amongst
my bookes for meditation.'[21] Baxter could not have avoided a feeling of
kinship here. He would later acknowledge early marital tension on just
such an issue:

> I had been bred among plain mean people, and I thought that so
> much washing of Stairs and Rooms, to keep them as clean as their
> Trenches and Dishes, and so much ado about cleanliness and trifles,
> was a sinful curiosity, and expense of servants time, who might that
> while have been reading some good book.[22]

In Mrs Gell's case the transfer of interest from self to husband and children had only been a transfer of fears. She was willing to be martyred
herself, but became paralysed with grief at the thought that her children should suffer when she heard of a smallpox outbreak in town or
the like. She felt that her hysteria blemished her religion.

Baxter's reply a month later explained that 'most women are of
more sensible passionate dispositions than men.' He knew that all the
reason in the world could not persuade a child, who is disposed to cry-

ing, to change his disposition. He had a homely personal instance of this: 'I can remember since I was a child, when my master whipt me to make me give over cryinge, which I thought unreasonable dealinge, seeinge it force me to cry the more.'

Self-reproach will therefore get her nowhere. Prayer has the effect of hindering the attendants of such fears — 'as murmerings against God, unseemely speeches and the like' — but cannot remove the fears themselves. Baxter believes that their sudden risings can hardly be avoided. His own fear of the dark is instructive:

> When I was younge (yea till 20 yeares of age) I durst not have gone into a darke roome alone; or if I had, the feare of it would have made me even tremble. I knew the folly of this, and both Reason and (I think) Grace did contradict it; and yet I was not able to overcome it, no nor one moment to forbeare it, if I might have had the world. Even such doe I take your case to be: feares and griefe above all passions are least at the command of reason and will.

Baxter concludes with reference to the sad case of Lady Rous, his dear friend, 'so far from over-much passionate sensibility in most women that ever I knew', who fell into a fever on report of her husband's illness and died, while he recovered.[23]

Katherine Gell writes back on 10 November 1657 to say that she is recovering from her depression, but fear of the dark affects her too: 'any little noise doth of late soe affright me that it makes me start from the place.'[24] A month later Baxter shares in her pleasure at recovery, but urges her to put down her feelings at present in writing as a comfort against any future relapses. He had spotted the significance of her quickness to take up his anecdote about the dark — 'I perceive that your nature hath that melancholy disposition still.' He admits his own fears of the dark are not totally banished, but they are as nothing compared to what they were. Though reason and faith helped, Baxter set more store by 'some change in my temperature by age'. So his advice was: avoid the dark and await — with age — for the season of deliverance. Moreover he had found comfort himself in the past from the thought that, if the Devil appeared in person, it would free him from the temptations to infidelity which had been agitating him and so would represent a victory for piety. Mr White of Dorchester had shown the way to rout the Devil:

> In the meane time I know you remember that Satan is but a con-

quered chained enemy, and should God suffer him to appeare to you, it would be but for some great advantage of your owne. What say you to such a man as Mr. White of Dorchester, who (as Mr. Clarke hath printed) living in a house at Lambeth that was wont to be haunted (for want of a better) the Divell one night appeared as standing at his beds foot. When he had stood there a while saith Mr. White to him [If thou hast nothing else to do stand there still] and so settled himself to sleepe, and the Divell vanished as ashamed of the contempt.

Baxter wanted Mrs Gell to aid self-examination by keeping a diary, but this too could be a snare for the melancholic:

But I would not advise you to spend so much time as the thoughtfull recounting and writing downe of every ordinary infirmity would require, for such, alas, we carry them with us so constantly, that we need no writings to tell us that we have them, and the frequent recording the same infirmity over and over, will make us as customary and sensles as if we recorded them not, or else will tempt us to dispare because we live still in the same recorded sins. And the time so spent may be better improved.[25]

Some six months later Mrs Gell reports that prayer is not working. She looks forward with apprehension to thirty years more of such suffering, and expresses her willingness to die. She had sought private counsel with her minister but found that in the eyes of her neighbours this was worse than 'gaming or mixed dancing or bare breasts'. She knew that the same people would consult with physicians, lawyers or bishops; ordinary clergy were, however, considered to be beneath them. 'Most of the gentry of England are now come to be of this straine,' she lamented, and this anti-clericalism intensified her depression.[26] Her complaint drew from Baxter a week later a sympathetic response:

they know not it is the Ministers office to oversee each members of the flock and to bee a stated Director for mens salvation, for all to goe to in their needs, as Physicians care for mens health and lives.[27]

This was the sombre background against which Baxter would write his *Holy Commonwealth*. The prejudices which Mrs Gell described were to receive their most powerful articulation in the writings of James Harrington.[28]

Baxter is at his finest as the physician of the spirit. One correspondent spoke for many grateful victims of melancholia: 'I doe from my soule blesse the Lord, he hath raised a second Calvin.'[29] Samuel Young mercilessly lampooned Baxter in 1696, but his regret, that the published *Reliquiae Baxterianae* contained so little in the way of the casuist, seems for once to be genuine: 'When I took up the *Reliquiae*, I expected some excellent cases of conscience: About Men Melancholy, or cast down; for he much conversed with such, he wrote to them, they to him.'[30] Baxter wrote from the inside: some of the most sensitive observations he made on melancholia are to be found in his biography of his wife. They elicited an angry remonstrance from Devon in 1690. Edward Elys could not see why, in writing of Margaret Baxter, he should be so concerned about the perils of over-intensive introspection: 'What Ugly Conceit have you of God, the Beautie of Angells, and Immortal Souls.'[31] What Elys could not see, and Baxter could, was the necessity of 'vent'.

Margaret had a fear-ridden nature. Before Baxter knew her, she had four times been on the verge of death (once from smallpox). She had seen men killed before her eyes in the Civil War. She had lived by a churchyard, where she saw all the burials of the dead. She kept a death's head skull in her closet. Thus a combination of circumstances worked upon a susceptible temperament:

> Though she called it melancholly, that by all this was cast into, yet it rather seemed a partly natural, and partly an adventitious diseased fearfulness in a tender over-passionate nature, that had no power to quiet her own feare, without any other clod on her understanding. All was much increased by her wisdom, so stifling all the appearances of it, that it all inwardly wrought, and had no ease by vent.[32]

That was the rub. The more fine and sensitive the intelligence the more likely the fears would be repressed — only, without a 'vent', to break out in some more malignant form.

The good were often unstable, and as such were easy prey for unscrupulous Quakers and Fifth Monarchy Men. Mr Beal, an 'Auditor of Revenue', was one pious victim of melancholy. On 3 May 1674 Philip Henry records how he threw himself out of his garret window into his garden and died immediately in the fall. Henry noted that 'he was a good man and feared God above many,' called it 'an astonishing Providence', and exclaimed: 'Lord! how terrible art thou sometimes to thine own children.' He went on: 'Mr. Baxter, kissing the dead Body sayd, he did believe his soul to be as happy, as he did desire his own soul to bee.'[33] Did Baxter take a stern enough line against suicide? The question was brought home to him with some force by a correspondent, Thomas Morris, on 1 November 1687. Joseph Southmead committed suicide, and quoted Baxter in a dying letter to support him. When Morris looked at the text 'this poor soule' quoted from *Saints Everlasting Rest* he found little in it to support such an action. Baxter, having left the sinner 'inexcusable at the judgement of God', had added the tiny solace:

> Only, as we do by our friends when they are dead, and our words and actions can do them no good, yet to testify our affections for them, we weep and mourn; so will I also do for these unhappy souls.

Then he added: 'though man will not hear, we may hope in speaking to God.' Armed with this rather fragile comfort Southmead, a merchant down on his luck, prayed with his family and then locked himself in a room and shot himself in the heart. It was the most deliberate self-murder that Morris had encountered and was unusual in that Southmead could *not* have been said to have done it 'in a fit of Melancholy'. Morris hoped that Baxter could produce a more robust antidote to 'the Devil's Temptations', since suicide seemed the classic English disease: 'English people were more addicted to it than any other nation.'[34] Baxter described the case history of one melancholic 'gentlewoman in Worcester' in 1671. She had been claimed from a scandalous existence by Baxter's preaching, fell in with the Quakers and then penitently sought reconciliation with Baxter once more. But her penitence was over-dramatic:

> But all these deep workings and troubles between the several waies did so affect her, that she fell into a very strong melancholy; Insomuch that she imposed such an abstinence from meat upon her self, that she was much consumed, and so debilitated as to keep her bed, and almost famished.

This time it was the Fifth Monarchists' turn, instead of the Quakers, to reap the harvest of the melancholy, and she was duly written up by them as a success story. Baxter thought otherwise:

> I shall say nothing of any thing which is otherwise known, but desire the Reader that doth but understand what melancholy is, better than the Writers did, to read that book, and observe with sorrow

and pitty, what a number of plain effects of Melancholy, as to *thoughts*, and *Scriptures*, and *actions* are there ascribed to *meer Temptations* on one side and to God's *unusual or notable operations* on the other side![35]

The tragedy was that it was her piety that had left her vulnerable.[39] It was to this point that Baxter reverted, on 18 May 1690, when he wrote down his reasons for disagreeing with the millenarian speculations of his friend Thomas Beverley:

Very good men have thus overturned themselves in some singular studyes, that have bin wise and humble in other things. As some that are not of sanguine complexion, may have a boile ... the blood festering on one place: so may a man that otherwise is not of a proud but very humble spirit notably overvalue himselfe in some one point.

What was this but a variant on the doctrine of the 'vent'? These comments were not published, and two anecdotes to bolster his points were even crossed out in the manuscript. They show the drift of his mind very clearly, however, and are worth recording. One anecdote was of an ex-prisoner: 'I honour his name so much that I will not name him ... a man of eminent humility and eminent unquestioned sincerity.' A conformist until Charles II's accession, an enemy of the Parliament's war, he had become attracted to the idea of the Saturday Sabbath, then to Anabaptism and finally to 'professing that God raised him to be the Leading Prophet of the age, to begin a new Reformation.' And Baxter rubbed home to Beverley the point once more: 'he was of as honourable a family and patronage as you, I know not the man that walked more self-denyingly'. The second crossed-out anecdote referred to a 'very Learned anciente' doctor who came to Baxter, a few months after Charles II died, with the 'great and certain secret that England was the place where much of the Revelation was to be fulfilled'. He was no less confident of the timing of these events:

And the Antichrist should heere be cast down before March, and that the Protestant princes would pull him down by a confederacy: And before March the King dyed, but so did not popery: And though a confederacy of Protestant Princes followed since then, I ground not my expectations of the successe on this Learned mans prophecy.[36]

Since these warnings were addressed to Beverley in 1690 they could be represented as a late development in Baxter's thought: the fruit of his researches of 1686. They are no such thing. Baxter developed as early as 30 May 1654, in a letter to Henry Bromley, precisely the same themes, and similar anecdotal material to buttress them.[37]

His letter to Bromley was a passionate warning against the exploitation of the vulnerably good by Quaker, Familist, Ranter and Fifth Monarchist prophets. Good men like Bromley's brother Thomas, under the spell of the Familist Dr Pordage, were betrayed by their melancholy: 'Excessive solicitousnesse and thoughtfulness doth habituate some of them to Melancholly which gives the Tempter advantage to possess them with Deluding phantomess.' Baxter found proof that 'the Devill is now on the stage' in the proliferation of Ranter, Leveller and Quaker movements. He quoted the story of Major Wilkie as a moral lesson. Wilkie was a Scot who lived with Baxter in Coventry in the Civil War. He was a good linguist, had Scriptures at his fingertips and at first lived 'a Civill life, and attended the publique ordinances'. Most significant was his melancholy:

> He was of an Active, fiery Melancholly Complexion, such as is the usual foregoer of madnesse . . . But never shewed any Defect of free Reason in his discourse or Employment but rather a greater height of reason, than most others here. At last he began to make knowne to me in secret that he had constant familiarity and Converse with Spirits but most in the night. I persuaded him that it was but the Delusion of his Phantasye by Melancholly.

Wilkie, however, continued to assert that he had been in communion with angels between ten and twenty years. Baxter asked him if the angels were good or bad. Wilkie replied that he heard and saw both: one, his devoted guardian (whom he called his lord) and the other, his special enemy. Baxter asked when his first visitations had come. Wilkie told him that in Paris, as a student, he was accustomed to sleepless nights and rising 'in his shirt and walking about the chamber'. Here Baxter interposes: 'You may see by that he was melancholly.' On one such occasion Wilkie had a vision:

> in a Constellation the perfect similitude of a Lyon Rampant at the moone: which while he beheld one foote broake off and turned to the likenes of a cocke: and then broke off a 2nd and then a 3rd, and then the 4th.

While admiring this sight he was confronted with 'the similitude of a crowned glorious prince, and the moone did shine in its fullest glory'. Wilkie went back to bed, slept, and had the various signs interpreted for him in a dream. The cloud was 'a Calamitous darkness that should befall the Church'; the lion was 'King Charles who should persecute the Church'; the feet breaking off were the Church of England, Scotland, Ireland and Wales. The prince had special significance:

> the crowned glorious person that succeeded was one that he called the prince of The Nations: Of this Prince he interpreted many prophecies which wee commonly Interpret of Christ . . . It was Revealed to him, that Christ should come and raigne on Earth personally a 1000 yeares, and the Prince must prepare the World for his 2nd coming, as John Baptist did for the first: that person should be a Northerne man of meane parentage (he thought a Knight) and have a Certaine Mark on his Cheeke: and he should conquer and subdue the Nations, France, Spain, Italy and so pull down the Pope, and remove the Impediments of the Jewes Coming, and then at the end of his raigne Christ should come, and himself convert the Jewes and destroy the Mahometans . . .

Wilkie awaited three changes: the sign of the prince; Christ's return to usher in the millennium, which he called 'the time of the Restitution of all Things'; the end of the thousand years, which he called 'the time of the New Creation'. Wilkie knew by thunder whether Parliament would gain victories or not: 'which party of the Spirits would gett the better'. His last prophecy was at Easter, where he forecast 1648 as the 'beginning of a glorious Church and State'. His end was suitably ignominious: a drunkard, spending days in darkness, lying in bed on the Sabbath and ultimately being deported 'starke madd' back to his friends in Scotland.

The whole reads like a rationalist tract. After saying that he knew nothing further about Wilkie he added: 'one of his Revelations was, that he should live till the 2nd comeing, to raigne visibly at Jerusalem: and if that be true he is yet alive.' This sardonic spirit permeates the letter. Wilkie's confession that a vision at night was followed by a chamber pot full of blood in the morning prompted Baxter to explain: 'I told him the motion of the blood might stir his phantasye, and cause that dreame which he called a voice.' But it is a protest, not against speculation about the millennium, but against *the wrong kind of speculation*. The letter concludes with a denunciation of the way in which Jesuits prey on the melancholic in order to peddle absurd readings of

Revelation, and thus to take away the *true apocalyptic guilt* from their Church.[38]

The same curiosity that led Baxter and More to ghosts and apparitions led them to the millennium. The same care in scrutinising supernatural claims inspired both men when they came to speculate about the millennium. Baxter knew how the serious study of Revelation could be retarded by the idiocies of a Wilkie. He was not above suggesting that Wilkie was a Jesuit double agent whose aim was precisely that. More knew the dangers *of his own* unbridled fancies. That is why his biographer and friend, Ward, praised his caution more than any other virtue. More had anticipated converse between inhabitants of the ethereal and terrestrial regions in seven thousand years. Ward believed that this was 'his real Conjecture'. And yet he observed 'that in his Expositions on the Revelation, and in other Representations of the Glorious times, he wisely takes no Notice of it'. He was equally reticent about another childhood impression: 'that lying one Moon-shining Night in the Cradle awake, he was taken up thence by a Matron-like Person, with a large Roman Nose, saluted and deposited there again'.[39]

Baxter and More were right to be cautious about the millennium; such speculations were dangerous for untutored minds. But tutored minds were not sceptical ones. Baxter and More inhabited the same world of Matrons with Roman Noses, monster-begetting women, witches and apparitions. Thus when Edmund Whichcote wrote to Baxter in 1682 about apparitions in Herefordshire the information was relayed at the same time not only to his uncle but to Henry More as well.[40] It was necessary to detect the fraudulent apocalyptic claims in order to defend the real ones. Wilkie's belief that the progress of the Civil War could be measured by the quality of the thunder was an absurdity to Baxter. His own belief that lightning in Lower Devon only struck churches as a judgement on the Act of Uniformity seemed, on the other hand, a rational proposition.[41] Henry Jessey's three volumes of prodigies were a farrago of untested conceits and yet amongst the dross were valuable true insights such as 'the drying-up of the River Derwent in Derbyshire, upon no known cause, Winter, the Earth opening and swallowing a Woman near Ashburn in the same County, upon her own Imprecation, the Appearance of an Army to pray near Montgomery'.[42] Papists revelled in fantastic tales of miracles, signs, apparitions, hauntings, witches and ghosts; no reason for Protestants to 'shut their eyes against the workings of Providence'.[43] The snare for the melancholic was the challenge for the prudent. Caution, systematic collation, teams of investigators: those were the tools of Protestantism, and as precious to Baxter as to More.

There is nothing which has been described so far about the background to Baxter's clash with More in 1684 to prepare one for it. In fact More's first major publication on the Apocalypse in 1664, *A Modest Enquiry*, had won the admiration of Baxter. His approach was strikingly original. Most of the commentators on the Apocalypse — Brightman, Mede, Durham, More himself later — proceeded by line-by-line comment on the Books of Daniel and Revelation. A cumulative pattern emerged from the detailed exegesis. More knew that the *idea* of Antichrist had become debased by vulgar usage: 'smells as strong as of Onions and Garlick'. More set himself the task of rescuing the *idea* of Antichrist from its trivial status. The concept of Antichrist was not 'a mere Idea' but 'a lively Image'. He would not *try* to prove that the Pope was Antichrist; he would show what attributes Antichrist would be expected to display. If it so happened that the Papacy possessed these attributes that could not be helped; it would, incidentally, clear the Church of England from such imputations. He thus avoided

> the bungling practice of the ancient ignorant Painters, who not being able to draw their Pictures lively enough, were fain to write under one, *This was a Bear*, and under another, *This is an Horse*, or *a Lion*, or whatever other *Animal* it was intended for.

More offered instead proof by the indirect method.

How was Antichristianity to be defined? In a number of attributes: idolatry (the sun worship of pagans was more rational than bread worship of Papists); scrupulosity; credulity ('for a crucifix also to take some fifty miles journey through the same element in a night, were a pretty figment to furnish out The Faith of Fools'); pride; lack of purity; lack of charity. More only turned to the Apocalypse when he had made up his shopping-list:

> After this Description of the Idea of Antichristian, to make search into the Prophecies; to find out that their prefigurations of Antichrist are in the main strokes (for neither are the Prophecies concerning Christ's predictions of all his particular actions) most manifestly answerable to the Idea we have given . . . And it is as good and natural a method to prove the Truth of the Prophecies by the fulness of the Events, as to illustrate the Nature of the Events, by the Application of the Prophecies.

Thus More claimed that he complemented Mede, 'whose enterprise was to interpret the whole Apocalypse in order'. Fundamental to More's argument was the belief that 'the Church was not grown Antichristian till about 400 years after Christ.' Until that time it was 'Symmetral'. He claimed that these 'approvable Ages of the Church were the Pattern of our English Reformation' and that the folly of Grotius's well-meant attempts at reunion was in asking Protestants to be reconciled to the Roman Church 'before she be reconciled to the Primitive Church in those Symmetral Ages thereof'. More owned up to the difficulty of finding Antichrist in the text:

> I must confess that it is hard to produce any Text of Scripture where-in this Apostatized state of the Church is undoubtedly foretold under the very name of *Antichrist*, though that Name be found more than once in the Epistles of St. John. But though some doe, yet I dare not contend that this Antichrist or Antichristianism which I have hitherto described is so clearly pointed out in every one of those places.

This meant that the Book of Revelation was cryptic, but not unintelligible. The Papists are so cunning that the text *had* to be cryptic:

> If St. John had said expressly, that by the *Two-horned Beast* and by *The Whore of Babylon* he did understand a Succession of Bishops of Rome with their whole Hierarchy adhering thereunto; it would be a hard thing to conceive that this Oecumenical Prelate would not, to hide his shame, have been tempted to change his Seven-hilled See, that he might not seem to be the man at whom the Prophecie pointed.[44]

In later works — especially his *Apocalypsis Apocalypseos* of 1680 — he developed his interpretation of Revelation on more traditional, exegetical lines. Yet it is interesting that Baxter's manuscript replies of 1686 to More are couched very much on the lines of More's original work of 1664. For all the nit-picking over the meanings of particular verses and lines that he indulges in, his is not a systematic exposition of the text. As we have seen he apologises for his disorderly approach; perhaps that is merely the difference between an unpublished draft and a published work. And yet it goes deeper than that. Baxter *is* fascinated by the idea of Antichrist. It becomes the starting-point for his numerous raids on Scripture. His disagreement with the later More is fought on lines laid down by the earlier More.[45]

This is not merely guesswork. We have evidence from the preface to one of Baxter's pamphlets of 1670, *The Cure of Church-Divisions*:

> And if the Roman Kingdom (for so it is rather to be called than a Church) had not such Moral marks of Antichristianity (which Dr. More hath notably opened in his *Mysterie of Iniquity*) . . . I should in charity, fear to suspect them of Antichristianity, notwithstanding all the Propheticall passages which seem otherwise to point them out; because I should still suspect my understanding of those Prophesies, when the Law of *Loving my neighbour as my self*, is plain to us all.[46]

It is an interesting argument. Baxter, in 1670 at least, professes to believe in the 'propheticall' attribution of Antichrist to the Roman Church, but on grounds of charity would be reluctant to say so were it not for the 'Moral Marks' which More had found. Thus, even in a passage deferring to prophecy, Baxter puts more weight on the 'Moral Marks'. The advantage of More's scheme was that the identification of Rome with Antichrist did not depend upon a dubious textual attribution.

More blamed Baxter for breaking the Protestant apocalyptic consensus. He gratuitously put weapons into his Catholic opponents' hands, first by exposing the variety of Protestant interpretations of prophecy in his *Paraphrase on the New Testament*, and then by conceding in the same work that the Pope was not Antichrist. More called him a 'Wooden Soul' and 'Stony Heart'. He had acted from the most petty of motives. He was paying More back for his writings on apparitions and spirits. This charge wounded Baxter more than any other. In some bewilderment he wanted to know why More should think that 'his booke of spirits needed any revenge'. On the contrary, Baxter 'greatly valued and thanked him for his publication of the treatise of Apparitions (written by my sometimes much overvaluing friend, Joseph Glanvill)'.[47] But More saw him as a 'blasphemer' who had described the Apocalypse as unintelligible. In so doing, Baxter had broken with the Tudor Church of England tradition: 'Whereas this Antichristianity of the Church of Rome is a Doctrine own'd by the Church of England, and Jewel against Harding was ordered to be placed in every Parish Church.'[48] More's charges were to be repeated by other Protestant critics. Baxter comments sourly in an unpublished note about the general reception given to his *Paraphrase on the New Testament*: 'These filled the City with the murmers that I had written that the Pope is not the Antichrist, that not Papall but Heathen Rome is the Babilon, and the Heathen Empire the beast mentioned Rev.13 etc.'[49] Baxter's apostasy won him the nickname of 'Bellarmine Junior'. John Owen spoke for many Protestants in arguing that if the Pope were not seen to be Antichrist 'many would be very indifferent how you treat with them, or what composition you shall make for yourselves'. The 'undoubted truth' that the Pope was Antichrist was 'the principal means of preserving the Body of the people in an aversion unto Popery'.[50]

Baxter had an answer to this. It was enunciated in the 'Advertisement' of 12 November 1684 appended to his *Paraphrase on the New Testament*:

> When some do, before they see my Book, accuse me loudly, as if I pleaded that the Pope is not Antichrist, and that unseasonably. Let them know, that as I say nothing but what I have summarily said of that point in all my Books against Popery these Seven and Twenty years; so that it is a Question I little meddle with, having greater Arguments and surer against Popery: My ignorance of most of the Revelations, I profess, and long have done.

It is possible to test the accuracy of Baxter's claim by examining the occasions when he did discuss the question of the identity of Antichrist, although over a slightly longer time-span than he had suggested. He had claimed consistency over a period of 27 years before 1684. If we start with Baxter in 1653 we find an impeccably lukewarm approach to the whole question:

> I will not undertake to maintain that the Pope is Antichrist, professing my weakness and ignorance of those Propheticall Scriptures to be so great, that I dare not be confident in my interpretations of them: But yet our English Protestant Bishops have commonly been confident of it, and maintained it: and Bishop Downames Book, *de Antichristo*, deserves consideration: and if that hold then the case is clear.[51]

Baxter shelters behind the authority of Downame: an untypical but significant evasion. A year later, in a pamphlet on doctrinal matters, Baxter slips in as an aside: 'I will not call Zanchy a Papist, because he denied the Pope to be Antichrist.'[52] These were cautious statements and neither could be said to constitute a challenge to Protestant orthodoxy.

Yet that is how they were construed, according to one friendly correspondent, Henry Bartlett. He wrote to Baxter a remarkable letter, on
3 June 1654, to warn him of the peril he was placing himself in by his
failure to affirm that the Pope was *the* Antichrist marked out in the
Apocalypse:

> I lately was certainly informed, that one (that was a Parliament man
> after Prides purge and is in a great office, and expects to be chosen
> now) did say last weeke, that you should be questioned next Parlia-
> ment for the Popery in your bookes, whereby many good meaning
> men were deluded, and the Papists were encouraged, and that one
> that lately came from Rome informed, that your bookes were made
> much of theare, and they hoped they would serve for their turne,
> etc. I thought fit to acquaint you with this: that if your Confession
> be not yet out you may more particularly declare yourselfe against
> Popery: But as you well observe that our overdoers have been our
> undoers, so I find, they say, all are Undoers, that will not overdoe as
> they doe: that passage in your Concord, whereby you are not cleare
> that the Pope is Antichrist, how frequently have I heard it declared
> against, as if thereby you shewed your good liking to the Pope, as if
> we must be Papists; if we will not hold him to be Antichrist.[53]

If Bartlett had hoped for some public repudiation of his agnosticism
from Baxter he was disappointed. But certainly the letter did seem to
have the effect on Baxter of checking public expression of doubts. For
the next few years he left the subject alone. How much can be attributed to Bartlett's influence is open to doubt. One piece of evidence that
Bartlett was beating on an open door is provided by Baxter's own
letter to Bromley, referred to earlier, about the Mad Major Wilkie. We
know from that letter how haunted Baxter was in 1654 by the spectre
of Jesuits operating under the 'masks' or 'visors' of Quakers or millenaries. And Baxter wrote to Bromley four days before Bartlett wrote to
him. Although the first part of the letter seemed to be a straightforward
warning to impetuous youth not to be over-impressed by millenarian
cranks, in the last part of the letter he addressed himself to the motivation of Wilkie in telling men that 'a perfecter Revelation is to be expected'. Baxter's answer was that he did so in order to take men away from
apocalyptic certainties. By persuading men of new Babylons and Antichrists, he weakened Protestants' certainty in their own faith. And so
the rationalist tract ended as a sermon against Popery: 'tis more than
probably that there is some blacke Jesuiticall Art that hath drawne up

the whole designe.'

Baxter was haunted by the cunning of the Jesuits:

> The Jesuites are subtill and wicked; able to outreach 100 young men
> and make them believe that they converse with Angells, when they
> are but befooled by these Juglers ... he is blind that sees not the
> hand of Rome, when is so much of the Interest of Rome involved
> ... Their maine drift is to Disgrace the Scriptures as Insufficient ...
> which is the master point of our difference with them. If they gett
> this, they thinke they gett the day.

The belief that the Pope was not Antichrist was fundamental to the
success of the Papal Plot:

> don't you see the Popish interest in all. I confesse some learned
> Divines have doubted whether the Pope be Antichrist. Zanchy
> denied it. But the Jesuites well knew that if they could roote this
> opinion from the minds of the people, the day were halfe won. Its
> not the cleare Evidence and Reason of the matter that so much takes
> with Vulgar minds, even in best causes, as the Reputation of the
> matter with those whom they honor. The Common opinion that the
> Pope is Antichrist doth prevaile more with the Vulgar that can't dis-
> pute against particular doctrines of Rome, than all direct Arguments
> that are used.

The Jesuits are well aware of this, and use millenarian lies to obscure
apocalyptic truths:

> at least they are confident that if they do no more, they shall cert-
> ainly do this much: they shall make that so seeme a doubtfull con-
> troversy, which before seems to the people past question when tis
> seen that so many are of another minde, they will have the advan-
> tage of deriding our change and will tell us how many opinions
> about Babylon and Antichrist are among ours.

Baxter's letter to Bromley concludes with a massive attack on the
Quakers: they are men with 'distracted raptures' (like Major Wilkie);
they are the mask behind which Jesuits plot; they are the same sort of
people who are drawn to witchcraft.[54] Not surprising then that the
following year should see, in a pamphlet totally devoted to opposing
Quakerism, this aggressive statement from Baxter:

That [Quakers] remember yet that it was the disgracing of the Popish Clergy, partly by their own notorious ignorance and vitiousness and partly by persuading men that the Pope is Antichrist, which was the main advantage which the Reformers had for the ruining of the Papall Kingdom; And therefore they would, partly in Policy, and partly in Revenge, attempt the destruction of our Churches by the same means.[55]

James Nayler was forced into a denial that Quakers believed anything other than that the Pope *was* Antichrist.[56]

How nervous Baxter was about the whole subject comes out vividly in a letter to Henry Hickman on 28 May 1657. Hickman had issued questions about the validity of ordination as coming from Rome. Although Baxter would not concede an uninterrupted succession, he yet thought the ministry of the Roman Church as true to the extent that their 'just administrations' were not void. However, he carried this bitter warning to Hickman: 'But if you plead this, your opponent will carry you into a controversy of [the Antichrist] and do you wrong.'[57] Baxter's *A Key for Catholicks* was written in 1659, when his horror of Popery was at its strongest. He was hardly likely to interrupt the flow of his savage anti-Catholic invective to proclaim that the Pope was not Antichrist, and yet even here his scepticism came sneaking out:

But I must profess here to the Reader, that though my modesty and consciousness of my weakness, hath made me so suspicious, lest I understand not the Apocalips, as to suspend my judgment, whether the Pope be the Antichrist, the Beast etc., yet the reading of their serious immodest arguings, to prove the Pope to be the Vice-Christ on Earth, doth exceedingly more increase my suspicion that he is *The Antichrist*.[58]

The prospect after the Restoration of a Declaration of Indulgence that would embrace Popery elicited a different response from Baxter. No qualms about Pope as Antichrist now! Armed with verses from the Book of Revelation he pleaded in 1663:

We ought not at this time to set up Popery, when God seems (according to the prophesies that went before of it) to pull it down. What when Babylon is falling, shall we put our hand to uphold it, when the Kings who have given their Kingdoms to her, threaten her, shall we Indulge her?

He asked: 'Do we pray that Antichrist may be destroyed; and yet do we uphold him?' Even more fiercely he went on:

> methinks the blood of Martyrs cryes aloud, *no toleration of Popery*; the Millions that have been massacred in Ireland etc., cry *how long Lord, good and true, will thou not avenge our blood on them that dwell on the Earth*? shall God *avenge*? and will you *indulge*?[59]

Baxter concluded with his customary attack on the sects as 'visors' and 'masks' for Jesuits: part of the master plot hatched by Contzen, Campanella and Allen. Bishop Bramhall protested in 1672 at Baxter's lurid plots, and at his view of Charles I as a pawn in the 'Grotian' design to exonerate the Catholic Church from Antichristianity. Bramhall drew a distinction between 'that great Antichrist and lesser Antichrists' and did not see why his reluctance to call the Pope the first meant that he was part of a design to bring Popery into England.[60] When Baxter published his *Christian Directory* a year later he sounded much closer to Bramhall than to himself ten years earlier. He was arguing that the Pope was Antichrist in the generalised sense, that he was a usurper, but not in the specific apocalyptic sense. Nevertheless, near the end of that work, he asked himself the question whether Antichrist was excluded from Christians' prayers and love. His reply was astonishing:

> Those that (with Zanchy) think Mahomet to be Anti-Christ, may so conclude, because he is dead and out of our communion. Those that take the Papacy to be Anti-Christ (as most Protestants do) cannot so conclude: Because as there is but one Antichrist, that is, one Papacy, though an hundred Popes be in that seat, so every one of those Popes is *in via* and under mercy, and recoverable out of that condition.[61]

The parenthesis says it all. Baxter acknowledges that most Protestants think that the Papacy *is* Antichrist. Yet he makes the distinction between the office and the persons occupying the office: the Papacy is irredeemable; individual Popes are not. In 1674 he ducks the question by deferring to Downame, much as he did in 1653.[62] In 1675 he asks himself the question: 'Would you persuade us to a union with Antichrist?' Baxter's reply is a model of diplomacy. He speaks of the 'dark text' in Revelation or Daniel. He denies that he is persuading men that the Pope is not Antichrist. He stresses the need for caution, however, in reading evidence for that attribution. He sympathises with Calvin's deci-

sion not to go into these matters. But he concludes with masterly inde-
cisiveness: 'Though no doubt but the book of Revelations is a great
mercy to the Church, and all men should understand as much of it as
they can.'[63]

Scrutiny of Baxter's actions between 1653 and 1684 hardly leads
one to support unequivocally the claims offered in his 'Advertisement'.
Taken separately, some of the statements are true, but their cumulative
effect is to give an illusory picture of consistency. He played delicate
variations on his basic theme in those years, and those variations were
imposed by the political game. He may not have thought much of the
customary identification of Antichrist with Rome, but in 'unseasonable' times he was ready to stifle his doubts. The 'unseasonable' times
were when Popery was triumphing. Thus in the late 1650s when the
Quakers were on the crest of a wave, and again in 1663 when Papists
were hoping to shelter under the umbrella of a royal Indulgence, Baxter was robustly Protestant.

The overall impression is of a man who placed little credence himself
in the identification but recognised its centrality in Protestant apologet-
ics. The surprise about his public statement in 1684 is therefore not
about its content but about its timing. Baxter did not suddenly happen
upon his insight and his biographer, F.J. Powicke, was wrong therefore to see 1684 as a watershed, as part of a general softening of his
attitudes to Popery.[64] What is surprising is that the self-censoring mech-
anism ceased to work in 1684. It had operated effectively in 1653, and
in 1663, when times were 'unseasonable' for the ventilation of opinions
which could comfort the Popish enemy. But why did the self-censorship cease in 1684 of all dates, when Popery was about to come into its
own?

More asked that question, among others which he posed to Baxter in
1684. One answer which More himself suggested was that Baxter was
currying favour with the rising Catholic party. Baxter, on this view, was
warning his fellow Protestants to ignore the delusive comforts of prophecy: even their fond belief, that Antichrist was marked out there,
proved to be unsubstantiated.

The truth was the opposite. Baxter believed that his fellow Protestants *should take more heed of prophecy*. He himself had been remiss on
this count. It was largely a fluke that, at Humfrey's prompting, he had
come to paraphrase the New Testament, and then in the course of
doing so had been forced to come to grips with Revelation. Once having
done so, though, he became increasingly aware of the important truths
which were to be found in such a study for his fellow Protestants. The

more he valued these truths the less ready he was to debase them by joining them with propositions, like the identification of Antichrist, which might have been useful in the past but which now proved embarrassing to a man who wanted the prophetic texts to be taken seriously. In other words, his denial of the identification of Antichrist with Rome is prompted, *not by the desire to impugn Revelation, but to protect its special status.*

More had argued that the identification of Antichrist with Rome was the ark of the Tudor covenant. He had eloquently invoked against Baxter one of the four Elizabethan chained books, Jewel's defence of the Church against Harding. Baxter turned to another, Foxe's *Acts and Monuments*, whose eschatology hinged not upon a positive identification of Rome as *the* Antichrist (although it certainly was *an* Antichrist) but upon clear assumptions of the role of the Christian Emperor. And as Baxter developed in prison in 1686, through his apocalyptic researches, his *critique* of More, he came to realise how subversive of civil magistracy was the interpretation which More had offered. This was far from obvious at first sight.[65] More had explained 'seven thunders' in the Apocalypse. They were successively: the destruction of Babylon; the descent of the New Jerusalem and the laying hold of Satan; the millennial reign of Christ and the close imprisonment of Satan; the letting loose of Satan; the siege of the Holy City by Gog and Magog; the coming of Christ to defeat the besiegers; the conflagration of Earth by thunder and lightning; and salvation of the Saints. By More's reckoning the millennium was the third thunder; the New Jerusalem spanned the third, fourth, fifth and sixth thunders. No scope in this scheme for futurist interpretations: Mede had successfully expounded the *antemedial* and *medial* visions of the Apocalypse. More acknowledged that the *post-medial*, 'in a manner to come', were more obscure but by revising Mede slightly More was able to claim that the English Reformation was the rising of the Witnesses:

> After which immediately succeeds the seventh Trumpet, with which in gross or at large are contained, the Millennial Reign of Christ, the Litigation and Incarceration of Satan, the Palm bearing Company, The Time of the New Jerusalem, or of the Lambs Wife; And this is so firmly proved by Mr. Medes Synchronisms, that there can be no doubt but that these glorious and happy times of the Church upon Earth are yet to come, which is the main scope of the *Postmedial* Visions.

There is much in More's analysis to comfort the civil magistrate: the traditional identification of Rome with Antichrist; the revision of Mede to dramatise the importance of the Reformation; his dependence on the existing magistrate to enforce the piety and virtue that will accelerate the present 'partial and imperfect advance towards the Millennial Reign of Christ'.[66]

The magistrate as scoutmaster: that is where More's arguments seemed to point. Baxter's reading of the Apocalypse in 1686 suggested a more dynamic role for him to play than that in advancing towards the Millennial Reign of Christ. And the closer he analysed More's exposition the less satisfactory the role of the magistrate actually became. The emphasis which More placed upon the 'Symmetral' qualities of the Church before Constantine undercut the claims for magistracy. Worse: More argued that Antichristianity came in with Christian Empire. More argued for the Church of England, not on the grounds of its imperial tradition but of its inheritance of 'Symmetral' *pre-imperial* characteristics of the Ancient Church.

This was a sinister development in a European context. Baxter and his fellow Protestants had seen how Roman Catholics had operated under the 'mask' of Quakers and other sects in the 1650s. More recently, Titus Oates had exposed their designs for world domination. But at least in both periods their aim had been straightforward: to advance the Pope by discrediting the civil magistrate. But there was a new development in the 1680s in which the same ultimate aim — the destruction of the Christian Emperor — could be achieved by different means. 'Italian' Catholics could continue to nurture their fantasy of world domination through the Pope; more realistic 'French' Catholics based their hopes on conciliar supremacy over both Pope *and* Emperor. This was the dream of Grotius, and it represented a highly acceptable compromise to many High Church Anglicans. Union with French Gallicans could be worked for by men *who continued to believe that the Pope was Antichrist*. How real these fears were to Baxter and his friends is strikingly brought by a diary entry of Roger Morrice on 28 March 1682. He noted that the French Convention were undermining the Pope's temporal powers, and as a good Protestant rejoiced in that fact: 'will be very uneasy to the Spanish and Italian Papists'. But, as a good Protestant, Morrice also perceived the fragility of the victory: 'but in order to the perfecting of the Cassandrian and Grotian unity so long endeavoured by so many here, and there'.[67]

This theme of the 'Cassandrian and Grotian' unity is taken up by Baxter in his prison researches in 1686. From this view the real significance of More's interpretation is the harshness of his treatment of Christian Empire:

> If you ask, *what moveth you to write what here you have done*, I answer . . . I am a dying man and would not have my hopes in Christ shaken; which they would be much, if I believed that as soone as his Church was delivered from Pagan captivity it became Antichristian, as very many say; or before 400 yeares, as Mr. More saith.[68]

That Baxter should see his 'hopes in Christ shaken' if More's views on the Apocalypse became an orthodoxy speaks eloquently for the way in which in the course of two years a defence of a particular way of interpreting Antichrist has broadened into a rival eschatology. Baxter shaped that rival eschatology in prison as a result of a personal re-reading of the prophetic texts and of the diverse interpretations of them by previous commentators. But he was helped on that way by correspondence with his friends, much of which has survived. Particularly revealing is his prison correspondence with three men, Thomas Beverley, Drue Cressener and Increase Mather.

Baxter was always generous in his acknowledgement of his debt to Thomas Beverley. He would have seen the hand of 'Providence' in the dispensation which made the millenarian scholar, Thomas Beverley, a fellow prisoner with him in 1686. Baxter developed his arguments about the Apocalypse in the course of prison communication with Beverley. He has left a fascinating record of the process in the form of an unpublished prison note:

> the speciall helpe I had was from Mr. Thomas Beverley his Ms prepared for the presse, which being prisoner also, he freely communicated to me, and candidly perused my arguments against him, and oft by Letters debated the case: But Messengers searching for more matter of accusation against me, surprised me with many of his Letters and some papers of mine by which (besides my booke) they understood my judgment: on which Dr. More reported that I had *perfidiously in an Addresse sought the favour of the Papists* by telling them how I understood the revelatione.

Baxter and Beverley had a great mutual respect. Baxter said of Beverley: 'if he change not my judgment no man is likely to do it, so strong and candid is his judgment.' For his part, Beverley wrote to Baxter on 4 April 1691 — long after both men had been released from prison — 'you who are to mee more a Father, and a Bishop than many nominall ones.[69] It was not a respect founded on identity of views. Beverley believed in a future millennium; Baxter in a past one. Beverley believed that the Pope was Antichrist; Baxter did not. Beverley believed that the world would end in 1697; Baxter thought such speculations blasphemous. Beverley admired Dr Crisp's Antinomianism; Baxter thought it poisonous. One of the only two pamphlets which Baxter ever wrote on the millennium was written explicitly against Beverley. These were formidable differences, and yet there were also forces which drove both men together. One was a distrust for the new conciliar fad among High Church Anglicans; Baxter learned a lot from Beverley's criticisms. A more profound basis of unity still was their common conviction that the Apocalypse, when read right, proclaimed Christ's Second Coming. It is a fallacy to think that Baxter's amillennial historicism cut him off from such intimations. Dr Ball has pointed out that amillennialists like Baxter (and Foxe before him) who did not expect a future millennium shared with premillennialists (who believed that the Second Coming would usher in the millennium) and postmillennialists (who did not expect a literal return of Christ until the end of the thousand-year-reign of His Saints) common historicist assumptions of 'an uncomplicated future, the coming of Christ, an immediate day of judgment and the subsequent reward of the righteous'. He goes on to quote statements from such amillennialists as Thomas Hall, Hezekiah Holland and Joseph Hall to support his argument that 'it is not essential to accept the doctrine of a coming millennium in order to believe in the imminent advent of the Lord.' Throughout his study he emphasises the adventist strand in Baxter's writings, which is the more remarkable in view of the fact that he seems to be unaware of the personal papers of 1686. On the basis of his public writings alone, however, he is able to comment:

> Richard Baxter, whose works reveal an unexcelled rapport with the times, and who has come to be recognised as representative of the more conservative elements in Puritanism, left ample evidence in *The Saints Everlasting Rest* of his understanding of the second advent hope ... A careful appraisal of *The Saints Rest* lived almost daily in the expectation of death, makes it evident that this was not merely a theological concept for Baxter, but a vital element in his own personal faith. 'Hasten, O my Saviour, the time of thy return, send forth Thine Angels, and let that dreadful joyful trumpet sound,' he entreated. 'O blessed day ... how neer is that most blessed joyful day? It comes again, even he that comes will come, and will not tarry.'[70]

The great Victorian adventist, C.H. Spurgeon, would reprint extracts from *The Saints Everlasting Rest* under the title, *The Second Coming of Christ*. In one passage in his manuscript, which he subsequently crossed out however, Baxter had written:

> I say nothing against the millenary hope. The three first petitions of the Lord's prayer raise my hopes higher than the revelations. I find that the Christians of the first age did expect some notable visible reigne of Christ: And Christ did not much contradict their expectations.

This shared adventism permeates the correspondence of the two students of the Apocalypse.[71] Baxter told Beverley in a letter of 31 May 1686 that he was happier with Beverley's 'doctrine of the Millennium' than he was with the proposition that Pagan Rome was not the Babylon whom John described as fallen.[72] Baxter was even happier subsequently with Beverley's modification of the 'meere terrestriale Jerusalem and Millennium described by other Millenarians'.[73] Beverley's worry – confided in a letter to Baxter of March 1691 – was that Baxter might convey the false impression to other people of a bigger difference between them than was the case:

> All Xtians are generally speaking Agreed as in that of the Calling of the Jewes and in that of AntiXtian Apocalyptic Rome. All the main zealous Protestants Agree and those of the Cassandrian Grotian way stand off. Farr be it from mee to suppose that you, who have professed against that way, should mean it the least favour.[74]

Baxter's manuscript replies to More, although not intended as a concession to the 'Cassandrian Grotian way', diverged from Beverley's thoughts on both points which he mentioned: the conversion of the Jews and the identification of Antichrist. One reason for Baxter's scepticism about an imminent future millennium was a timetabling one. He worried about the length of time it would take for the Jews *en masse* to be converted to Christianity. Missionaries would need a great deal of time to learn the language, and even then would lack the fluency to carry conviction: 'Halfe their age must be spent in learning to speake: And when they have done, men will laugh at them for their ill accented broken language, as we do at foreigners and welshmen'.[75] According to one critic, Baxter had Welsh characteristics himself:

Why so many Letters on all occasions? when the substance of them
(if there be any there) may be exprest in a few lines. But to have the
same stories, arguments over and over is intolerable. Like the Welsh-
man, tell a tale, and begin it again.[76]

It would be wrong, however, to think that Baxter treated the problem
of the Jews' conversion simply as a *reductio ad absurdum* of the premill-
ennial thesis. In his *The Life of Faith*, first written in 1660, he outlined
his vision of a College for Conversion: a reminder once more of how
Baxter was caught up in the exciting milieu of the 1650s (so well portrayed by Charles Webster in his recent book),[77] of correspondence with
Eliot about converting Indians, with Lewis about founding universities,
with Poole – as we have seen – about collating news of prodigies, with
Durie about Church union.[78] Baxter argued that it was not enough to
pray for the conversion of the Jews:

> *Do not only pray for them, but study what is within the reach of*
> *your power to do for their conversion.* For though private men can
> do little in comparison of what Christian Princes might do who must
> not be told their duty by such as I. Yet somewhat might be done by
> Merchants and their Chaplains, if skill and zeale were well united;
> and somewhat might be done by history and translating such books
> as are fittest for this use: And *greater matters* might be done, by
> training up some Scholars in the *Persian, Indostan, Tartarian*, and
> other such languages, who are for mind and body fitted for that
> work, and willing with due encouragement to give up themselves
> thereto. Were such a Colledge erected, natives might be fit to teach
> the languages: and no doubt but God would put into the hearts of
> many young men, to settle funds sufficient to maintain them; and
> many Merchants would help them in their expedition. But whether
> those that God will so much honour, be yet born, I know not.[79]

Despite the cautionary note at the end, there is still a qualitative difference between the buoyant mood of the 1650s when all things seemed
possible, and his wry scepticism in 1686 about the possibility of 'obdu-
rate Infidel Jewes' being made wiser and better on a sudden than all
other Christians.[80]

Baxter was equally sceptical about More's identification of Antichrist. Like Mede before him, More had made too much of idolatry as
the Mark of the Beast, and from there had moved swiftly to Rome.
Baxter saw idolatry as a more venial sin:

I have oft had such indiscreet affectionate hearers, that have crept behind me with great desire but to touch my Cloake: If some such weake person should get a bone, or a picture, of Mr. Cartwright, Hildersham, Dod, Bolton, Preston, Jewell, Grindall etc. and should overvalue them are few religious people would call this Antichristianity and equall it with the worship of Devills and Pagan Idols.[81]

A nearer instance at hand were the Puritan sympathisers, who caught the blood of Prynne, Burton and Bastwick in their handkerchiefs, when the martyrs' ears had been cut off. The Catholic Kenelm Digby had in fact used the same example to make an opposite point: 'you may see how Nature leads men to respect relics of Martyrs.'[82] Baxter accepted that the Pope was *an* Antichrist but believed that Mahomet was *the* Greater Antichrist: he followed Foxe rather than More on this point. Baxter praised Bunny's revision of Parsons' book as the greatest formative influence on his early life, and found this to be true of other Nonconformists too.[83] 'If then the common doctrine that papists and protestants agree in, written by the most defamed of all English Jesuites, be so blest of God', argued Baxter, it would be scandalous to write the Roman Church off as Antichristian on dubious grounds.

But his scepticism about the specific attribution did not imply a softening of attitudes to Roman Catholicism. Indeed as part of his 'humble search into the sense of the Revelations', he recited an enormous catalogue of Papist atrocities. His weary comment was: 'And when and where it will stop God knoweth!' But for Baxter the important point is this: 'I do not believe that any text of Scripture tells us that any Antichrist should shed so much blood.'[84] It is not that the Papists are not bad enough to be identified with Antichrist; in respect of bloodshedding *they are too bad*. The Pope was obscene, but he was not Antichrist.

Baxter agreed that the Papacy could be called 'Antichrist' in a noneschatological way:

I doubt not but that since Popes claimed an universall Monarchy or Government of the whole world, as the Vice Christs, that they thereby usurpe Christ's prerogative and therefore may be called *Antichrists* in the same sense as a self-made usurping Viceroy may be called an AntiKing, that is, a traytor.[85]

But he disagreed with Beverley's judgement that these findings were crucial for 'the Cassandrian Grotian way'. It was true that many who were inclined that way also agreed that the Pope was not Antichrist; but not all of them, and certainly not More. But for men who favoured conciliar supremacy the identification of the Papacy was a side issue. The central issue was the power of the magistrate, and Baxter found Beverley as wanting on this principle as he had found More.

Beverley was a shade politer about Constantine than More had been. But only a shade. He had forecast the End of the World in 1697. Baxter had forecast in 1686 that Beverley would have some explaining to do after that date to show why it had not happened.[86] Beverley proved equal to the task. In 1711 he proclaimed 'at the Barr of Reason' his lack of disappointment. Some adjustment of dates was necessary; allowance had to be made for a time-lag between the events and the notice taken of them: 'As then the Great Change by the Christian Empire did not appear, till some time after Constantines Imperial State.'[87] Even if their appearance was belated, Beverley in these words was acknowledging that great events had flowed from Constantine's Empire. In 1691 he had written of the transition from Pagan to Christian Empire as 'a sure Pledge of that Great Millennial Kingdom'. And yet, quite as much as More, Beverley trounced the humbug in exalting Constantine, the Christian Emperor: 'at the same Door, that those things came in, the Christian Purity, Humility, Mortification, Self-denial, Contempt of this World went out.' Beverley moreover jeered at the illogicality of making 'the 1260 years of the Apostasie the 1000 Years Kingdom of Christ'.[88] In reply Baxter expressed surprise at Beverley's slighting references to magistracy:

> Would we not have Christian Kings? Was not Constantines Reign a grand blessing to the Church? who knoweth not that it was he by advancing Christians that let in the Crowd of Hypocrites. And that they will come in when ever prosperity and Godly Princes do invite them: The most will be on the upper side. Shall we therefore be against the Kingdom of the world becoming Christ's Kingdome? Or wish the Church to continue persecuted? If that be best, why write we against the Beast for persecuting? Why pray we not for persecution but against it?[89]

Beverley, as much as More, was shaking Baxter's hopes in Christ by failing to recognise the great change brought into the world by Christian Empire.

Another student of the Apocalypse who crossed swords with Baxter was Drue Cressener. He contacted Baxter in the flush of fulfilled prophecy. Had he not prophesied the Protestant deliverance of 1688 from Revelation, when the faint-hearted had followed Usher in predicting the triumph of Popery for the immediate future? Moreover this was not wisdom by hindsight. Was he not able to produce in 1689 a whole gaggle of bishops who testified that Cressener had contacted them a year *before* the Glorious Revolution with his prophetic insights?[90] In 1690 he wrote against the 'Expedient for Catholick Union of all Christian Churches by the Compliance of the Roman' and believed that his reassertion of Protestant apocalyptic traditions would show the fallacy of claims 'that Grotius was Divinely Inspired, and that Mr. Baxter is the Greatest Man in England among the Protestants for seconding him'.[91] This did not prevent him from making an extraordinary appeal to Baxter in a private letter on 2 June 1691:

> You have given publick testimonies of the great ingenuity of your spirit in yielding sometimes to new information even to the forsaking of a former judgment, which is so very rare a thing, that I much admire it in you. And I should think it a very happy advantage to the Reformation, if after your former opposition of it you should now impartially owne, That its great Adversary is so pompously set forth to the world in the Prophesy, As the Great Antichrist.

Cressener went on to say that his own investigations into the Apocalypse were 'intended for such scepticall, and searching Heads as yours'. Therefore he had handled the subject 'in the closed mathematical method', relying upon the inexorability of logic rather than upon varieties of proofs. Even though, with a rare flash of modesty, Cressener did not put their establishment in the same class as the demonstration of proofs from geometry and arithmetic, he thought that his apocalyptic conclusions were irresistible.[92] For Baxter the trouble was that, on the way, he was asked to accept some extraordinary propositions. Thus Cressener's exposition of the vials proclaimed the first as the victory of the Reformation, and thereafter succeeding vials followed at some forty-year intervals. The second, 'the sea of blood' was the time of the Armada, the French Wars of Religion and the Revolt of the Netherlands; the third, 'the River of blood', was the time of the Thirty Years War; the fourth, the 'man of fire', with its obvious reference to the power of the sun to scorch, must indicate the Sun King, Louis XIV. Now Cressener was aware that Protestants more commonly saw Louis XIV as the 'advancer of the Interest of the Beast'. But Cressener pointed out 'that all that he is regarded for in this vial is that part of his history wherein he has been a plague to the Confederates, and supporters of the Beast'.[93] Baxter was withering about Cressener's identification of the 'German Emperor' with the Beast:

> from whence it followeth that King William with England and Scotland and all the Protestant Princes and States are now Confederates with the beast and fighting for him; that the King of France and the Turks and the Tartarians are fighting against the Beast: And that all the praying people of England and Scotland pray for the Beast that pray for the Emperor's success against Turks or French.[94]

So much for Cressener's 'new information'.

It was one thing to dismiss a Cressener; another to put aside the objections of a revered fellow-inquirer into 'Providences' in Increase Mather. Baxter thought so highly of Mather that *before* publishing his *Glorious Kingdom of Christ* he allowed Mather to see it in manuscript. We have Mather's notes of 16 December 1690 on Baxter's pamphlet, and a letter from Baxter to Mather in that same month. Mather was as sharp as Cressener had been about Baxter's equation of Apocalyptic Babylon with Pagan Rome: 'This notion will mightily please the Papists, like Grotius and Dr. Hammonds endeavour to shew that the pope is not Antichrist.' Mather pointed out that the Kingdom of God was not tied down to the precise span of a thousand years ('I take the 1,000 yeares to be only the morning of that day') and Baxter wronged his opponents in assuming that they thought along such lines. Moreover, his denial of a future general conversion of the Jews put him in opposition to 'the judgment of the greatest divines'. Finally Mather rejected his amillennialism:

> I can not think that the 1,000 yeares are expired ... If the chiliad is past, then Antichrist and his clergy (the beast and the false prophet) are in Hell. For at the end of the 1,000 years they are found there, Rev.20.10, but we know they are still on earth.

This is the difference between millennial and amillennial eschatology. Yet although Mather worries about the fillip that Baxter gives to Grotius and Hammond, he is not seriously accusing him of straying outside the Protestant fold altogether into preterism or futurism. This becomes clear near the end of the letter when Mather counsels him to publish – with one reservation. He wants him to expunge some of the sharper allusions to opponents. Mather makes clear why Baxter and he can differ within a broader area of agreement:

> I would not discourage you from printing . . . because (1) As to the mayne wee agree. You believe that after the Judgment of fire there will be a new Heaven and earth and that of long continuance, wherein righteous men shall dwell, and the creature be restored to its paradisean state. (2) Tho' in some things we differ, yet they are such matters as we may have differing . . . *in salva fide iet charitate.*[95]

Mather pays here a tribute to Baxter's adventism in his recognition of their shared faith in 'the new Heaven and Earth' that would succeed the Judgement of fire.[96]

Such a fine act of judgement was required about publication that it was possible for another correspondent to share much the same general premiss with Mather, and to draw a radically different conclusion from it. John Faldo begins with an apology: he has read as much of Baxter's papers 'as the shortness of the time and my pressing occasions at present would permit'. Unfortunately the letter is undated but his comment that, 'for the severall reasons you menconed, I think you should be best to suppress it,' sounds like a direct reply to Baxter's agonisings in 1686 about whether his thoughts on the Apocalypse should reach a wider audience. He approves of Baxter's desire in expounding the Apocalypse, 'to keep the main scope of it in the eye', but on several grounds disagrees with Baxter's version of 'the main scope'. In particular he asserts that Christian Rome, not Heathen, is described in Chapter 17 of Revelation; that the thousand years of the twentieth chapter cannot be past; that the Albigensians were not the first to call the Pope Antichrist. Although he seems to side with Baxter when he concludes, 'You say well, that we lay not our opposition to Popery chiefly on the dark Revelation prophesy or on the question who is the Antichrist, but on the plain word of God,' the effect of this is spoiled by the writer's conviction that the 'plain word of God' does proclaim a *future* millennium.[97]

We can understand Baxter's change of mind in 1691 in the light of this correspondence with Beverley, Cressener and Mather. There was a case for repressing material which might accidentally benefit Popery, when a Popish King was on the throne. Baxter's own past record showed a keen sensitivity to the harm that could be inflicted on Protestantism by querying the identification of Papal Rome with Antichrist. With the deposition of James II the case for self-censorship was weakened. Even so he did not proceed without taking counsel. That counsel was conflicting, it is true, but Mather's judgement weighed most with Baxter. Baxter's two published works on the Apocalypse in 1691 are a reworking of his 1686 material. I have found no significant modification of his earlier principles. He leaves out a lot of the detailed textual points and — perhaps heeding Mather's advice — expunged some of the more caustic replies to More. The difference between 1686 and 1691 is not a difference of political theory but of political judgement; to publish or not to publish hinged in the end upon a sensitive political judgement about when it was safe to shout that the Pope was not Antichrist.

But were the fruits of Baxter's researches only the strengthening of a scepticism about the identification of Antichrist with Papal Rome which, we had seen, was lurking only just below the surface from as early as 1653? We have emphasised this negative aspect which certainly was important. But there was a positive side too, and ultimately this would be more important. Baxter had always respected the role of the civil magistrate: deeper research into the Apocalypse in the 1680s convinced him that, even so, he and fellow Nonconformists of the seventeenth century had seriously underrated the power of the Christian Prince. One fruit of this insight was his concept of 'National Churches': so important to him that he published in 1691, besides his apocalyptic pamphlets, a whole treatise under that title. We shall see what Baxter meant by this concept, and how profoundly it affected his leadership of Protestant Nonconformity, in the fourth chapter of this book.

Baxter thanked Beverley and 'my harder study of the Apocalypse' for his revaluation of civil magistracy in an important letter (unfortunately undated) to Joseph Boyse. Baxter had come to recognise that Tudor conformists had a surer instinct than even Nonconformists of his own time in the power that they would confer on the civil magistrate:

> the old Reformers in the dayes of K. Henry and Edw.6 and Q. Eliz. were sounder in this than the Nonconformists mostly; and that popery is mainly built on the denying or obscuring it, and confining church power to the sacerdotal.

Baxter explained the apocalyptic roots of civil magistracy:

> God instituted a holy magistracy before Abrahams time, in Abrahams time, in Moses and the Judges, in Saul, David, Solomon and he never repealed it, tho' he repealed the Lawes of Mosaicall Jewish Administration he altered not the form of constitution . . . Kings are obliged to be sacred persons in exercise, continually to read the Law

of God, and to meditate in it day and night. Moses understood it better than Aaron: they are as sacred persons as priests, tho' not priests: they are God's anointed, both as Types and officers of Christ: they are bound to punish false deceiving prophets and priests, and therefore to know where they offend. Our old writers Jewel, Bilson, Bp. Buckeridge, Abbot, Andrewes . . . etc. have fully proved that Kings now have as much power about religion as Asa, Hezekiah, Josiah, Nehemiah, Zorababel etc, had of old . . . Almost the whole book of the Revelations describeth him as punishing and conquering the pagan, captivating Idolatrous Babylon by his sword and setting up his government by a Christian Empire.

We have seen how Increase Mather, the millennial, could still recognise in Baxter's amillennialism a shared vision of the New Jerusalem; from the other way round, Baxter, the apologist for magistracy, could still honour in his millenarian colleagues a shared vision of a royal kingdom:

The description of the New Jerusalem and of the finall judgment fully proveth that Christs Kingdome as instituted and consumate conteineth his sword government, of which Angells and men are officiall substitutes. All the millenaryes maintaine the Royall Kingdome, except they be grosse self-contradicters. He that denyeth that it is the Duty of King and Subjects to be Christians is Antichristian. And if Kings and Subjects be Christians, they are Christian Kingdomes . . . If Episcopall, Presbyterians or Independents or Anabaptists deny this Royall Administration of Christ, and confine his Kingly Government only to the Priests, they serve Popery, and are so far Antichristian.

Baxter turns to a Tudor bishop, Thomas Bilson, for support for the argument that the civil/ecclesiastical distinction is false, and that the true distinction is between *sword* and *word*, or *force* and *doctrine*. Therefore he argues: 'nothing can take down popery but restoring princes to the sacred power of bearing the sword as the officer of God and of Jesus Christ in the ministeriall exercise of Christs kingly power by the sword.' Erastus, Selden and Lewis du Moulin went too far against clergymen but they could not go too far in their respect for magistracy: 'far be it from any Christian to reproach King Jesus, King of Kings, and to deny his Royalty, or his Royall officers, by the name of *Erastian*, and so deny an essential part of Christianity.'[98]

If we turn back to 1657 we can see how far the Apocalypse has taken Baxter in his support of magistracy. In December 1656 Thomas Horne had written to Baxter for his views on the Apocalypse.[99] Baxter's reply, on 11 January 1657, was in a sense predictable: that these were speculations that excited him more when he was young: 'my juvenile fancye being more daring and more confident than now I find myself disposed to be'; that the Apocalypse was not unintelligible, 'but it followeth not that so you or I understand it'; that to proclaim that the end of the world was coming on 25 March 1657 was a rash judgement that could be soon put to the test. He was particularly scornful of Horne's belief that the bishops could be a bulwark against Rome; especially — interestingly enough — those bishops who had denied that Rome was Antichrist. He went on: 'But seriously do you thinke, if Magistrates hold their sword still, and preachers hold their tongues and pens still, that Episcopacy and Ceremonies (which the Papists all awe and love) will pull down the Pope'. Yet Baxter was writing in 1657, when he was haunted by the spread of Popery, and when he was hungering for the magistrate to use his sword: 'it is not for want of Bps, but it is for want of the Magistrates restraints which workes most on those kind of people.'[100] This was the dilemma: Baxter wanted the magistrate to pull down the Pope, but he lacked *status*. The deeper study of the Apocalypse was the way out of the dilemma.

Foxe had shown the way. The more Baxter studied the Apocalypse, the more he respected Foxe's achievement. When he wrote publicly against Beverley in 1691 he appealed to Foxe:

> I once more intreat the Reader to read John Foxe ... who was no Papist, and thought Prophetical, when he told Mrs. Honiwood despairing in Melancholy how she would recover and live to be old, when in unbelief she threw a Glass to the Wall or Ground, and took it up whole, and fulfilled his Prophesie.[101]

This was the prophet whom advocates of a future millennium would ignore at their peril. And earlier, on 18 May 1690, responding irritably to the confident way that Beverley and Jurieu expounded their revelations, he confided to his manuscript the observation that they had no monopoly of illuminations from the Almighty:

> If extraordinary Light or Inspiration may embolden confidence, who can plead more than John Fox, what man more holy, more humble, more ripe in experience, more averse to Popery. Who yet professed ... that God did by Revelation by sudden irresistable impress (equal-

ly to a voice, tho' not a voice) tell him that the 42 months must be numbred as Daniels weekes by sabbaths of years; And the good man appealeth to God with an Oath that it is true. And that there upon he found that the time ended at the death of Licinius, just the same yeare that the pagan persecution ended. And that then he thinkes began the 1000 years of the Dragons binding, and ended the first yeare of the Ottoman Empire. And he thinketh that the great Beast (7-headed and ten horned) was the Pagan Empire and Mahomet the greatest Antixt and the pope the 2nd Beast and the Western Antixt: I justifie not this: But who hath a more plausible plea for credibility? I thank you for them, and I have read all your books: and can say that I am able to say much more against your exposition than you have yet said against John Foxes.[102]

Baxter might have been here discussing the visions of Major Wilkie, although the 'equal to/though not' distinction in the above passage was perhaps crucial. Certainly Baxter was fascinated by the process by which Foxe attained his apocalyptic insights: it is a topic to which he returns on other occasions. He quotes from 'that holy credible man John Fox' his own account of the process:

Thus being vexed and turmoiled in spirit about the reckoning of these numbers, it so happened that on a Sunday in the Morning I lying in bed and musing about these numbers, suddenly it was answered to my Mind as with a Majesty, thus inwardly saying within me, *Thou foole, count these months by sabbaths as the weeks of Daniel are counted by Sabbaths.* The Lord I take to witness thus it was.[103]

Baxter had formulated a schematic pattern for the reading of Apocalypse; Foxe's experience was one way in which it broke down in practice. He argued that there were five ways of expounding the Apocalypse: 'Meerly Literall' ('contrary to Reason'); 'Cabalisticall' ('fictitious and presumptious'); 'Conjecturall' ('by reasons which seem plausible to each man as prejudice and fancie dispose him'); 'Rationall' ('fetcht from the context of former prophecies'); 'Revelationall' ('By propheticall Inspiration or Vision'). Baxter believed that his own practice was rational with a dash of conjectural:

But I joyne the Rationall way about the great substantiall points of the prophecy (and I am therein cleare). And the *Conjecturall way* about some few but dark phrases or circumstances such as the *666 Number* the time and half time etc., . . . As for the Cabalisticall and unproved and Revelationall wayes, I will not censoriously oppose them. But take up with things certaine, and leave the rest to the proofe of the wise or more self-conceited.

Baxter would seem to have bracketed 'Revelationall', with 'Literall' and 'Cabbalisticall' interpretations, but in reality his mind was open on the subject. There is an almost wistful note in his reference to 'Revelation-all' interpretations: 'This last John Foxe sweareth by an Appeal to God that he had . . . And some others too have bin as confident as if they had Visions: I can boast of no such thing.'[104] Yet his description of the genesis of *Aphorismes of Justification* — his first published work — had Foxe-like intimations. A dying man at the end of 1646, he had started writing *Saints Everlasting Rest* in convalescence at Rous-Lench. He had reached page 68 — on the need to see in what sense men are called righteous — when the revelation came: 'An over-powering Light (I thought) did suddenly give me a clear apprehension of these things, which I had often searched after before in vain. Whereupon I suddenly wrote down the bare Propositions'. The parenthesis — 'I thought' — takes some of the immediacy from the experience; he often in fact repented later of the pamphlet's hasty and ill-digested presentation. But this was a genuine turning-point in his career, and he never repented of the experience itself.[105] To set the 'rationall' Baxter against 'revelation-all' rivals is once more to miss the genuine sense in which Baxter was part of a movement which he was also criticising.

Against preterist and futurist interpretations, Baxter stressed the value of historicism. An illusory past and an impossible future were routed by an historical understanding. The best antidote to the false peddler of visions was a true insight into Church history:

He that is but furnished with the historicall knowledge of past matters of fact and then impartially readeth over the booke it selfe, will have cause to thank God that he hath a clearer expository light than most expositors give him, and that he hath escaped their obscu-ring self devised expositions.[106]

In *The Life of Faith* he expressed his passion for a better teaching of history:

Therefore the writing of Church-history is the duty of all ages, because Gods Works are to be known, as well as his Word: And as it is your forefathers duty to write it, it is the childrens duty to learn it (or else the writing it would be in vain). He that proveth not what state the Church and world is in, and hath been in, in former ages, and what God hath been doing in the world, and how errour and sin have been resisting him, and with what success, doth want much to the compleating of his knowledge.[107]

Those without knowledge of Church history are condemned to ignorance of a millennium which had been located in the past. No wonder they failed to do justice to the achievements of the Christian Empire since the time of Constantine:

I cannot imagine unlesse it be to see Christ and Angells, what any Millenary (called Fifth Monarchy men) can reasonably expect as to outward administration than what was then given to the Church. Would they have Christ visibly reigne by Christian Rulers. So he did then. Would they have the civil and ecclesiasticke power. So it was then. Would they have all their enemies forced to submit to them as their Lords. So it was then. Would they have Christianity publickly possesse the Country of Judea. So it did more plentifully and splendidly than any other nation on earth, proportionally. Would they have the Churches have the full power of Church discipline, to separate the precious from the vile. So they had. Would they beate the swords into plow and be out of the danger of pagan persecution, and need to learne warr no more, as being under the defence of Christian Magistracie: so it then was.[108]

Baxter's search into Revelation to redress the historical wrongs done to magistracy brought him up against the real crime of Popery:

It is a great cause of all our Church confusions, that the usurpation of the Romane Clergy hath by appropriating to themselves the title of the CHURCH and the ministers or Vicars of Christ, obscured the true dignity of Christian Princes and Magistrates, and blinded the world (and too many Rulers) with a false and base conceit, that Princes are but for the Body, and Priests only for the Soule, and so that the office of every priest is as much above the Kings as the soule is above the body: And as the Soule must rule the Body, so must the Pope, prelates and priests rule Kings and Magistrates: And hereby the Glory of Christs Kingdome as set up in Power, by Christian Emperors and Kings is clouded, and the sense of the Revelation perverted, by Papists and too many Protestants, who call for the exercise of Christs Kingly office by a vile mistake as if it were only in the hands of pope, prelates, presbyters or popular congregations.

The perversion of Revelation is the clouding of this imperial truth, grasped more firmly by Foxe and Jewel than by those who came after them:

> And God hath given the world too few good Princes, because we do not sufficiently value and pray for such. Whereas a due consideration of Scripture would tell us, that Christian Princes are as sacred persons as priests, and are bound as such to understand the Law of God, and are the Rulers of Priests by the sword, the priests may guide them by the word as their physicians when they choose may direct them for their health ... That Christs Kingdome was but in its Infancy till he visibly ruled by the sword, by Christian Princes. And as God did in the time of the Judges rule by Prophets and Inspired Deliverers, till Kings were Setled, and then let Government run in the naturall course, so did he by propheticall Apostles and Inspired Teachers keep up his Church, till he had ripened it for a Christian Empire, and then let it run in the naturall channel.[109]

For Baxter the apostolic church was kept up until it 'ripened' into a Christian Empire; for Beverley and More it was the 'Symmetral' model for reform before Antichristianity *came in* with Christian Empire.

Baxter meant it when he said to More that his 'hopes in Christ' would be shaken if he accepted More's view that the rot set in with Christian magistracy. Historically the defence of Christian magistracy had been linked to the concept that the Pope was Antichrist. Baxter took the bold and imaginative step of breaking that historic link *in the interests of Christian magistracy*. The Laudians had done so from opposite motives. The more he studied the Apocalypse in 1686, the more convinced he became of the power of the Christian magistrate, the more unconvinced of the identification of Papal Rome with Antichrist. He knew what he was doing when he printed his doubts about Antichrist: that is clear from his earlier letters and pamphlets. Moreover, just before he published his controversial *Paraphrase on the New Testament* he was in the thick of acrimonious disputes with Anglicans like Dodwell, Sherlock and Thorndike. He had been reading the recently published biography of Laud by Peter Heylyn and he could guess where his opponents of the 1680s drew their inspiration from. He knew the significance of the Laudians' retreat from their predecessors' faith that the Papacy was Antichrist. He knew that it was meant to facilitate the 'Grotian' type of unity – on terms laid down by Rome – which he had always distinguished sharply from his own ecumenical hopes.[110]

He knew the risk he took when he affirmed publicly that he did not believe the Pope to be Antichrist. It was a risk which he might not have been prepared to take, paradoxically, if it had matched a parallel disregard for apocalyptic research as a whole. The contrary was true: the more excited he became by what the Apocalypse taught him about the powers of the magistrate, the significance of 'National Churches', the more important it became not to entangle these truths with propositions which were dubious, even although they seemed to be convenient. Mather believed that Baxter was wrong to have doubts about Antichrist but from equally profound adventism recognised the sincerity of his desire to honour the Apocalypse. That is why he thought Baxter should publish his notes, even although Catholics might incidentally make political capital out of them.

Baxter agreed with Mather in 1691; it had been his own belief– and practice – with the publication of his *Paraphrase on the New Testament* in 1684. In between these dates – in 1686 – he had sought to conceal his researches. The common-sense explanation of his secretiveness is largely correct: truths that helped Catholics became 'unseasonable' when a Catholic sat on the throne. And yet if the unseasonable truth had *only* been that the Pope was not Antichrist he would seem to be making a lot of fuss about little. For the damage had already been done. He had already named the unmentionable in public. He could heap *further proofs* to show that the Pope was not Antichrist, but they would hardly in themselves justify all the mumbo-jumbo – instructions to literary executors, scrutiny by an impartial divine, and the like.

Another explanation is possible. The presence of a Catholic King on the throne challenged those insights into magistracy which the Apocalypse was teaching him. There is a very real sense in which Baxter's published writings of 1691 are the fruits of his apocalyptic studies of 1686. *The Glorious Kingdom of Christ* and *A Reply to Mr. Thomas Beverley's Answer* are direct replies to Beverley's reading of the Apocalypse; *Of National Churches* extends his changing views on magistracy and Church government; *The Certainty of the Worlds of Spirits* continues Mather's inquiry into signs and providences. Finally his pamphlet, *Against the Revolt to a Foreign Jurisdiction*, defends the removal of James II. It was not only the brash Cressener who had seen 1688 as the fulfilment of prophecy. Beverley described the unfortunate James as 'intolerable to prophecy', whereas William of Orange had been 'borne upon the wing of prophecy'.[111] Such language − or thinking − was not for Baxter. This did not mean that he did not *use* the Apocalypse against James II; but he used it in a very different way.

The Apocalypse did not open up new insights into magistracy so much as invest old ones with a new status. We shall see in the next chapter how highly he regarded the Christian Prince throughout his career. This regard was compatible with an unsentimental awareness of the defects of individual Christian Princes. There was a case even for Nero. Constantine had been no saint: 'Emperors also had their odious crimes; even Constantine killed his Eldest Son Crispius, and after his Step-Mother for accusing him and banished Athanasius: shall we therefore be unthankful for a Christian Empire, which was Christ's own Visible Kingdom?'[112] Was there then any crime odious enough to cost the Emperor his job? There was only one: failure to fulfil his imperial role. 1686 was the time of supreme embarrassment for Baxter: when his regard for magistracy was raised to a higher apocalyptic pitch at the same time that a Papist King sat on the English throne. How he resolved the embarrassment becomes clear in his published, and even more in his unpublished, writings of 1691. He came prepared for that task, not only by his researches in prison in 1686, but by earlier hypothetical resolutions of this problem. We shall see in the next chapter how Baxter's attempt after the Restoration, to explain the origins of the English Civil War, is much more a rehearsal of these later debates than has commonly been supposed.

Notes

1. (DWL) *Baxter Treatises*, ii, f.103; vii, f. 296.
2. Ibid.
3. (DWL) *Baxter Treatises*, vii, f. 294v.
4. B.W. Ball, *A Great Expectation* (Leiden, 1975), p. 110.
5. (DWL) *Baxter Correspondence*, vi, f. 123-5.
6. Keith Thomas, *Religion and the Decline of Magic* (London, 1971), p. 110, notes the parallel between Poole's project and the Royal Society's attempts to collect and classify natural phenomena.
7. (DWL) *Baxter Correspondence*, iv, f. 255 (Baxter: Matthew Poole, 31 August 1657).
8. Thomas, *Religion and the Decline of Magic*, p. 111.
9. (DWL) *Baxter Correspondence*, 1, f. 217v (Baxter: Increase Mather, December 1690).
10. This was a collection of anti-Royalist prodigies, issued in three parts in

1661-2 as *Mirabilis Annus*. The work was a continuation of Henry Jessey's *The Lords Loud Call to England* (London, 1660), and may have been partly written by Jessey. See C.G. Whiting, *Studies in English Puritanism* (London, 1931), pp. 547-51; Thomas, *Religion and the Decline of Magic*, p. 111; Ball, *Great Expectation*, pp. 111-14.

11. Baxter, *The Life of Faith* . . . (London, 1670), p. 142; Baxter in Matthew Sylvester (ed.), *Reliquiae Baxterianae* (London, 1696), ii, pp. 432-3.

12. Baxter, *The Saints Everlasting Rest* . . . (London, 1650), pp. 261-2.

13. Baxter, *A Key for Catholicks* . . . (London, 1659), pp. 184-5.

14. (BL) *Egerton MSS* 2570, f. 88v.

15. Baxter, *The Successive Visibility of the Church* . . . (London, 1660), pp. 164-5.

16. Baxter in Sylvester, *Reliquiae Baxterianae* ii, pp. 431, 364-5.

17. G.F. Nuttall, *Richard Baxter* (London, 1965), pp.42-3, has a balanced discussion of Baxter's infirmities.

18. Samuel Young, *Vindiciae Anti-Baxterianae* (London, 1696), preface, p. 61.

19. (DWL) *Baxter Treatises*, xiv, f.4-4v (Baxter: John Warren, 11 September 1649).

20. Baxter, *The Saints Everlasting Rest*, p. 117.

21. (DWL) *Baxter Correspondence*, v. f.3.

22. Baxter, *A Breviate of the Life of Margaret* . . . (London, 1681), p. 80. There is a fascinating glimpse of his wife's sovereignty in the household in Baxter's dispute with a wayward servant: (DWL) *Baxter Correspondence*, iii, f. 290v (Baxter: John Griffith, 19 July 1681).

23. (DWL) *Baxter Correspondence*, v, f.11-11v.

24. (DWL) *Baxter Correspondence*, v. f.28.

25. (DWL) *Baxter Correspondence*, iv, f. 183.

26. (DWL) *Baxter Correspondence*, v. f.5-6.

27. (DWL) *Baxter Correspondence*, v. f.9.

28. On which, see Chapter 3.

29. (DWL) *Baxter Correspondence*, v. f.55 (R. Beresford: Baxter, 2 January 1660).

30. Young, *Vindiciae Anti-Baxterianae*, p. 247.

31. (DWL) *Baxter Correspondence*, i, f. 119.

32. Baxter, *A Breviate of the Life of Margaret*, pp. 44, 45.

33. Philip Henry, *Diaries and Letters*, ed. M.H. Lee (London, 1882), p. 268.

34. (DWL) *Baxter Correspondence*, v. f.140-140v; Baxter, *The Saints Everlasting Rest*, p. 141 (at least this contains the only paragraph in 'Ch.7 Sect.6' which seems to make sense in the context of Morris's letter).

35. Baxter, *A Defence of the Principle of Love* . . . (London, 1671), pp. 58-60.

36. (DWL) *Baxter Treatises*, vii, f. 45-45v.

37. (DWL) *Baxter Treatises*, iii, f. 302-9. Baxter, *A Defence of the Principle of Love*, p. 55, has a reference to the Major in the context of warnings against melancholy. G.F. Nuttall, 'James Nayler: A Fresh Approach', *Friends' Historical Society Journal Supplements*, 26, 1954, pp. 1-20, has a good discussion of Thomas Bromley in relation to James Nayler's milieu.

38. (DWL) *Baxter Treatises*, iii, f.302v, 303, 303v.

39. A. Ward, *Life of Henry More* (London, 1710), pp. 132-4. On St Augustine's distinction between 'prophetic inspiration' and 'conjecture of the human mind' (*City of God*, xviii, p. 52), see R.E. Lerner, 'Medieval Prophecy and Religious Dissent', *Past and Present*, 72 (1976), p. 8.

40. (DWL) *Baxter Correspondence*, i, f.215v-216 (Edmund Whichcote: Baxter, 4 March 1682).

41. Baxter, *Saints Everlasting Rest*, p. 246.

42. Baxter in Sylvester, *Reliquiae Baxterianae*, ii, pp. 432-3.

43. Baxter, *Confession of his Faith* . . . (London, 1655), p. 3.

44. Henry More, *A Modest Enquiry* . . . (London, 1664), preface, pp. 44, 54, 59, 82, 133, 134, 180, 181, 189, 200, 203, 207, 212.

45. This did not mean that Baxter was uncritical of More's methodology. Far from it. He put his finger on its essential weakness: 'If their Imagery, ambition, viciousness, persecution make not the Greeks or any others to be the Babilon and Beast, it will not prove Rome such, till the Pope claimed as vice christ to governe all the world: And if it begun but then, it was too late to be the same Babilon that is in Apocalypse': (DWL) *Baxter Treatises*, v, f.93v. Yet it is the *idea* of Antichrist – usurper, viceroy, idolater – that is as much the focus of Baxter's ideas as it is of More's. More saw the inconsistency in this: 'Philicrines Parrhesiastes', *Some Cursory Reflexions Impartially Made Upon Mr. Richard Baxter His Way of Writing Notes* (London, 1685), p. 14.

46. Baxter, *The Cure of Church-Divisions* . . . (London, 1670), dedicatory epistle.

47. (DWL) *Baxter Treatises*, vii, f. 295. For examples of Baxter's close relationship with Glanvill, see characteristic letters from Glanvill to Baxter: (DWL) *Baxter Treatises*, i, f. 170-4. There is an interesting letter from Glanvill to Baxter on 21 January 1663 about psychic investigation (ibid., v, f.177) and an equally interesting letter from Baxter to Glanvill on 18 November 1670 about witches and apparitions (ibid., ii, f.138). Cf. also Baxter in Sylvester, *Reliquiae Baxterianae*, ii, p. 378.

48. 'Philicrines Parrhesiastes', *Some Cursory Reflexions*, pp. 10, 18; More, *Apocalypsis Apocalypseos* . . . (London, 1680), p.vi; More, *Paralipomena Prophetica* . . . (London, 1685), preface.

49. (DWL) *Baxter Treatises*, i. f.81v.

50. John Owen, *A Brief and Impartial Account of the Nature of the Protestant Religion* (London, 1682), pp. 27-8.

51. Baxter, *Christian Concord* . . . (London, 1653), p. 69. Baxter includes as an appendix to his pamphlet, *The Safe Religion* (London, 1657), pp. 381-455, a translation of the seventh chapter of Downame's proof that the Pope was Antichrist. Cf. also an excited anonymous comment: 'A large booke written by Dr. Downame to prove that the Antichrist is already come, and the Pope he' – (East Sussex Record Office) *Frewen MSS* 598, f.401.

52. Baxter, *Richard Baxter's Admonition to William Eyre* . . . (London, 1654), p. 8.

53. (DWL) *Baxter Correspondence*, vi, f.122.

54. (DWL) *Baxter Treatises*, iii, f.306v, 306, 309.

55. Baxter, *The Quakers Catechism* (London, 1655), dedicatory epistle.

56. James Nayler, *An Answer to a Book called The Quakers Catechism* (London, 1655), p. 13.

57. (DWL) *Baxter Correspondence*, i, f. 266. See how cleverly at this time Baxter *associates* himself with Protestant orthodoxy on Antichrist without *committing* himself, and getting in a thrust at the Quakers into the bargain, in this attack on Papists: 'And though their errours are so many and great, that most Protestants take the Pope to be the Antichrist, yet are they so arrogant as to pretend to Perfection, as the Quakers do' (Baxter, *A Winding Sheet for Popery* (London, 1657), p. 12).

58. Baxter, *A Key for Catholicks*, p. 301.

59. Baxter, *Fair Warning* (London, 1663), pp. 16, 17, 18, 19.

60. John Bramhall, *A Vindication* . . . (London, 1672), p. 35.

61. Baxter, *A Christian Directory* (London, 1673), p. 847.

62. Baxter, *Full and Easie Satisfaction* . . . (London, 1674), p. 188. He adds a

charming disclaimer: 'Every man should be best at that which he hath most studyed.'

63. Baxter, *Catholick Theologie* (London, 1675), ii, p. 293.

64. F.J. Powicke, *A Life of the Reverend Richard Baxter . . .* (London, 1924) pp. 258-61.

65. And More did not intend that it should be obvious. See, for instance, how cleverly he forced opponents on to the defensive: they had to protest that *their* interpretation of the millennium did not do down magistracy (Joseph Beaumont, *Remarks on Dr. Henry More's Expositions* (London, 1690), preface).

66. More, *Apocalypsis Apocalypseos*, p. 328.

67. (DWL) *Morrice Entering Book P*, f. 331.

68. (DWL) *Baxter Treatises*, vii, f. 295v.

69. (DWL) *Baxter Correspondence*, v. f.239-40.

70. B.W. Ball, *A Great Expectation* (Leiden, 1975), pp. 72, 75, 163, 28, 29. The best recent critical survey of writings on this topic is Hillel Schwartz, 'The End of the Beginning: Millenarian Studies, 1969-1975', *Religious Studies Review*, 2, 3 (July 1976), pp. 1-15; Paul Christianson, *Reformers and Babylon: English apocalyptic visions from the reformation to the eve of the civil war* (Toronto, 1978), is a valuable work of synthesis.

71. (DWL) *Baxter Treatises*, vii, f. 288v.

72. (DWL) *Baxter Correspondence*, i, f.61.

73. (DWL) *Baxter Treatises*, ii, f.187-187v.

74. (DWL) *Baxter Correspondence*, i, f.64v.

75. (DWL) *Baxter Treatises*, ii, f.180v.

76. Young, *Vindiciae Anti-Baxterianae*, p. 116.

77. Charles Webster, *The Great Instauration* (London, 1975).

78. Examples of each respectively in: (DWL) *Baxter Correspondence*, i, f.59; i, f.127; iv, f.255; v, f.199-199v.

79. Baxter, *The Life of Faith*, p. 536; although reprinted in 1670 with additions, the substance was written in 1660.

80. (DWL) *Baxter Treatises*, vii, f.299v.

81. (DWL) *Baxter Treatises*, ii, f.116v.

82. *Calendar State Papers Domestic, Charles I, 1637*, p. 332.

83. (DWL) *Baxter Treatises*, vii, f.298v. The debt of Baxter and other Nonconformists to Parsons prompted Dr Bossy to argue that, in the early seventeenth century, the popular mission of the Catholic clergy was more effectively to English Protestants than to English Catholics: J. Bossy, 'The English Catholic Community, 1603-1625', *The Reign of James VI and I* (London, 1973), pp. 104-5.

84. (DWL) *Baxter Treatises*, vii, f.277.

85. (DWL) *Baxter Treatises*, ii, f.112v.

86. (DWL) *Baxter Treatises*, vii, f.45. How men respond to the shattering of their eschatological predictions has been observed in: L. Festinger, H.W. Riecken and S. Schacter, *When Prophecy Fails* (Minnesota, 1956); (in fiction) Alison Lurie, *Imaginary Friends* (London, 1967). Cf. also R.E. Lerner 'Medieval Prophecy and Religious Dissent', *Past and Present*, 72 (August 1976), pp. 17-18.

87. Thomas Beverley, *The Grand Apocalyptic Question . . .* (London, 1711), preface, p. 46.

88. Beverley, *The Thousand Year Kingdom of Christ . . .* (London, 1691), pp.33, 32.

89. (DWL) *Baxter Treatises*, vii, f.125.

90. Drue Cressener, *The Judgments of God Upon the Roman Catholick Church* (London, 1689), preface. A specimen from several such testimonials: 'These are to certifie, That the Commentary upon the Revelation of St. John, to the Nineteenth Chapter, was sent to me by the Author, and read over by me, near

a Year ago; when there was not so much a Thought of what is since come to pass in this Kingdom, March 22, 1689, Simon Patrick, Dean of Peterborough.'

91. Drue Cressener, *A Demonstration of the First Principles of the Protestant Application of the Apocalypse* (London, 1690), preface.

92. (DWL) *Baxter Correspondence*, iii, f.15-15v.

93. Cressener, *The Judgements of God Upon the Roman Catholick Church*, pp. 200-7.

94. (DWL) *Baxter Treatises*, vii, f.302v.

95. (DWL) *Baxter Treatises*, vii, f3, 3v, 4v, 7.

96. Cf. (DWL) *Baxter Treatises*, vii, f.290, where Baxter says: 'I firmly believe that (its like after 1000 years) there will be a blessed Sabbatisme and that there will be a new heaven and a new earth in which shall dwell righteousness . . . such a Kingdom of God I hope for: but not for a meere 1000 yeares but as the everlasting sabbatisme.' Beverley also recognised the common apprehension of a 'New Heaven and New Earth' with Baxter: see (DWL) *Baxter Correspondence*, v, f.239v, Beverley: Baxter, 4 April 1691.

97. (DWL) *Baxter Correspondence*, v. f.161-2.

98. (DWL) *Baxter Correspondence*, ii, f.11-12v.

99. (DWL) *Baxter Correspondence*, v. f.156.

100. (DWL) *Baxter Correspondence*, iii, f.115, 117, 118.

101. Baxter, *A Reply to Mr. Thomas Beverleys Answer . . .* (London, 1691), p. 12.

102. (DWL) *Baxter Treatises*, vii, f.45. Baxter found the *confidence* of commentators like Brightman, Jurieu and Beverley intolerable. On Brightman, Baxter commented: 'I loathe such expositions as Brightmans that say [This Angel was Thomas Cromwell, and that Angel was Cranmer, etc.]. He that will feigne that I meane English when I expound Gods words that speaks of all or other Churches, will judge his own words and not mine': (DWL) *Baxter Treatises*, i, f.82. And in the course of confuting Jurieu's '35 characters of Antichrist' he claimed that he was 'marvellously confident in his exposition of these prophecies upon uncertain grounds, yea improbable': (DWL) *Baxter Treatises*, vi, f.356v. Beverley attempted to counter Baxter's criticisms with remarks such as: 'I know not a phenomenon that I have not solved': (DWL) *Baxter Correspondence*, iv, f.286, Thomas Beverley: Baxter, 21 May 1686. Baxter, for his part, wished that critics would be more ready to 'confess their uncertainty': (DWL) *Baxter Treatises*, vi, f.357v.

103. (DWL) *Baxter Treatises*, ii, f.132v-3.

104. (DWL) *Baxter Treatises*, ii, f.103v.

105. J.I. Packer, 'The Redemption and Restoration of Man in the Thought of Richard Baxter', unpublished D. Phil. thesis, Oxford, 1954, p. 233, quotes this passage and argues its importance as a genuine traumatic break in Baxter's life.

106. (DWL) *Baxter Treatises*, ii, f.111.

107. Baxter, *The Life of Faith*, p. 374.

108. (DWL) *Baxter Treatises*, ii, f.172v.

109. (DWL) *Baxter Treatises*, vii, f.300v.

110. Baxter, *The True History of Councils Enlarged and Defended* (London, 1682), pp.18-19, 88, 187.

111. Beverley, *A Memorial . . .* (London, 1691), no pagination; Beverley, *The Command of God to his People* (London, 1688), dedicatory epistle.

112. Baxter, *The Glorious Kingdom of Christ* (London, 1691), p. 7.

2   BAXTER AND THE ORIGINS OF THE ENGLISH CIVIL WAR

The English Civil War began as a constitutional conflict and ended as a religious one. That was the thesis which Richard Baxter advanced in his autobiography. It has been taken up and expanded into an ambitious reinterpretation of the English Revolution in a long essay by Dr Manning. Dr Manning even accepts Baxter's judgement on when the change took place: in 1643 with the publication of a pamphlet called *Plaine English*. The author of the pamphlet is not named by Dr Manning, but the argument which it sustains — that the issue of the war was 'liberty or tyranny, Popery or true piety' — marks for Baxter (and Dr Manning) a decisive change in the character of the Parliamentarian cause.[1]

The author of the pamphlet was Edward Bowles. In the same year in which he wrote *Plaine English* he wrote *The Mysterie of Iniquity*. He addressed himself in that pamphlet exclusively to the question of whether Charles I was implicated in the Irish Rebellion of November 1641. The evidence offered was slight and the author's tone was apologetic and defensive. He was exploring 'a Mystery, a worke of darknesse'; it was not to be expected that the proofs which he offered would stand up to court-room standards of scrutiny. Moreover men like Falkland, who had really drafted the King's Answer to Parliament's Nineteen Propositions, were moved by a sincere desire for peace. But at Newry the rebel leaders, O'Neill and Macguire, had claimed the King's support for their Papist Rising and produced royal commissions in his name to authenticate that claim. The King had said that the commissions were forged. Why should he have given the rebels such backing? Bowles argued that the rebels knew — better than Falkland a few months later — the slipperiness of Charles I's character. They needed, in other words, to bind him to them. Moreover, there were no limits to the lengths to which Papists would go to deceive Protestants. On the other hand, they dealt openly with each other. Bowles noted that Charles failed to dissociate himself convincingly from the rebels until as late as January 1642; his actions in the intervening two months belied his professed horror at the rebels' actions. His promise on 8 April 1642 to chastise 'those wicked and detestable Rebels' was the minimum he had to offer in order to conceal his real convictions. Nothing in the course of the Civil War gave that promise plausibility.[2]

The tone of the pamphlet is far removed from Baxter's sober reconstruction of events, as we shall see. But how divergent were they in reality? A curious exchange of correspondence in 1679 points a different moral. Edmund Borlase had just published a successful exposé of Irish Papist atrocities. He sent a copy to Lewis du Moulin. He was assured of a sympathetic response from such a doughty anti-clerical controversialist.[3] Du Moulin predictably praised Borlase, in his letter to him on 2 September 1679, for a style which was 'strong and current and well worded'. But he went on to say that he had 'seen and read (but I have it not now) an order and declaration of the Counsell about my Lord Antram declaring he had done nothing but what he had order and letters for'. He then correctly recalled Bowles's pamphlet with its information on the commission given by Charles I 'to the Irish (not to massacher) but to stand upon their armes and to oppose all those that were in this warr for King and Parliament'. He had also seen the pamphlet, *Murder Will Out*, which concentrated on the specific commission given to the Earl of Antrim by Charles I. Du Moulin believed that there had been such a commission. But since he had also spent a lifetime attacking the way in which clergymen in general (and Papists in particular) weakened the magistrate's authority, he was prepared in this case to defend the King's right to issue such commissions. He concluded that, on the whole, Borlase 'did prudently to decline to speak out'.[4]

That decision had not been Borlase's to take. We know now that Borlase possessed information on the Antrim commission and that Sir Roger L'Estrange had intervened on 20 February 1679 to prevent such material from being published because of the damage it could do to the Crown.[5] On the other hand, it is clear that Borlase had not then read *Murder Will Out* because a letter has survived, addressed to him from Richard Parr on 4 September 1679, in which he explains that 'I have sought for that pamphlet you mention vizt Murther will out but cannot meete with it yet, when I do you shall have it.'[6]

In the chapter that follows I shall try to show why the Antrim commission, the pamphlet *Murder Will Out*, and the allegations of O'Neill and Macguire should continue to excite fevered speculation among men who wanted to find out why the Civil War had happened, long after the events which they were discussing had taken place. I shall argue that Baxter shared du Moulin's interest in Bowles's revelations. Bowles's circumstantial evidence on the Irish Rebellion was prefaced by copious allusions to the Book of Revelation: the proper context in which to place Papist perfidy. In the previous chapter I showed how important it was to Baxter to read the prophetic texts correctly. That interest brought him closer to Bowles's reading of the Civil War than has commonly been recognised; closer than Baxter himself would be prepared to concede when he came to write his autobiography after the Restoration.

A recent historian has written of the 'almost religious reliance' placed by later generations on Baxter's dissection of the Civil War parties.[7] The charm of Baxter's interpretation lies in its magnanimity. The story, as he develops it, is not melodramatic but tragic. The English Civil War was not willed by Papists. It was rather the outcome of a long series of misunderstandings, whose roots go back to previous reigns. On both sides there were good men. The dividers *on either side* were the real culprits. There is a good retrospective case for neutrality. This is a memorably lukewarm analysis, and its fairness and objectivity have won it respect from many quarters. It becomes a key text in R.B. Schlatter's thesis that Baxter was the constant champion of mixed government.[8]

Whatever its superficial attractions it is not a thesis which should command an almost religious acceptance. It was written long after the events which it described. Baxter himself acknowledged the limitations which this imposed: 'distance disadvantageth the apprehensions.' Some of the best things in it were cribbed from his friend, John Corbet, who had at least produced his analysis of the Civil War in Gloucester at the time when the events occurred.[9] Most damaging of all, they were written after the Restoration by a man who had already burned his fingers badly in Commonwealth politics: not the ideal time to fling mud on the memory of Charles I.[10]

What are the grounds for setting aside the published version in Baxter's *Autobiography*, with its recollection in tranquillity of a breakdown of the constitution, as being a misrepresentation of what Baxter actually felt in 1642? The highest grounds would be the discovery of personal papers which survived from that time which contradicted his later assertions. That discovery has not been made, nor is it likely to be. Baxter's earliest published writing dates from 1649; there is little in the way of personal correspondence before that date to throw additional light on his position. We have to fall back on inferior evidence. This may be divided into three separate sections. The first section is an analysis of the text of his *Reliquiae Baxterianae*. It requires us to look at the circumstances in which his memoirs were composed, and the way in which his original manuscript was treated by successive editors. The second section looks at these findings in the context of his other writings on the Civil War. Baxter wrote about the origins of the Civil War on other occasions than the famous version in his memoirs. Many of these writings were produced even later in time than that account — and so were even further removed in time from the events described — although one of them, his *Holy Commonwealth*, actually antedates the Restoration. In private correspondence with friends after the Restoration, however, Baxter is notably less discreet than in his public statements. The third section deals with the discovery of one undated and unpublished treatise among his private papers. From internal evidence it was composed some time after the accession of William III and Mary. He never finished it, and it may have been among the last works which he wrote. I would like to see it as the summing up of almost a lifetime's obsession with the origins of the Civil War. But to make my point stick I must show how the evidence from the text of the *Reliquiae Baxterianae* and that of his writings do point in the same direction as this unpublished treatise, his *Political Catechise*.

We will begin with the text. There are four major versions of Baxter's famous autobiography. In chronological order we should list: *Baxter I*, the original manuscript version, unfortunately not complete; *Baxter II*, the published version edited five years after his death in 1696 by his friend, Matthew Sylvester, the famous *Reliquiae Baxterianae*; *Baxter III*, the abridgement of Sylvester by Edmund Calamy, first published in 1702, with subsequent enlargements in 1713 and 1727; *Baxter IV*, the Everyman abridgement of Sylvester by J.M. Lloyd Thomas of 1931 (the new edition by N.H. Keeble in 1974 has a revised introduction but the text follows the Lloyd Thomas abridgement in its entirety).[11] If *Baxter I* had survived in its entirety we would have faced no problem. That problem, it is true, has been lessened by the conscientiousness of Sylvester: *Baxter II* has been widely accepted as a faithful transmission of Baxter's original material. Where the text has survived, and we are able to compare the manuscript version with Sylvester's edition, the changes are slight. Indeed the criticism of Sylvester is that he has been all too faithful. Even on 3 February 1692, John Tillotson read the danger signs. He wrote then to Sylvester with the delicate warning: 'I would not have you make too much haste in it (to which many will be pressing you) but take time enough to do it well.'[12] Poor Sylvester was hag-ridden by fidelity to the memory of his beloved Baxter. Nothing was left out and *Reliquiae Baxterianae* was the result: the victory of loyalty over literature. Calamy produced *his* edition in reaction to Sylvester's sprawling monster. He made no pretensions to accuracy. By judicious *omissions*, he sought to produce a more manageable book. He did more: by judicious *additions*, he sought to produce a more coherent and logical one. The most easily accessible of the Baxter texts is *Baxter*

IV: the Everyman edition, which omits passages from Sylvester in much the way that *Baxter III* did, but without the interpolations that marred the Calamy text.

These textual variations are important when measuring the response of contemporaries, who did not warm to the balance and moderation of the analysis, as later historians would; many deplored it, rather, as a mischievous assault upon the integrity of Charles I. It almost seems as if they were talking about different books. And perhaps they were. For example, when we read a particularly venomous attack on 'Black Saint Baxter' for his calumnies on the King, we find that the edition under attack is *Baxter III*.[13] Calamy was quite open about the liberties that he took with the text: 'sometimes I have kept pretty much to his language and sometimes I have taken the freedom to use my own. I have divided the whole into Chapters, and given things a little connexion.'[14] A flagrant example comes from Baxter's explanation of the Civil War. His paragraph on the Irish Massacre begins in *Baxter I*, *Baxter II* and *Baxter IV* in an identical way: 'But of all the rest there was really nothing that with the people wrought so much as the Irish massacre and rebellion.' That same sentence appears in *Baxter III*, but minus the phrase 'of all the rest'. This radically alters Baxter's sense. Moreover in *Baxter III*, at the end of this same paragraph, comes an additional passage not found there in the other three editions:

The Irish declar'd They had the King's Commission for what they did: And many even at that time, weighing all Circumstances, believ'd as much, while others represented it as an horribly Unjust and Scandalous Aspersion upon His Majesty; but as Providence ordered it, a certain Memorable Particularity help'd to set the Matter in a just light. The Marquess of Antrim, who was a Noted Man among the Irish Rebels, having had his Estate Sequestered, tho't fit, upon the Restoration of King Charles the Second to sue for the Restitution of it. The Duke of Ormond and the Council judg'd against him as one of the Rebels. Whereupon he bro't his Cause over to the King, and affirmed, That what he did was by his Father's Consent and Authority, the King referr'd it to some worthy Members of his Privy Council, to examine what he had to shew. Upon examination, they reported, *That they found he had the King's Consent, or Letter of Instruction for what he did*, which amaz'd many. Thereupon King Charles wrote to the Duke of Ormond and the Council, *To restore his Estate*, because it appear'd to them appointed to Examine it, that what he did was by his Father's Order or Consent. The Lord Mazarine, and others in Ireland, not fully satisfied with this, tho't fit so far to prosecute the matter, in that the Marquess of Antrim was forc'd to produce in the House of Commons a Letter of King Charles the First, by which he gave his Order for the taking up Arms, which being read in the House produc'd a general silence. The whole account of it, with a great many surprizing Particulars, was publish'd in a pamphlet call'd *Murder will Out*. At the time when the Barbarity was committed, all England was fill'd with fear.[15]

We are thus introduced in this passage to those revelations about Charles I's commission to the Earl of Antrim which we have seen had caught the imagination of Borlase and du Moulin.

We now can understand Royalist anger at Baxter's memoirs. Even after the Restoration it would appear that he was prepared to snatch at a weak, circumstantial tale from a dubious source in order to link Charles I with Irish Catholic rebels in 1641. But we have seen that this perception was rooted in a misunderstanding. Ostensibly from Baxter, the tale had been fathered on him by Calamy.

But this cannot be true either. Some of the Royalist anger at Baxter pre-dates the appearance of *Baxter III*.[16] We see why: this Antrim story *is* in *Baxter II*, but at a much later place in the text, with an apology to preface its inclusion out of turn: 'I had forgotten one passage in the former War of great remark, which put me into an amazement. The Duke of Ormond and Council had the cause of the Marquess of Antrim before him.' Then follows the story – as Calamy had told it – but with a cautious marginal note: 'We are not meet Judges of the reasons of the Superiours actions.'[17]

Thus Calamy is vindicated. He had not minted something new, but had merely restored the Antrim episode to its intended place in the text. Indeed one critic, Thomas Long, writing in 1697, found it difficult to believe that Baxter could simply have forgotten to include the Antrim story in his interpretation of the origins of the Civil War.[18] Did Sylvester exercise editorial control and place the story at a more innocuous point in the text? Could he have added the craven marginal note? Either or both is possible. If Sylvester had doubts, it might be objected that the simplest solution would have been to omit the Antrim story altogether. This is to misjudge the man. Total suppression might have seemed to the conscientious Sylvester of a different order from judicious rearrangement of material already there. Certainly his preface reveals a touching concern to scotch the myth that Baxter was a hater of Charles I. Moreover he showed himself willing to insert additional

material to humour John Owen's widow. Motive and opportunity therefore were not lacking. Since the manuscript material for this later part
of *Reliquiae Baxterianae* is missing, we cannot be sure.

But we do have *Baxter I* for an earlier part of the narrative, when
Baxter also refers to Ireland. And this is one point where we can catch
Sylvester out in a deliberate omission. In the passage Baxter placed a
parenthetical comment, which Sylvester *deliberately* left out. The passage runs as follows:

> (And now lately some nameless author hath gone about to persuade
> men that it was true, by publishing a Letter of the present King, and
> the Lord Deputy or Commissioners in Ireland, *in the behalfe* of the
> Marquesse of Antrim (one of the Irish Generals) to absolve him from
> sequestration, and being found uppon examination that what he did
> was for his fathers service and by his consent) . . .[19]

Baxter had thought that the Antrim episode was important enough
to be included in his explanation of why the Civil War had happened,
even if it was wrapped in brackets. Sylvester simply expunged it from
the record.

Modern scholarship has confirmed the importance of the Irish Rebellion in the origins of the Civil War. Charles I was not directly involved
with the leaders in promoting the 1641 Rising and the commission that
Sir Phelim O'Neill produced at Newry was almost certainly a forgery.
Charles's guilt was at a different level: his negotiations with the Irish
nobility in the summer of 1641 made possible the later *coup*. The coin-
cidence of timing of events and the rebels' claim to be acting with royal
authority made plausible fears of a royal-inspired 'Popish Plot', which
Pym was not slow to exploit.[20] Thomas Long was one of the earliest
critics of *Reliquiae Baxterianae* for reviving an old *canard*: 'The King is
represented as a Papist and Authorizer of the Irish Insurrection.'
Although the story rested on no stronger documentary basis than the
regicide pamphlet, *Murder Will Out*, Long saw the blessing of Baxter as
instrumental in elevating its status. Writing in 1697 he noted that 'it
was beginning to pass as Common Discourse in Cabals and Coffee-
Houses.'[21] The enemy that Long must have had in mind was a man like
Samuel Young who, a year earlier, had hailed Baxter's Antrim revelations with enthusiasm:

> If this will not convince the World of the Righteousness of our Civil-
> War, I know not what will. I pray all advocates for that worst of

Kings, consider it. I am ready to prove him a Popish, Perjurd, Arbitrary, Tyrannical, bloody Pseudo-Martyr.

Young saw how Antrim smashed the argument for non-resistance: 'You cannot doubt, but he that gave him one, gave others too, though they came not so to light. Was there not reason for the Parliament to prevent a Massacry here?'[22]

Young was making a brave attempt to explain away one weakness in the case against the King: the absence of similar warrants to other Rebel leaders. There were other flaws. Long pointed out one of them: why did Parliament not use this charge, in their exhaustive researches for their case against the King?[23] Ludlow was able to use the Antrim story in his memoirs with the words, 'thus the mask was openly taken off,' but in the speech which John Cook *almost* made at the King's trial the proof is blatantly circumstantial:

If I meet a man running down stairs with a bloody sword in his hand, and find a man stabbed in the chamber, though I did not see this man run into the body by that which I met, yet if I were of the jury, I durst not but find him guilty of the murder.

Cook blusters: 'Many strong presumptions, and several oaths of honest men, that have seen the King's commission for it, cannot but amount to a clear proof.' Later critics, like Long, were not impressed. Moreover there was the evidence that Sir Phelim O'Neill had retracted his claim to royal support at his trial. This was the point that impressed William Binckes in a sermon to the Commons on 5 November 1705. He saw Charles I as victim of a Popish Plot that brought him to the scaffold.[24] Benjamin Bennet, writing in 1723, was equally sceptical about the claim that the King gave a commission to the Irish rebels, but this did less well for Charles I than might appear. For while Bennet thought that Papists were quite capable of forgery to make the King odious, that same capacity for equivocation made O'Neill's retraction worthless. Bennet's conclusion was thus:

I don't suppose the King gave a commission to the Irish rebels, for the purpose they us'd it, and for the work they did; all that I suppose is, that he might encourage, and authorize them to take up arms, and assist him in the circumstances he was then in.[25]

This was much more sophisticated than the anonymous pamphleteer of

1702, who used Charles's commission to the Irish to flesh out his picture of Charles I as the shedder of blood.[26] Such melodrama could be avoided — as it was even by Cook in his near-speech and by Baxter himself in 1659 — by portraying Charles I as personally innocent, but the dupe of a 'Grotian' Papist design. Whether Charles I was knave or pawn, the right of Parliament to resist was incontestable. To contest the incontestable, the premiss had to be challenged: the Antrim story had to be exploded.

This was where Thomas Carte came in. His refutation of Baxter was published in a pamphlet of 1715, *The Irish Massacre Set in a Clear Light*. He named Ludlow's memoirs and *Murder Will Out* as the sources for the story; quoted Arlington's testy letter to Ormonde on 30 January 1664 on the damage done by the rumour; showed how O'Neill and Macguire retracted their claim to royal backing; pointed out that the warrant was not concerned with the *beginning* of the Rebellion and that Charles II's meaning had been perverted by the libellers.[27] It is a good piece of critical analysis; but it represents the tip of the iceberg. Carte's private papers, both before and after 1715, show the lengths to which he went to get at the truth.[28] Carte made copious notes on the collections and memoirs of Castlehaven, Nalson, Lilly, Bramhall, Howell, Holles, Rushworth, Heylyn, Burnet and other writers to show the groundlessness of the allegation; the ace in the pack was the omission in the charges against the King in 1649 of specific reference to the commission for the Rebellion in 1641.[29] In October 1717 correspondence reaches Carte of the harm done by preachers raking up the Antrim story, and who still 'urge very much what Baxter etc. did'.[30] On 1 May 1719 another correspondent is transcribing chunks of Long's pamphlet for Carte's benefit and says of Baxter, 'I have his *Holy Commonwealth* and will transcribe any thing you send for.'[31] Earlier, on 16 February 1713, Carte writes to Richard Cresswell about his successful use of oral history, and gives this vivid account of O'Neill's trial:

> I went to enquire of Mr. Newburgh as you directed about the charge against the King, Ch[arles] the First. He says, that his Uncle was present at the trial of Sir Phelim O'Neal in the Chancery — Court of Dublin where the High Court of Justice satt, but there was a Committee in an adjoining room called the Chancery-Chamber, who directed the Commissioners what questions that they propose to O'Neal etc. They pressed him very earnestly to plead the King's Commission for his rebellion, but he answered, He would not increase his crimes by accusing an innocent man who was dead, a messenger was appointed

to goe constantly from the Commissioners to the Committee and represent to them all proceedings in the Court. He spoke thro' a square hole in the wall, and received their instructions on every occasion, but nothing was soe much insisted on as endeavouring to extract from O'Neal an accusation against the King. He owned He had publickly show'd a pretended Commission, but that he said was of his own framing, he having been bred in the Laws of Court in England and the great Seal affixed to it was taken from an old Patent. The tryal was drawn out to a great length, that he might be wrought upon. Mr. Newb[urgh] thinks it lasted severall dayes, but be persisted in his defence of the King's innocency agt. all the temptations thrown in his way. And since he was the first Author as well as the chief Generall of the Rebellion his Testimony was received without dispute.

Carte was less successful with the Antrim letter:

Mr. N[ewburgh] does not know anything of the pretended Letter about the Marquis of Antrim, he remembers that Ld. was restored to his Estate, which he allways apprehended was done only in respect to the Marquesses assisting Montross as Siding with the Duke of Ormond against the Pope's nuncio when the pacification was made with the Irish Rebells.

He concluded with a defence of Charles I's integrity:

you may remember the character which Mr. Vines after the Treaty in the Isle of Wight gave the King to Mr. Gilbert the Presbyterian of Coventry who related it to my father. I mentioned it in a former Letter to you, and one part of it was in these words, Of all the Kings of Israel and Judah there was none like him.[32]

A similar attempt by Carte to obtain verbal support from Antrim's nephew met with heart-breaking failure, as he recounted in a letter of 6 August 1717. He had intended to use the good offices of a friend to win him an introduction to the Marquis, but a series of unfortunate coincidences forced him to seek the meeting earlier than he had intended, without such support. He knew what he wanted:

for as my desire was to have such a Authentic Account of the M[arquis] of A[ntrim] Trial before Court of Claims on August 20

1663 and of the Case as it appeared to the Court wch pronounced him Innocent, as I might oppose to the very scandalous and false account of it published in the pamphlet called Murder will out, which was first printed in 1663, reprinted in 1689 . . . As I desired nothing else but this and copyes of some of the papers presented by the M[arquis] to the Council: in his own defence when his Cause was there (the originals whereof were burnt in the Fire at Whitehall, as the Records of the Court of Claims were in another that happened some years ago in Dublin). I desired 'em for no other end than the Interests of Truth and Justice . . . But as his Lordship was pleased to reject and scarce to hear of my Request, I am perfectly at a loss what to do in this Case.

Poor Carte had to set against his accounts not only a wasted journey to Ireland in pursuit of the elusive Antrim but 'the Expense of a London journey purely for the End of search of Council Books for Accounts of the several hearings before the Council, and collected Materials for the purpose'.[33] As late as 10 April 1718 the search continued, as a letter to Viscount Ikerrin, in Carte's possession, of that date testified:

I can only acquaint your Lordship, that I have search'd the Journals both of the Lords and Commons house from the year 1660 to December the 16th 1665 and for more years before and after, and I doe assure your Lordship there is not any such letter, nor the least mention of the Marquis of Antrim directly or indirectly in the Lords or Commons Journals. Mr. Worthington is Keeper of the Commons Journals, and Mr. Enoch Hearne keeps the Lords' Journals; I would have had a certification under their hands about this affair, but they told me that was a demand which was not practis'd nor could it be granted me: since I received yours, I have made it my business to peruse Sir James Ware's and Mr. Richard Cox's History of Ireland, they both agree as to the time of the passing of the act of Explanation, Sir James Ware does not mention the Marquis of Antrim but one Paragraph; his words are these he says that July 1663 (he does not set down the day of the month) the Lord Lieutenant and Council received a letter from the King in favour of the Earl of Antrim which they answered, these are Sir James's words; Mr. Richard Cox (who is the best writer of the two) takes noe manner of notice of the Marquis, this is what I thought proper to acquaint your Lordship with.[34]

For Carte and his correspondents the truth about Antrim meant fresh light on the origins of the Civil War. Baxter gave the story credence by publishing it in his memoirs: lost in the Sylvester edition, it became a key passage in the Calamy edition. But Calamy had grounds for protest at the way he was subsequently traduced: 'if they would consider that I report it from Mr. Baxter it might abate their Censures. If he was imposed upon in this matter, I cannot help it.'[35] The editor who tampered with the original text was Sylvester, not Calamy. He used his editorial discretion to delete Baxter's parenthetical aside about Antrim. His preface contained the significant words that

Mr. Baxter is charged by some as *being against King Charles the First in the past War, and too much a Fomenter of it.* To this you have his Reply, in the History itself; and thither I refer the Reader.[36]

But the most misleading of all the Baxter editions may be the most modern one. Certainly in Baxter's original hand there is considerable material on the role of the Irish Rebellion in the coming of the Civil War — quite apart from the Antrim Commission — which found its way into both Sylvester's and Calamy's editions, but not into the *Everyman* edition, which is probably the one most familiar to general readers. In particular there is a long section in *Baxter I* and *Baxter II* which begins: 'And now we come to the main matter, What satisfied so many of the intelligent part of the country to side with the Parliament when the War began.' This section is not to be found in *Baxter IV*. Baxter breaks down the causes of the war into eight points. The second he names as the 'Murder of 200,000 Protestants in Ireland and their friends so Bold in England'. The sixth is the belief that Charles I had forsaken his Parliament and wanted to protect Delinquents, 'but it is the Irish, the Papists and those guilty persons who would *ruine* all and save themselves from Justice, whom they accuse, and not the King'. The eighth, and most significant for an understanding of his political theory, is the denial that passive obedience is the only possible response to the triumph of Popery if 'unchristian rebellion' is ruled out:

The Protestants Patience was that which pleased the Irish: or (if a King must be brought in as a party) the French Mens Patience in the *Parisian* Massacre pleased Charles IX and the Executioners: And if in all countries the Protestants would let the Papists cut their Throats, and die in the Honour of Patience, it would satisfie those bloody Adversaries; who had rather we die in such Honour, than lived without it. But if such Patience would be a poor excuse for a Father that fought not to preserve his Children, much less for the Parliament that stood still while Papists and Delinquents subvert both Church and State.[37]

A disservice to Baxter is done by omitting such passages from the Everyman edition: often the source for historians' comments on the motive of Baxter (and sometimes, by inference, of his fellow Puritans) in fighting a Civil War on the side of Parliament.[38]

Even in the Everyman edition Baxter's interest in the Irish Massacre is not wholly obscured. We have seen that the passage is retained where he surveys the various issues which led to Civil War and says: 'of all the rest there was nothing that with the people wrought as much as the Irish massacre and rebellion.' He added that, *at the time*, he had shared this astonishment and that this had swayed his judgement. But the distancing effect of using such phrases as 'of all the rest' and 'with the people' does its work in relegating the Popish issue to a minor part in the story.

But Baxter could not leave the issue alone, to judge by the way he took up the Antrim revelations after the Restoration. Matthew Sylvester did his best to cover up for his friend and in part succeeded. But Thomas Long and Thomas Carte were two men who had no illusions about Baxter. He was in their eyes quite simply one of the perpetrators of the most damaging libel on monarchy which circulated in the seventeenth century.

We need now contextual evidence to put these textual findings in perspective. How far was Baxter's interest in the Irish Massacre, and the Antrim commission, a lonely exception to his general readiness to put constitutional matters first? Quite apart from the passages in his memoirs, Baxter pontificated on the causes of the Civil War on a number of occasions. We ought to be quite clear about when he was saying it, and to whom; the emphases change with time and audience.

The first group of writings date from the last years of the Commonwealth. In his *Holy Commonwealth* of 1659 he emphasises the self-preservative nature of the war:

And when we saw the odious Irish Rebellion broke forth, and so many thousands barbarously murdered, no less (by a credible testimony) than a hundred and fifty thousand murdered in the one Province of Ulster ... If you say, *What was all this to England*? I answer, We knew how great a progress the same party had made in England.[39]

He would never be quite so frank again about the connection between the two events or about what might have happened if the Royalists had won the Civil War: 'His impious and Popish Armies would have ruled him, and used him as other Armies have done them that entrusted them.'

In another pamphlet, *A Key for Catholicks*, written a few months before *A Holy Commonwealth*, Baxter showed how it was not necessary to believe that Charles I was a Papist to recognise how he *could be used* by Papists. He denied that Charles was a 'flat Papist' and believed that his execution speech cleared him of that charge. But the Jesuits had shown exceptional skill in infiltrating Protestant antinomian sects: 'We fear the Masked Papists and Infidels, more than the bare-faced, or than any enemy.' Charles's ingenuousness could be exploited by unscrupulous men, 'who take on the several shapes and names'. The Jesuits excel at covert warfare: 'the principal design that the Papists have upon our Religion at this day is managed under a sort of "Jugglers".' Baxter was especially concerned that many Levellers were now Royalists: a splendid 'vizor':

And whence came it that Sexby and others, that have been soldiers in our Armies, have confederated with Spain to murder the Lord Protector? And whence are the Jesuitical Treasonable Pamphlets (such as Killing no Murder) provoking men to take away his life?[40]

In another pamphlet at this time Baxter made clearer how Charles I, without being a 'flat Papist', could promote the Papist cause: 'while he as a Moderate Protestant took hands with the Queen a Moderate Papist, the Grotian design had great advantage in England, which he himself boasted of.' And when his usefulness came to an end, the Papists put him to death.[41]

His writings after the Restoration are markedly different in tone. They had to be: Baxter was a highly suspect figure, not least because of his *Holy Commonwealth*. To save his political skin he had to disown that work. Answering Bishop Morley's charges against him on 9 July 1683, he was able to cite his *Christian Directory* of 1673 as his act of atonement for writing his *Holy Commonwealth* earlier. He singled out with pride in the later work his 'large confutation of R. Hooker (as to *singulis maior et universis minor*)'.[42] This is the line which he also peddled in his memoirs: that many clerical simpletons like himself had been over-impressed by Richard Hooker's arguments against absolute monarchy. This in turn led to such follies as Baxter's flowery dedication of his *Holy Commonwealth* to Richard Cromwell. The moral he repeatedly drew after the Restoration was that clergymen (like himself and Hooker) should keep out of politics, and leave such matters to the lawyers.

Such an analysis was consistent with a view of the Civil War as being primarily a muddle over the constitution. Because this worked to Baxter's personal advantage it should not be discounted as insincere. On the contrary it is clear that it touched a deep chord in Baxter. He did believe that a populist fad had deceived many men of his generation; he did believe that the magistrate's authority must be upheld at all times (except one, which we shall come to in a moment). The insincerity comes in the pretence that between 1659 and 1673 lies an abyss. If he failed to convince opponents like Bishop Morley of this, however, he was in deep political trouble. He had somehow to convince them that his *Holy Commonwealth* belonged to the days when he took Richard Hooker's liberalism seriously. If the earlier work had indeed been an apology for Hooker and the philosophy of *singulis maior et universis minor* his confutation of both in his *Christian Directory* would have been a spectacular *volte-face*. It is not, because a glance at the *Holy Commonwealth* will show that he offends monarchy in that work not by emphasising its closeness to tyranny but its closeness to Popery. But throughout the *Christian Directory* he acts as if he *were* repudiating a formal liberal self. His *Christian Directory* lacked the offending dedication to a Lord Protector, but in no other way does it show a significant shift in his political thinking. Advice continued to flow from his pen to the politicians of the day: this time though in the form of 'Memorandums' rather than 'Directions' to rulers; in his new chastened mood he contented himself with 'Memorandums'. The distinction was a very contrived one. 'Memorandum 14' for the magistrate reads: 'Keep the sword in his own hand, and trust it not in the hands of Churchmen.' It was by no means clear why magistrates should heed 'Memorandums' but not 'Directions', nor why they should ignore Churchmen in general but listen to this one Churchman in particular. The truth was that Baxter wrote as much or as little about politics after the Restoration as he had done before. Nor was the message conveyed radically different. Baxter did, at one point in the *Christian Directory*, acknowledge as much when he said that although he regretted writing his *Holy Commonwealth* he did not recant 'the Doctrine of it, which is for the Empire of God, and the Interest of Government, Order and Honesty in the World'.[43]

What Baxter meant by the 'Empire of God' — and what he defended in both pamphlets — was the unfettered authority of the magistrate. The enemy was Roman Catholicism, which sought world domination through the destruction of the civil magistrate's authority. His contempt — as much in 1659 as in 1673 — was expressed for common lawyers and liberal Anglicans who dissuaded the magistrate from using his powers to the full. Baxter never sounded more like Hobbes than when he was pouring scorn on the feeble compromises of a Hooker. Even the Emperor Nero had his points. He had weaknesses, it is true, but at least he knew how to use the sword and how to keep the mob in check. His tyranny cost *hundreds* of victims their lives, but the count would have risen to *thousands* if the rabble had been let loose. Bad government was better than no government.[44]

We should not be in doubt about Baxter's 'Toryism', although we should be in doubt about using the term. Baxter rebelled against the use of such a term in his reply to Dr Sherlock of 1682,[45] but it was 'downright plain Toryism' that Samuel Young found in Baxter's posthumous memoirs when he reviewed them in 1696. Young was disgusted with the lengths to which Baxter went in his praise of the sacredness and inviolability of magistracy. He saw Baxter's career as the pilgrim's regress:

> Once he was a Chaplain in the Army against the King, and a notable Clarificator he was. Kings did stink in the Nostrils of God, etc. And when he write his Saints Rest; the wonderful appearance of God in that cause, was an Argument to prove the truth of the Scriptures by. Oh what a Confirmation it was to his Faith! And after all this, in the Reigne of Charles the II, he turns Non-Resister, calls in his Political Aphorisms; and then he wrote the Book, now printed, when a Tory ... For he saith ... that the Person and Authority of the King is inviolable, that he cannot be Accused, Judged, Executed by any having Superior etc.[46]

Young may have falsified Baxter's *motives*, but not his *sentiments*. The most vigorous statement of Baxter's regard for magistracy comes in his *Christian Directory* of 1673, but it might as easily have come from Hobbes's *Leviathan*:

> Because the multitude of the needy, and the dissolute Prodigals, if they were all ungoverned, would tear out the throats of the more wealthy and industrious, and as Robbers use Men in their Houses, and on the Highway, so would such Persons use all about them, and

turn all into a constant War. And hereby all honest industry would be overthrown, while the point of Mens labours were all at the Mercy of every one that is stronger than the owner; and a Robber can take away all in a Night, which you have been labouring for many years, or may set all on a fire over your heads. And more persons would be killed in these Wars that sought their Goods, than tyrants and persecutors are to kill (unless they be of the most cruel sort of all). And it is plain, that in most Countries, the universal enmity of corrupted nature to serious Godliness, would inflame the rabble, if they were but ungoverned, to commit more murders and cruelties upon the godly, than most of the Persecutors in the World have committed.[47]

Young was clearly not exaggerating the deferential nature of Baxter's political theory. But he was wrong to see it as an apostasy from 1659. His *Holy Commonwealth* of that date is the product of the same nightmarish world: a world which, I will argue, Baxter inhabited throughout his life. There was the same terrifying vision of anarchy only warded off by the sword of the magistrate; the same revulsion from democracy and overweening clerical ambition. Harrington's democracy was the ungovernability of the rabble given the fig-leaf of respectability by his Utopian elaborations: as unpalatable in 1673 as it was in 1659. The difference lies not in the diagnosis but in the remedy. The solace for the faithful offered by Baxter in 1673 is only that even the most vicious tyrants are a better bet than mob rule. His *Holy Commonwealth*, on the other hand, we shall see in the next chapter to be a legitimate fulfilment of the millenarian hopes of the 1650s (however he tried to play this down at the Restoration): a millenarian hope in magistracy only properly to be rekindled in 1686 with the discovery of 'National Churches', and rediscovery of the Christian Emperor, as one by-product of his researches at that date into the Books of Daniel and Revelation.

What I am arguing is that Baxter's respect for the magistracy is more than Vicar of Bray opportunism: it is the ark of his faith. If, as we have seen, it reached the lengths of asserting that judgement even on a Nero should be left to history, were there no limits which Baxter would have placed on the powers of the magistrate? Certainly not the limits which would have interested a Hooker, but those which would have interested Hooker's great contemporary, Thomas Bilson. They represented the Whig saving-clause to a High Tory constitution. The magistrate forfeited obedience, not by excessive use of his powers, but by misdirecting them. Treason, not tyranny, was the critical issue. If a magistrate were to become a Papist, and use his authority to deliver his realm into the hands of a foreign power, then the point of his having had those powers in the first place would have been quite negated.

It followed that the interest in Charles's probable complicity in the Irish Rebellion which Baxter voiced in 1659 owed nothing to Hooker's populist theories and everything to Bilson's imperial theories. It was indeed compatible with a reverence for magistracy as an institution. Therefore, after the Restoration, High Tory sentiments about monarchy also were compatible with a continued interest in possible Royalist complicities in Popish Plots. The times were not ripe for their strident assertion, however.

A letter from Baxter to John Humfrey in 1669 reflects his dilemma. He is worried that Humfrey, in understandable revulsion from the Clarendon Code, is coming too close to resistance theorising. He welcomes Humfrey's entry into the field of politics; one which he ruefully claims to have vacated after his one disastrous excursion in that direction in his ill-timed refutation of Harrington. His welcome is tempered by fears that Humfrey may have fallen into similar miscalculations: he is wrong to claim Jewel and Bilson for resistance theories, and it would be better to ignore John Williams, Laud's enemy, who was 'a Coward'. 'Let this sleepe' is his counsel, especially when Humfrey dares to re-open the old wounds about the King's commission to Irish rebels:

> It is perillous to put such instances as [what if the King should commission the papists to cut the throat of the Protestants] and then put it off without an answer, when it is knowne that the Irish murdered 200,000 uppon that false pretense that they had the Kings Commission for it: Either therefore silence this, or answer it.[48]

Critics would make fun of the ease (or so it seemed to them) with which Baxter wheeled round to support of Charles II at the Restoration.[49] But Baxter was not a Samuel Parker or a Roger L'Estrange. His support for the magistrate on the throne stemmed from his principles, not from his lack of them. His knowledge that no greater barrier to Popery existed in the English constitution than the power of the civil magistrate inspired a deep mistrust of anything which might weaken it. That went for Calvinist resistance theories, clerical ambitions (Anglican or Presbyterian), egalitarian doctrines and even milder (but in Baxter's eyes, more insidious) 'liberal' ideas of a balanced constitution and the consent of the people. Better to soldier on with the magistrate in office, repress doubts and stifle rumours about his competence, and shore up his position in the people's esteem. The historian could square the accounts later. In his letter to Humfrey of 1669 Baxter could write off John Williams as a coward without being guilty of double-think. His letter was emphatically not an apology for cowardice; it *was* an apology for sustaining in power a magistrate who should be given the benefit of the doubt, however unpalatable many of his actions were. We shall see how he modified that position in the course of the reign later in the chapter, although again a fuller explanation must wait upon a detailed discussion of the controversies after the Restoration in the fourth chapter. But Baxter's was not an unconditional surrender. The conditions were imposed by recognition of the Jesuits' mastery of the political game: their ability to change sides and to don masks required corresponding agility in their Protestant detectors. Logically their end was the destruction of civil magistracy: when (according to Baxter) Henrietta Maria's confessor waved his sword exultantly as Charles I's head rolled off we were in the privileged position of seeing *Popery with the mask off*. But think of the infinite deviousness of the Jesuit mind in the preparations for 1649: Gondomar's ascendancy over James I; the attempted Spanish Marriage; the influence of Henrietta Maria; the exploitation of Laud; the (real or false) alliance of Charles I with the Irish Rebels. Who was to say that what they had done with the help of one sovereign they would not do again with another?

We now see the dilemma of the imperial Protestant. To think ill of the magistrate was to play the Papist game. Humfrey's response to the provocation of the Five Mile Act was thus a gift to Popery. Not to think ill of the magistrate — to the point where the security of the realm was threatened — was also to play the Papist game. Protestants nearly left it too late in 1641 and could do so again.

Fortunately a sixteenth-century bishop had provided the classic resolution of the problem. Thomas Bilson had defended 'Christian Subjection' and denounced 'Unchristian Rebellion'.[50] One right only he had denied to the Prince: 'to subject his Kingdom to a foreign Realm'. This was not a theory of resistance, but common sense, and Bilson made short shrift of those who claimed different: 'We may not so much as hide our hands, nor pull our necks out of the greedy jaws of that Romish Wolf, but the foam of your unclean mouth, is ready to call us by all the names you can devise.'[51] But many did claim different: Bilson provided a favourite text in the Civil War for resistance theories. He exerted a life-long fascination over Baxter, who was angered at the way his message had been misunderstood. Thus Baxter quoted Bilson's warning against the Romish Wolf only a few sentences on from his own

Hobbes-like hymn to magistracy. Bilson had not seen the two principles as antithetical; nor did Baxter: 'He that can read such a Book as Bilsons for *Christian Subjection against Unchristian Rebellion*, and yet deny him to be a Teacher of Subjection hath a very hard forehead.' This was how Baxter saw *himself*: as a 'Teacher of Subjection'. The limits to that subjection were set, not by the sovereign's fidelity to some mythical balanced constitution, but by his fidelity to Protestantism. When a kingdom was 'palpably designed to ruin', self-preservation was common sense. But until that point was reached, the magistrate must be given the benefit of any possible doubt. To do otherwise was to emasculate magistracy: to make it vulnerable to every passing rumour and suspicion. That was why Baxter attached supreme importance to the distinction between the 'true Historian' and the 'Self-Avenger'. Evil rulers could be reproached in private or posthumously publicly disgraced by the historian; yet, while they ruled, no breath of scandal must touch them:

> There is a great deal of difference between a *true Historian* and a *self-avenger* in the reason of the thing, and the effects: To dishonour bad Rulers while they live, doth tend to excite the People to Rebellion, and to disable them to govern. But for Truth to be spoken of them, when they are dead, doth only lay an odium upon the sin, and is a warning to others that they follow them not in evil.[52]

Given such a philosophy it is impressive that, even in his *Christian Directory*, a pamphlet which Baxter himself saw as a classic apology for magistracy, he does not repress the question: 'If a Prince should go about to subject his Kingdome to a foreign Realm', nor is he afraid to turn to Bilson for the answer. It was not enough that Baxter did not believe that Bilson *was* an apologist for resistance; he knew that, in the eyes of most commentators on the Civil War, his role was precisely that. Baxter was not above capitalising on this prejudice when it suited him: against Anglican taunts of regicide, he would frequently invoke the names of the Church's two favoured sons, Bilson and Hooker, as the true architects of the Civil War. There was, however, a clear distinction between them, in Baxter's eyes: one taught subjection; the other, rebellion. It was as Bilson's pupil that Baxter responded to the difficult challenge of the Restoration Settlement.

The Restoration posed difficulties because of unresolved doubts about Charles II. On 6 October 1673 Baxter wrote a letter to Edward Eccleston. It was the same year that he published the *Christian Directory*, and the letter movingly captured his dilemma:

> I once in a great congregation where many approved of these doings,
> did preach against the causelesse silencing of the ministers, which
> was accepted with so much (open) applause by the approvers, as too
> much pleased me; and severall times after (about the Imposing of the
> *et caetera* oath) I did the like: And I am to this day in doubt whether
> the publick disclaiming of such publike sins will more justifie what I
> did, or the stirring up of people thereby to taste the preachers who
> did it, do more condemne what I did.

In 1673 he had no doubt which was the more venial sin:

> But I am now so sensible of the later, and how bad it is to catch a
> distast of Rulers (though in a sort usurpers and persecutors) while
> they are tolerable, as that I have oft alreadie Recanted what I did of
> this kind, and Printed my Repenting retraction.[53]

It was consistent with his desire not 'to catch a distast of Rulers' that
he should rebuke Humfrey in 1669 for his outspoken attack on the
Five Mile Act, or indeed that in the same year of 1673 he should discuss
with Edmund Hough ways of *shoring up* the authority of the magistrate.
He told Hough that Hooker had fatally weakened subjects' obedience
to their rulers, and advised him to be equally wary of theories of pater-
nity, primogeniture and conquest as 'by that you will exceedingly
wrong the King':

> If you put him to make good his Right by primogeniture, as being of
> the family which was the originall of his three Kingdomes, you will
> deale too hardly by him. And if you make conquest a title you will
> give Cromwell a right or any other successful usurper.[54]

Baxter was writing on all three occasions in private to Nonconformist
friends, and it is clear that he was not urging his friends to submit to
authority on grounds of political prudence, but on grounds of principle.
He objected to the Royalist argument from conquest, not because he
wished to magnify the subjects' right of consent but because he thought
that *it did not go far enough* in expressing the sovereign's authority.
This was clear in a manuscript that he composed in prison. In 1686
Baxter read an anonymous treatise, arguing for sovereignty by conquest.
Baxter did not know the name of the author but lamented the damage

that he had done to the authority of monarchy. The author was in fact James I. Baxter commented:

> There is a little booke written by a namelesse Scot, 1603, called the Law of free Monarchies against all Rebellion which containeth much of what I have said. But when he foundeth the originall right of Monarchy uppon *strugle and conquest* by which only Kings are made Kings, and then they only make all Laws and are prime proprietors of the land, I shall say (1) that I dare not think Hobs and Spinoza in the right that thought right was nothing but strugle to get and keep possession, (2) nor dare I so farre encourage Rebels, nor did I ever believe that Cromwell's conquest gave any usurper Right (3) Nor while France is stronger than England, Holland or other Kings, I dare not say that if that Kingdom conquer them he is their rightfull monarch, lest such doctrine entice him to attempt it.[55]

The man who could serve Nero, and who felt that James I said too little for monarchy, was not the man to rebel against Charles II. Behind his reverence for magistracy lay a profound pessimism about the nature of mankind. The task of the magistrate was not to draw out man's good qualities, but to police his bad ones. The best expression of this philosophy is in the *critique* of Petrus Pomponatius's *Tractatus de immortalite animae*, of 1516, which is among his unpublished and undated papers. Pomponatius had argued that virtue was its own reward, vice its own punishment, and that ethics were not contingent on belief in the immortality of the soul. Baxter was scornful:

> Is human nature made to be ruled by this doctrine. Let him trie his wife, children and servants with it, and tell them if you be lyars, thieves, fornicators, drunkards, gluttons, idle, you shall have the punishment only of being such and see whether they will be such as he would have them be.

And he saw the practical consequences of such beliefs:

> O how this doctrine will encourage those that say the killing of a tyrant ... or breaking an oath to save the Commonwealth is the greatest virtue ... And this will encourage no man to any secret good, nor harden them from any secret villany: for unknowne things bring neither honour nor dishonour.[56]

In a pamphlet of 1667 Baxter painted a sombre picture of life on earth without the prospect of future punishment:

> And all those that princes cannot please, would Plot, revenge, or play their game another way; and subtil Men would think it easie to Poison or Murder secretly Princes and Nobles, and any Enemy that stood in the way of their own Designs, if once they were out of fear of a Life to come.

He adds a marginal note: 'A fortnight after the writing of this, London was burnt.'[57]

Until the second half of the 1670s – in response to the arguments of Dodwell, Sherlock and Heylyn in particular – Baxter was primarily worried about 'liberal' Anglicans emasculating magistracy, not about 'totalitarian' Anglicans exalting it. This was why Baxter was irritated by his Nonconformist friend's defiant pamphlet against the Five Mile Act: John Humfrey's *A Case of Conscience* of 1669. Baxter remonstrated with his friend in private for his claim that Bilson and Jewel were apologists for resistance. When Humfrey went so far as to quote Jeremy Taylor this drew from Baxter the outraged comment: 'This unkinging is worse than resisting.' When Humfrey wished to claim that the King was *maior singulis, minor universis* Baxter exclaimed: 'Are you in good earnest? As bad as Hooker!'

This private letter of 1669 shows the tenacity of Baxter's belief in the power of the civil magistrate. Hence his antipathy to those 'liberal' Anglicans like Jeremy Taylor and Hooker who would weaken the magistrate's power. For Baxter, the King was *maior universis* as well as *singulis*: he must be encouraged to extend, not restrain, his powers. The libel on Bilson must be cleared:

> You both wrong your cause and wrong Bp. Bilson: you wrong your cause by mentioning his opinion, wch being in the best treatise that ever was written against Rebellion, and accepted by Queen Elizabeth, will countenance the adversary, and might better be concealed: you wrong him, by intimating that the King may be deposed, when he expressly professeth that an hereditary K. may not be deposed, even when he saith Lords and Commons may by armes defend their Liberties against him.

But Bilson had left the loophole: what if a King should alienate his own kingdom by surrendering it to a foreign power? This was no idle hypothesis, as Humfrey argued, when 'it is known that King John resigned it to the Pope.' Baxter commented: 'Either silence these dangerous passages or answer them, lest you seeme to prevaricate.' And we have seen that he was equally brusque when Humfrey, by implication, seemed to raise the Antrim spectre with the hypothesis 'wt. if the King should commission the papists to cut the throat of the Protestants.'[58]

The exchange with Humfrey brings out well the reasons for Baxter's reliance on Bilson. Bilson had no truck with limited monarchy, a balanced constitution or popular sovereignty: he had written the most celebrated apology for obedience. 'Christian Subjection' was compatible, however, with pulling 'our necks out of the greedy jaws of that Romish Wolf'. Bilson might superficially be coupled with Hooker, but their cases were quite different. Baxter genuinely believed that many men had entered the Civil War through a mistaken dependence on Hooker's ideas of limited monarchy. He had clouded Bilson's subtle truth. Inasmuch as the case against the King was formulated on Hooker's terms — that he was *maior singulis, minor universis* — Baxter could sincerely repudiate those terms, and with it the Parliamentary cause, both before and after the Restoration. This was not the *volte-face* that Whig critics like Samuel Young supposed. To be for the King on Bilson's terms was a curious kind of royalism in 1641, and would prove to be so again in 1688.

When he defended the Nonconformists' political theory in 1676 he drew the distinction well between these two authorities:

> Did ever any of us that now address our selves to you, go farther in our Principles than Bishop Bilson did, even in his excellent Book of *Christian Subjection*? we detested all that went beyond him in his Doctrine of Resistance: or did any of us ever go near so far as your famous Richard Hooker in his *first* and his *eighth* Book of Ecc. Politie . . . whose over Popular Principles one of us, long ago, at large confuted.[59]

Bilson had gone as far as Nonconformists wanted to go; Hooker went over the top. A letter has survived from Baxter to his old school friend, Richard Allestree, of 20 December 1679, in which this distinction is recognised. They had both attended the same school at Donnington. Allestree went on to become Regius Professor of Divinity at Oxford and eventually Provost of Eton. Rather touchingly Baxter owned up to the motive of wanting the good opinion of an old school friend, and justified in this private letter his reasons for taking Parliament's side in the Civil War:

> The newes of 200,000 murdered by the Irish and Papist strength in
> the King's armies, and the great danger of the Kingdom, was pub-
> lished by the Parliament . . . I thought that both the *defensive part*,
> and the *salus populi*, lay on the Parliament's side . . . my principles
> were the same with Bishop Bilson's (of subjection) and Jewel's, but
> never so popular as R. Hooker's.[60]

He made an identical point in a pamphlet of 1682: that he had never
thought that Parliament was blameless; he had nevertheless supported
its cause on the principles of Bilson; he never went so far against the
King as Hooker did.[61] In the unpublished treatise on magistracy, which
Baxter composed in prison in 1686, he had exalted magistracy to the
skies. This was the pamphlet which had scolded James I for not giving
enough power to the magistrate. Revelling in the insights into magistracy thrown up by Revelation, Baxter still did not let go the doctrine
of self-defence: 'These men expect that as I have confuted much in
Richard Hooker, so I should the rest and condemne Bp. Bilson's treatise of Obedience, of Barclays and Grotius doctrine of resistance.'[62]

On 1 October 1691 Baxter wrote a treatise proving that King James
II had abdicated the Crown, and it is interesting to see how much he
drew upon the ideas of his papers of 1686. With hardly a nod to
Hooker, he extended Bilson's imperial theory. He was plainly irritated
at the poor job his rulers had made of justifying their case; he was not
interested in contractual notions of consent, or such fantasies as the
idea that James, through flight, had vacated the throne. James's offence
had simply been that of 'delivering himself and his Kingdom to a
Foreign Jurisdiction'. Baxter suggested that the rulers' present nervous-
ness to bring this into the open might stem from the mistaken notion
that they were therefore conceding that this was a 'war for Religion':

> Perhaps they might think that had they opened how much of the
> abdication consisted in delivering up the Kingdom so far to a For-
> eign Jurisdiction as Popery doth, by professing the extermination of
> the nation on account of Religion, the Emperor, and the Kings of
> Spain, Portugal, Poland, The Duke of Bavaria, Savoy, etc. might have
> thought that it was a war for religion and so would by consequence
> be as against them.

Baxter wanted to scotch the idea that imperial self-defence *was* 'a war for Religion'. This is important: when Baxter said that the Civil War became by 1643 'a war for Religion' he was not saying (as Dr Manning seemed to suppose) that before that date it was constitutional issues that mattered. He was saying that, after that date, King-killing theories (often imported from Scotland) associated with Calvin, Paraeus, Buchanan and others gained popularity in the Army, especially among the sectaries in Cromwell's regiments. The advantage of the theory of imperial self-defence was that it gave no blessing to such theories, which Baxter sincerely deplored. The Emperor Nero remained irresistible:

> Objection 2. He was not worse than Nero and such princes whom Christians would not resist. Answer 1. Christians were not the Roman Commonwealth but a small party of dissenters. Therefore to destroy them was not to destroy the Commonwealth.

An extraordinary passage later comes as near to a justification of even Mary Tudor as ever came from the pen of a disciple of John Foxe:

> Objection 4. Was not Queen Mary a lawful Queen, though a Papist, and changed King Edward's religion and laws. Answer. King Edward ruled so short a time that it was but a small part of the Kingdom that were protestants at his death: almost all the Parish Priests were the same that had been Mass Priests. Either the body of the Kingdom was then protestant, or not? If not, it's nothing to our case. If they were, could their resistance have prevailed, I am not he that could have proved it unlawful. But reputation followeth success. If Queen Jane, or Sir Thomas Wyatt, had prevailed, history would have honored and justified the undertaking. But indeed the small number comparatively that submitted to be burnt for their religion tells us that then the protestants were but a small part of the Nation.[63]

This was not novel doctrine — he had said as much in his *Christian Directory* of 1673[64] — but then it might have been attributed to a prudent desire to keep on the right side of authority. He had no such inhibitions in 1691, but both his apology for Nero and his half-apology for Mary Tudor are to be seen as examples of the lengths to which he would go in support of the magistrate. The sixth objection he set himself to answer was that 'the Church of England must not lose the honor of her enmity to rebellion, and her being for passive obedience'; the imperial Protestant replied that 'we are all of the Church of England, and all against rebellion, and resistance of the King. But what's that to a public enemy that is no King.'

The seventh objection was the deadly one: 'by this we shall justify the Parliament rebellion against King Charles I which we have with so much zeal condemned.' Baxter had almost conceded as much when he had justified self-preservative action to save a Kingdom 'palpably designed to ruin', by a direct allusion to Ireland in 1641. His answer was very carefully phrased:

> Answer. Either the case was the like or not. If not, it is no justification of it. If yea, then what can I say but as the Rulers to Judas, that cryed 'I have sinned in betraying innocent blood' 'See thou to it: what is that to us?' ... Will you not rather disgrace your old cause by such equaling King Charles I and King James II?[65]

He had been equally careful in 1683 when he was trying to clear himself from charges of sedition by the Oxford convocation:[66]

> *The Twenty-Seventh Proposition* is charged on me — *King Charles the First made war upon his Parliament, and in such a case, the King may not only be resisted, but he ceaseth to be King.* The first part I retracted long ago; the last I cannot find that I ever said.

But, even with his life at stake, Baxter kept true to Bilson:

> Where I went furthest in these retracted sayings, it was but this, that when it is not 1. bare hurting but destroying and 2. That not single person or a party, but the whole nation or the very essence of the republic and common good and 3. that not by a passionate act, but a resolved course, then every republic or Kingdom hath by the Law of Nature a self-defending power ... And the Bishop of Winchester [Bilson] well saith, *None but a madman will do it* ... And when the Irish murdered two hundred thousand, it's like they would have destroyed a protestant nation if they could.

Baxter even touched on the King's commission in 1683, although he did so by saying that he would not touch on it: 'Whether the false pretending the King's commission made it unlawful for the two hundred thousand murdered protestants to have defended themselves against the Irish, or whether they might have done had it been true, I meddle not with that.'[67] The consistency of Baxter's views in 1683 and 1691 is remarkable. He was defending himself from the charge of being a resister on one occasion, and defending resistance on the other. It is impressive to see *how far he leans to resistance* on the first occasion, and *how much he is prepared to give to the magistrate* on the second. It would be wrong then to see Baxter's caution as the product of expediency: rather, it is the caution of a man who accepted Bilson's proposition that only a madman would be self-destructive; that when he is proved to be mad, he must be prevented from such self-destruction; but until that point is reached the definition of lunacy must not be widened to encompass every distasteful action which that particular ruler took.

The twenty-seventh proposition of the Oxford Convocation charges of 21 July 1683 not only comes closest to Baxter's real reservations about magistracy — although only posthumously in 1696 with the Antrim reference in his autobiography, and even more so in 1702 with Calamy's revised edition which gave it much greater prominence, was its full implications for Charles I brought out — but it is probably the *only* proposition which can make any plausible link between Baxter and sedition. It is worth looking briefly at the other 26 to see how little they touch Baxter. The first condemned proposition was that civil authority was derived from the people: a view condemned by Baxter in his *Holy Commonwealth* and *Christian Directory*. The second, of a 'mutuall compact' between Prince and subjects is not found in Baxter. The third, that if lawful governors become tyrants, they forfeit their subjects' obedience, is attributed to Baxter along with Bellarmine, Buchanan, Milton and Goodwin. Unlike the other four writers, however, Baxter believed that Nero should be obeyed; the *historian* could withhold the allegiance which the *subject* could not waive. The fourth proposition, that the King had a co-ordinate power as one of three estates, is developed by Hunton and Rutherford, who are named alongside Baxter, but is hardly touched on by Baxter except for some defensive responses to Dodwell's 'Leviathan' in the late 1670s and early 1680s. The next five propositions — that blood does not give entitlement to rule; that Covenants may be taken in self-defence; that self-preservation is the supreme justice; that subjects may resist religious persecution; that Christians are not obliged to passive obedience — are not attributed explicitly to Baxter and are in fact rejected by him. The self-preservative principle that they attack is that to be found in Hobbes: this is radically different from the qualified reserve position of a Bilson, which Baxter elaborated on in his reply to the twenty-seventh charge. Baxter is linked with Hobbes, Owen and Jenkins in the tenth charge, of believing that 'possession and strength give a right to Govern': a view that Baxter expressly repudiated when he declined the Engagement in 1650. Four Hobbesian principles follow – the State of Nature is a state of war; the sovereign's authority is created as an answer to the anarchy of the State of Nature; the citizen has the right of self-defence; oaths are not binding. The last, though attributed to Hobbes, is a misreading of Hobbes and would be disowned by him as it would be by Baxter. Baxter, particularly in his pamphlet *A Christian Directory*, has much of Hobbes's pessimism about the origins of society, and fears of anarchy if the magistrate's authority is not sustained. But both also have a more exalted concept of magistracy in terms of its *apocalyptic* justification in a *Christian* Commonwealth.[68] The fifteenth proposition, drawn from Baxter's *Holy Commonwealth*, that later Covenants made even with a dispossessor have a validity over earlier ones made with the legal sovereign, is probably the most damaging to Baxter, apart from the twenty-seventh. As we shall see in the next chapter, no amount of blustering by Baxter could conceal the extent to which he had moved from his frigid position of 1650 to one where he was seeking active co-operation with the Protectorate in 1659. Then followed propositions all roundly condemned by Baxter: all oaths are unlawful against God; oaths oblige is the sense of the taker, not the imposer; dominion is founded on grace; worldly powers are usurpations upon Christ's; Presbyterian government is incompatible with the Royal Supremacy; superiors have no right to impose any thing other than essentials to the worship of God; human authority and the need to offend a weak brother impose contrary constraints; the ungodly ruler must be deposed and excommunicated; tyrannicide upon private inspiration is justified; new rules for men came with a new dispensation from Revelation; Charles I was lawfully put to death.[69]

Most accusations against Baxter for disloyalty have the imprecision and wrong-headedness of nearly all the clauses of the Oxford Convocation's charges; only the fifteenth and the twenty-seventh press upon Baxter's most vulnerable points. One is repeatedly struck by the triviality and the contrived nature of the attacks on his loyalty; not only the notorious wresting of his *Paraphrase on the New Testament* by Roger L'Estrange in 1685 (itself only the climax of a long campaign in his news-sheet, *The Observator*) which inspired his trial and subsequent imprisonment, or the bullying extension of L'Estrange's charges by Judge Jeffreys in the course of the trial itself, but on numerous other occasions.[70] It seemed as if contemporaries conceived of only two ways in which authority of the sovereign *could* be undermined: by emphasising the legal restraints on kingship or by emphasising the subjects' right to rebel. Baxter identified the first with Hooker and deplored it as a principle which began the Civil War; he identified the second with Calvinist regicide theorists and deplored it as the principle which extended the Civil War after 1643 into a 'war for Religion'. Faced with such opposition to the two basic tenets of the rebels' creed, opponents could only argue that Baxter was insincere in his opposition. Typical of the tittle-tattle which Baxter was subjected to, and *faute de mieux* became the substitute for the regicide views which they could not trace directly to his writings, were the claims that he had killed a man in cold blood in the Civil War, when the worst that he had ever done was to wrestle with a friend in his youth and accidentally break his leg;[71] the L'Estrange libel that he had stolen a medal from a man whom he had shot in the Civil War (still an effective *canard* as late as 1704);[72] that Pym and Hampden were among the saints whom he looked forward to meeting in Heaven, in his *Saints Everlasting Rest.*[73] By a self-fulfilling prophecy, provokers like Roger L'Estrange, Samuel Parker, Dodwell and Heylyn almost succeeded in implanting in him the sentiments which they professed to abhor: 'But yet while I thought they went on Bilson's Principles, I was then on their side, and the Observator (Parker) almost tempted me to Hooker's Principles, but I quickly saw those Reasons against them, which I have since published.'[74]

In 1691 he wrote *Against the Revolt to a Foreign Jurisdiction*. Two themes were combined in one: there was the 'revolt to a foreign jurisdiction' in James II's efforts to make England a Catholic realm, and which justified self-defence in his subjects; there was the allied 'revolt to a foreign jurisdiction' in the exaltation of universal conciliar government by Anglicans like Thorndike, Dodwell and Heylyn. Baxter believed that the French Papists were more deadly than the Italian. The Italian offered straight Popery and toleration; the French cried down toleration, put Council above Pope, and promoted coalition on Grotius's terms. The war was on two fronts: against a King who had favoured *Italian* Catholicism, and prelates who favoured *French* Catholicism.[75] His pamphlet was dedicated to John Tillotson. At the end of his life Prynne too turned to Tillotson for comfort: he left him in his will some of his own turgid writings.[76] Tillotson (and Baxter bracketed Isaac Barrow with him) stood for that old Protestant tradition in the Church of England. They were the heirs of men like Jewel, Usher and Bilson, who took the Pope for Antichrist and would have 'none of his Jurisdiction here.' The Thorndikes and Dodwells were heirs of another tradition: Heylyn's biography of Laud emphasised that other continuity. Laud was to 1641 what Thorndike was to 1688. Baxter did not now flinch from these resistance parallels:

These distances between the old Church-men and the Laudians having increased to that which they came to in 1641 suddenly on October 23 the Irish Rebellion Murdering Two hundred thousand, and Fame threatening their coming into England, cast the Nation into so Great fear of the Papists, as was the Cause (whereever I came) of Mens conceit of the *necessity of defensive Arms*.

Baxter vividly described the *grande peur* which preceded the resort to arms:

But the most odious injury that ever they did him, was by pretending his Commission for that most inhumane War and Massacre in Ireland; when in time of peace they suddenly Murdered two hundred thousand, and told men that they had the King's Commission to rise as for him that was wronged by his Parliament; the very fame of this horrid Murder, and the words of the many fugitives that escaped in Beggery into England (assisted by the Charity of the Dutchess of Ormond and others) and the English Papists going in to the King was the main cause that filled the Parliaments Armies: I well remember it cast people into such a fear that England should be used like Ireland, that all over the Countreys, the people oft sate up, and durst not go to Bed, for fear lest the Papists should rise and Murder them.

Baxter's argument is still, at this late date, based on the premiss that the Papists did Charles I a grievous disservice by forging his name. Even his *Holy Commonwealth* of 1659 had cast Charles I as a hapless victim, though hardly innocent in view of the service he had already performed for the 'Grotian' design. Only the Antrim revelations brought the guilt closer to the sovereign himself. And until Calamy produced his edition, Baxter's interest in Antrim was not widely known to his reading public. Baxter's references to the Antrim commission were, as we have shown, repressed from Sylvester's edition at one place in the manuscript, and possibly transposed to a less conspicuous place from another. But the fact that Baxter documented them in his manuscript at all shows the suspicions of the sovereign that were not far from his consciousness; they were rekindled by further revelations about the reigns of both his sons. And so to a text, lamenting the Papist injuries to Charles I's memory, Baxter added this much cooler postscript:

I knew not when I writ the Book, 1. of King James's Paper published as found in King Charles the Second's Pocket, and the Testimonies that he died a Papist, nor what was witnessed of his Engagement for them. 2. I knew not of Archbishop Bramhall's Letter . . . confidently assuring Archbishop Usher, that on his certain Information, the Papists in 1647 got into Cromwell's Army, and confederated with the Papists at Oxford in the King's Army to have the King put to Death: And whether they went beyond Sea for Approbation, and obtained it.

Armed with this *post hoc* wisdom, Baxter saw the prelates who had accompanied Charles II overseas as privy to his (now revealed) Papist designs; saw how close this 'slow way' had come to the success which James's precipitancy had lost them. By his clumsiness James II had provoked a Protestant revival:

> They had not forgotten Queen Maries Days: Fox's Book of Martyrs was in the hands of many: Nor had they forgot the French Massacre, or the Greater Murders formerly committed by Wolves in Sheep-Skins who were knowne by their bloody fangs and Jaws.[77]

The image may have been a conscious echo of Bilson's 'greedy jaws of that Romish Wolf', which Baxter had quoted with such approval in his *Christian Directory*:[78] and the 'Frenchmen's Patience in the Parisian Massacre' was what Baxter had deprecated in that passage on the origins of the Civil War which was left out of the Everyman edition.[79]

Pace Thorndike and Dodwell, Baxter maintained that 'the Church of England is nothing but a Protestant Sovereign, and a Protestant Kingdom of Subjects guided by Protestant Ministers of the Word, Sacraments and Keys'. This was a definition which deprived James II, or any Papist sovereign, of the claim to head a 'National Church'. Royalists, who think that Parliament has no part in the legislation and sovereignty, cannot accept that a 'National Church' exists at all; while, for those who think otherwise, 'it is but a National Church *secundum quid*, in respect to the power of Parliaments and Laws'.[80]

Foxe's *Book of Martyrs*, Bilson's 'Romish Wolf', the St Bartholomew's Day Massacre, the meaning of 'National Churches': these were the preoccupations of Baxter's last years. They were predictable preoccupations of a man who believed that the Antrim commission was the key to the Civil War. They were not to be predicted of a man who saw the Civil War as a conflict over the constitution. But these preoccupations were characteristic of Baxter's earlier years also. Thus in 1675, in his *Catholick Theologie*, he recalled the alarm that he and fellow

Protestants had felt over the spread of Arminian doctrines:

> Being under these apprehensions, when the Wars began, though the
> Cause it self lay in Civil Controversies, between King and Parliament,
> yet the thoughts that the Church and Godliness it self was deeply in
> danger by Persecution and Arminianism, did much more to byass me
> to the Parliaments side, than the Civil interest (which at the heart I
> little regarded).

It is a wonderfully revealing passage, making the crucial distinction
between the received wisdom about the origins of the Civil War and
what had moved Richard himself to arms. In case we should miss his
point he follows this up later in the same pamphlet with an anecdote
about two Nonconformist ministers. Both had supported Parliament
in the Civil War, but wondered afterwards whether they had been right
to do so. They assiduously read up all the available documents –
'Statute-Book', 'Common Law-Books and Cases' and 'all the History of
our ancient Governments, and of our late transactions'. They were
honest and conscientious in their search, but they reached totally opposite conclusions. For one, the subsequent adversities suffered by the
Saints was God's Judgement on Parliament's cause; for the other, a
blow had been struck against the tyranny 'that kept up Popery and
kept out Reformation'. Baxter pointed out that these preconceptions
governed their reading of the documents: a sardonic insight which puts
his much-trumpeted readiness after the Restoration to defer constitutional questions to the lawyers in proper perspective. This was the man
who 'at the heart' little regarded the civil interest.[81]

The question remains: did *he* view these matters after the Restoration as a chastened victim of God's retributive justice or, rather, did he
continue to believe that a blow had been struck against Popery?

By 1679 in his *The Nonconformists Plea for Peace* – itself a passionate polemic against the tyranny 'that kept up Popery and kept out
Reformation' – the Irish Massacres are given pre-eminent place in the
factors that precipitated the Civil War.[82] Charles's own complicity is not
indicated, however: it was not until 1690 that he could once more raise
the question of Charles's commission to the rebels. In his pamphlet of
that date, *The English Nonconformity*, he restated the case made by
Anglican persecutors against his fellow ministers: 'They say that you
took part with the Parliament against the King, and invoked the Land
in blood, and have still the same Rebellious Principles.' Instead of playing his familiar post-Restoration tune – that Presbyterians *revere* monar-

chy and that it was *Anglicans* who began the war — Baxter switched to the offensive and invoked the spirit of 1659:

> And when the Irish had Murdered Two Hundred Thousand Protestants, falsly pretending that they had the Kings Commission, and threatening to finish their work in England, there were many formerly tempted to fly in fear to the Parliament for safety; being ignorant that the King's bare word, notwithstanding the Papists Strength and Interest, was more to be trusted with our Laws, Lives and Religion, than all the Lawyers, Courts and Parliaments.[83]

James II's reign had shown how much Protestants could rely upon 'the Kings bare word' for their salvation; throughout his writings of 1690 and 1691 Baxter hints at the parallels between the actions that Protestants took for self-preservation in 1641 and 1688. After showing, in an unpublished treatise of 1 October 1691, how James II undermined confidence in his assurances to his Protestant subjects by his actions, he put the case for precipitate counter-moves: 'A kingdom thus palpably designed to ruin, or endangered, may not on pretences of uncertainty delay their self-preservation till they are past remedy (as in Ireland 1641 it fell out very near).'[84]

In 1691 it was easy. James II had vacated the throne. The Kingdom *had* been 'palpably designed to ruin'. With hindsight, the Protestant reaction in 1641 could be seen to have been not only justified but almost to have come too late. The fifty years between these two decisive moments presented much more difficult challenges. There was still a palpable design to ruin in the activities of the Jesuits — Baxter never slackened his belief in the conspiratorial power of Popery — but it required considerable finesse on the part of the Protestants to grasp the direction which that design would take. In 1691 Baxter could see that the Protestants of 1688 were right to take action against a sovereign who was working in partnership with the Jesuits. In 1641 Protestants were equally justified in taking the action they did against a King who was, at best, an innocent victim of Jesuit treachery; at worst, an ally; and most probably — somewhere between the two — a 'moderate Protestant' collaborator with a 'moderate Papist' wife in a Grotian mish-mash design. But what of his execution? A blow against Popery? Not necessarily: the Jesuit plan was to switch to *collaboration* with the extremist regicide elements who, to Baxter's anguished apprehension, had as early as 1643 captured the soul of the Parliamentary Army. Thus Baxter produced his documentary evidence that the regicide was a Popish Plot. As early as 19 March 1664 William Prynne had written to Peter du Moulin to convince him that the rumours, that Charles I had been done to death by Papists, were justified. That du Moulin was convinced we know from his *A Vindication of the Sincerity of the Protestant Religion* of 1671:

> Mr. Prynnes intelligence confirmed mine. He saith that our late excellent King having assented in the Treaty of the Isle of Wight to pass five strict Bills against Popery, the Jesuites in France, at a general meeting there, presently resolved to bring him to Justice and take off his head, by the power of their friends in the Army.

The fourth chapter of Peter du Moulin's work analyses the struggle between Pope and Emperor throughout history. 1649 is one landmark in that struggle: 'Indeed Charles the I our holy King and Martyr, suffered for his Religion.' Sir William Morice wrote to Peter du Moulin to assert that 'the irreligion of the Papists was chiefly guilty of the Murther of that Excellent Prince.'[85] The Catholic, Davenport, regretted the credulity of ordinary people and tried to stamp on the rumour circulating among them, ever since the regicide, that Henrietta Maria's confessor had waved his sword in jubilation on that occasion: 'but seeing it lately confirmed by two sober and eminent persons, Mr. Prynne in his *Good Old Cause* and Mr. Baxter in his *Key for Catholicks*, I began to suspect the worse.'[86] Bramhall wrote to Usher on 20 July 1654 to tell him that the Parliamentary Army had included a hundred Romish clergymen who were instructed daily 'to correspond with those Romanists in our late King's Army'. They were obeying instructions from the Sorbonne that the King must be removed. This story circulated in a pamphlet of 1681 in the context of Usher's grim prophecy of more Papist massacres to come, and was treated by Baxter as 'proof' of the Papist responsibility for the regicide, in an undated manuscript which has survived.[87] Baxter's fullest development of the theme is in a letter he wrote to the Catholic, Hugh Cressy, in 1666. Cressy was stung by the frequent references 'in old gazets' to the Jesuit game of 'playing in the dark' under the disguise of Seekers, Quakers, Anabaptists and the like. He challenged Baxter to prove it 'now since I reade it attested by a Sober and Learned man'.[88] The letter in reply has survived, although Baxter crossed out the following passage:

> Sir, I am not talking now to the world, but to you in secret. Therefore you cannot say that I stirre up the King against you. You know

I am further from his eares than you: and you may choose whether any of this shall be seene: And I will let you see what things I have *long concealed* of your party.

He then reproduced the letter from a Gloucestershire minister, James Stansfield, who testified that a 'Gentleman of good worth and quality' in the country had fallen in with a Jesuit minister who introduced him to a group of Catholic converts:

And they there falling into discourse about the late Kings death, He told him, that the Kings death was contrived and designed by Cardinall Mazarin and the Jesuites in France: And that a Councill of Priests and Jesuites, in number about 50 gave debate and consultation about it in London; by order from Mazarine. And then and there the said councill concluded with those of France, that he should die; And that there were but two of the said Priests and Jesuites dissented, which was himselfe and one more, as foreseeing sad daies to their native Countrey, if that should be effected. According as they concluded, the King suffered etc.

Baxter had further proof of the story:

Afterwards the minister called on me, and told me this Gentleman was Mr. Atkins brother to the worthy Judge Atkins; and unkle to Sir Robert Atkins: and that he was not willing to appear in it, because it was disingenuous to wrong his friend who was since preferred to be Head of Douay Colledge. He gave me this Letter to print with his attestation, but I never published it. But once about 1661 being in talke with Dr. Thomas Goad of Hereford, I told him of it. And he told me that he was so familiarly acquainted with Mr. Atkins that he was resolved to ask him of it. The next time I met him, he told me that he had askt Mr. Atkins, and he averd it all, except the number of the Priests and Jesuits, which was but thirty.

Baxter told Cressy that he would not publish this story but would keep it as a secret, which he told him only because 'you summoned me to name dissemblers, and because you lay so great a stresse upon this point.'[89] However the letter appears in substance in *Reliquiae Baxterianae* with this additional comment:

I would not print it without fuller Attestation lest it should be a wrong to the Papists. But when the King was restored and settled in Peace, I told it occasionaly to a Privy Counsellor, who not advising me to meddle any further in it, because the King knew enough of Mazarine's Designs already, I let it alone.[90]

This was the point at which Coleridge's patience with Baxter snapped:

Richard Baxter was too thoroughly good for any experience to make him worldly wise; else, how could he have been simple enough to suppose, that Mazarine would leave such a question to be voted *pro* and *con*, and decided by thirty emissaries in London! And how could he have reconciled Mazarine's having any share in Charles's death with his own masterly account.[91]

Baxter's 'masterly account' is actually rather generalised and brief. The original manuscript has not survived at this section, and therefore unfortunately we do not know whether Sylvester left anything out. What he left in was a rapid summary of the political background to the execution and then this portentous moralising:

Where-in appeared the severity of God, the mutability and uncertainty of worldly things, and the fruits of a sinful nation's provocations, and the infamous effects of error, pride and selfishness, prepared by Satan to be charged hereafter upon Reformation and Godliness, to the unspeakable Injury of the Christian Name and Protestant Cause, the Rejoicing and Advantage of the Papists, the Hardning of Thousands against the Means of their own salvation, and the confusion of the Actors when the day is done.[92]

Calamy was starker still. That passage may have been rather general in its scope, but it was still too round a rejection of the regicide for Calamy's taste. Calamy left the whole passage out, disclaimed Presbyterian responsibility for the execution of the King, and transferred the guilt to Papists (with marginal references to Peter du Moulin, Morice and Atkins).[93] Here again one may query whether Calamy violated the *spirit*, as opposed to the *letter*, of Baxter's writings. Baxter never did subsequently make much fuss about the regicide except when protesting against the libels on Presbyterian loyalty or when underlining the menace of the Catholic conspiracy. There is missing from his writings a respect for Charles's personal sanctity: no prolonged meditations, as with so many of his contemporaries, on Charles's sufferings and last days. This did not mean that he believed that Charles I deserved to die. Even in his *A Key for Catholicks* – written in 1659 when he was furthest removed in sympathy from the Stuart cause – he denied the rumour that Charles was 'a flat Papist' and cited 'his speech at death' as part of the contrary evidence. His conclusion then was that 'I think we may be confident that he was no nearer to Rome than was the reconcilable part of the Greeks.'[94] But even that was too near for comfort, and it must be remembered that the passage comes in a pamphlet which warns that the Papists now manage their operations 'under a sort of Juglers',[95] and that their successes have been made possible by the mistaken 'Grotian' collaboration of men like Charles I and Laud. The Irish rebels in 1641 may have forged Charles I's commission but how many tears could be shed for a man who had allowed himself to be manoeuvred into a position where such charges could seem plausible? Charles was a martyr in the sense that he was put to death by Papists, but it was only in that sense that he was a martyr; no extravagant personal cult of the Royal Martyr is encouraged by Baxter's austere prose. Coleridge was wrong therefore to see Baxter's 'masterly account' as incompatible with belief in Mazarin's plot. The year 1649 complemented 1641: a politically naive fellow-traveller was first exploited, and then discarded, by men who were artists of disguise. Between the origins of the Civil War and its conclusion there was not the gap that Coleridge assumed. The evidence from the various texts of the *Reliquiae Baxterianae*, and the contextual evidence from Baxter's other writings, would suggest as much. But we have one final archival piece of evidence: the survival among his private papers of an unfinished treatise which he had entitled *A Political Catechise*.

He began by standing on its head his usual argument that divines ought not to meddle in politics; that they should leave it to the politicians. This was a useful defence that Baxter had previously invoked on numerous occasions. He had backed the wrong side in the Civil War because he had not known enough law; he had backed Richard Cromwell in the Commonwealth because he had not understood the complexities of political life; he should have left such arcane matters to his legalistically-minded friends like George Lawson and other such subtle minds. On this premiss he had built the rather dubious distinction of 'Memorandums' and 'Directions' in his *Christian Directory* of 1673. Now, however, he argued that politicians *needed* 'monitors' or 'reprovers' of their morality. But more than that: who was to tell the magistrate that *regere* and *perdere* are inconsistent? The obvious answer was: the lawyers. Baxter gave them a half-tribute – they were better than the foppish nobles of other countries, who spent their time whoring, hawking and hunting when they should have been counselling princes, and so gave a spurious respectability to alternative theories of oligarchy and democracy. The trouble with lawyers was that they studied the laws of England, not 'the Nature, the Originall, efficient order and End of government'.[96] He made the same point in his pamphlet of 1691 proving James's abdication: lawyers 'never well study what the nature, original, measure and ends of government in *genere et specie* are, nor what a law is'.[97] He now wanted lawyers not to study the laws of England until they had studied what politics *are*, and steeped themselves in writers like Grotius, Bodin and Suarez. But whatever the shortcomings of *lawyers*, Baxter recognised the value of *laws* as a restraint upon rulers. What of the argument that wit and honesty were all that was required in the governor, and the forms and restraints could take care of themselves? This was very much the theme of his *Holy Commonwealth* in 1659, when in the face of the Jesuit threat Baxter wanted all good men to stifle their scruples and rally round the most effective form of government. Now he was saying that good men with good intentions were not enough:

> I will confesse to you that all the Politicall doctrines and good Laws, will not cause good government and a happy Commonwealth without Witt, and Honesty, in the Rulers. But wit and honesty will not serve without good Lawes and politicall knowledge.

Bad men may be bad 'under all your Laws and Politicks' but laws can shame, and tame, them. The dangers of unlimited magistracy weighed heavily on him: 'In Moscovy all preaching is forbidden lest the ministers should preach sedition, and only Liturgies and Homilies allowed, and so an ignorant ministry set up.'[98] This was the very image that had haunted him in his battles with Morley, Dodwell, Sherlock and Heylyn, which he pithily expressed in his *Nonconformists Plea for Peace* of 1679: 'all Christian Kingdoms conform to Moscovie when the Prince commandeth it.'[99]

For Baxter it was the Pope's usurping powers which made him an Antichrist:

> While one man will claime a right of Governing all the world, and being a *Vice God* as some call him, or a *Vice Christ* as others, and so to be an Antichrist, while he usurpeth the pre-rogative of Christ, which no mortall man, and its like an Angel is capable of.[100]

The many times that Baxter showed that the Pope was *an* Antichrist as a usurper, in his researches of 1686 in the Apocalypse, may still not have received proper recognition because they were invariably coupled with assertions that the Papacy was not *the* Antichrist of prophecy. This made the lesser claim seem weak and insincere, a fall-back position, when in reality it demonstrated the implacability of his enmity to Rome. The more evidence he accumulated for the worth of the Christian Emperor, the more intolerable a usurper's rival claims became. Not only Papal claims to supremacy were intolerable; the French Catholic ideas of conciliar supremacy, taken up by Sherlock, Dodwell, Heylyn and other 'new Conformists' in the late 1670s, were equally abhorrent. To both, Baxter opposed the concept of 'National Churches', which he had discovered through studying the Apocalypse.

The Civil War was itself the consequence of false political principles. Baxter saw Bishop Morley as a forerunner of the 'new Conformists', blazing trails for Dodwell's 'Leviathan':

were it but the two politicall controversies handled between my silencer Bp. Morley and my selfe, you may easily see what caused our civil warre that is 1. *Whether the whole Legislature Power be in the King, and none of it in The Parliament* And 2. *Whether the King's Power be absolute and unlimitted, or not.* How can a Kingdome avoid a Civil Warre that is not agreed about such points as these and no better knoweth its owne Constitution?

Baxter drew more closely the parallels between the imperial resistance of Charles I, and of James II:

And now our parliaments of 1689 and 1690 are come nearer that in 1642. The Longest Parliament swore the subjects, and made all the clergy subscribe, that *It is unlawfull on any pretence whatsoever to take armes against the King, or any Commissioned by him in the execution of the Commission.* But our later parliaments think If the King commission a French army and Navy to invade the land they may resist them. Yea the Bps. and Lords and K. James his owne select Army thought they might joyne with the Prince of Orange that resisted him: And the English Parliament have sent soldiers into Ireland to resist him theare; (where his Abdication and the Cause was much more dubious).

Resistance was the extreme medicine, not the daily bread, of the constitution. Baxter revered magistracy too much to speak of resistance in anything but whispers: he knew from first-hand experience the horrors of civil war, which is why he thought that bad government was better than no government (even if he baulked at Muscovy totalitarianism). Civil war was terrible, because soldiers were devils: no light epithet this, when at this very time he was publishing *The Certainty of the Worlds of Spirits*: 'Devils that haunt houses seldome hurt or much impoverish any but only affright them by noises of apparitions. But soldiers (men Devills) rage, blaspheme, domineere wound and kill and take away all that they can carry.'[101] Baxter had told Mrs Gell how Mr White of Dorchester banished the Devil by telling him to stand still at the bottom of his bed if he had nothing better to do. No such easy method for banishing the men-Devils of the Civil War! And Baxter knew who were the ultimate losers of civil war: the poor. Again it is worth remembering that it was at this same time that Baxter was composing *The Poor Husbandman's Advocate*,[102] and his compassion for the poor comes out forcibly in this eloquent passage against the military:

> They keepe the poore in terrour night and day, and when they have burnt their houses and taken all their goods and cattell, leave them to seeke as beggars, to some other Country for entertainment, if they do not kill them to prevent that distresse.

Baxter referred to Germany 'after the warre in 1632 when men were faine to watch the graves in the church yards, lest the famished people should dig up the dead to eate'.[103] Baxter used the terrible experiences of the Civil War as a sermon against pride in his *Christian Directory*:

> He that had seen what the late doleful Wars did often shew us, that the fields were strowed with the carkasses of men, and when they lay by heaps among the rubbish of the Ditches of Towns and Castles that had been assaulted, would think such loathsome lumps of flesh, should never have been proud.[104]

And he knew how much of what his own wife called her 'melancholy' had its roots in her dreadful Civil War experience; of how her mother's house was used as a garrison, of how it was stormed while she was in it and houses burnt all around, and of how she saw before her very eyes men being killed, threatened and stripped of their clothes.[105] When Baxter thought that bad government was better than no government, Nero better than anarchy, he wrote with the Civil War experience etched into his soul. He wished even that the resisters of La Rochelle had heeded the caution of 'Great Morny du Plessis, and Peter du Moulin': 'the description of whose case cannot be read without horrour'.

This did not mean that he approved of a man being fined for saying that *salus populi suprema lex est*; he pointed out that this was not only a principle derived from Roman Law but 'is the essence and definition of Government', and wondered if Hooker would have been fined if he were alive at the end of the seventeenth century for saying just that. He claimed that his *Holy Commonwealth had* got the balance right; it was an argument *against* democracy, not *for* it; it had been traduced by 'ambitious secular court preachers' who 'made it as a football in their sermons'. Bilson was right to show that *regere* and *perdere* were incompatible, but 'rebellion is so heynous a sin, that we have 100 times more reason to cry it down (as I have done at large in the aforesaid Treatise) than to tell the people when they may resist.' Crying down rebellion — with awareness of all the dreadful implications of a civil war — was compatible with refusing to acquiesce in a Muscovy tyranny.

Self-preservation was the ultimate justification for taking up arms. Baxter acknowledged that this was true for himself when he disposed of the objection that subjects must not support a King with an ill cause, against a foreign King. His revealing comment was 'that seems to be against the maine reason that engaged me to the Parliament in the Warre.' He went on to explain why self-preservation was so important:

> I confesse did K. Charles, James or K. William wrong the Turk, the Algeriane, the K. of France and it came to a warre, and if he be conquered we may expect slavery, popery and common ruine, I would exhort all subjects to fight under the bannere of their King, declaring that we owne not his faults, but we will defend ourselves and our posterity and deserved not ruine by his misdoings. He that may not destroy us himselfe by his soldiers at home, may not by every fault expose us to be destroyed by foreiners. A Kingdom hath yet the right of self-defence.[106]

Baxter acknowledged how much 'of the peace of my conscience' rests on this issue. He sincerely admired George Lawson's political treatises but found them wanting here. Lawson offered a constitutional explanation for the Civil War, which was admirable up to a point. Baxter had certainly been glad earlier to invoke Lawson as the political analyst whom divines (like himself) could follow with profit. Lawson had believed that the Civil War was a quarrel over the militia.[107] How gladly Baxter himself had seized on this thesis when he had wanted to deny that the Civil War was a 'war for Religion'! Lawson had argued that when Parliament issued the Militia Ordinance and the King, Commissions of Array, government was dissolved. A vacuum was created; into which in some cases Grotius would argue that a conqueror could assume authority. Baxter would have none of this:

> I thinke this is a dangerous errour; for want of distinguishing the *species* from the *individuall*, and the peoples right from the princes, and the just ends of a war from the unjust. The Constitution of the Government being settled in King, or Parliament, hath a Virtuall Existence in the minds, conscience and obligations of all the Kingdome: And therefore if one King abdicate or forfeit the species or Constituted forme surviveth in the Contract and Consent and obligation ... The present full exercise of a Government may be interrupted, and yet the species not dissolved, nor the people let loose to alter it: for the dead or abdicating King hath rightfull Successours, Or, if none, the people may choose such.

This was a marvellous argument for continuity. Lawson's dissolution of government had become a hiccup; the King abdicates or forfeits the allegiance of his subjects; their right to self-preservative action is maintained but the people are not 'let loose'; magistracy passes on to a successor, or if there is none, the people may choose one. Thus Baxter had reconciled respect for magistracy, horror of rebellion, fear of the people and a refusal to endorse slavery.

But his quarrel with Lawson was at a deeper level still. Lawson stood for that sober political analysis which missed the whole point of a Civil War:

> And because many are of the opinion of my highly valued friend Mr. George Lawson (a most judicious Politician) ... that saith, *The Government was dissolved when the King set up his standard against his Parliament, and they were divided about the militia* (which I deny, And because many judge by the issue that the Parliament warred on that supposition.[108]

Much in the way that in 1673 he had lectured a young student, Edmund Hough, on the need to be *there* to understand how the Civil War began, Baxter poured contempt on those 'that now in a dry house do talke of the stormes that we then underwent, without that sense which experience would have given them'. To remedy this, Baxter proposed to append a petition of 1643 which he felt captured the Parliamentary mood *at the time*, even although he would not now care to endorse every sentiment expressed in it. Alas, we shall never know what that petition was: the manuscript breaks off shortly after this point. Baxter hoped that men on the Parliamentary side would never again be provoked in a like manner, or that would-be persecutors would never again 'try whether Bees have stings by pulling downe the hive'. It would be good to have that petition: to see what Baxter thought had provoked the bees to sting. All we know is that it had nothing to do with divisions over the militia, the dissolution of government and the world of George Lawson.

It is George Lawson's world that is evoked by R.B. Schlatter in his final judgement on Baxter's political theory:

> His choice, consistently, is the mixed species of government which he considers the best as well as the true, historical, English form. He supported the Parliament in the Civil War because he thought Charles I was trying to undermine the old government of King, Lords and Commons; he opposed Oliver for destroying that government; he supported Richard's Protectorate as a kind of revival of that government; and he supported the Restoration because it offered the only hope of bringing back the true, English, mixed government.[109]

It is possible now to offer a revised version of that judgement:

> His choice, consistently, is the sovereign imperial power of the Christian Magistrate, which he considers the best as well as the true, historical, English form. He supported the Parliament in the Civil War because he thought that Irish Papists with the real (or forged) consent of Charles I were determined on the destruction of the Protestant Kingdom; he opposed Oliver as a regicide and a usurper; he supported Richard's Protectorate as a kind of revival of the 'holy commonwealth' ideal; and he initially supported the Restoration because it then offered the only hope of bringing back the true, English, imperial government.

The next two chapters will try to substantiate these last two claims.

Notes

1. B. Manning (ed.), *Politics, Religion and the English Civil War* (London, 1973), pp. 120-1. For a critique of his reliance on Baxter (and Corbet) see J. Morrill, *The Revolt of the Provinces* (London, 1976), p. 50.

2. Edward Bowles, *The Mysterie of Iniquity* (London, 1643), pp. 3, 31, 39, 41.

3. See below, p. 133.

4. (British Library, henceforth BL) *Sloane MSS* 1008, f.208-208v.

5. (BL) *Stowe MSS* 82, f.325-6. See Appendix A.

6. (BL) *Sloane MSS* 1008, f.212.

7. Joyce L. Malcolm, 'A King in Search of Soldiers: Charles I in 1642', *Historical Journal*, 21, 2 (June 1978), pp. 252-3. The thesis advanced in her article reinforces the interpretation of Baxter's motives in 1642 which is offered in the rest of this chapter.

8. R.B. Schlatter, *Richard Baxter and Puritan Politics* (New Brunswick, 1957), p. 26.

9. Noted by Royce McGillivray, *Restoration Historians and the English Civil War* (The Hague, 1974), pp. 153-4.

10. A point made by Schlatter, *Richard Baxter*, p. 6.

11. Respectively: (BL) *Egerton MSS 2570*, reproduced in (Dr Williams's Library) *Baxter Treatises*, xxii; Matthew Sylvester (ed.), *Reliquiae Baxterianae* (London, 1696); Edmund Calamy (ed.), *An Abridgement of Mr. Baxter's History of his Life and Times* (London, 1702); J.M. Lloyd Thomas (ed.), *Autobiography of Richard Baxter* (Everyman, London, 1931).

12. (DWL) *Baxter Correspondence*, ii, f.76.

13. Charles Leslie, *A Case of Present Concern* (London, 1702), p. 4.

14. Calamy, *An Abridgement*, preface.

15. Ibid., p. 44.

16. E.g. Thomas Long, *A Review of Mr. Richard Baxter's Life* (London, 1697).

17. Sylvester, *Reliquiae Baxterianae*, iii, p. 83.

18. Long, *A Review*, pp. 207-8.

19. (DWL) *Baxter Treatises*, xxii, f.11.

20. K. Lindley, 'The Impact of the 1641 Rebellion Upon England and Wales, 1641-1645', *Irish Historical Studies*, 18 (1972-3), pp. 144-75; R. Dunlop, 'The forged commission of 1641', *English Historical Review*, ii (1887), pp. 529-33; J. Lowe, 'The negotiations between Charles I and the confederation of Kilkenny 1642-9', unpublished Ph.D. thesis, University of London, 1960, pp. 12-13; A. Clarke, *The Old English in Ireland* (London, 1966), pp. 165-8; T.C. Barnard, *Cromwellian Ireland* (Oxford, 1975), p. 4.

21. Long, *A Review*, dedicatory epistle.

22. Samuel Young, *Vindiciae Anti-Baxterianae* (London, 1696), pp. 194-5, 230.

23. Long, *A Review*, p. 205.

24. William Binckes, *A Sermon preach'd before the Honourable House of Commons* (London, 1705), p. 15; cf. also William Baron, *A Just Defence of the Royal Martyr* (London, 1699), p. 68.

25. Benjamin Bennet, *A Defence of the Memorial of the Reformation* (London, 1723), p. 85.

26. Anon., *Animadversions on the Two Last 30th of January Sermons* (London, 1702), pp. 8-10. I am indebted to my former student, Mr Mark Goldie, for the references in this footnote and also in footnote 24 above.

27. Thomas Carte, *The Irish Massacre Set in a Clear Light* (London, 1715), preface, p. 5.

28. (Bodleian Library) *Carte MSS* 225, f.219-f.292a. For the text of *Murder Will Out* – and Carte's rejoinders – see *Lord Somers Tracts*, ed. W. Scott (London, 1811), v, pp. 624-64.

29. Ibid., f.257v.

30. Ibid., f.274.

31. Ibid., f.266v.

32. Ibid., f.276-f.277.

33. Ibid., f.278-f.279.

34. Ibid., f.260-f.260v.

35. Calamy, *An Abridgment* (London, 1713), p. 44.

36. Sylvester, *Reliquiae Baxterianae*, preface; i, pp. 34-6.

37. Ibid., pp. 34-6.

38. Manning, *Politics, Religion and the English Civil War*, p. 120.

39. Baxter, *A Holy Commonwealth* (London, 1659), pp. 473, 478.

40. Baxter, *A Key for Catholicks* . . . (London, 1659), dedicatory epistle, pp. 316, 327, 330, 321.

41. Baxter, *The Grotian Religion Discovered* (London, 1658), pp. 106-8.

42. (DWL) *Baxter Treatises*, iv, f. 276v. Morley had published his *Bishop of Winchester's Vindication* in the first half of 1683; Baxter's manuscript reply, entitled 'Bishop Morley's great mistakes', was written on 9 July 1683.

43. Baxter, *The Christian Directory* (London, 1673), pp. 722, 725, 727.

44. Ibid., p. 736.

45. Baxter, *An Answer to Mr. Dodwell and Dr. Sherlocke* (London, 1682), p. 158.

46. Young, *Vindiciae Anti-Baxterianae*; preface.

47. Baxter, *The Christian Directory*, p. 736.

48. (DWL) *Baxter Correspondence*, iii, f.11-f.12v.

49. Young, *Vindiciae Anti-Baxterianae*, p. 47.

50. He still awaits his biographer. I tried to sketch something of his immense influence on the seventeenth century in an earlier article, 'The Rise and Fall of Bishop Bilson', *The Journal of British Studies*, v, 2, pp. 22-32.

51. Baxter, *The Christian Directory*, p. 745.

52. Ibid., p. 733.

53. (DWL) *Baxter Correspondence*, ii, f.211.

54. (DWL) *Baxter Correspondence*, i, f. 70.

55. (DWL) *Baxter Treatises*, i, f.172v. James I produced his treatise anonymously five years before the officially accredited publication: see J.N. Figgis, *The Divine Right of Kings*, ed. G.R. Elton (London, 1965), p. 138.

56. (BL) *Egerton MSS 2570*, f. 81.

57. Baxter, *The Reasons of the Christian Religion* (London, 1667), p. 50. This was a slight variant on the stock theme that Papists caused the Great Fire. Cf. the anonymous correspondent who informed Baxter in 1666 about a Mr Light who 'having some discourse with one Mr. Langhorne of Middle Temple Barrister reputed a zealous Papist, about the February last; After some discourse in disputation of Religion; he took him by the hand and said, you expect great things in sixty five and that Rome will be destroyed; but what if it be London? – (DWL) *Baxter Correspondence*, vi, f. 179.

58. (DWL) *Baxter Correspondence*, iii, f.11v-f.12v.

59. Baxter, *The Judgment of Non-Conformists About the Difference Between Grace and Morality* (London, 1676), p. 114.

60. Rebecca Warner (ed.), *Original Letters* (London, 1817), p. 5.

61. Baxter, *The True History of Councils Enlarged and Defended* (London,

1682), p. 43.

62. (DWL) *Baxter Treatises*, i, f.205.

63. Baxter, 'King James His Abdication of the Crown Plainly Proved' in R.B. Schlatter, *Richard Baxter and Puritan Politics* (New Brunswick, 1957), pp. 159, 172, 173.

64. Baxter, *The Christian Directory*, p. 736.

65. Schlatter, *Richard Baxter*, pp. 174-5.

66. (DWL) *Morrice MSS P*, f.373-f.374.

67. Baxter, 'A Sheet in Reference to the Judgment and Decree of the University of Oxford Passed in their Convocation' in Schlatter, *Richard Baxter*, pp. 150, 151, 155.

68. (DWL) *Morrice MSS P*, f.373. For a detailed analysis of Hobbes's eschatological defence of magistracy, see J.G.A. Pocock, 'Time, history and eschatology in the thought of Thomas Hobbes' in J.H. Elliott and H.G. Koenigsberger (eds.) *The Diversity of History: Essays in Honour of Sir Herbert Butterfield* (London, 1970), pp. 150-98.

69. (DWL) *Morrice MSS P*, f.374.

70. Cf. (DWL) *Morrice MSS P*, f.461, f.465, f.515, f.516, f.593.

71. (DWL) *Baxter Treatises*, xviii, f.75v; Baxter in Sylvester, *Reliquiae Baxterianae*, ii, p. 378.

72. (DWL) *Baxter Correspondence*, v, f.14v (Baxter: Major Thomas Jennings, 27 May 1682);'Philethes' (i.e. Isaac Sharpe), *Animadversions on Some Passages of Mr. Edmund Calamy's Abridgement* (London, 1704), p. 24; John Barnard, *Theologo-Historicus* (London, 1685), p. 48.

73. Charles Leslie, *A Case of Present Concern* (London, 1702), p. 9. Jane, the Bishop of London's Chaplain, had preached in June 1676 around the text that Baxter *'had sent as bad men to Heaven as some that be in hell'*: Baxter in Sylvester, *Reliquiae Baxterianae*, iii, p. 177; (DWL) *Baxter Treatises*, vii, f.23-f.23v.

74. Baxter in Sylvester, *Reliquiae Baxterianae*, iii, p. 151.

75. Baxter, *Against the Revolt to a Foreign Jurisdiction* (London, 1691), dedicatory epistle.

76. S.R. Gardiner (ed.), *Documents Relating to Proceedings Against William Prynne* (Camden Society New Series), xviii, p. 98.

77. Baxter, *Against the Revolt to a Foreign Jurisdiction*, pp. 53, 25, 26, 78, 86, 87, 320, 326, 360, 429. For circumstantial evidence of Baxter's personal responsibility for anti-Catholic hysteria in 1641, *see* R. Clifton 'The Fear of Catholics in England 1637-45' (unpublished Oxford D.Phil. thesis, 1964), pp. 148-50.

78. Baxter, *The Christian Directory*, p. 745.

79. Baxter in Sylvester, *Reliquiae Baxterianae*, i, p. 36.

80. Baxter, *Against the Revolt to a Foreign Jurisdiction*, p. 433.

81. Baxter, *Catholick Theologie* (London, 1675), i, preface; ii, p. 175.

82. Baxter, *The Nonconformists Plea for Peace* (London, 1679), pp. 125-6.

83. Baxter, *The English Nonconformity* (London, 1690), p. 215.

84. R.B. Schlatter, *Richard Baxter and Puritan Politics* (New Brunswick, 1957), p. 164.

85. Peter du Moulin, *A Vindication of the Sincerity of the Protestant Religion* (London, 1671), pp. 64, 65, 116.

86. 'Sancta Clara' Davenport, *A Cleare Vindication of Roman Catholicks from a Foule Aspersion* (London, 1659), p. 45; Prynne related the story of the Queen's Confessor in full on two occasions: *A True and Perfect Narrative . . .* (London, 1659), pp. 62-3; *A Brief Necessary Vindication of the Old and New Secluded Members . . .* (London, 1659), p. 45. Cf. Baxter, *The Grotian Religion Discovered* (London, 1658), p. 108.

87. Anon., *The Prophecy of Bishop Usher* . . . (London, 1687), pp. 6-9; (DWL) *Baxter Treatises*, i, f.269.

88. (DWL) *Baxter Treatises*, iii, f.293.

89. (DWL) *Baxter Treatises*, iii, f.261v-f.262v.

90. Baxter in Sylvester, *Reliquiae Baxterianae*, ii, p. 373.

91. S.T. Coleridge, *Complete Works*, ed. Shedd (New York, 1854), v, p. 347.

92. Baxter in Sylvester, *Reliquiae Baxterianae*, i, p. 63.

93. Calamy, *An Abridgement*, p. 57.

94. Baxter, *A Key for Catholicks*, p. 327.

95. Ibid., p. 330.

96. (DWL) *Baxter Treatises*, vi, f.286-f.286v.

97. Schlatter, *Richard Baxter*, p. 158.

98. (DWL) *Baxter Treatises*, vi, f.286-f.286v.

99. Baxter, *The Nonconformists Plea for Peace*, pp. 89-90.

100. (DWL) *Baxter Treatises*, vi, f.287.

101. (DWL) *Baxter Treatises*, vi, f.288-9.

102. On which, see Chapter 4.

103. (DWL) *Baxter Treatises*, vi, f.289.

104. Baxter, *The Christian Directory*, p. 200.

105. Baxter, *A Breviate of the Life of Margaret* . . . (London, 1681), p. 44.

106. (DWL) *Baxter Treatises*, vi, f.291-3.

107. George Lawson, *An Examination* . . . (London, 1657), p. 32: 'The seeds of this division were sown and begun to appear before the wars, and the opinion, that all these were only in one man, that is the King absolutely, some say, was the greatest cause, not only of the last, but also of other civil wars in former times . . . Our several opinions in Religion have heightened our difference, and hindered our settlement, *yet Religion is but pretended*' (my italics). On Lawson, see: A.H. Maclean, 'George Lawson and John Locke', *Cambridge Historical Journal*, xi, I, 1947, pp. 68-72; J.H. Franklin, *John Locke and the Theory of Sovereignty*, (Cambridge, 1978), *passim*.

Baxter wrote his *Holy Commonwealth* of 1659 in answer to James Harrington's *Oceana*. For R.B. Schlatter it was the classic defence of the concept of mixed government. When he published a selection of Baxter's writings, *A Holy Commonwealth* accordingly commanded more space than any other single work. This did not mean that he reprinted the whole of even that pamphlet. What Schlatter gave the reader was 85 pages from a total text which ran to 517 pages. However, Schlatter claimed that the two chapters of that work which he did print 'contain the heart of what he had to say'.[1] This should be amended to: contain the heart of what he had to say *about mixed government and James Harrington*. How peripheral both are to his main concerns will be argued in the rest of this chapter.

I see his *Holy Commonwealth* in a different light: as a fiercely anti-Catholic work suffused with millennial intimations. In this sense it complements the argument of the two preceding chapters: it is after all what one would expect from the student of the Apocalypse and the discoverer of Popish Plots. There is another sense, however, in which the work is rich in surprises. Baxter's millennial hopes rest upon the Protectorate of Richard Cromwell. Ten years earlier this would have seemed inconceivable. Baxter had attacked the regicide, declined to take the Engagement Oath to the new Commonwealth régime, and believed that the exiled Prince Charles was the rightful ruler in England. Yet not only is his *Holy Commonwealth* of 1659 unctuously dedicated to Richard Cromwell: it is clear that the whole strategy outlined in that book hinges upon action by the Protector.

The analysis of *A Holy Commonwealth* which follows is, therefore, also an analysis of the ten years of Baxter's life under the Commonwealth. It is impossible to understand the process by which Baxter moved from frigid hostility to the usurper Cromwell to the partisan endorsement of his son without detailed examination of the controversies he engaged in during this period, the causes he embraced and the practical schemes he initiated. We are fortunate for this period in the wealth of documentation which is available. It is possible to trace Baxter's gradual change of mind in the letters which he wrote to friends during this time, as well as in his published works. The topics which are there raised seem to have only a tangential relationship to the great themes of *A Holy Commonwealth*. Yet I hope to have established their connection by the end of this chapter.

We should begin with doctrine, for that is where Baxter himself began. His initial dislike of Oliver Cromwell, and of his Fifth Monarchist crony Harrison, lay in their fluency in expounding the concept of Free Grace which they barely understood. We saw in the last chapter how certain Baxter was in the knowledge of when the Civil War turned sour. 'Now begins the change of the old cause,' he wrote of the period after 1643.[2] This was when the Civil War became a 'war for Religion', meaning not that it had been about legal matters before that date, but that a legitimate war of limited self-defence had been transformed into King-killing aggression. When Baxter accepted the invitation in the summer of 1645 to serve as chaplain in the regiment of his friend Edward Whalley he learned at first hand the nature of the change. During the following year of military triumphs with the New Model Army Baxter was fighting his own internal war with fellow ministers. It was a struggle which would only cease in February 1647 with the collapse of his health, the loss of 'a Gallon of Blood by the Nose', convalescence at Rous-Lench and the genesis of his first published work *The Aphorismes of Justification.*

How a political reaction was transmuted into theology is made clear by Baxter in his writings. A letter survives from Baxter to some of his old Army colleagues. It is written in despair:

> And you must thinke that a man would not be very prone to oppose that partye, with whom he hath so zealously joyned in their greatest adversity, and endured so many cold stormes, and unseasonable marches, and laine out of doores so many rainy nights together, and bin in so many bloody fightes, as I have been in the space of 4 yeares and a halfe; and contracted so many sicknesses to my body, and at last even death it selfe; which is to me even at the doore in all probability, occasioned by those distemperings of my body, and especially by the losse of a gallon of blood which did force me from you.

Their antinomian refusal to be bound by human vows was the quality that repelled Baxter:

> To say an ill oath is better broake than kept, is a plea for a conscience that hath long bin under the hott-iron. To swear to defend Parliament, though fallible, is no ill oath: And some ill oathes, though not all, are better kept than broaken . . . Only the Anti-scripturists among

you can reconcile the Actions of these 2 yeares with their principles.[3]

Baxter's protest might have ended at that point: a peevish disgruntlement with former comrades. He took the decisive next step — and arguably transformed the rest of his writing life — by relating their backsliding to bad theology. Baxter himself looked back on that week of convalescence at Rous-Lench as a watershed in his life: 'I discovered more in one weeke than in seventeen yeares reading, hearing and wrangling.' He uses the language of religious conversion to describe the 'overpowring Light' which struck him when he had reached page 68 of the manuscript of his *Saints Everlasting Rest*. At a certain point he reached in the argument — discussing in what sense men could be called righteous — he was blessed with a 'clear apprehension'.[4] It was the only time in his life that he would come near to the excitement of his great teacher, John Foxe, when unravelling the Apocalypse. His *Aphorismes of Justification* was the product of this experience: originally intended as an appendix to *The Saints Everlasting Rest*, but published in its own right as his first work.

Baxter described in a later work, his *Catholick Theologie* of 1675, how he had grown up with an uncritical antipathy to Arminianism: 'all my reverenced acquaintance (save one) cryed down Arminianism as the Pelagian Heresie, and the Enemy of Grace'. The Army saints forced on Baxter a painful re-examination of himself:

I there met with some Arminians, and more Antinomians: These printed and preached as the Doctrine of Free Grace, that all men must presently believe that they are Elect and Justified, and that Christ Repented and Believed for them (as Saltmarsh writeth). I had a little before engaged my self as a Disputer against Universal Redemption, against two ancient Ministers in Coventry (Mr. Craddock and Mr. Diamond) that were for it. But these new notions called me to new thoughts.

Why his 'new thoughts' should take the form of his *Aphorismes of Justification* is not self-evident from that passage. He may have met with more Antinomians among his enemy Saints, but he had conceded that some also among them were Arminians. He put it even more strongly in a later pamphlet of 1684. He then suggested that there were *equally* as many Arminians as there were Antinomians among the leftwing Army chaplains.[5] There was therefore no statistical compulsion on Baxter to put the blame so squarely on those who preached too strongly on predestination rather than on those who shied away from the doctrine.

But this is what he did. His *Aphorismes of Justification* was a conscious effort to reverse the Calvinist tide. And since he saw Oliver Cromwell as the spokesman for Calvinist sectarianism, he was at the same time consciously setting himself to oppose any experiment in 'holy commonwealths' which sprang from that tainted source. Two points illustrate the power of this obsession. He was haunted by the rise of Quakerism in the early years of the Commonwealth period. He was convinced that they were masked Jesuits and thrashed wildly about for documentary proof. He found it in the argument that the Quakers did not think that the Pope was Antichrist. This was doubly discreditable in Baxter. Nayler protested on behalf of the Quakers that they did think that very thing; on the evidence of the first chapter, it is dubious if Baxter himself shared that confidence.[6] Yet the obvious doctrinal affinities between Quakers and Jesuits were played down. Secondly, he even made little of the commitment to free will in Catholics themselves. He argued that they put much less emphasis on personal merit than the majority of Protestant critics supposed. And if the Jesuits had overstressed free will, their Dominican rivals had gone equally far in the opposite direction.

Baxter's double standard is nowhere more strikingly illustrated than in a private letter to a colleague, Peter Ince, on 21 November 1653. It was supposed to be a testament of his revulsion from Arminianism, and it began in promising vein: 'I cannot pray well with the Arminian doctrine: For sure if I thought free will did so much and grace so little I should pray with little life.' Immediately he adds a softening afterthought as he recollects that 'millions' of godly men of that opinion (his own estimate of numbers) did not have this inhibition. But they came from other countries, and that makes the difference:

> And doubtless, one reason why they were so bad in England was, that the godly being first entered into another schoole, and so running one way (much by the force of example and affection and much by divine grace) the others were temporizers that took up the opinions for worldly respects ... Its generally acknowledged that in France and Belgia the orthodox are too loose, so that Arminians at first carried it much by more than ordinary piety.[7]

Little of comfort here for an anti-Arminian, even if Baxter concedes that 'divine grace' as well as 'example and affection' pushed the English godly in an anti-Arminian direction. The crucial point was *that Armini-anism and impiety were not causally related.* The impious took it up as a reflex response to the prevalent pious orthodoxy. In another country, at another time, it could be the turn of the *pious* to adopt Arminianism.

A few months later Baxter was pamphleteering against Antinomian-ism: the contrast could not be more marked. The relationship between Antinomianism and impiety is seen as a causal, not a contingent, one. Antinomianism is the voice of the ungovernable rabble, the assertion of natural man:

> I seriously profess, to my best observation it appears to me, that the Antinomian Doctrine is the very same in almost every point, which I find naturally fastned in the hearts of the common profane multi-tudes, and that in all my discourses with them I find, that though the ignorant cannot mouth it so plausibly, nor talk so much of free Grace, yet have they the same tenets, and all men are naturally of the Antinomian Religion; and that very work of preachers (when Christ's death and the Promise of pardon and Life is once revealed) is principally the cure of naturall Antinomianism; and this is that we call the work of conversion.[8]

Baxter did not always reason this way. In 1690 he would even argue of Antinomians, that 'it is the Piety and Strictness of the lives of many of them which hath drawn many well-meaning ignorant persons to their Errors.' He would then cite Bunyan, 'an unlearned Antinomian', as the type of an 'honest, Godly man'.[9] But in the 1650s Baxter was incapable of such magnanimity. While Arminianism might have been taken up *by* wicked men, Antinomianism was the religion *of* wicked men.

The argument was frequently advanced by contemporaries that such was Baxter's vehemence against Antinomianism that he over-reacted, and actually did become an Arminian. Dr Bossy has called him 'the father of a rational and humanist "Arminianism"' who had begun 'the process of detaching English Presbyterianism from its Calvinist roots'.[10] Baxter himself claimed to have steered a middle course between both extremes. Samuel Young thought that the compromise had not been very successful — 'a meer Gallimophery, a Hodg-podge Divinity' — but at least gave him credit for having attempted to incorporate elements of Calvinism *and* Arminianism into his 'Baxterianism'.[11] Perhaps we should not make too much of Baxter's repeated boasts that he had found the middle way: it is not often enough remembered that Edward Fisher, the most influential of all hard-line anti-Arminian writers, had claimed to have discovered that same golden mean.[12]

The howls of protest which greeted his *Aphorismes of Justification* — which would continue to reverberate down the years in his correspondence — would seem to confirm Dr Bossy's judgement. But to call him an 'Arminian', or to say that his principles necessitated a detachment from 'Calvinist roots', begs a number of questions. Predestination never had the primacy for Calvin that it had for many who came after him. It became the badge of orthodoxy when the majority of delegates at the Synod of Dort (supported by James I's delegates from England) voted down the Arminian alternative. It became the badge of heterodoxy when Archbishop Laud and a group of bishops imposed their Arminian beliefs as the new orthodoxy in the England of the 1630s.[13] But there were always men who were highly critical of the predestinarian theory without joining either the ranks of the defeated at Dort or the victorious Laudians. Among the most influential and interesting of these were Cameron and Amyraut (quoting Calvin against Beza), Davenant and Ward (subtly distinguishing their position from that of their fellow English delegates at Dort: Carleton, Balcanquhalle and Goad), Sibbes and Preston (among the leading 'covenant' theologians of the 1620s and 1630s).

All had their influence on Baxter; none more so than Davenant. He still awaits his biographer, but his 'hypothetical universalism' proved resilient against the ideologues of both camps. At Dort, Davenant preached universalism against a rather restrictive concept of predestination; twenty years later, against his Laudian critic, Samuel Hoard, he was to insist on its hypothetical nature. The crucial distinction for Davenant — as it was for Baxter — was between *sufficient* and *efficient* Grace. Thanks to *sufficient* Grace *all men* get the chance to be saved (which sounds Arminian); the fact that they will not all take it up is a consequence of their human frailties without redeeming *efficient* Grace (which sounds Calvinist). The *hypothetical* nature of this universalism means not only that it is not Arminian; it is not even full 'covenant' theology. Davenant emphasises the 'infrustrability' of election, compared to the mutuality of the 'covenant' between God and Man in the theology of Preston. Preston emphasises that he is talking about 'so small a condition' but the Antinomian Saltmarsh recognised the importance of the loophole: to attribute to man some small part in his own salvation is really to put salvation in his power entirely'.[14] The hypothetical universalist escapes this snare, but at the price of common sense in the eyes of the Arminian. As Hoard put it to Davenant, if everybody who receives *sufficient* Grace is certain to abuse it, what is the point in granting it? An Arminian of the Left, John Goodwin, would have a similar objection in 1651:

> So that to affirme and grant, that Christ died *sufficiently* for all Men, and yet deny that he died intentionally for all Men, is to speak contradictions, and to pull down with the left hand, what a Man hath built up with his right.[15]

Perhaps it was *the consciousness* that Baxter *was* taking from Davenant and Dort, from Cameron and Amyraut, and even from the covenant theologians, which was his greatest crime in the eyes of his opponents — more than the particular principles themselves. When Baxter began writing in 1649 challenges to strict predestinarian beliefs were in the air. The trouble was that, when they were not tainted with associations with a discredited Laudian past, they were tainted with associations with an equally disreputable 'fringe sect' present (Quakers, General Baptists, Walwynite Levellers). Even John Goodwin had a soiled regicide image[16] and, although he would point out inconsistencies in some of the decisions at Dort, he lacked Baxter's instinct for exposing these inconsistencies in order to develop, via Davenant and Ward, his own version of what had happened at Dort. Baxter had a good sense of working within a tradition.

He did something more: he treated the Laudian episode as a false intrusion into that tradition. In 1649 he resumed the debate at the point where it broke off with the irrelevancy of Laud: in other words, when the implications of Dort could still be explored courteously within a common Protestant framework. Davenant, Usher and Hall were bishops, at the time of Laud, who could have checked Antinomian tendencies by preaching universal redemption; instead of which, their energies were spent in defending *their* orthodoxy against the Arminian-inspired attack of their own colleagues. Hoard attacked Davenant, Montague attacked Carleton, and Cosin and Montague could look forward to the day when a 'half-Puritan' like Bishop Hall could be a victim of *their* Inquisition.[17]

A remarkable feature of Baxter's doctrinal writings is the paucity of reference to the Laudians. Under the catch-all label of 'Arminian', opponents had lumped together a number of features of that régime which had only a tenuous link with doctrine. Prynne is a good example: even when he writes anti-Laudian pamphlets on doctrinal themes (and he cares very much about these doctrinal themes, and he will go back to Pelagius to prove his case), he still includes a whole host of unrelated issues (bowing at the name of Jesus, the placing of the Communion table and the like). And Baxter would himself confess later that much of his earlier zeal against Arminianism derived from ignorance about what it was. But Prynne, at his most eclectic, never forgot that there *was* a doctrinal argument against Laudianism. Baxter's doctrinal pamphlets in the 1650s, however, are stripped of reference to Laud, Cosin, Neile, Wren, Montague and Hoard, which seems an excessive overcompensation. They almost might never have existed. Not unreasonably, some opponents deduced that he was now secretly partial to their views. This was wrong. His detestation of Laudianism was sincere. But it was a rejection at a personal, rather than ideological, level. This was the importance of his refusal to see a causal link between their doctrine and their actions; so unlike his response to Anabaptist chaplains in the Roundhead Army. The Laudians were wrong but irrelevant. And even, in the late 1670s, when he read Peter Heylyn's biography of Laud against the background of increasingly sinister manoeuvres by Laud's spiritual heirs (Thorndike, Dodwell, Sherlock), he raised the spectre — not of assaults on doctrinal purity — but of a renewed submission to a 'foreign jurisdiction'. The Antinomian, not the Arminian, remained the enemy.

Throughout the Commonwealth period Baxter was obsessed with the problem of 'natural antinomianism'. It coloured his dealings with the Baptists. He had great sympathy with their position until he joined the Army regiment. Only a few years earlier the good women of Kidderminster had almost stoned him to death for having asserted that 'hell was paved with infants' skulls.' Hazlitt witheringly recorded the sequel: 'But, by the force of argument, and of learned quotations from the Fathers, the reverend preacher at length prevailed over the scruples of his congregation, and over reason, and humanity.'[18] Once, however, Baxter had made the connection between adult baptism, Free Grace and bad behaviour, he pursued former colleagues, like John Tombes, with considerable venom. Saltmarsh and Dell were Antinomian heirs of the Anabaptists of Munster; Coppe, the leading Ranter, had 're-baptised more than any one man that ever I heard of in the Countrey'. Some of his arguments were pruriently silly: he claimed that Baptist ministers, for instance, like Tombes, were driven by the ambition of baptising naked 'all the maids in Bewdly'.[19] As he conceded that the very mention of this was immodest, this shows how far he was prepared to go in defeating Antinomianism. Again the double standard operates: when Baxter attacks Baptists, he attacks Calvinist Particular Baptists, not Arminian General Baptists. His famous dismissal of the Quakers as 'nothing but the Ranters' has similar psychological roots. Coleridge was incredulous: 'observe the *but*'.[20] Coleridge was incredulous in part because the Quakers of his time were the domesticated animals of George Fox's later years, and not the wild beasts of the early Commonwealth period who did truly, as Christopher Hill has shown, have affinities with Calvinist Ranters of 'the world turned upside down'.[21] Therefore Baxter's identification was less myopic than Coleridge had supposed. Even so that identification was itself based on doctrine. Baxter had made his analysis of the troubles of his time: they sprang from an over-rigid devotion to predestinarian doctrine. Only by seeing the Quakers as an offshoot of the Ranters, the most extreme Calvinists of the day, could they be accommodated within that analysis.

Baxter's debates with colleagues over their claims to control admission to the Sacrament of the Lord's Supper were shaped by similar fears. He was against common admission: this was to abandon the attempt to discipline 'natural antinomianism'. But he was equally unhappy with the 'deeper discoverie' demanded of communicants by Independent colleagues (and by an increasing number of Presbyterian ministers). This was not because he was shy about asserting clerical discipline; it was simply *the wrong kind of assertion*. However noble the aims, the practical results of over-keen ministerial scrutiny were similar to common admission: except for a handful of the pure, the vast reprobate majority were excluded from the comforts of clerical discipline. Ministers must seek 'order and decency' in those who attended the Lord's Table: there was a middle way between promiscuity and élitism.

In pursuit of that middle way Baxter separated himself from Erastian colleagues, with whom in other respects he seemed to have much in common. There are two ways in which the word 'Erastian' is used: in the technically correct sense, of identifying with Erastus's views on clerical discipline; in the popular (pejorative) sense, of identifying with Hobbes's views on unlimited powers for the civil magistrate. Scottish ministers used the second label to discredit opponents who attacked them on the first ground; unfairly, since Erastus's interests in the powers of the civil magistrate went little beyond the quiet aside, that the civil magistrate was capable of doing many of the things that clergymen claimed could only come through an increase of their disciplinary powers. Gillespie and Rutherford caricatured their opponents, Prynne, Coleman, Lightfoot and Selden, when they called them 'Erastians' in the Byzantine sense of the word. The Erastians of 1645 were following Erastus himself in his quarrel with Wither (and translating his writings to get it right) in a primary concern about misuse of clerical powers rather than about any desire to extend the power of the civil magistrate. Even Prynne, who did believe that the civil magistrate should have far-reaching authority — and said so in his pamphlet of 1647, *The Sword of Christian Magistracy* — was an 'Erastian' in the *correct* sense of the word.[22]

Baxter, on the other hand, comes closest to being an 'Erastian' in the *incorrect* sense of the word. Like Prynne, he was prepared to commit to the magistrate formidable discretionary powers; like his friend Lewis du Moulin, he had a deep historic sense of the injustices which an over-ambitious clergy had perpetrated in taking power from the civil magistrate; like them both, he feared over-zealous ministerial control of admission to the Sacrament. But in the correct sense of the word, Baxter was profoundly 'anti-Erastian'. He opposed Prynne's advocacy of open admission; he tried to persuade du Moulin to withdraw his writings against excommunication.[23] He was enough of an 'Erastian', in the popular sense of the word, to relish that side of Hobbes and Harrington which found outlet in their exalting the civil magistrate and in their denouncing clerical meddlers in politics. No man was more enthusiastic than Baxter in denying the civil/ecclesiastical distinction as the basis for clerical ambitions. But he was enough of an 'anti-Erastian', in the correct sense of the word, to deprecate, in both Hobbes and Harrington, an anti-clericalism which went beyond a legitimate political grouse to a far-reaching denial *of ministers' pastoral disciplinary functions.*

One of his most vigorous defences of clerical discipline was made in a letter to John Eliot in January 1669, which drew upon his Common-wealth experiences. The 'talke of one or two in a parish' angered him: the assumption, made by Independent ministers and Presbyterian ones too, that only a few were fit for Church communion. They had not undergone the necessary, laborious task of house-to-house, man-to-man catechising. They had gathered the faithful into communion. They had shown no interest in the excluded, unless to catch them out in a ques-tion, if they met them by chance, to confirm them in their judgement. But, said Baxter proudly, 'we had lately in England' a mixture of Epis-copalian, Presbyterian and Independent ministers, 'set upon union and addicted to no party.' These by agreement either got all their people to come to them, or went to those, who either *would* or *could* not come, by house-to-house visiting. Baxter left a graphic record of the pastoral achievement:

In my parish were about 4000 soules, and neere twenty miles circuit of ground. We finish it in a yeare, setting apart two dayes a weeke (two or three of us) on purpose. We dealt not with them captiously to disgrace them, but tenderly and patiently to instruct them in all the principles first, and then sent all home by earnest conviction and exhortation. By this meanes there were very few in all the parishes whose measures of knowledge, and affection, and parts, and lives, wee had not a competent acquaintance with. And wee found abundance that were not noted for any extraordinary profession nor even came to private meetings to be solid godlie people: Some had superiors who forbad them; and some had Callings which hindered them; and some had an invincible bashfulnesse etc. And we found some noted professours, constants at our private meetings, who were utterlie ignorant of the essentialls of Christianity (about the person and office of Christ). And abundance that we found ignorant seemed in a little time instructed and resolved for a holy life.

Through the work of the ministerial associations in extending this discipline on a county basis England was a land fast becoming holy, until the political upheavals of 1659 changed everything: 'And this course was first set up, and beginning to spread all over England (8 or 9 counties had begun by agreement to attempt it) in 1659 when confusion buryed all etc.'[24]

There is thus a logical thread, which was not at all apparent at first, between his writing *Aphorismes of Justification* in 1649 and *Political Aphorismes* in 1659 (the alternative title of his *Holy Commonwealth*). *His Aphorismes of Justification* was a brave challenge to the Calvinist doctrines of the men who were creating a new Commonwealth; his *Political Aphorismes* was his testament of faith in the possibility of that Commonwealth becoming 'holy'. What connects the two seemingly disparate positions is a common evangelical mission, starved by the prevailing orthodoxies of the early Commonwealth period and richly fulfilled in the ministerial associations and ecumenical designs of the later period. This point can be made more strongly after a more detailed study of his controversial writings and actions in this period.

If the Antinomian enemy had to be personified for Baxter, he would have looked very like the Ranter, Coppe. Baxter remembered him, as a zealous Anabaptist neighbour, when he was preaching to the garrison at Coventry in the Civil War. Coppe progressed, from rebaptising more men in Warwickshire, Oxfordshire and parts of Worcestershire than any other minister, to trance-like states, in which he cried down moral duties as 'plaguy holiness' and advanced the theory, that as one of God's Elect, he was free from normal restraints: he can 'swear a full mouth'd oath, and can kiss his Neighbours wife in Majesty and Honour'. Worse: he pleaded for common ownership of property and went up and down the streets of London 'with his hat cockt, his Teeth gnashing, his eyes fixed, charging the great ones to obey his Majesty within him'.[25]

This was a memorable portrait of a psychopath. But behind the psychopath lay a mistaken ideology, in which faith as well as good works had been systematically denigrated, the capricious nature of God's Grace had been exaggerated, and a minority had been encouraged to believe that they were exempt from the rules which governed their fellow creatures. Behind the disreputable Coppe were eminently respectable divines, like Twisse, Crisp and Fisher, who would certainly have disapproved of his behaviour, *but who had made a phenomenon like Coppe possible* by their own doctrinal teachings. Baxter identified the 'master-points' of Antinomianism in their writings:

> [That Christs satisfaction is ours *qua praestita* before the Application; and that so far, as that we are actually Pardoned, Justified, Reconciled and Adopted by it before we were born, much more before we believe: yea that Adoption and Remission of sin are immanent acts in God, and are so for from eternity, even before any death of Christ, or efficacy of it: That pardon of sin is nothing but Justification *in foro conscientiae*, or the sense of that in our hearts, which was really ours from eternity, or from Christs death, or both: That justifying faith is the feeling or apprehension of Gods eternal Love, Remission and Adoption] I say, take heed of these master Points of Antinomianism.[26]

Many of these ideas, taken singly, were unexceptionable; particularly when articulated by a revered minister like Twisse, whom Baxter acknowledged had influenced his own early views inordinately. But cumulatively they provided the intellectual crutch for a Coppe.

Baxter's achievement in writing his *Aphorismes of Justification* in 1649 was to re-open a debate which had been artificially frozen in the 1630s by the Laudian counter-revolution. To be 'anti-Arminian' then meant being against bowing at the name of Jesus, against placing the Communion Table in the east end of the Church, against Ship Money — all features of Laud's rule which had but a tenuous connection with doctrine. But the situation had changed by 1649: the 'anti-Arminianism' of the 'Country' party of the 1630s was very different from the Antinomian excesses of the Ranters in the 1640s. In this changed situation Baxter wanted his fellow Protestants to look with fresh eyes at the

Arminian doctrine. John Humfrey's letter to Baxter on 11 May 1654 conveys the liberating impact of this message on some of its hearers: 'and how the doctrine of good workes hath hung in our protestant divinity (before your Aphorismes put some reason in it).'[27]

To put some reason in it was not the same thing as totally accepting it: Humfrey was under no illusions about this, although other supporters and opponents of Baxter's doctrine of good works would not be so perceptive on this as he was. But if Baxter had identified the main characteristics of the Antinomian challenge of the late 1640s he had also identified five major principles to invoke against the challenge. The main outlines of his reply are indicated in his *Aphorismes*, but they would go on being refined in subsequent debates and revisions right up to his death. It is time now to summarise these main elements in Baxter's challenge to orthodoxy. They were as follows: that God was both a *dominus* and a *rector*; that Christ had died *sufficiently* for all men, but *efficiently* for the Elect; that Christ's sacrifice had brought a 'new law' of salvation to the world; that such an offer was conditional on faith; that the fear induced by the prospect of Hell was a legitimate part of God's armoury.

This was more complex than a restatement of the doctrine of good works: contemporaries who recognised that fact also frequently resented the complexity. Baxter was seen with justice as a man who loved spinning ever more subtle distinctions, almost for their own sake. But Baxter had a serious purpose in mind in offering his distinctions, and to discover that purpose, and to assess its relationship to his later pursuit of a 'Holy Commonwealth', we must stay with theology and with Baxter's fine distinctions for some pages to come.

The hardest thing for contemporaries to grasp — and yet in a sense all his other propositions flowed from this one — was his conviction that God was, at one and the same time, both *dominus* and *rector*. This distinction — so vital to Baxter, if one is to understand the nature of his compromise — was best expressed in his *Catholick Theologie* of 1675, although he uses in this passage the terms *'Creator and Motor'* rather than *'Dominus'*:

God hath as Creator and Motor become the Voluntary Root or Spring of Nature and natural motion, and accordingly established all second causes as natural agents under him, and doth by them operate in a natural necessitating and constant way: And this is antecedent to his Laws to free agents: And this natural course of agency we must not expect that he should alter, but rarely by miracles . . .

But God being secondarily the Rector of free-agents, and making their Laws to Rule their own volitions and actions, he doth by these Laws oblige their reason and will, to restrain and resist some natural or sensitive appetites and inclinations, and so to resist some natural motions of God in nature, in which he is pleased to operate by second courses but *in tantum* and resistibly.

Baxter gave both these facts great status. It is important to emphasise that neither was slipped in as a concessionary point. He would never sound more totally at one with Grotius than when he was expounding God's rectorial function:

God as Rector (though he vary his Laws in some things to severall ages and places, and promulgate the same Gospell, with inequality, on severall accounts yet) according to the respective Laws that they are under, dealeth with all men in a certain equality, which is called Justice: that is, His Laws antecedently to mans acts make not difference; and as Judge he maketh none, but what mans different actions require according to the said Laws and Justice.

Nor would he ever sound more like Twisse than when he was developing the theme of God's power as *dominus*:

But yet as Owner and as Benefactor he is free (not against, but) above his Laws, to make many inequalities, which are no injustice; they being not acts of formal Government: and so he may do *with his own as he list.* And thus though God give all their due according to his Law of Grace, yet he giveth to his Elect such proportions of Grace, as he gave them no *antecedent Right to by his Law* (or at least to many of them, passing by the controversie now, whether he do so to them all).[28]

And Baxter would continue to believe, with Twisse, in unconditional election, the total depravity of man, the final perseverance of the saints. It is true that he introduced certain Arminian elements into the superstructure — the *rationale* for instance of God's laws and punishments being found, not in His nature, but in His rectorial relation to man — but he parted from Grotius in his emphasis on God as *dominus*. All men are redeemed in the sense that they live under the new law of Grace in virtue of Christ's death, but only the Elect believe *and are saved*. The gift of faith is a fruit of election, not redemption: this was the tragic sense of inequality recognised by Baxter in the words, 'the elect shall obtain it, though the rest are hardened.' In this sense Baxter's 'middle way' is as fraudulent as Hoard had alleged was the 'hypothetical universalism' of Davenant in England and of Cameron and Amyraut abroad. They all held to the essential Calvinist point: that God's *secret* will includes the unconditional particular election of certain men to salvation. And that was why one correspondent, Thomas Good, writing to Baxter on 23 March 1655, dismissed the supposed compromise as 'rigide Calvinism in a softer dresse'.[29]

That might be a fairer description of the compromise than to call it straight Arminianism, but that would not be fair either. It is true that the submission of man before the inscrutable *dominus* was absolute: 'No man or Angel can merit of God in Commutative Justice as Proprietor: But only as Rector. All is (as is before said) of free gift from God as Proprietor and Benefactor.'[30] But it did not follow (the common fallacy) that His rectorial power was negligible. To deny this power is 'to deny the whole frame of his Sapiential Government'. The false antithesis of Law and Grace vitiates the meditations of Sir Henry Vane. For Baxter, Vane subverts true theology by taking all spoken and written precepts or laws, to be 'the law, which is distinguished from Grace, which is meer Alteration to the Soul'. Baxter, on the other hand, saw 'the Law' as the instrument for signifying God's mind, 'the Spirit' working with and by it on our minds, and both going together before the Fall and under Christ:

> But to conclude hence that this is the difference between the Old Covenant and the New, and the Righteousnesse of each of them (of men under them) that one is obedience to a written Law, and the other is the effect of the Spirit, is not sound: for under each Covenant there was both Law and Spirit, though with difference.[31]

Baxter was able to bring this belief into pastoral service when he dealt with the melancholia of the ever-troubled Mrs Gell. We saw, in the first chapter, how Baxter had had to wrestle with her doubts. Now that the big doubts were over, she persisted in worries about post-conversion stolidity and dullness. This was how Baxter reassured her, in a letter of 7 June 1656:

> But in this life, even Grace itselfe doth usually worke accordinge to the way of nature: for commonly it doth only turne all naturall powers to their right objects, and our actions into the right streame,

rather than adde any more of the same kind to the naturall powers (I speake of Nature as Nature, and not of Nature as Corrupt). And therefore we see those that were of quicke and active dispositions about worldly things before Conversion, are usually so about spiritualls after.

There could not be a greater contrast than with the strenuous efforts of Bunyan, for instance, in his *Grace Abounding* to establish the demarcation lines between the self before conversion and the self after. Yet Baxter himself conceded that, without such strenuous efforts, hypocrites were often content with a 'seeming assurance' that they were to be saved, 'when once they are past the feares of damnation'. Mrs Gell was to be congratulated for refusing to settle with mediocrity, but that refusal should be regarded itself as speaking a 'high degree of Grace' rather than as a sign that she should tax her brain with further morbid self-scrutiny.[32]

The danger between distinguishing God as *rector* from God as *dominus* was that the rectorial justice would be seen as negligible; similarly, the danger between distinguishing *sufficient* Grace, by which all men are to be saved, from the *efficient* Grace, by which only the Elect are to be saved, was that the sufficient grace would be seen as negligible. It is important, therefore, to see how far sufficient Grace reaches in Baxter's scheme of things:

> Remember that all sufficient Grace is effectual, but not effectual to the act: It doth *efficere potentiam*, *enableth* men to act: but doth not cause the act it self, unless it be *efficax ad actum*, as well as *ad potentiam* ... *no man in the World hath grace sufficient for Salvation*, that is, *Glorification*, an hour before he dieth: for he *cannot be saved* without *more*; that is, without the Grace of perseverance to the end. But every believing Protestant hath Grace sufficient and effectual to give him a *present Right to Salvation.*[33]

If in the eyes of many Reformed Protestants this was to put *sufficient* Grace altogether too high, an even greater offence would be Baxter's distinction between two forms of righteousness. There was the legal righteousness, not personal, but in Christ; there was also, however, the *evangelical* righteousness which was personal and qualified men for salvation under the terms of the new covenant. Baxter maintained that this evangelical righteousness was no less necessary for man's salvation than the righteousness of Christ which procured him the first covenant.

Baxter even used in 1670 the loaded term 'Merit' for this 'reasonableness' or 'Evangelical worthiness'. Antinomians were dependent on Christ's legal righteousness solely and had discounted personal evangelical righteousness. Behind the disagreement lay different concepts of Christ's sacrifice. Owen saw Christ's death as vicarious personal suffering, a penal substitution; Baxter saw its effect as the procurement of a new law of grace by which evangelical righteousness was imputed to the believer. He saw in the contrary position the germ of Antinomianism; Crisp's rigid view of 'personal imputation', in which the sinner becomes righteous in Christ, begets in process of time Coppe's proclamation that there is no sin in the Elect.

For Baxter, faith was the protection from such dangers: the condition upon which evangelical righteousness was imputed to the Elect. An *act of will* was central to Baxter's concept of faith. Omission of the will was at the root of man's sins: Baxter claimed that it was what made Usher die with his last words, 'But Lord, in special forgive my sins of omission.'[34] This was one respect in which Baxter quarrelled with the 'hypothetical universalists': Cameron had undervalued the free agency of the will; he had mistakenly rooted the viciousness of man in *understanding*, not *will*. In a pained way Baxter recognised affinities between 'great and excellent healing Cameron' and Hobbes in a failure to see the importance of physical renewal of will and in a contrary readiness 'to make the Will as such necessitated by a train of natural *second causes*'.[35]

When determinism was taken up providentially by Hobbes and Spinoza its evil consequences could more easily be calculated than when voiced by a good man like Cameron. For this same reason Baxter was to become haunted in 1675 by the prospect of a revival of the doctrine through the writings of Cromwell's chaplain, Peter Sterry. Sterry was a Harry Vane with metaphors: a man whose generous imagery seduced men away from the task of combating sin:

And if I did believe that sin, death, hell; and holiness, life, Glory are in the world but as Winter and Summer, Night and Day, and, as Origen, that the wicked are but in a State of Revolution, and shall come about again into a state of hope; or, as he here seemeth, that their sin and misery is but like the dying of a flower in the fall, that shall in the Spring again be as before (or rather another in its stead;) and that it is but the retiring of Christ from the Creature, as the spirit of the Tree in Autumn from the Leaves, I should then be ready to receive his *Necessitating Predetermination to Sin*, and fit all the rest of my opinions hereunto.

Strip away the fine words and what is left but Hobbes? —

> I take the root of his error to be, his overlooking and undervaluing
> Gods Design in Making and Governing free Intellectual agents, by his
> Sapiential Moral Directive way: He supposeth this way to be so
> much below that of Physical Motion and Determination, as that it is
> not to be considered but as an instrument thereof ... thus looking
> only at Physical Good, Being and Motion, and thereby thinking
> lightly of Sapiential Regency, is the summ, as of his, so of Hobbes,
> Spinoza's, Alvarez, Bradwardines, Twisses, Rutherfords and the rest
> of the Predeterminists errors herein.

Sterry's floridity provoked Baxter into his most emphatic assertion of
free will, and reverence for the 'sapiential' rule of God as governor:

> Accordingly I think, that God made man a free self-determining
> agent, that he might be capable of such Sapiential Rule: And that it
> is a great Honour to God, to make so noble a Nature, as hath the
> power to determine its own elections. And though such are not of
> the highest rank of Creatures, they are far above the lowest: And
> that God (who we see delighteth to make up beauty and harmony of
> diversities) doth delight in the Sapiential Moral Government of this
> free sort of Creatures: And though man be not Independent, yet to
> be so far like God himself, as to be a kind of joint-determiner of
> many of his own Volitions and Nolitions, is part of God's Natural
> Image in Man. Accordingly I take Duty to be Remarkable and
> Laudable; and sin to be odious as it is the Act of a free agent: And
> that the Nature of Moral Good and Evil consisteth not in its being
> the meer effect of physical premotion, but in being a Voluntary
> Conformity or Disconformity to the Sapiential Rule of duty, by a
> free agent that had Power to do otherwise.[36]

The 'independency' that man has attained is not separable from God:
'this rank and state of free *agens* is Gods own wisely-chosen work in
which he is delighted.' Does God then *permit* that which he foresees?
Baxter shows the limits of that freedom:

> It is far from a full permission. He doth all that belongeth to a Rec-
> tor to hinder it ... He sets Heaven and Hell before them daily; and

is this *permitting* it? He doth indeed in this sense *permit* it, in that
he doth not all that he can against it, or doth no more than as aforesaid.[37]

Baxter embraced Hell because he shrank from determinism. If the
ministers did not constantly keep before their congregations the immi-
nence of eternal torment, the freedom that man had been granted, by
God's willingness to exercise His functions as a *rector* and not a *dominus*, would degenerate into 'natural antinomianism'. When Baxter wrote
The Saints Everlasting Rest he acquired notoriety by looking forward
to encounters with Brightman, Hampden, Pym and other saints in
Heaven. But his vision of Hell is more dramatic and emetic, and in
reality more worthy of notice:

> an angry sin-revenging God above them, and those Saints whom they
> scorned, enjoying the glory which they have lost; and about them
> will be only Devils and damned souls; Ah, then how sadly will they
> look back and say, Are all our merry Meetings, our Feasts, our Plays,
> our wanton Toys, our Christian-Games and Revels come to this?
> Then those Ears which were wont to be delighted with Musick, shall
> hear the shrieks and cries of their damned companions.[38]

The price of man's liberty is eternal clerical vigilance. Without ministers
carrying out God's rectorial work, setting Heaven and Hell before them
daily, ordinary men would abuse their freedom. Ministers must not
relax the pressure on them:

> Sinners shall lay all the blame on their own Wills in Hell for ever.
> Hell is a rational Torment by Conscience, according to the nature of
> the Rational Subject. If sinners could but say then [it is long of God
> whose Will did necessitate me, and not of me] it would quiet their
> consciences, and ease their Torment, and make Hell to be no Hell to
> themselves. But to remember their wilfulness will feed the fire, and
> cause the worm of Conscience never to die.[39]

Coleridge called Calvinism 'the lamb in the wolf's skin' and Arminianism 'the wolf in the lamb's skin': a surprising reversal of normal preconceptions. But Coleridge's point was that Calvinism might offer to
the race a bleak and pessimistic judgement, but comfort to individuals;
Arminianism, on the other hand, offered a generous and optimistic view
of mankind, but was cruel to individuals 'for fear of damaging the race

by false hopes and improper confidences'.[40] Wesley offered to the eighteenth century precisely this combination of Arminianism and Hell-fire. It is clear that Baxter felt the need to balance his view of God the *rector*, who revelled in the freedom permitted to His subjects, with the 'angry sin-revenging' *dominus* who punished defaulters with eternal Hell-fire. Free activity in the classroom; but the cane resided in the Head's study.

It is possible to trace the reactions of contemporaries to Baxter's anti-Antinomianism in pamphlets and correspondence. The first critical response to his *Aphorismes of Justification* came from John Warren on 27 August 1649. Warren sounded a note that would soon be familiar: Baxter was too scholastic in his distinctions and too abusive of those who did not understand the difference between *legal* and *evangelical* righteousness.[41] In his reply, on 11 September 1649, Baxter thanked Warren for his candour which compared well with old friends' behaviour, who were criticising him behind his back. Familiar Baxter notes were also struck early: complaints about his health; the claim to have offended extremists on both sides by having found a middle path between them; excuse for rough language by the *tu quoque* argument (he quotes Walker's assertion that 'it is Socinian heresye to make faith the Condition of the New Covenant'). He anticipates the partiality of his later attack on 'natural antinomianism' (in his letter to Ince of 1653) in the statement – as early as 1649 – that it was the 'vulgar sort' who were attracted to Antinomianism; that it was conceivable that a learned man could succumb to the Arminian error, but not to the Antinomian.[42] Two months later, on 7 November, Baxter was developing for him the important distinction between *ius* and *eventus* in a follow-up letter to Warren. It is not the same thing for God to say *This you ought to do* and *This shall come to pass*: both duty and event may be present undivided in God's Will, but they must be distinguished. And consideration of God as *dominus* must go before consideration of Him as *rector*; His purposing will as *dominus* extends to all His creatures and actions, His legislative will as *rector* only to His rational creatures. Thus man's personal freedom as a subject of God's rectorial rule must not be confused with man's subordination to God's proprietary rule; his ability to challenge *prescriptions* in one sphere – with the penalty of Hell-fire to pay as a consequence – must not be confused with his ability to challenge *prophecy* in the second.[43] A critic in 1681 would crudely comment on Baxter's ability to 'distinguish himself into a Fart',[44] yet through such distinctions Baxter sought to avoid the Arminian and Antinomian polarities. Hell-fire, or even 'a fitt of the stone',[45] would cure critics of blandness in the face of evil: a theme which he developed at length in his *The Saints Everlasting Rest*.

But Hell would hold no terrors as punishment for the unbeliever, if belief were reduced to 'nothing but suffering'. This was Baxter's complaint, in a letter of September 1650 to an anonymous correspondent. A 'Pelagian Anabaptist' had boasted to him how easy a thing belief in Christ was: attainable by any man with the power of natural reason. Were it true, the case for infant baptism would be unassailable. But if such *were* the grounds for infant baptism, he would be against it.[46] The whole letter is sharply anti-Arminian in the development of his criticisms of passive faith, and is indeed unusual in its recognition that General Baptism was a much his enemy as Particular Baptism.

On 29 October 1650 Robert Abbott wrote a letter to Baxter expressing his belief that they shared an affection for 'a Regulated Episcopacy' and for Cameron's 'middle way' in doctrine.[47] A flurry of letters between Baxter and Richard Vines in 1650 and 1651 established that, to one respected friend at least, the 'middle way' leaned altogether too heavily towards Arminianism and John Goodwin, and even drew from Baxter the admission that 'I see now J. Goodwin is a flatt Arminian.'[48] George Lawson was another admired correspondent who, in Baxter's opinion, veered too close to Arminianism in a shared antipathy to Antinomianism. Baxter came to appreciate Lawson's greater understanding of constitutional points — ultimately this became his standard excuse for keeping out of politics — but in this early letter to him, of 6 August 1651, he is puzzled by the inference Lawson had drawn from his own scholarship. Baxter was trying to avoid two extremes: that God's threatenings *must* be executed; that God could relax a law as soon as He made it. Lawson believed the first, but had demonstrated that a Law-giver, in making laws, did not part with his power above the laws, to abrogate, interpret or relax them. This argument reinforced the second extreme position — which Baxter associated with Twisse — which shifted all responsibility from man to God: 'lay all on God, and say, He might have pardoned us freely, if he would.' But there was one sense in which Baxter was clearly with Twisse against Lawson. He quoted Davenant and the Synod of Dort to support his argument 'that in that Vocation a giving of faith to some and not to others, doth first appear the great Mystery of Predestination'. Against Lawson, Baxter had to affirm not the universal redemption of God's revealed will (about which they agreed) but the limited election of God's secret will: 'It is most fitt that the Covenant Grant should be universall, though God intend not Salvation to be universall.'[49] Baxter explained the successive steps: the law makes no distinction between men, before believing; 'supernaturall Grace flowing from election' comes in and makes the difference which the 'new law' recognises; whilst all are still unbelievers, even though some are Elect, no man has more interest in Christ than another; 'Electing Love' gives the faith to some men only, upon which follows their legal interest. Therefore 'in Law sense' redemption *is* universal; but it is not universal 'in respect of the Redeemers Intent of saving men eventually thereby'.[50]

A few months later, on 22 October 1651, Baxter is defending his 'middle way' against the opposite flank. He is pleased that Warren denies that God *can* justify or pardon before faith — unlike Owen, who believes that 'we have an actuall right to the benefits of Christ's death' — but worries that Warren confuses justifying faith with the mere willingness to receive justification. This is to put altogether too low an estimate on faith, and one which undercuts pastoral discipline. Congregations are all too willing to assume that they have justifying faith. Sterner tests are required from the communicant: evidence that Baxter would not welcome 'common admission' to the Sacrament of the Lord's Supper. As Baxter put it: 'That which any Reprobate in the world may have (who believes that God offers him pardon) is not the Justifying faith. But such is the meere Accepting of Justification.'[51]

In the *Aphorismes of Justification* Saltmarsh's failure to define faith properly — 'that it is nothing else but a persuasion more or less of God's love' — was seen by Baxter as an Antinomian 'master-point'.[52]

Hobbes's determinism stung Baxter into retaliation. From Trinity College, Cambridge, Thomas Hill wrote to Baxter on 13 February 1652: 'Your deepe detestation of Hobbes his Leviathan hath awakened some of us to consider what is fitt to be done therein.'[53] In reply, on 8 March, Baxter stressed the connection in his own mind between Twisse and Hobbes:

> Had I time I culd show, that the denying of Redemption to the Non-Elect in Davenant sense hath a Multitude of Intollerable Inconveniences. I speake of the evill of Denying Christ's Doctrine to be a Law, in that most of the Horrid consequences in Hobb's Booke arises from that Principle: viz. ergo Xt Doth but teach and Princes command ... ergo Scripture is no further a Law (saith Hobbs) than Soveraignes so make it: Nor Ministers have any power of Governing, or Comanding, Nor Christ any Kingdome now on Earth; but only in preparing men by Doctrin for one hereafter, and 100 the like Hobbes abounds with.[54]

Baxter's answer to Hobbes soared far above the book-burning that Hill had seemed to hint at; that too, no doubt, but he recorded his grief 'that now All's done' (a cryptic allusion to a more settled political scene?) rulers were still doing nothing to settle the Church, ministers nothing to promote agreements between Churches. He asked the Master of Trinity College to draw up a petition to Parliament to set up a healing conference between Episcopalians, Presbyterians, Independents and Erastians. This is an extremely interesting letter, bridging as it does earlier efforts to involve Hill and others in work of conciliation, with the meeting of ministers in Worcester later in the summer of 1652, which is the true origin of the Association of Ministers. And even at such an early date as March 1652 Baxter's desire to see the magistracy taking the initiative in furthering holiness, and routing Hobbism, was working against his initial determination to stay aloof from government by usurpers.

'I beseech you in the bowels of Christ', began Henry Bartlett in a letter to Baxter of 3 November 1652.[55] The plea that followed was for another edition of *The Aphorismes of Justification*, and a request for him not to hide his talents. The request had a new urgency and bite a few months later, on 28 June 1653, when Bartlett got wind of the manuscript that Crandon was preparing in which Baxter was to be lampooned as a 'Papist Jesuit'. Moreover another minister had met Bartlett recently 'who was hot, that in the point of justification you wear so popish'.[56] Bartlett's efforts to dissuade Crandon from publication by a private conference with him proved groundless, as he recognised in a letter to Baxter on 21 October. He had worse news. Crandon was carrying opposition to the point of contacting eminent ministers in several counties to publicise his work. Bartlett was relieved that Gataker had approved his writing, but there was now a clear onus on Baxter to give the lie to Crandon, and to show how different his ideas of justification by works were from Papists'.[57] Bartlett had suggested that he show his affinity with the Protestant school of Cameron and Amyraut, but Peter Ince, writing to Baxter four days later, intimated that he was *too close* to Davenant and Amyraut. He reminded Baxter of the moral fibre of the men who had opposed Arminianism in the 1620s and 1630s.[58] This drew from Baxter, on 21 November 1653, an unexpected response. He denied undue dependence on Cameron, Amyraut and Davenant; feared, rather, that he might have over-valued them because their prejudices happened to coincide in many respects with his own; and claimed that he had deserted Twisse, not for Arminians, but for the Synod of Dort. The unexpected element in the letter was the suggestion that Arminians in England (as opposed to France and the Netherlands) were 'temporizers that took up the opinions for worldly respects'. In other words, he defused the ideological issue as emphatically as ever Bishop Morley did with his notorious joke that what the Arminians held was 'all the best bishoprics and deaneries'.[59] No wonder Ince was not convinced, in his further letter to Baxter of 8 December, that Baxter *had* met his objections: he still valued Amyraut too highly; the Anabaptists' excesses may have been to Baxter a warning against Twisse's way, but Ince persisted in the belief that the Arminians' excesses of the 1630s were equally as much a warning against *their* way; Ince was pleased to hear from Bartlett that Baxter was intending a brief reply to Crandon.[60]

On 11 May 1654 John Humfrey expressed to Baxter his disgust on reading Crandon's work, *Mr. Baxters Aphorismes Exorcised*, and said how it offended him 'to see what manner of spirit men are off'.[61] One of the interesting features of Crandon's savage attack is that he identified Baxter as one 'professing himself a zealous Presbyterian' but who, when 'this vizzard' falls from his face, stands revealed as 'the Anabaptized Jesuit, taking his station there from whence he thought to have most advantage to promote his Popish doctrines'. Thus the Popish 'mask' makes its first appearance as a description *of* Baxter, not *by* him. Well before the Association of Ministers had developed a momentum, Crandon was haunted by the prospect of a network of Baxter's 'Circumsoraneous Legates' linking up all over the country to propagate his false doctrine:

> (which having their Provinces assigned either of one or more Counties, are still Circling and Compassing them, first to dispense this his Mystery of iniquity with such accusations, that there may be no one that hath the repute of a pious Gentleman or Minister a stranger to it; and then by their frequent visitations to examine how the Baxterian Faith thrives in each person, and to hold them fixed to it). These returning once in six or seven Moneths out of their Circuits to their Grand Master may possibly speak in things which they know not, what they think may be plausible to him.

Crandon went on to remonstrate against the cult of Baxter: the pilgrimages to Kidderminster, to bless and be blessed by him; the veneration of him as a 'matchlesse and super-eminent Saint'; the Popish scholasticism of his writings. Crandon actually agrees with Baxter's condemnation of Saltmarsh but believes that he exaggerates his importance and will not have it that Saltmarsh's Antinomianism *is* the logical development of

Twisse's predestinarian doctrine.[62]

Baxter dedicated one of his writings of 1654 to his friend, Colonel Sylvanus Taylor, who had seventeen years earlier detected the significance of the rise of Antinomianism in London and in New England. Baxter reproached himself for his own slowness in relating bad theology to bad conduct: 'bad opinions are not so innocent as some men suppose them: when it bringeth men, and such men, men to be Ranters, Shakers, and I think, possessed with Devils.' After Twisse, Saltmarsh: Baxter was unrepentant. The sins of the nation were legible judgements: monsters in New England, Ranters in Old England, were as much confirmatory evidence as Christ's miracles had been to His generation − and as difficult probably for later generations to credit. Above all, to fly from Arminianism to Antinomianism is to 'go out of the ashes into the fire'; truth borders close to error and therefore is *close to* Arminianism.[63] William Duncombe wrote to Baxter, on 3 April 1654, to speak of his liking for the 'middle way' of Cameron, Amyraut and Davenant, but added that he saw the way 'but darkely' and had tried in vain to get copies of Amyraut's writings.[64] On 23 March 1655 Thomas Good urged Baxter to draw up three columns showing the Calvinist and Arminian positions, together with the 'middle way'.[65] Baxter had promised to carry out such a design in the introduction to his *Saints Everlasting Rest*: Good was not the only correspondent to urge him to redeem that promise.[66] Henry Bartlett, for example, writing to Baxter on 10 May 1655, passed on a request from Ministers of the Western Association in Dorset for an enlargement of *The Aphorismes* with three columns and the truth in the middle.[67] There was a worrying factor behind Bartlett's request. A month earlier, on 4 April, he had told Baxter how many of the young ministers were committed to preaching free grace. Through reading Crandon, and misunderstanding *The Aphorismes*, they thought of him as another Grotius, intent upon 'some Cassandrian Syncretisme'.[68] The Association movement was being seriously impeded by the prejudices aroused by his anti-Antinomianism. The Dorset ministers' hopes from his demonstration of a 'middle way' had a touch of desperation about them. Good had been urging him, on 23 March, to publish a 'middle way', but from quite different motives. The Dorset ministers wished to be reassured that he was not too far apart from their ideas of free grace; Good's worry was that the compromise offered was merely tarted-up Calvinism.[69] Perhaps with this in mind Baxter was careful, when drawing up his *Confession of his Faith* in 1655, not to make a shibboleth of the 'middle way':

I never thought that when ever men differ, it is my duty to go in a middle between both (for so that middle will be next taken for an extream, and men must seek out another middle to avoyd that).[70]

In the same year John Owen published his *Vindiciae Evangelicae*, with scorn for the efforts of Amyraut, 'whom I looke upon as one of the greatest wits of these daies', to find a 'middle way'. He deplored the easy way in which those who do not follow any particular 'middle way' are labelled as 'rigid'.[71] Despite Baxter's recognition that Owen had a point, his *Confession of his Faith* does have a number of pages divided into three columns: 'Antinomian', 'Truth', 'Papist'. It is interesting that 'Papist', rather than 'Arminian', is seen by him as the opposite extreme to 'Antinomian'.

Baxter's *Confession of his Faith* provided an opportunity for him to refine the views expressed in his *Aphorismes* in the light of criticism. He now repented of his use of the term 'Covenant of Works', and although he had made it clear in his first pamphlet that no man was capable of being justified by that Covenant or promise, he had not then seen so clearly that the promise itself was null. Faith as the condition of salvation remained his shield against Antinomianism; the arbitrariness of the gift of faith remained his shield against Arminianism. Baxter explained:

The Law threateneth or curseth the Elect as well as others, while they are Infidels and unregenerate: For all Christs satisfaction, and Gods Decree, and the certainty of the future pardon when they believe, and for all God hath foretold that he will call and pardon them.

Opponents said that Baxter was thereby putting Believers under the curse of the Law. No, said Baxter, except when 'new sins are by these believers committed'. This would seem at odds with Calvinist faith in 'the perpetuity of the regenerate person's estate' — to quote the title of one of Prynne's first pamphlets — except that it is immediately followed by the reassurance:

they are in a sure way for the pardon of future sins, when they are committed: seeing as the Morall Law doth bind them to punishment, so the Remedying — Law of Grace dissolveth that obligation, and pardoned them when they have sinned.

Which would seem to have opened Antinomian floodgates if he had not added, 'they having Faith and Repentance, which is the Condition'.

The more labyrinthine Baxter's argument became the more he recoiled from his own subtlety: these fine distinctions culminated in a plea for practical divinity. Against ingenious disputers who 'pretend to be more exact' Baxter urged young students to turn to the great Puritan casuists, Thomas Hooker, Bolton, Rogers, Hildersham and Fenner. Truth, lost in scholastic disputations, is recovered in 'sober practice'. What he admired in the 'covenant theologians' of the 1620s and 1630s was the practical advice which they gave to their parishioners about the actions which lay within *their* responsibility.[72] The 'new notions' of Free Grace had called him to revise his first thoughts as an opposer of the Coventry ministers, Craddock and Diamond, when they had preached Universal Redemption: he had become alarmed at men's willingness to abdicate *personal* responsibility for their actions, and put all on God. Although Cameron's moderation and charity had a great appeal to him he came to perceive that he was tarred with the same brush: 'his Resolving the cause of sin into necessitating objects and temptations, laid it as much on God (in another way) as the Predeterminants do.' The point was that godly men's *prayers* and *sermons* gave the lie to this renunciation of personal responsibility of the will. On Coleridge's copy of Baxter's *Catholick Theologie* — from which this passage comes — he has added enthusiastic marginalia:

> For *me* this would be as weighty an argument as it was for Baxter — possibly, even a more convincing one, thro' my conviction that in prayer and earnest practical enforcement of the truths of Godliness the Spirit acts more *collectively*, is more total and entire, than can be in any simply intellectual effort.[73]

The assurance of the Elect comes, not from the fact that there are no conditions, *but from the certainty that he shall fulfil them*. Prayers and sermons keep men up to the mark by reminding them of their need to fulfil the conditions: Hell-fire is a good reminder of the consequences of failure. Edward Fisher's *Marrow of Modern Divinity*, first published in 1645, was to establish itself as the classic statement of the unconditionality of the Covenant of Grace. It is significant that, ten years after its publication, Baxter should still identify it as the main enemy in his *Confession of his Faith*. Eternal Hell-fire was as real a punishment to the godly who did not fulfil the condition of faith as it was to the reprobate:

> So the *Marrow of Modern Divinity* . . . earnestly presseth believers
> not to look at their sins *as making them lyable to Gods everlasting
> wrath and Hell-fire, nor to crave pardon and forgiveness for them
> that thereupon they may escape that penalty*.

Since the 'Marrow men' conceded that the Elect were taught in the
Lord's Prayer to pray for forgiveness of sin Baxter felt that this could
not be squared with 'perfect pardon' or the view that Christ had made a
'perfect satisfaction' by His vicarious sacrifice.[74]

The most sympathetic recent study of 'Marrow divinity' has been
made by Professor Torrance.[75] He believes that the doctrine of conditional grace was imported into Scotland by Baxter and Daniel Williams.
The rot had set in with the fatal leanings to 'federal theology' in the
1645 *Westminster Directory for the Public Worship of God*. Baptism
and the Lord's Supper came to be seen less as Seals of the Gospel, or
converting ordinances, than as Seals of Repentance. Faith interpreted
in contractual terms led to a 'fencing of the table' with the clear implication that communicants were welcome only upon their fulfilment of
certain conditions. This was Crandon's case against Baxter and all other
ministers who

> affright the poor soules from all hope of entring . . . no prophane or
> unclean person hath right to meddle with this Grace. No, first they
> must have such heart — preparations, pacifications and prejacent
> qualifications, before they draw neer to partake of mercy, must first
> cleanse and cure themselves, and then come to Christ afterwards;
> must be cloathed with an inherent Righteousnesse first, and then
> expect to be cloathed upon with a Righteousnesse imputed.[76]

There is a broad sense in which both Professor Torrance and Crandon
were right to see Baxter as a champion of conditional grace: in the final
analysis we shall see that Baxter throws his weight against the protagonists of common admission to the Lord's Supper — men like Humfrey,
Prynne and Morice. But it is only in the final analysis, and on the way
he shows a genuine sympathy with much of their case. Crandon's picture of strenuous 'heart-preparations' is a ludicrously overdrawn picture
of Baxter's requirements of communicants. Baxter indeed shows a
marked dislike for the austere demands imposed by ministers like Gillespie, Owen and Nye. Where Professor Torrance is on surer ground is in
claiming that many of the traits identified with the triumph of so-called
'rigid Calvinism' between 1648 and 1651 — the discontinuance of the

Sacrament of the Lord's Supper and ministers' abandonment of personal devotions, reading of the Lord's Prayer and daily services — represent rather a defeat for 'Marrow divinity'. Similarly it was not the men who believed in unconditional grace who needed to emphasise the torments of Hell-fire; it was those who believed in conditional grace who needed to show sinners the dreadful consequence of abusing the freedom that they enjoyed. Eternal Hell-fire went with a Contract-God, not a Covenant-God.

There were friends of Baxter who applauded his attack upon 'Marrow divinity' and yet deplored the wounding and sarcastic way in which he waged it. Robert Abbott, for instance, wrote to Baxter on 7 June 1655, as one 'from the first, an hearty imbracer of your Aphorismes'. He had chatted with Dr Kendall at the funeral of Whittaker and expressed the hope that they were moving closer together in doctrine. Kendall replied that he had not yet read Baxter's latest works, but he had heard that 'he hath horrible rayled upon mee'.[77] Abbott warned Baxter against giving gratuitous offence. Kendall's introduction to a sermon by Obadiah Howe, printed in the same year, makes clear in fact his desire for solidarity with Baxter against the Arminianism of John Goodwin; we have seen that Baxter had recognised, as early as 1651 in correspondence with Vines, that Goodwin *had* gone too far.[78] It is therefore in a more conciliatory spirit that Baxter makes clear, in a letter to John Milner of 24 January 1657, that he is on the side of Calvin and Beza against Amyraut in asserting his belief that 'I cannot fulfill the Law, it beinge above my strength even as Regenerate: And so I cannot be justified by Law. And so I thanke God that he abrogated it, and freed me and all believers from it.' There was nothing novel in the statement. He had said as much in his *Confession of his Faith* when he sought to withdraw the provocative phrase 'Covenant of Works'. Moreover, he acknowledged to Milner that this was *not* the crucial divide in Reformed theology. Nevertheless his argument showed a sensitivity to the dangers of over-reacting against predestination in the way that John Goodwin was seen to have done.[79] Thomas Doolittle revealed another danger, in a letter to Baxter on 9 May 1657, which may have been the more telling because it eschewed abstractions and dealt with problems at the level of practical morality. As a working preacher, Doolittle put the classic objection to the preaching of universal redemption to his congregation: 'how can I in my constant preaching offer Christ to the worst in my congregation and promise him eternall life upon his believing and Repenting.' The classic response is: we do not know who is to be saved and are not, therefore, in a real sense preaching to *all*. Doolittle is not satisfied. There is a statistical probability (almost amounting to a certainty) that there is at least one reprobate in the congregation who shall never be saved: can Doolittle say to such a man (even although not knowing which one it is) that, if he repents and believes, he *shall* be saved?[80]

Nevertheless, in 1657, Baxter published one of his most vigorous defences of 'this Middle way of Universal Redemption'. He was stung by a contemporary reference to him as Amyraut's only English proselyte, and which heaped further indignity on him with the assertion that Archbishop Usher had 'thought so contemptuously of Amyraldus Method'. On the contrary, Baxter claimed that he had behind him the authority of the Synod of Dort, many of the Westminster Assembly divines, the hypothetical universalists (Cameron, Amyraut, Davenant) and the 'practical preachers' (Preston, Stoughton, Fenner, Ball, Culverwell and Vines). To these names he added that of Usher himself. Much of the confidence of his counter-attack comes from the assurance that he had Usher on his side.[81] One can still feel the excitement of his discovery in 1653 that the man, whom he revered more than any other, concurred with him on this doctrinal issue too:

> And a reverend, learned, eminent Doctor of Cambridge tels me, that Bishop Usher is of the same Judgement, and he was never taken to favor of Arminianism. And to confirm me in it, I have lately received from a pious judicious Gentleman, a Manuscript of Bishop Usher in resolution of the question of universal Redemption, determining just as Martinius, Davenant and the rest, most solidly and excellently shewing the two extreams, and the danger of them.[82]

In London in 1654 Baxter had met Usher, then over seventy years old, who had 'owned my judgment' in nearly everything. Now, in 1657, Baxter from a position of authority cleared a libel on the dead. He had Usher's manuscript of 3 March 1617, at Dublin, asserting the 'middle way' of Davenant and Cameron. He had Usher's word that he had written this to Culverwell. He had Dr Kendall's testimony that he was present when Usher boasted of his influence over Davenant and Preston. An early Davenant biographer had claimed that his 'middle way' at Dort predated acquaintance with Usher. In fact Usher had met Davenant and Preston in 1609, when they were both firm friends and Fellows of Queen's College, Cambridge. It is clear that Baxter came to Usher via Davenant; but it is quite a reasonable proposition that the true lineage *was* Usher-to-Davenant-to-Baxter-to-Usher. With such a lineage behind him Baxter could refute the claims of Thomas Pierce, the apologist for bishops, that Arminianism was the only alternative to predestinarian doctrine. Pierce identified Calvinism with such views as: the Dominican concept of physical predetermination; supralapsarianism; limited atonement. But the Synod of Dort 'owneth none of these' and Baxter emphasised that it is that Synod that is the test of the Calvinists' anti-Arminianism.[83] Pierce persisted in his facile identifications of 'Calvinist' and 'Arminian'. Thus, in his reply of 1659, he quoted from Baxter's strictures in his *Saints Everlasting Rest* against 'such as were spruce in their apparel, and delighted in May-games, Morice-dancers, Shewes, or Stage-Playes'. Pierce presumed that Baxter's willingness to consign all such offenders to 'the pains of Hell' stamped him as a 'Calvinist'. We have seen that Baxter had argued for Hell-fire specifically *against* Fisher's *Marrow of Modern Divinity*. This did not prevent him from being bracketed with Fisher by Pierce: 'There is a Book intituled, *The Marrow of Modern Divinity*, which hath dangerously built upon your foundation, and is publicly commended by some of your way.' The 'some of your way' were exponents of Free Grace, which Baxter had rejected; *The Marrow*, far from building on Baxter's foundations, was written before Baxter had produced a single pamphlet; Baxter's compromise had been fashioned in part *in response to* Fisher's theology. The antinomian consequences that Pierce drew from the doctrine — he showed how an idle maid could chew 'upon this bit of marrow' and justify her lascivious behaviour with the thought that God would love her nevertheless — were no different from the inferences that Baxter himself drew from 'Marrow divinity'.[84]

Pierce's caricature in 1659 of the 'anti-Arminian' position is significant because it anticipates the unwillingness of many of the post-Restoration bishops to distinguish between their opponents, to differentiate a Twisse from a Baxter, when once they were in the saddle. Their insensitivity was matched by their opponents. In 1659 the 'Arminian' position was caricatured by those who were *then* in the saddle. The fear of a Calvinist-inspired witch-hunt moved Benjamin Woodbridge, in a letter to Baxter of 6 January 1659, to take up the case of one White. He was coming before the commissioners on grounds of scandal or insufficiency. Woodbridge presumed (wrongly, in this case) that it was his criticisms of Free Grace which had made him suspect:

And the reports of his being an Arminian discouraged mee the lesse, because I know his principall adversaryes put that name upon what doctrines they please: insomuch that my selfe am fallen under suspicion of that heresy with them, for nothing in the world, but because I lately preached from Heb.10: 35, 36 that the heavenly kingdom is given to none but as a reward of their precedent service (unlesse they want age and naturall abilityes to performe it).[85]

On the eve of the Restoration 'Arminianism' was being defined by the persecutors of Woodbridge in terms that would have been comprehensible to Pym and his Parliamentary colleagues, whilst Pierce used the term 'Calvinism' with the sweeping imprecision of a Laud. For all the fierceness of the invective on both sides (and we have seen that it was not Baxter, but his opponent Crandon, who began the identification of Papist 'vizors'), the debate which Baxter had helped to launch with his *Aphorismes of Justification* had been fought along different lines. The extremist *social* implications of theological beliefs, it is true, were never far from the protagonists' minds, *but the theology stayed in the foreground*. Between 1649 and 1659 a number of ministers went to a great deal of intellectual trouble to tease out the implications of resolutions passed in the Synod of Dort or the Westminster Assembly. The search for a 'middle way' compromise, although it reflected the ecumenical mood of the time and could have ended up as sentimental waffle, was translated into hard-headed scrutiny of writers like Cameron and Amyraut. When compared with what went before it, and what was to come after it, it is hard to resist the conclusion that these ten years were a high point in Protestant theological debate.

The doctrinal debate spilled over into other areas of controversy for Baxter in the Commonwealth, and that is why we have stayed with it for so long. These other disputes take on a different dimension when we view them from Baxter's hard-won doctrinal perspective. His controversies with Baptists like Tombes, Haggar and Kay in the early 1650s have a breathtaking crudity about them. We have already seen that Baxter imputed to Tombes the motive of wishing to baptise the nude maidens of Bewdley. Shopkeepers in London, especially women 'that take but little of the cold air', would be killed off in their thousands by dipping in cold water. Covetous landlords would therefore encourage Baptist conversions as good for trade.[86] The level of reply was no more edifying. Henry Haggar suggested that Baxter's sensitivity to the plight of shopkeepers and delicately-brought-up ladies derived from knowledge that they had the fattest purses. Baxter's suggestion that Baptism was prized as a homicidal weapon established him in Haggar's eyes as a 'Mountebanck'.[87] John Tombes, his Baptist neighbour who disputed with him at Bewdley, lamented the way that Baxter handled the debate.

He particularly objected to Baxter's contingent of supporters who 'cry up a Baxter, as if they had bin a company of Boys at a game'.[88]

All this is to give a misleading gloss on the controversy. Baxter had only baptised two children of godly parents before he came to doubt the legality of infant baptism, and for ten or eleven years suspended the practice altogether. He was won to the cause by his reading of pamphlets in Coventry and by his experiences in the Roundhead Army. He did not feel that he could accept full pastoral responsibility until his doubts were resolved; the Antinomianism of Coppe provided a powerful reinforcement for his prejudices in favour of infant baptism. But even in 1654 – at the height of his exchanges with Tombes, Haggar and Kay – he wrote that Anabaptism was not nearly so dangerous and divisive a force as Antinomianism.[89] Correspondence between Baxter and Thomas Gataker in October and November 1653 showed how many of Baxter's earlier reservations were not totally banished and how differences could be explored within a framework of mutual respect and courtesy.[90]

Three years later Baxter remained worried, and open-minded, on the issue of whether infants of true believers were in a justified state or not, and whether they might fall from it. He acknowledged to an equally worried colleague, Thomas Vaux, that although the Synod of Dort, Davenant, Ward and Amyraut thought so, 'I have dealt with some learned men about it, but yet am not fully satisfied my selfe.'[91] And, for all the fury of his exchanges with Tombes, there is evidence that by 1654 he was more worried by the 'loose Doctrine of Baptism' argued by Thomas Blake. Once accept Blake's latitudinarianism – that 'common faith' gives right to baptism – and the progression to Arminianism seems logical and not as such to be welcomed by Baxter. For it is easy to argue that 'common faith' gives right to the *ends* of baptism, at best remission of sin: 'And so upon the good use of common Grace, God should be in Covenant obliged to give them special Grace: which is taken for Pelagianism.'[92] Blake makes of baptism *too much*; Kendall, *too little*. This was the opposite extreme to avoid: 'How small a matter is left for Baptism to seal and exhibit, as to Remission, when all sin was tantamount remitted from Eternity.' In developing this aspect of his case against Baptism Baxter reworked the territory of his *Aphorismes of Justification* and restated the case against a doctrine which took away the disciplinary weapon of fear:

for if all your sins were pardoned as soon as Christ died, then what need you pray for pardon, or Repent, or Believe or be Baptized for pardon? then God loved you as well when you were his enemies as since; and then how can you be restrained from sin by fear?[93]

Thus the knock-about exchanges with Tombes and Haggar do a disservice in obscuring the seriousness of his intellectual involvement with Baptism in this period. It was complicated by his emotional involvement with Baptism as a young man; in his exchange with Kendall, he acknowledged the depth of his previous attachment to the views of Twisse. But he was repelled as much by Blake's looseness as by Kendall's rigidity; he urged Baptist inclusion in schemes of accommodation in 1671 precisely because they were 'Godly men', who differed with him and others on a point of great difficulty, but who were not 'the Munster Anabaptists';[94] and, true to that insight, he could write to William Mewe on 6 August 1659 that he had all but achieved a reconciliation scheme with many London Baptists when the change of government dashed ecumenical hopes.[95]

We shall see that there were a number of reasons why Baxter's hopes of a 'Holy Commonwealth' were to prove illusory; but the naked maidens of Bewdley cannot be counted high among them.

It would only be a slight exaggeration to claim that the debate over admission to the Lord's Supper in the Commonwealth period determined the character and fortunes of Puritanism for the rest of the century. Two great opposing principles tugged at Puritans' loyalties: the 'church-type' ideal was expressed in the case for common admission to the Sacrament; the 'sect-type' ideal was expressed in the case for unmixed communion. The strength of the 'church-type' argument was its appeal to all who yearned for a National Church, who recognised that the wheat and the tares were indistinguishably mingled together (until the Last Judgement), and who saw the inclusion of hypocrites as a small price to pay for good order and stability. Baxter felt the force of all these arguments. There were three common counter-claims. One, the argument was seen as a plea for promiscuity. This was not true. Advocates of common admission recognised the need to exclude the scandalous *impenitent*; the debate was over the rights of the scandalous *penitent*. Blake thought that a profession of visible penitence was enough; Baxter wanted more, and looked for a 'justifying faith'; Owen wanted more still and looked for an 'inner certainty'. Two, the argument was seen as anti-disciplinary. This also was not true. Those who opposed the ministers' suspending and excommunicating powers in the late 1640s had not renounced discipline but questioned the clerical use of it. When Prynne recognised that the Presbyterian ministers' strict discipline 'really reforms very few or none'[96] he was expressing the same moral concern as his colleague, Thomas Coleman, and the spiritual ancestor they had in common, Erastus. Three, the argument was seen as anti-clerical. This was the most telling objection. But the grief that Erastus, Coleman and Prynne felt about clerical *abuse* of power was different in kind from the pleasure that men like Hobbes and Selden derived from tweaking clergymen's noses. Prynne had held a great respect for London Presbyterian ministers and he launched his attacks on suspension in 1645 only when he came to believe that, in the rest of the country, the Presbyterian ministers were not in the same class as their London colleagues. His anti-clericalism in the Commonwealth period was tempered by the fear that he would be aiding the Quakers in their efforts to discredit the ministry. Baxter, for his part, recognised that Prynne was not a Hobbes. It was therefore all the more traumatic for him when, towards the end of the Commonwealth period, Prynne urged that ministers should not be paid tithes. Its effect on Baxter was to confirm his suspicion that the case for common admission − whatever its other incidental virtues − was vitiated by its prejudice against clerical status.

This did not mean that Baxter was enthralled with the contrary advocacy of unmixed communion. Its appeal was to a narrow exclusiveness of spirit. It encouraged ministers to get above themselves. 'Who would not rather live in Algiers?' asked Coleridge, when he sympathised with Baxter's mistrust of over-rigorous discipline.[97] It was an Independent principle, which had been borrowed by the Scottish Presbyterian, George Gillespie, in his anti-Erastian arguments of the late 1640s. But the Commonwealth period provided a much more congenial environment for Gillespie's ideas. At the centre was a vacuum. Cromwell deliberately refused to impose a religious policy. There was a much more plausible case for ministers to exercise disciplinary powers when the alternative was not direction by the Commons − as in the late 1640s − but anarchy. These were the tendencies that worried Baxter. The abandonment of the attempt to discipline the reprobate struck at the Presbyterian 'church-ideal'; the growing reluctance of men to pay tithes to their ministers alarmingly demonstrated the narrowing of the Presbyterian base, even although in Prynne's case it sprang from his anger at the infrequency with which clergymen of his day offered communion to their parishioners.[98]

To understand the force of Baxter's reaction, one must see the political scene in 1657 as he saw it. Everywhere Popery was on the march. Only the clergy could halt the spread of 'natural antinomianism'. Yet they were made the objects of ridicule: savaged by Hobbes, Harrington and Vane; denied tithes by Quakers, who were themselves but Jesuits in disguise. The success of the Association of Ministers showed that clergymen were nevertheless capable of leading a moral reformation. At this critical point in time, Prynne swung his weight behind Hobbes, Harrington and Vane and joined the Quakers in denying tithes to the ministry. In changing his mind about tithes, Prynne demonstrated what critics of common admission had always maintained: that the real objection to ministerial discipline was *not to the power, but to the office.*

The more sharply that Baxter distanced himself from the champions of common admission in order to defend the ministerial office, the more vulnerable he became to charges that he had sold out completely to the other side, to the 'sect-ideal'. Although Baxter sought to belittle the importance of the Erastian movement − 'all that I know of, since Dr. Ward is Mr. Blake, Mr. Humfrey and John Timpson; and John Timpson, Mr. Humfrey and Mr. Blake' − he had to admit that it had chalked up some powerful propaganda successes. In particular, the writings of Blake had persuaded many of his friends that Baxter favoured the 'deeper discoverie' of Philip Nye and his Independent colleagues:

> I hear that some Reverend Godly Men of his acquaintance are so confident that hee is in the right, that they marvel that ever I should hold the contrary, and blame mee as defending a principal point in the Independent caus.

Particularly damaging were the libels that Blake cast on the Worcestershire Association:

> As fairly doth hee cast his censures, on the credit of his informers, at the Worcestershire combination (as hee termeth it) [*that the most prophane, where the Minister carries any Authority are as forward as any*] with more of the like ... And he was publickly told by them and mee, that wee were not gathering Churches or taking in members, and therefore not discovering who were meet; but only discovering who did account themselves as such, and profess themselves such already.[99]

But, in a letter to Baxter in October 1657, Humfrey repeated Blake's point: his Worcestershire Association admitted to communion only those who felt that they were of the Elect and were so regarded by the ministers. Baxter had attempted a distinction between 'a profession that my faith is indeed saving or sincere' from the profession of *justifying* faith that he sought. Humfrey called such a profession 'that old customary roade of formality and lying'. His letter concluded with a vigorous defence of Prynne and a complaint that Baxter's arguments succeeded in cutting his adversaries *to* the heart rather than succeeding in pricking them *at* the heart.[100]

Baxter's reply of 13 March 1658 was a moving testament of his failure to find a 'middle way'. His first correspondence with Humfrey four years earlier had assumed that he *could* capture the mean between regeneration and hypocrisy. His 'preparatory state to true Regeneration' may have seemed too tame to a Nye or an Owen, but went considerably further than Humfrey or Blake had in mind. Despite Baxter's great emotional sympathy with Humfrey's case — 'a greater inclination to it than the contrary' — he knew on which side he would fight when the barricades came down. Prynne's apostasy may have made the critical difference: the ministerial status must be preserved. Baxter's hatred of separatism could not take him to the point of acceptance of mixed communion. For that was the renunciation of discipline, which was the task of *distinguishing* the clean from the unclean.

Baxter's letter — following his pamphlet of 1657 — is important as it finally marks upon which side of the line his sympathies would fall. He put the question to Humfrey that was for him decisive:

> When you have lett in all the rabble into the Church that will make your profession which costs them nothinge, what will you do with them when you have done? Will you exercise the Discipline that the Scriptures, and all the ancient Canons of the Church prescribe, and the old Churches used, or will you not?

From 'the smart of daily experience' Baxter warned of the dangers of men coming to the Sacrament before they were ready for it. The analogy was with the boy, learning his ABC, thrust prematurely into advanced classes in Greek: 'he will scarce thanke you for your cruell mercy, that prefer'd him thither before he was ripe'. If he failed to make the grade, he would be whipped. If he was not whipped, discipline had been abandoned. Whereas the true way of dealing with the scandalous, outwardly penitent, was to let him 'stay among the Catechumens' untroubled by discipline or ordinance, until the minister had his 'eares and affections' and has him 'in a way of hope'.[101]

Peter du Moulin wrote to Baxter from Oxford, in June 1658. He criticised the stringency of Baxter's requirements for admission to the Sacrament. He pointed out that, if all ministers were of 'that Christian mildnes and happy dexterity' of Baxter, the fear of entrusting ministers with such disciplinary powers would be groundless. But the majority of the ministers did not match Baxter's calibre; therefore, separatism and neglect of the Sacrament would be the consequences of his policy. Du Moulin was arguing like Prynne in 1645, when he recognised the futility of measuring all Presbyterian ministers by the quality of those who worked in London.[102]

Yet, only a few weeks later, Michael Edge was writing to claim that the attempt to pull down the barriers to admission to the Sacrament, or to pass off the ordinance as a converting instrument, were part of the tactics of the 'rigid Episcopall Brethren'. Edge hoped that the disciplinary requirements of the Worcestershire Association would serve as an antidote, and this view was welcomed by Baxter in his reply.[103] Henry Stubbe had warned in 1659 that Anglicanism and Presbyterianism could come together 'out of the profits arising from a destroyed – Sectarian – Toleration': really the same point as Edge's.[104] And in another pamphlet of the same year John Beverley argued that the future of Presbyterianism was best secured in an understanding with Independency. In a preface to Beverley's pamphlet John Stalham, warning readers against the baleful influence of Prynne and Timson, revealed that, had Beverley lived, he had planned a reorganisation of church government in his area, based upon an understanding between those Presbyterians and Independents who shared the 'sect-ideal'.[105] It is notable that, in the pamphlet itself, Timson and Prynne were labelled as 'Erastians', not, in the correct sense, for their advocacy of common admission, but in the incorrect ascription to them of the view that there could be no order in the Church without the magistrate. The less Baxter believed the first, the more he inclined to the second. But the important point was that he turned to the civil magistrate *not as the alternative to clerical discipline but as the means of making that discipline possible.* Those who believed in common admission could rely upon the converting powers of the ordinance to secure the discipline; those who wished to safeguard the purity of the ordinance could remain detached from the problem of disciplining the excluded majority (in Saunders' words, 'we leave them to themselves'); only those – like Baxter – who depended upon ministerial control to secure the discipline required quite so much reinforcement from the civil magistrate. If by the end of the Commonwealth, Baxter could seem 'Erastian' in his dependence on the magistrate (unlike Prynne who was withholding tithes and conspiring against the Protectorate) it was for the most 'un-Erastian' of reasons: the protection of clerical discipline. This did not make his support of civil magistracy insincere. Indeed, his horror of clerical intrusions into what was properly the civil magistrate's sphere was so genuine that he would warm *to that aspect* of Hobbes's and Harrington's writings; it was when the clergy's disciplinary powers, as opposed to their political ambitions, were under attack that he parted from their critics. Hobbes and Harrington would have argued that clergymen's political ambitions *were* indissolubly linked with their claims to exercise discipline; Baxter was never less 'Erastian' (in both senses of the word) than in his denial of that thesis. His hatred of clericalism came by a different route: a historical sense of the way that Popes and bishops had usurped functions which had belonged to the Emperor and which, incidentally, distracted them from precisely that pastoral, disciplinary role which should have satisfied them. The worst aspects of ambitious clericalism (which Baxter hated as much as Hobbes) were *not therefore extensions of pastoral overseeing on to a wider canvas, but were rather a consequence of their neglect of such functions.*

Only a month after Edge and Baxter were agreeing that more stringency in discipline would check a High Anglican revival, John Beale was pointing out to Baxter the practical embarrassments of seeking to narrow the base:

A younger brother of Colonel Birch did in much heate urge it, That wee must invite and take in (as far as could obtain it) all the ministers into this Association; or wee did in effect judge them, that were not received, scandalous or insufficient.[106]

Too narrow for Birch, the requirements were still too broad for John Howe, who in May 1658 wrote to Baxter that the profession of visible faith which Baxter required of his communicants fell short of the 'deeper discoverie' which Philip Nye thought necessary.[107] Howe's judgement was confirmed a few months later with the Declaration in favour of unmixed communion drawn up by the Independent ministers at their Savoy Conference on 12 October 1658.[108] Baxter's reaction to the Declaration was an appalled one, as we shall see: it cruelly terminated hopes of an understanding along the lines of his correspondence with Edge. The Declaration may have been a worse blow to Baxter than Prynne's defection on the other side. Baxter was hurt by Prynne because he admired the man. But it was the action of an individual which, at worst, only confirmed Baxter's suspicions about the anti-clericalism which clung to the advocacy of common admission. The Declaration was, however, a collective slap in the face to Baxter from a formal body. It cast doubt upon the substance of the achievement in co-operation which had been painfully built up in the past few years through the Association of Ministers.

The drive towards ministerial associations in the Commonwealth was initially defensive. Baxter had no love for regicides and usurpers, but as early as 1650 he was petitioning the Commons as part of his campaign to establish ministerial discipline. The Rump was unlovely, but Antinomians, Quakers, Ranters and Jesuits were worse. The less bad was better than the worst. Parliamentary initiatives were pursued in tandem with conferences aimed at bringing Presbyterian and Independent divines together. Ironically the pamphleteering efforts to find a 'middle way' in doctrine and to agree upon qualifications for admission to the Sacraments were intended to bring men closer together, although the effect was often to achieve the reverse. The initial *defensive* nature of the drive was never lost: among his last letters in the Commonwealth are hysterical fears for his life at the hands of Papists. But another element was added to the drive at an early date: a *positive* yearning to establish a New Jerusalem. The two elements were not contradictory, and the one never totally cancelled out the other. The more successfully 'natural antinomianism' was held at bay, the more possible it became to envisage positive programmes of moral reform. The positive element is most marked in Baxter's correspondence with the ecumenist, John Durie, or the missionary, John Eliot, or with the Welsh Justice of the Peace, John Lewis. Too much could not be expected from the Rump. Their execution of the Presbyterian Royalist minister, Christopher Love, on 22 August 1651, made even his low expectations of them seem too high. Like other conservative Puritans, however, he had rallied to the Rump once more by the end of 1652, when much worse alternatives seemed imminent. The Barebone's Parliament, from July to December 1653, confirmed his worst fears, but when that 'Pageant' was played out Baxter became increasingly drawn into closer co-operation with the experimental, *but more conservative*, regimes which succeeded it. Not only in correspondence with Durie, Eliot and Lewis — where one would expect it — but in less obvious places one catches an increasing excitement in Baxter's letters in the later years of the Commonwealth. In part, this reflects the millenarian excitements of the time, from which Baxter was not immune; in part, this reflects his pride in the solid *positive* achievements that could already be put in the credit column. Because these achievements had been precariously won, and because he never underrated the subtlety of the Jesuit, the defensive note is never totally lost. But what he expects from Richard Cromwell's Protectorate is in a different league from what he had earlier asked of the Rump. The success of the ministerial associations is the essential bridge between his efforts to combat a prevalent narrowness of spirit in the rulers in the early years of the Commonwealth (his attacks on Antinomian doctrine, Baptism, Quakerism and the polarisation of positions in the Lord's Supper controversy) and the very real hopes of commitment to a 'Holy Commonwealth' in the rulers in the last years of the Commonwealth. By looking in detail at the progress of the ecumenical idea through the ministerial associations we can document the gradual change in Baxter.

The Worcestershire Association was launched in September 1652, at a point almost midway between Christopher Love's execution and the calling of Barebone's Parliament. In between these two low points, Baxter tried to agitate the Rump into more decisive action to strengthen ministerial discipline. On 22 December 1652 Baxter was active in the manoeuvres which preceded the petition from Worcestershire to the Rump on behalf of a godly ministry. On 22 March 1653 Bartlett could report that Hampshire were following suit, with a petition of 8,000 signatures; they would be followed in turn by petitions from Dorset, Wiltshire, Somerset and Sussex. There was an impressive orchestration about the campaign – recalling something of the sweetness of the 'root and branch' operation in the early 1640s – which was cruelly terminated with the dismissal of the Rump.[109]

Baxter continued to promote moral discipline by other means. His earlier ecumenical schemes, raised in correspondence with men like Thomas Hill and Gataker as early as 1649, were beginning to bear fruit. Between 1652 and 1654 Baxter and Durie collaborated on schemes for the holding of a conference to promote Christian unity. Using first Hill, and then Durie, as instruments of his plan, Baxter wanted Cambridge University to back his idea of a petition to Parliament, setting up a committee drawn from Episcopalians, Presbyterians, Independents and Erastians. Two years of negotiations culminated in 1654 in a bastard compromise: the committee shrank to five representatives each, but drawn from Presbyterians and Independents only; the steam went out of it with Durie's departure between 1654 and 1657 to promote Christian unity abroad. In its way as significant as anything else was the way in which Baxter and Cromwell were converging: seven of the ten were appointed to Cromwell's newly formed Committee of Triers (much praised by Baxter for their promotion of godliness later) and at least two had been present at earlier unity meetings launched by Cromwell. Baxter grudgingly came round to the acceptance of office as a Worcestershire Assistant to the Triers: an important step towards reconciliation. Moreover he was among the ministers summoned to London in November 1654 to assist the subcommittee appointed to confer with the Protector about the articles of religion in the Instrument of Government. The conference was abortive. Baxter was nominated by Broghill as Usher's substitute but found himself outmanoeuvred by some of the 'rigid' Independent divines, who were unforgiving of his *Aphorismes of Justification*. The way in which they expanded the 'Fundamentals of Religion' was a foretaste to Baxter of the rigidity which would mark their Savoy Conference Declaration of 1658.

The success which eluded him on the wider front was achieved to a large extent on his home ground. Seventy-two ministers joined his Worcestershire Association in the first three years of its existence; monthly meetings were planned to be held at Bromsgrove, Evesham, Kidderminster, Upton-on-Severn and Worcester; there were quarterly meetings at Worcester. The ministers, conferring with each other on discipline and controversy, were drawn from Independents, Baptists and Episcopalians, over half of whom eventually conformed at the Restoration. Baxter was the driving force behind the association and it spread beyond the boundaries of Worcestershire. Wiltshire, Hampshire, Dorset, Somerset, Kent and Devon by the end of 1655 had formed Associations along the lines of the Worcestershire model (it was not until the summer of 1653 with the publication of Baxter's *Christian Concord* that details of the Worcestershire agreement became widely known). Cambridgeshire, Cornwall, Sussex, Essex, Herefordshire, Staffordshire and Norfolk would be added by 1659. There was nothing monolithic about the movement. Not only were there important regional variations (ordinations took place only in Cambridgeshire, Cornwall, Cumberland, Devon and Westmorland); the Cheshire Association, like those of Cumberland and Westmorland, had come into independent existence and was closer to Presbyterian classical movements in the inclusion of lay elders.[110]

It has been said that 'for a mixed organisation of this kind' there was 'no previous precedent in England'.[111] In a sense this is true, but in another sense Blake was saying more than he may have meant when he termed it 'the Worcestershire combination'.[112] In his *Gildas Salvianus* of 1656 Baxter referred to the seminal inspiration of Grindal's combination associations: 'that excellent Letter of Edmond Grindal Archbishop of Canterbury to Queen Elizabeth for Ministeriall meetings and exercises (such Bishops would have prevented our contentions and wars)'.[113] Professor Collinson has drawn attention, in a pioneering article,[114] to the importance of the combination lectureships as an underrated feature of the institutional vitality of the Jacobean Church; the more that research dispels our ignorance about these developments, the more likely we are to appreciate the traditions — outside the Presbyterian classical movement — that Baxter could draw upon *from within the Church of England*. It is certainly of interest that Baxter could see his brotherly associations as the true heirs of Grindal.

The earliest of Baxter's writings show his fear of tolerance. Defending his Worcestershire Petition in 1653 to the Parliament, he deplored the freedom which men enjoyed to attack the clergy. If scolds are punished with 'grumble-stools' why should the attackers of ministers escape? 'Powder Plotting Papists' were able to claim indulgence for tender consciences. When doctors could earn as much as a thousand pounds a year, why should ministers be reviled as 'greedy Dogs' when they merely wanted enough to live on? The attack on tithes had its sinister social side. 'Landlords rent and tithe rent will stand or fall together,' Culmer had observed; Prynne called tithes 'a charge, debt, duty, as well as their landlords rent'; Baxter believed that the repeal of tithes would be analogous to the abolition by law of debts and rents. No tithes, no property: 'Ah, poor England, that is grown so Lunatick, as to be taken with such arguings![115]

Christian Concord was written in 1653 by Baxter as the answer to such lunacy. It published an alternative practical strategy to the search for the elusive doctrinal 'middle way', although this remained his long-term aim. The Association of Ministers was not a *substitute* for that search, which went on; it was a short-term expedient to shore up those points where agreement could already be reached by practical steps. Presbyterians were wrong to see the movement as a challenge to their classical system. Outside London, Lancashire and Shropshire, where *classes* had Parliamentary authorisation, many Presbyterians had in a mistaken spirit of austerity denied their congregations for some years the comfort of the Lord's Supper. The Association was open only to 'those Parties who acknowledge a Discipline', which not only excluded such austere Presbyterians, who denied that there could be a discipline that was not of the classical kind; but also Independents who were only interested in a gathering of the pure, and finally Episcopalians who were 'Cassandrian Papists', and who followed Grotius in schemes to reunite with Rome. Some Episcopalians were converted to the Catholic faith, but they were not the main problem:

> But some have more wit than these and think they may do that Party more service by staying in England, under the names of Episcopall Divines, a great deal than they can do by declaring themselves Papists . . . he is stark blinde that doth not see so strong a design laid for the introduction of Popery.[116]

Thomas Good warmed to this theme in a letter of 12 October 1653 to Baxter. He hoped that the Worcestershire Association would spread 'betwixt al moderate conscientious orthodoxal protestant ministers, before the prophane Atheist and subtle Jesuit take al'.[117]

By 1655 Baxter was becoming uneasy about the passivity of the magistrate. The ministerial associations were *an* answer to those who felt that 'because the Sword doth not enforce it, they think nothing can be done.' But they were not *the* answer. What of the ministers who did not respond to the Worcestershire lead, and who failed to explore pastoral and disciplinary care through brotherly associations? The neglect of ministerial *rule* was as grave as the neglect of preaching: 'why the Magistrate should not punish *such negligent ones*, as well as the other, I yet know not.'[118] This point became the eighth in twenty he urged Parliament to adopt in a sermon to them on Christmas Eve, 1655, in Westminster Abbey. It was the ministers, not the magistrate, who exercised the ecclesiastical discipline; but it was the magistrate who punished ministerial 'maladministration'. Clearly Baxter was becoming less bothered by 1655 at the prospect of *too much* direction from the top. The consequences of non-intervention, rather than the abuses of too much intervention, provided the theme of his sermon. Baxter looked for tighter laws to restrain 'scorners', and a burning of books — 'Specially Hobbes his Leviathan'. He wanted to see the ministry regularly paid, and their disciplinary powers respected. He wanted to see good laws for the Sabbath upheld. Sitting in the stocks was too tame a punishment for 'swearers, drunkards and prohibited Ale-sellers': Baxter wanted the magistrate to introduce a programme of systematic whipping of offenders. The 'free use' of ministerial associations (his fifth point), and a liberty given to them to ordain ministers (his sixth point), were commended in the context of a more active disciplinary role for the Christian magistrate. His sermon culminated in specific recommendations for the appointment of Catechists in every parish in the land, working two hours a day, at a salary of between £12 to £20 per annum, 'which may be imposed on the people to pay'.[119]

He had prepared a sermon earlier in the same month to be delivered at Worcester. For health reasons he had been unable to deliver it, and it was eventually expanded and published in the following year as his famous *Gildas Salvianus*. When Quakers, Papists and Hobbists were so ready to denounce the clergy, Baxter hesitated about exposing their shortcomings. He cited Prynne, however, as an example of the 'plain dealer', who wins ultimate respect for his integrity: Charles I, shortly before his execution, called him 'the Cato of the Age'. His proposals were on the same lines as his Christmas Eve sermon. He wanted more private instruction from the ministers, rather than public sermons: the tutorial rather than the lecture. The neglect of private instruction should be seen as no less scandalous than omitting sermons: 'if these lazy worldly hypocrites were but quickened to their duty by a Sequestering Committee'. Preparation for the tutorial required *more*, not *less*, effort than the lecture. Clerical discipline could be exercised independent of the magistrate: 'But what if the Magistrate will not help us? Nay, What if he were against it? So he was for about 300 years, when Discipline was exercised in the primitive Church.' In 1686 Baxter would be offended when Henry More said much the same thing.[120] Nothing could be more hurtful to the imperial cause than the admission that the Church had done rather well *before* Constantine came on the scene. The Ministerial Associations recognised the point of Henry Hammond's plea for more private conferences between the Minister and his flock, which Baxter defended as the working out of Grindal's aspirations. Parishioners saw the pulpit as a stage 'where Preachers must shew themselves and play their parts'; only when ministers 'said it personally to their faces' did they see 'that you were in good earnest' and apply the strictures to their personal lives.[121]

On 20 January 1657 Baxter appealed to Eliot to turn from converting Red Indians to persuading Presbyterians and Independents to unite. Baxter made the interesting point that whenever unity seemed imminent it foundered on one issue: 'whether they should or should not, take members promiscuously out of all Parishes'. Baxter believed that the issue was as much sociological as theological: in country areas, they said no; in towns, they were more flexible.[122] On 5 May 1657 Baxter was corresponding with John Lewis 'about a Colledge with Academicall Priviledges for Wales': Red Indians and Welshmen were alike in being infidels ripe for conversion. This was no novel venture. As he reminded Lewis, ten years earlier he had tried to interest Colonel Markworth; six months earlier, Major General Berry. Berry promised to help him, 'but the want is money'. A childless Shrewsbury man worth £40,000

living in London had been marked out by Baxter as a possible founder/
victim. Once financial assistance had begun, Baxter expressed no doubts
to Lewis about the attitude at the centre: 'I make no doubt to procure
Authority from the Protector and Parliament.'[123] In other words,
although Baxter might have faced hypothetically in the previous year
the possibility of a hostile or passive partner, the realities of the
common search for reconciling schemes between parties, and advancement of morality, were pulling Baxter and Protector closer and closer
together. Cromwell was still a usurper; their couple of four-hour sessions
closeted together had not transformed their *personal* relationship;[124]
but there were ties deeper than politics and personalities.

The threat to unity would come from another source. One of Cromwell's chaplains, John Howe, spelled out a development which was
more ominous than a clash of personalities in a letter to Baxter on 23
May 1658. He informed him how Philip Nye disliked Baxter's concept
of visible belief as 'a credible profession of faith and holinesse' in antithesis to 'such a deeper discoverie as hee would thinke necessarie'.
Howe quoted Nye's pessimism about whether 'there would never bee an
agreement about that matter'. Since this dispute was about requirements for communicants in the Association movement it was a disturbing letter for Baxter to receive. His hopes for understanding between
Presbyterians and Independents, in their common recognition of ministerial discipline, were based on the assumption that Owen had no more
claim to represent the Independent point of view than did Humfrey and
Blake the Presbyterian. Howe was saying that Owen spoke for Nye: a
crushing reply to Baxter's original letter to Howe, of 3 April 1658,
which had asked the Protector to accelerate the drive towards unity.[125]

More heartening for Baxter was the letter from Durie, written a day
after Howe's, which enclosed a number of papers to be distributed
among members of the Worcestershire Association, tying up Reformed
Churches in Switzerland, Germany and the Netherlands with the ecumenical impulse of the Association movement. Enclosing a general
reply on 18 August 1658, Baxter explained the slowness in answering
by the mechanics of the movement. The particular associations met
monthly, but the General Meeting met quarterly and were only able
now to despatch a proposed 'Confession of Faith' and 'Profession of
Brotherhood' as the basis for further discussion. Baxter's letter to Durie
has this remarkable aside:

> If this way will not doe, I know of none its like to doe it, but Princes
> correction of intemperate Divines. We may easyer thus sattisfie them

by writings than by confused passionate debates in great Assemblies. And you or I may not hope to live to see an Assembly of all or most of the Churches for this worke.[126]

Ecumenical associations and the use of the magistrate's corrective sword lay within the sphere of practical politics; a universal healing Assembly did not.

On the same day that Baxter was restating his faith in the ministerial associations, Michael Edge was writing to him of the strains imposed upon that development by the behaviour of some 'rigid Episcopall Brethren'. Their triple plan was to undermine respect for the ministry, revive Arminian doctrine and 'pull downe the hedge which our Divines have endeavoured to set about the Lord's Supper'. Edge noted how Pierce's pamphlets were being handed 'from one neutrall Gentleman to another'.[127] Baxter's reply, on 24 August 1658, offered the success of Durie's ecumenism on the Continent as the answer to Pierce's attacks on the Association. His letter of the same day to John Beale made the same point: 'The correspondencye desireable betweene the Churches at home and abroad (which Mr. Dury is so earnest for, who is just now gone from me) cant be carryed on with any but Associated Churches.'[128] Beale, in his letter of 9 September to Baxter, did not need persuading of the philosophical case for the movement: 'a necessary step towards Mr. Duryes designe, which is to mee in precious esteem'. His worry was at a more mundane level of practicality: his first attempts at forming an association a year earlier had foundered on the 'sharpeness and narrownesse of some, and the dullnesse and unsensiblenesse of others'. Beale confirmed Edge's diagnosis: the wreckers of the movement were the Episcopalian high-fliers:

> They denyed themselves to have power or spirite from Christe to restore or erect any kind of presbytery, or to act in their owne congregations, or in any association to separate the Communicants from the scandalous, or to exercise or countenance any other brand of discipline. Soe they received the Comunione parochially without any regard to discipline, and as their duety.

A year later the situation was no more promising. Profiting from the first experience, ministers began more warily. They were now seeking more evidence of fitness and preparedness before admitting colleagues to the Association. Beale knew that there were two potential wreckers, who were notoriously profane and unlearned. Before Beale could caution them, one had insinuated himself into the movement and was already provoking disturbances: 'I see cause to feare more, and worse.'[129]

Edge and Beale were preparing Baxter for the attack from the 'Right': *iure divino* Anglicans were pulling down the disciplinary barriers which the Association ministers were trying to set up. But the attack, when it came, came from the 'Left': the Declaration of Independent ministers at their Savoy Conference on 12 October 1658 endorsed Nye's view that a 'deeper discoverie' was needed of communicants than Baxter's profession of visible faith. How deeply cast down was Baxter by the development is apparent in some notes that have survived in manuscript: 'How low then hath this laid our hopes of Reconciliation.' He had not heeded Howe's warning about Nye and saw the Declaration as an affront to 'the moderate healing concessions of Mr. Norton, Mr. Cotton and others of New England; yea of Mr. Nye and Dr. Goodwin'. The most worrying aspect of the Declaration was its formal status: 'And the worke being done by Agreement in such an Assembly, we can no longer say, these are but the opinions of some few among them, but the Partie now seemeth Engaged in them.'[130] In his autobiography, written some time after these events, he was particularly bitter about the loss of Paradise, through the captiousness of the Independents as well as through the perfidy of the Anglicans: 'England had been like in a quarter of an Age to have become a land of Saints, and a Pattern of Holinesse to all the World, and the unmatchable Paradise of the Earth.' The original culprits were the five dissentients from the Westminster Assembly – Nye, Thomas Goodwin, Simpson, Bridge and Burroughs. Burroughs expiated his sins with his later irenicism, but after Burroughs' death Owen was 'not of the same spirit': 'by whom and Mr. Philip Nyes Policie our Flames were encreased, our Wounds kept open, and carried on all, as if there had been none but they considerable in the World'. He then saw the Savoy Conference – with its claim *That we are justified by the Righteousness of Christ only, and not by any Works* – as the product of the intransigence of Owen and Nye, and the logical development of the spirit that had cooked up 'New Fundamentals' in earlier efforts at reconciliation.[131]

John Durie had not despaired. A couple of months after the Declaration he was writing to Baxter on 20 December 1658 about his hopes for a joint Public Declaration from both universities and London Synod, together with the release of correspondence between the Association ministers and the Swiss Churches, which would counter something of the unfavourable impact of the Savoy Conference. Hopes for unity would revive with such a commitment, and the Independent ministers would, he believed, associate themselves with the movement:

> The Congregational Brethren who mette at the Savoy have promised faire, that they will concurre with the rest in this worke; but they delay the performance; and walke not so openly with me in the business as I did expect.

Durie nevertheless hoped that they would release their Confession, and other matters in preparation, as the basis for negotiations. The Baptists, despite internal divisions, were favourably inclined: Durie knew that Lamb and Allen had been in close contact with Baxter. He was waiting for things to ripen before involving the Protector. The timetable thereafter was clear:

> and then I shall desire a reference from him to some of the Counsell whom I shall name who may consider upon the Information which I shall give them what may bee fitter for him to doe in it? how farre he appeare for the encouragement of the worke? in what way hee should assist it at home and abroad? how farre to owne me, or without taking notice of mee (which I think more expedient) to owne the business so we may not give any state Jealousie to those that will bee startled at the full appearance of a reall unitie amongst us.[132]

It is a remarkable passage, breathing the sophistication of the insider. This was collusion very close to the centre of power.

If a synod were to be called, Durie wanted Baxter to co-operate with his friends to see that Church unity was made its peculiar business. But he accepted it as unlikely, unless there was full agreement with the Protector, and between themselves, that one should be called. If there were to be no synod, Durie wanted a committee appointed to enquire into the business, with powers to investigate how Parliament could be involved in the encouragement of Church unity. A month later, Thomas Manton was asking Baxter whether it would be advisable to move for a synod 'considering the present posture of affairs'. Manton, in framing the request, claimed to be the mouthpiece of 'many of your Friends in parliament who upon my motion were very importunate that I should write to you'.[133] Baxter's reply, of 1 February 1659, was contemptuous of General Assemblies: 'they will doe less in a month than one or two men would doe in a day or two.' Assemblies were at the opposite end of Baxter's spectrum from associations: the one thriving on rhetoric and exposure of differences, the other on discipline and the patient realisation of unity. He had two stipulations for a synod: no members were to be chosen from the last Assembly of Divines; there were to be free elections to such an Assembly not by Parliament, but by the 'Lawfull Ministers of England'. The second stipulation was negotiable; the first was not.[134]

Baxter's last letter on the theme of the Ministerial Associations in the Commonwealth period makes melancholy reading. He writes to William Mewe on 6 August 1659, with almost all his hopes dashed, and fearing physically for his safety at the hands of Papists. He tells Mewe of a 'hundred threatnings I have had from all parts of the land' although 'yet I have suffered nothing by violence.' The ubiquitous Romish menace was its source: 'I never came in danger till I set against the Papists. *They do all, that are seene in nothing.*' He looks back on reconciliation schemes with Independents and Baptists, and says that if anything could have prevailed on them it had been attempted. Agreement with Baptists in London was all but complete a week before 'the change of government'. He claims that 'all the Ministers of our Association likt it'. The political revolution altered the debate — 'the turne set them up' — but Lamb and Allen were still for peace. He complained of being left, a lone Promethean figure (apart from his friend, Henry Hickman), to battle with 'Pierce, Stubs and the Papists and sectaries of all sorts': work which he would continue to perform until the Papists deprived him of his liberty.[135]

There was nothing novel about Baxter's alarm at threats from ubiquitous Jesuits; what was novel in 1659 was the fatalism with which he met their assaults. His letter to Mewe shows what he lost when Richard Cromwell resigned his Protectorate. No longer was he sustained against his adversary with the supporting sword of the Christian magistrate.

Earlier on in the Commonwealth period his dependence on that magistrate was less marked. Correspondence between himself and Richard Vines in July 1650 established their agreement not to take the Engagement: no allegiance was due to a blood-stained usurper.[136] Nearly two years on, a different note is struck. When he wrote to Thomas Hill on 8 October 1652 it was with ill-concealed irritation that the Commonwealth was not doing more to promote Church unity and moral reform.[137] His Worcestershire petition to the Rump in 1653 on behalf of the ministry was an illustration of how far he was sliding into a policy of collusion with the established government. This went further than filling a vacuum. Baxter was responding to the excitement of the age. Abraham Pinchbecke was no Winstanley, but his letter to Baxter of 5 August 1653 communicates something of that excitement:

> doe not we see in Common Weales how after ages perceiving the faileing of their people in the observation of some precedent laws doe ad remedies to such transgressions and new conditions to old laws, or make new laws where the other are imperfect, or the present condition of affaires require? and for invention have we not some whose braines have brought forth some new formes of government very rationall?[138]

It was difficult for Baxter to remain untouched by this excitement; and even more difficult when he read Henry Oasland's letter to him in January 1654. Oasland was grateful for Baxter's contributions on faith, works, redemption and justification: 'the world knows your mind in them fully ... but the world doth not know your mind fully in this point, especially how far the magistrate is interested and where his work lyes.' Oasland wanted Baxter to explain the powers of the magistrate. It is interesting *why* he wanted him to do so: because ministers were now so unpopular. Oasland complained of being 'hissed at in any work beside pulpit worke'. Once congregations understood the extent, and limits, of the magistrate's authority, there would be less resentment at clerical discipline. But first the clergy themselves must know how far these powers stretched. From his letter it is clear that Oasland was not expecting a Byzantinist tract which reduced the clergy to ciphers, but neither was he happy at the way that Scottish divines especially had developed the counter-argument:

> The ignorance of most Ministers how far the Magistrate is interested, may stirre you up to inform us. For my part I am not ashamed to say I am ignorant but dare not compare others with my selfe, yet most that I meet with are in the same judgment. Mr. Rutherford hath a piece which is dark to mee and difficult to find out the truth, in his contest with Erastus.

Oasland was concerned that the magistrate was likely to neglect his disciplinary role unless it were made clear to him. Baxter shared the premiss of this letter, and his subsequent writings upon magistracy reflect this. Unlike Gillespie and Rutherford, Baxter did not see the authority of the civil magistracy as a *rival* to clerical discipline, but as its *prerequisite*.

Oasland concluded with some very practical advice. When Baxter had written his piece, he should dedicate it to Parliament and to all Christian magistrates. He should let other ministers know about it, in order that they can second his efforts and 'insinuate' it 'into the hands of the Godly Magistracy'. Finally, he should change his booksellers, or make them charge less for his books. Not, he added hastily, that they were not worth it, but he was in danger of pricing himself out of the reach of potential customers. Some four years before it happened Oasland was asking for a *Holy Commonwealth* and fixing the price in advance.[139]

A month after Oasland gave the theoretical case for co-operation with the civil magistrate, Durie gave the practical case. He had this consolation for Baxter in their ecumenical efforts:

> But there are more engaged in these thoughts than wee; through the good hand of God I hope over his people: for my Lord Protector is foreward in the worke, and this very day there is a meeting of Ministers and of some from the Universities at his Lodgings in the Cockpitte: Let us pray for the spirit of Truth and Peace to rest upon them.[140]

The greater the co-operation with Durie in ecumenical activity the easier it was for Baxter to appreciate the Protector's good faith. But was Cromwell tough enough on the Quakers? In a number of pamphlets at this time Baxter, drawing heavily upon Prynne's sources for proof, demonstrated that Quakers were masked Jesuits. The day after Guy Fawkes' Day in 1654 Bartlett was discussing plans with Baxter to petition Parliament against the spread of Popery;[141] an earlier letter from the same source had warned Baxter of the bad impression he had made on some influential Parliamentarians by his flabby refusal to identify the Pope with Antichrist.[142] Meanwhile the Quakers, Goodaire and Farnworth, were breaking up Baxter's sermons and were being sent to prison for their pains. A stormy meeting, in which the Quaker Edward Bourne remonstrated with Major General Berry about this betrayal of Commonwealth principle, found Baxter a broodingly enigmatic observer, saying nothing but standing by the fire with his hat over his eyes.[143] The magistracy must not sleep while the Quaker menace grew. Baxter was not physically present when the Protectorate Parliament debated the Nayler case; but spiritually he was, and nothing recorded in Burton's diary matches the unforgiving violence of Baxter's pamphleteering.[144] So much so that, in May 1656, Morgan Lloyd put this plaintive question

to Baxter: 'You condemne the generation of the quakers. If I were intimate with you I might better aske, Why?' Baxter did not wait for inti-
macy to flower. He told Lloyd on 10 July what he had against the
Quakers. They were the enemies of Scripture, the clergy and sobriety.
He bracketed them with Vane. They spoke in allegories and instead of
an ordered system of belief provided 'incoherent scraps'. Baxter begged
Lloyd to 'studiously avoid Allegoryes, metaphors and uncouth phrases
except where necessity compelleth you to use them'.[145]

How far would Baxter go in co-operation with a government that
held back the Quaker menace? In September 1656 he was invited to
clarify his position. His friend, Colonel Edward Harley, wanted to know
what course to follow in the coming second Protectorate Parliament.
Baxter's reply of 15 September is important as a bridge between the
concerns expressed in earlier petitions to the Rump and the programme
outlined in his *Holy Commonwealth*. He first urged on Harley that
religion *was* the business of the forthcoming Parliament, and that it
should not wait on other business. He proposed setting up a Committee
for Religion to prepare business for the Parliament. He looked to the
passing of an Act, presented to the Protector for the securing of religion,
as the best way of dispelling secular reservations about the régime. Toleration must be avoided and with it the offensive argument that the
magistrate should not intervene in religion:

> Its not the believing of untruths that must be restrayned (would,
> that could be done!) nor yet the professinge what a man believeth
> when he is comanded or called to it: But it is the seducinge others
> by the teaching of those untruths. And this may be restrayned in
> consistency with the Liberty that is granted in the Instrument of
> Government.

Popery can claim no privileges under the banner of that liberty:

> yet Popery resteth so much on humane strength and violence, that it
> must not have the same forbearance or easye exposition, as many
> other errors, which in themselves may seeme as bad: for they can
> have so much countenance, and maintenance and supplyes from
> beyond seas, that may beare downe a bare discountenance at home.

Baxter wanted to see the work of the Committee for approbation of
ministers strengthened. They had done much good, which must not be
diluted by over-fragmentation into numerous committees. The admission

of the unworthy was a Papist aim. The Committee for ejecting scandalous ministers must likewise be strengthened: additional commissioners and assisting ministers should be 'Pious Carefull Men' (not always the case in the previous Parliament). Failure to exercise discipline should be seen as much a badge of ministerial negligence as the failure to preach. Visitors appointed to each county – on the university model – could supplement information to the Commissioners for Ejection about the competence of ministers. The Commissioners should have more teeth: be given the power to coerce witnesses. Large parishes should have more ministers. There should be more up-to-date assessment of the financial capacities of tradesmen, lawyers and doctors: the clergy must be better supported, and their tenures secured from alienation. The Association mission must be supported and extended: ministers should be given the power to ordain. Ministers should be supported in their task of admonition of notorious offenders. Assisting ministers could join lay commissioners in determining whether censures were too severe or too lax. Baxter thought that fears of ministerial abuse were in any case exaggerated: 'But in the meane time I see, that Jealousyes and vaine suppositions of ministers overdoinge, doth raise horrid apprehensions of things that are seldome like to come to pass.' Ministers and Justices of the Peace, or officers appointed by Parliament, could collaborate in 'the disposall of the Church (the place of meeting)' in order to avoid the infiltration of undesirable persons. Slanderers of the clergy should have no more protection than libellers of lawyers and doctors: 'for the life of the Papists Cause doth lye in this designe'. To strengthen discipline, Baxter looked to the passing of measures against profanity – 'some law against the scorninge at Godlyness' – and the reinforcement of the punitive resources of the Justices of the Peace. Baxter wanted to see a 'standinge Examiner', subordinate to Justices of the Peace, in every Parish which had not got one: 'One or more of the faithfullest inhabitants, and of best understandinge, would thus commit more offenders in a yeare than Justices doo in many; because of the distance and trouble of prosecution and other reasons.' Baxter wanted the Associations of Ministers to be supported in their attempts to unify the nation. 'A free chosen Convocation is best in its season,' but the autumn of 1656 was not its season. Instead the Committee of Religion could consult one or two leading 'Reconcilers' from each persuasion. The Westmorland and Cumberland Agreements were good working models. Two years earlier he and Usher had agreed on everything in half an hour. Finally, Parliament should authorise a reformed version of singing psalms: 'the old ones are not tolerable when better may be had.' London ministers lived among men of different minds and were told by Episcopalians that they lacked authority to make changes. The problem of the vacuum required resolution: 'All look to you. A word will do it.'[146]

Baxter had moved from hostility to forbearance to collusion. No wonder Sir Francis Nethersole got a dusty answer from him when he tried to enlist Baxter to the old Royalist and Episcopalian cause! An embarrassed postscript to his letter suggested that Baxter himself wondered whether he had gone too far in his attachment to the Protectorate: 'To do nothing against our Allegiance and obligations to our Lawful Governors, I take for granted we are agreed on: yea to do all for them that by lawfull meanes we can.' The text of the letter belied the postscript. 'To do all for them that by lawfull meanes we can' became in the text an apology for *inaction*. If his duty to oppose were clear, it would be inexcusable for him to shrink from it. But he explained to Nethersole that he measured means by ends. Government is a means: its end is 'Gods Honor in the prosperity or good of Church and Commonwealth'. Anything which tends to the destruction of that end is not acceptable to Baxter as a means. Factors which influenced Baxter in believing that active opposition to the present régime (albeit not 'our Lawfull Governors') was to be deprecated were: 'the way in Church and State before the Warres'; 'the strange streame of Providences, through all the change in all the three Nations'; the revengeful character of the politicians of Restoration; the debased quality of the ministers of Restoration. Baxter trembled at the thought of running 'into the fire' with such an opposition:

> And I am able sincerely to Profess, that if in this I be mistaken it is for God and for the Church and not for myselfe or any worldly thinge. So that I take myselfe to be called by God to stand still, till he make plaine my way. I dare not goe against his precept on one side; nor dare I strive against a streame of Providence for the apparent destruction of the Church, on the other hand. The Prediction of a certaine captivity ... disobliged Jews from many actions which otherwise they were obliged to in obedience to their Kinge, and in defence of their Country.[147]

To set the 'streame of Providence' in antithesis to legal obligations was dangerous talk, and showed how far Baxter had gone from his principled objection (with Vines) to the Engagement in 1650. Moreover that sort of language could be used as effectively against himself. Thus in December 1656 Thomas Horne sought Baxter's support for the view that England was fulfilling the prophecies in Revelation. Horne's belief in the 'streame of Providence' inspired the apocalyptic hope:

> these so wondrous transactions of ours in Britain may probably have beene pitched upon by the spirit for the character of this age (these beinge without exception, the most remarkable that have befallen Christs Kingdome (the Revelations peculiar concernment) in the age of Man).

Nor was it strange that, after Rome's defection, England should be the Elect Nation: 'The Reformed Church (and Brittaine cheifly in that worke) is sure the choicest (Though not the largest) part of christendome, and consequently the fittest for the Divine stage of present transactions, as Rome hath beene for the former.' The pattern of recent politics vindicated prophecy:

> Whether it can bee easily digested that the Late commotions in Britain could have beene agitated to and fro with so rare a springe of swift and active motion, had not some energeticall prophecy lyne underneath, which wee have found by experience was allwayes wont to quicken and invigorate the progresse of affaires upon the appointed mutation of each Severall Monarchy, answerable to those powerfull revelations which Holy Daniels prophecies have acquainted us with.[148]

Baxter was not too happy at this turn of events. Providence was a good brake on Cavalier zeal, but a dangerous accelerator for speculative minds. He replied frigidly on 13 February 1657 with the comment that 'it is not meet to enter upon Revelation controversyes.'[149] When Horne came back to the attack in June 1657 Baxter replied with more specific criticisms. He wrote off his earlier interest in the millennium as a 'juvenile fancye' of twenty years ago. He had lost that earlier confidence; now 'in a certaine despondency' he had almost 'laid by that study'. He did not believe that the Apocalypse was unintelligible but doubted that he or Horne understood it.[150] The rest of the letter was taken up with detailed criticisms of some of Horne's suggestions. He ridiculed Horne's belief in 25 March as the Day of Judgement. This was an easy target, comparable later to Beverley's expectations of 1697.[151] More interesting was his scorn for Horne's faith in bishops as the best bulwark against Rome. Their reluctance to call the Pope Antichrist established their bad faith in Baxter's eyes: three years earlier, Bartlett had reported that Members of Parliament were saying the same about Baxter.[152] Baxter's letter to Horne is in its way as uncompromising as his snub to Nethersole. It shows the same unsentimental rejection of the past, and confidence in a magistrate-directed present. A difference is the care which he takes, in writing to Horne, to separate the appeal to the magistrate's sword from apocalyptic readings of providence, which was implied, although not fully stated, in the earlier letter to Nethersole. The separation of the two became more difficult to sustain as his own hopes of Church unity and reform expanded. In his *Gildas Salvianus* of 1656 he jubilantly exclaims: 'I finde that we never took the rightest course to demolish the Kingdom of Darkness till now.' This was, of course, not a reading from Revelation despite the language; the claims instead derived specifically from his catechising achievement. But the language he chose to use has its own significance. He explained how the pastoral care worked. Mondays and Tuesdays from morning to night were spent in catechising, taking in fifteen or sixteen families in a week, and throughout the period about eight hundred a year. No family *refused* to come: only a few made excuses for not coming. At the delivery of catechisms, Baxter took a catalogue of all understanding persons in the parish. The clerk sent a week before to every family to tell them when to come, and at what hour. He would see them normally *as a family*; only rarely would outsiders be present. Baxter rejoiced at the results: 'I bless God for the change that I see in the Countrey; and among the people, even in my own charge.'[153] That change could be destroyed by the Jesuits. Operating under the mask of Quakers, they were most seductive to good but melancholic men: that was the point of Baxter's homily, on 30 May 1654, to Bromley about the Mad Major.[154] Baxter was increasingly drawn closer to the magistracy in a common aim to stamp out Quakerism. Clement Writer was a Quaker who fell foul of Baxter. He described how he was summoned to Worcester to debate with Baxter in his chamber, with a clerical minion as witness. Writer reported Baxter's taunt to him: '*What, dare you not declare your Fault? You must not fear any thing now in this time of Liberty.*' This was reported speech from a prejudiced source. Even if it were an accurate verbatim record, it is open to different interpretations. Baxter was far from welcoming a 'Liberty' which took in Quakers, Jesuits, Ranters and Anabaptists. But even if spoken in irony, the exchange rings true at a different level: as in the parallel case, when Bourne confronted Major General Berry and Baxter acted the *voyeur*. Baxter was collaborating with the régime in ever more pronounced ways.[155]

The results of that involvement were at times confusing. Several of the Ministerial Associations took part in ordinations, but neither Baxter nor the Worcestershire Association ever adopted the practice, although Baxter recommended that Parliament should make it legal. At the same time Baxter was anxious that unnecessary scruples should not stand in the way of the primary task: of strengthening ministerial discipline. Thomas Willis complained, in a letter of 14 December 1657 to Baxter, that his elasticity had been exploited by Thomas Brooks. According to Willis, Brooks was spreading the word that Baxter thought that soldiers and the like *could* be constant, ordinary preachers. Willis presumed that Baxter was referring to a *de facto* rather than *de jure* position. In his reply of 17 December, Baxter reaffirmed his judgement for ordination, 'though not for the absolute necessity of it to the very Being of the ministry in all times and cases'. He disliked *'Preachinge Soldiers'*, but soldiers joined with commissioners were legitimately participating in ministerial efforts to keep out the unworthy. He wanted 'to stop the mouths of unjust objectors' by reciting what was being done; he of all people was not wishing to revive the reign of Saltmarsh and Dell. Willis's reply on 22 December was gracious but indicated that he felt Baxter had largely missed the point:

> I suppose you are as fully sensible as my selfe that the Designe of This Age, managed by Jesuiticall Agents and their Instruments, is against the very Foundation of the Gospell-Ministry, and they have prevailed with 1000s to the drawing them quite off from the true Ministry (O the sad state of such Soules!) upon the Account of the pretended Falsnesse of the Call as Popish and Antichristian, the chiefe Argument I have had to doe with in this Controversye.

On 24 December Brooks was giving *his* side of the story. Willis had got it wrong. Brooks was not arguing that any Tom, Dick or Harry could preach. On the same day Willis wrote again to Baxter with the request that he should ignore whatever Brooks wrote to him. Baxter's reply to Brooks, on 2 January 1658, was pragmatic and conciliatory: 'with you, perhaps judicious Auditoryes refusinge to hear such men may restraine them.' Baxter's own experience was something of a different nature: 'But with us it is but stoppinge into Herefordshire or the skirts of Wales and allmost any man that can talke loud may be applauded.' But Baxter was pleased that Brooks was for ordination, and now that he had established that Willis was not arguing for the necessity of ordination *at all times*, he could see no reason why both — professing they agreed with Baxter — should not join together to prevent public scandal.[156]

The time of Papist advance was not the time for self-indulgent squabbles. Nor was it the time to do or say anything which might cast odium on ministers or on the magistrate. That belief — which was to inspire his *Holy Commonwealth* — was expressed most powerfully and succinctly in a letter which Baxter wrote to John Howe on 3 April 1658:

> I would have you very tender and cautelous in publishinge any of the neglects of Governors: A time there is for open plaine dealinge: but as long as the case is not palpable, desprate and notorious, and you have leave to speake privately, that may suffice you. The well-fare of the Church and Peace of the Nations, lyes as much on the publike Reputation of good Magistrates which therefore we should not diminish but promote. I would awaken your jealousyie to a carefull (but very secrett and silent) observance of the Infidells, and Papists, who are very high and busye under severall garbes, especially of Seekers, Vanists and Behmenists. Should they infect our vitalls, or get into the saddle, where are we then?

Baxter then launched into a eulogy on Cromwell, far surpassing the public dedicatory epistles to his son later in the year which caused him so much opprobrium after the Restoration:

> The Protector is noted as a man of a Catholike spiritt, desirous of the unity and Peace of all the servants of Christ. We desire nothing in the world (at home) so much, as the exercise and success of such a disposition.

To further the work of peace, Baxter wanted Cromwell to consider some healing principles, to win the consent to them of one or two leading men of the Episcopalians, Presbyterians, Congregationalists, Erastians and Anabaptists, have them published and a freely elected Assembly discuss and adopt them. His letter concluded with a reaffirmation of his trust in Cromwell: 'I am confident as I live that (by Gods Blessinge) he may happily accomplish so much of this worke if he be willinge, as shall settle us in much peace, and prevent and heale abundance of our distempers.'[157]

Baxter's concern about Popery was driving him into the arms of Lauderdale as well as those of the Protector. Their curious friendship began with a service that Lauderdale performed for Baxter, while he was himself a prisoner in Windsor Castle. Lauderdale could read French, and he became an invaluable help to Baxter in translating works which would otherwise be inaccessible to him. In one letter to Baxter on 11 June 1658, Lauderdale warned him against being over-charitable to Papists: a correspondent in Holland had been horrified at Baxter's hope that thousands of them would be saved.[158] A week later Baxter wrote to Peter du Moulin for a translation of his father's anti-Papal writings. Lauderdale had not sated Baxter's thirst:

> I am the more urgent because I am confident the Papists are playinge their games in England as busyly this day as they did in times that we accounted worse: and therefore we have but need of helpe consideringe the advantages that our Liberty, confusions, and sects do give them.[159]

In his correspondence with Mrs Gell in August and September of 1658 they agreed about the lamentable lack of respect shown to the clergy, when Mrs Gell's private consultation with her blameless minister, Woodbridge, was as censurable an act in her neighbours' eyes as 'mixed dancing or bare breasts'.[160] Some clergy had deserved their low esteem. In a letter to the Laudian Peter Heylyn, on 20 October 1658, Baxter welcomed his assurance that he was not of the 'Grotian' religion, and hoped that more of the Protestant divines would disown it.[161]

The death of Oliver Cromwell was not the end of Baxter's hopes. The accession of his son, Richard, promised a renewed war upon Popery, and its Grotian twin, and a more immediate realisation of ecumenical aims. That was the gist of Durie's letter to Baxter on 20 December 1658, when he discussed with him the best way of exploiting the new Protector's goodwill.[162] John Swinfen was one of Baxter's friends elected to Richard's Parliament, which met in January 1659. Baxter wrote to him on 17 February, whilst in the process of writing his *Holy Commonwealth*, and his advice touched on similar concerns: the spread of Popery under various masks; the belief that a fully free Parliament, *democratically elected*, would ensure the triumph of the ungodly; the ideal of clerical discipline exercised by ministers (whether Presbyterian, Independent or of whatever party) in association with magistrates' officers; the next-best state, as stringent a qualification for electors, *as for the elected*, in the *Humble Petition and Advice*; a settlement of a godly militia in each county; an elective or successive government. If elective, Baxter wanted Parliament to choose a Standing Council of

State; from that Council four men be chosen to succeed the Prince, one of whom would be chosen by lot. If successive, Baxter relied on education by godly tutors to make him 'more ours than his father's'. The letter ended with the familiar lament at the spread of Jesuits and the encouragement which they received by pleas for democracy. He pleaded with Swinfen to take up the cause of the imprisoned Lauderdale.[163]

The concerns expressed in his private correspondence were reflected in three of his public writings: *The Grotian Religion Discovered; A Key for Catholicks* and *A Holy Commonwealth*. All three were composed between 1658 and 1659 as a *concerted* exposure of the ramifications of Popish Plots. In the first pamphlet Baxter showed how the 'Grotian' plans for unity with Rome, favoured by the Laudians, had produced the Civil War. The second work placed this design in its historic setting of Papist plans for world domination. The general hostile reception given to it was one of the reasons (according to the 'Meditations' of 25 April 1659 that he appended to *A Holy Commonwealth*) that he never in the end completed that third work.

His attack on the 'Grotian Religion' was sparked off by his controversies with Pierce. As proof 'that England hath befriended the design of Grotius', Baxter referred to various writings of William Prynne. He wrote of his debt to Grotius for many insights, and approved of his pacificatory ends. He compared these ends to those pursued by Eliot in New England, Jesuit missionaries, Hall, Davenant, Morton and Amyraut. Unfortunately Grotius had chosen the wrong means for those ends: he had sought unity by acceding to Rome's terms. But the end of unity was the increase of holiness, whereas Popery *decreased* holiness. Baxter did not want peace at any price: 'I had rather have a contention that promoteth Holiness and Salvation, than a Peace that doth destroy it. For its no Means with me that destroyeth the End.' He referrred to his *A Key for Catholicks*, 'not yet Printed, but finished, and going to the Press', in which the full Romish strategy stands revealed. In the meantime he drew attention to worrying features of Papal advance. He owned to 'a strong suspicion that the Papists had a finger in the Pie on both sides', and found support for that belief in Prynne's proof, at Laud's trial, that Richelieu promoted the Irish Rebellion, and Bramhall's cryptic remark that 'there was a Bishop in the world' who 'did help to kindle that unnatural war', which Baxter took to be an allusion to Richelieu. The Papist infiltration into the sects, 'especially the Quakers and Seekers', was particularly disturbing. Baxter estimated that there were hundreds of them at work 'under the Vizor of any of these sects, playing their parts in England'. He believed that it was 'the Grotian design' which was 'the cause of all our wars and dangers here in England'. The King was not a Papist, but who better than a 'Moderate Protestant' married to a 'Moderate Papist' to further the Grotian design? When he had served their purpose, they put him to death.[164]

A Key for Catholicks – like *A Holy Commonwealth* – was dedicated to Richard Cromwell. Attempts later to pass off the gesture as a pious convention are belied by the urgency and personal nature of his appeal to the Protector:

> I beseech you therefore that you receive not this as you would do a Scholastick or Philosophical Disputation about such things as seem not to concern you, but as you would interest your self in a Disputation upon the Question, Whether you should be deposed or murdered as a Heretick?

The invisibility and ubiquity of the enemy made the task of the godly supremely difficult: 'We fear the Masked Papists and Infidels, more than the bare-faced, or than any enemy.' Even if Baxter would have preferred to suspend judgement on whether the Pope was Antichrist, Richelieu's manipulations confirmed that he was. Baxter's recital of Jesuit plots was lifted bodily from Prynne:

> I had rather you would read in Mr. Prins *Works of Darkness brought to Light*, and *Canterburies Tryall* and his *Romes Masterpiece* and his *Royall Favourite*, than have it from me: And if any reader be disaffected to the writer of it, let them at least peruse impartially the *Evidences* produced by him.

Prynne had blotted his copy-book with his recommendation against tithes, but he remained Baxter's seminal influence. He quoted at length Prynne's revelation of the fulsome language of Charles, as Prince of Wales, when addressing the Pope and commented: 'So far prevailed they with Prince Charls, our late King.' He gave equal space to the Habernfeld Plot, discovered by Prynne, even although it had the blemish of being a Popish Plot *against* Laud. He quoted excitedly from the Jesuit's letter, found by Prynne in Laud's study, which gave the declaration of intent: 'We shall procure the odium of King-Killing to fall upon them.' Baxter thought of this as 'the frame of the Papists plot'.

How to *prove* Papal power and interest in the King's armies, and then in his enemies'? Baxter becomes embarrassedly circumlocutive at this point:

It will be expected that he that asserteth any thing in matters of this moment, should prove it by more than moral evidence of greatest probabilities: and therefore I shall be sparing in my Assertions: but yet I shall say in general, that tho' the business would be troublesome, chargeable and tedious, to call together the Witnesses that are necessary, yet Witnesses and Evidences may be had, to prove that the Papists have had more to do in our affairs, than most men are aware of, without any positive Assertions.

Levellers-turned-Royalists were not a surprising phenomenon to Baxter. Sexby and his colleagues were working with their natural collaborators in Spain to take away the Protector's life: 'And whence are these Jesuitical Treasonable Pamphlets (such as Killing no Murder), provoking men to take away his life?' Baxter turned for 'copious Proofs' back to Prynne and to his anti-Laudian material. The Jesuits' design was now 'managed under a sort of "Juglers" ', helped by their enviable capacity to metamorphose themselves into any shape and size they wanted to adopt.[165]

It would be a mistake to sever *A Holy Commonwealth* from its anti-Papal background. A bitter personal postscript makes the point that it was 'written while the Lord Protector (prudently, piously, faithfully, to his immortal Honour, how ill soever you have used him) did exercise the Government'. It was, in other words, written at a time of hope: when the Christian magistrate could repel the Jesuit advances. The fear of Popery permeates the pamphlet. Contzen's and Campanella's plans for restoring Popery are printed in the preface to *A Holy Commonwealth*. His attack on Vane's *Healing Question* echoes Prynne's fear that the Jesuits' tactics were working — 'have plaied their game under vizor of other Sects'. Their design to keep the magistrate from interfering in matters of faith and worship was 'the present setting up of Popery in England'.

It was an anti-millenarian work. Baxter saw millenarianism as a Popish Plot:

> Which I perceive some Papists of late very busy, under their several masks, to indigitate, partly in order to persuade men that the Church is a Body that hath a universal visible Head, which must be Christ's Vicar, but in the interspace betwixt his first and second coming.

This was consonant with his warning to Bromley in 1654 about Papist interests in encouraging the millenarian wild men. It was besides a distraction — he declared *himself* almost neutral about the subject — which

took men's attentions from what was possible *now*. His treatise was on
the contrary sober and pragmatic: holiness was within men's immediate
grasp. What was needed was the programme outlined already to Harley
and Swinfen: the right sort of voter, and 'Parliaments of the wisest and
most pious men'. To make a Commonwealth holy required no elaborate
fantasies: 'Be awakened then, ye Christian Magistrates, to keep the
sword in your own hand.' Baxter was indifferent to niceties of politics:

> And we will not contend either for or against such jingles as Mr.
> Harrington and others do lay so great a stress upon. Monarchy,
> Aristocracy or Democracy will serve us (though a mixed Govern-
> ment, or limited Monarchy we judge best; and Democracy worst, in
> most places) so we may be secured in the main.

It is hard to see in these words a resounding commitment to the theory
of a balanced constitution. For all his revulsion from Hobbes's anti-
clericalism he *shared* the basic belief that inspired it: that the Church/
Commonwealth distinction was a false and mischievous one; that
priests' claims to elevate themselves above princes on the analogy of the
superiority of the soul over the body had been responsible for most of
the misfortunes that befell England in recent years. Baxter defined
approvingly a 'Theocracy' as a state 'when Princes govern *From God,
By God*, and *For God* in all things', not disapprovingly as one where
princes had the shadow of power and priests had the substance. The
chief punishment for crimes was reserved for the after-life, but that did
not prevent murder and theft from being punished on earth. Notorious
impiety should likewise not only be punished in the hereafter by God,
but also here and now by the magistrate. Against the fashionable 'Utopias' and 'Cities of the Sun', Baxter offered a pragmatic insistence on
the value of excluding the unworthy from elections, whether as choos-
ers or chosen. Thus for him the ministers' disciplinary task of separating
the precious from the vile was not a theocratic challenge *to* the magistrate's office (as it was to Erastus, Coleman and Prynne), but the necessary complement *of* the 'theocratic' (in his understanding of the word)
nature of the magistrate's office. Where ministers went wrong was, not
in exercising their discipline, but in meddling in state matters which
were not their concern. Baxter looked to a civil officer, or censor,
working in every parish, and to a magistrate exercising his veto, to prevent clerical high-handedness, or as Baxter put it, to 'stop the Erastians'
mouths'. Baxter believed that magistrates should not abdicate *their*
responsibility — a theme to which he would return with particular force

after the Restoration with his *Christian Directory*: 'It would long ago have quieted the Clubs, if the Magistrates had kept their power to themselves, and also had not made themselves the Prelates' executioners.' To satisfy their ambitions, the clergy have often made a great deal of fuss about the abuse of power by the civil magistrate. Emperors like Nero have had a consistently bad clerical press. But Baxter asked their misdeeds to be set in perspective: 'Where the Emperors killed an hundred christians, had they but turned loose the vulgar rabble, they would have killed a thousand, or made an end of this.'[166] He would say the same later in his *Christian Directory*: 'I do not think Nero or Diocletian, martyred near so many as the People turned loose upon them would have done.'[167]

By printing only the eighth and ninth chapters of Baxter's *Holy Commonwealth* in his volume of Baxter's writings, R.B. Schlatter conveys the misleading impression that a concern for the balanced constitution was at the heart of his philosophy. In these chapters, it is true, he develops the constitutional safeguards which he found lacking in Harrington's *Oceana*. It is equally true that his *preference* was for 'a mixed Government, or limited Monarchy'. But he showed a cheerful willingness to work any constitution – monarchy, aristocracy or even democracy – which secured godliness. The crucial issue was Popery: under which form of government could the Jesuit threat be best countered? The twelfth chapter – 'Of due Obedience to Rulers' – reveals Baxter's concern, not to impose limits on the sovereign's authority, *but to take fetters from him*. Even a Nero did not justify resistance. And although his thirteenth chapter – 'Account of the Reasons that persuaded me (and many others) to take up Armes in obedience to the Parliament in the Late Warres' – dutifully recites the constitutional objections by Parliamentarians to the extensions of the King's powers, in much the same way as he would do later in his autobiography, nobody reading it could be under the illusion that this was what the Civil War was *primarily* about. As he himself said, 'The Warre was begun in our streets before the King or Parliament had any Armies.' And the war was begun in the streets – first in Ireland, and then in England – by men who would obey a Nero, but not a 'Popish Royall Favourite'. Quoting fully from Prynne's revelations of Royalist complicity in past Popish Plots, Baxter adds. 'I will forbear to rake any further into these calamities.' Not quite however: he then shows how the Irish Rebellion had to be related to the progess which 'the same party' had made in England; how if Baxter and his fellow Protestants had not taken up arms, a victorious King would have been ruled by his 'impious and popish Armies'.[168]

A Holy Commonwealth is an unfinished work. His 'Meditations', written on 25 April 1659, explain why. He had been discouraged by the fall from power of Richard Cromwell and by the hostile reception to his *A Key for Catholicks* (written only months before *A Holy Commonwealth*). Both were inimical to the strategy of the later work: men would understand the need for a Holy Commonwealth when Baxter had exposed in *A Key for Catholicks* the dimensions of Catholic intrigue; and with Richard Cromwell as Protector the existing Commonwealth could be made holy overnight — no Utopias, no Oceanas, needed — *if only the magistrate used his full powers*. The clergy were one obstacle to magistracy. Baxter may not have liked the disrespectful language that Hobbes and Harrington used when speaking of clergymen, and yet he shared their insight that good government hinged on the subordination of the clergy to the civil magistrate. Professor Pocock has noted Harrington's 'vain search for the clerical adversary to answer him' and his failure to make 'a vigorous rebuttal' of Baxter's *Holy Commonwealth*. This may have been caused by Harrington's recognition that Baxter's concern, that clergymen should be respected and that their disciplinary powers over their flock should be strengthened, was not the same thing as a defence of clerical claims to *superiority* over the civil power.[169] Indeed Baxter's objection to Harrington was not that his democratic fantasies were an affront to mixed monarchy, *but that they were an expression of crypto-Popery*. One critical passage from Baxter's manuscript omitted by Sylvester refers to Harrington and Nevill in the following terms: 'he and his helper seeme by the contrivance to be of the old religion, I meane that of old Rome, though something as if they were Christians be intersperst.'[170] Dr Nuttall has already drawn attention to Sylvester's omission of Baxter's manuscript references to John Owen's part in the downfall of Richard Cromwell.[171] Baxter felt that Owen's intrigues with Army grandees were part and parcel of the same captiousness which had succeeded in expanding the concepts of 'fundamentals' in religion to the point where prospects for unity were wrecked, and which had produced the intransigent Savoy Conference Declaration. Here was a good example of the clergyman meddling in politics, to the ruin of the civil magistrate, which Baxter deplored every bit as much as Harrington or Hobbes did.

Meddling divines were one obstacle to good magistracy; meddling soldiers were even more of a nuisance. Baxter's emphasis on franchise reform did not represent his search for limits to be placed upon the Protector's absolutism. Rather, they were his way of strengthening

Parliamentary support of the Protectorate against the Army. Baxter would spend a large part of his later political life in efforts to explain away the provocative passages in his *A Holy Commonwealth*. His real regrets were of an entirely different nature. He believed that he had helped to destroy the Protectorate with that treatise. This was quite contrary to his *intentions*, of course, but the *effect* of his writings was to alarm opponents to the need to take preventive action swiftly, if a Holy Commonwealth were not to be established. In manuscript Baxter would record after the Restoration his real thoughts about both *A Key for Catholicks* and *A Holy Commonwealth*:

> And those two books as proved the meanes of the protectors down-fall (which was not my intent) partly by enraging the Officers (to whom I had lent them) by charging them with the Kings blood, and partly by provoking Our turbulent leading sectaries against him, when they thought that he would close with those whom they called Presbyterians (though the Government pleaded for in my disputations is not Presbytery, but the primitive Episcopacy).[172]

Sylvester had more excuse for leaving this passage out of his *Reliquiae Baxterianae* than the Antrim reference.[173] Baxter himself had crossed it out in manuscript, as perhaps revealing more than he intended. But even if he had not crossed it out, it is difficult to see how Sylvester could have let it stand in the published autobiography – any more than his swingeing attacks on Owen, his references to the Antrim commission or his rejection of Harrington as a Papist. Sylvester wanted to show that Baxter was not the anti-royalist that opponents made him out to be. He was as anxious, as Baxter himself was to be after the Restoration, to demonstrate that *A Holy Commonwealth*, in opposing Harringtonian democracy, was a tract *for* monarchy; that the dedicatory epistles to Richard Cromwell were the lapses in good taste – and no more binding than that – which happened when a clergyman was let loose into politics; that the most regrettable effect of the treatise was in making Cromwellian rule seem respectable, not in killing it off (which we see was Baxter's real grief).

A Holy Commonwealth is an anti-Papal work. Did Baxter really believe that Harrington was 'of the old Religion', as he confided in his manuscript? There were two possible answers. One, which Baxter pursued with the zeal of a Marxist theologian, was that *objectively* a Protestant fanatic could advance the Papist cause which *subjectively* he deplored. By weakening Protestant certainty in the identification of Rome with Antichrist, a daft millenarian like Major Wilkie became an instrument of the Jesuit design. But there was also a second argument which Baxter pursued with equal devotion: that radicals among the sects were *literally* metamorphosed Jesuits. This proposition did not seem incredible to the man who later would write *The Certainty of the Worlds of Spirits*. Baxter pursued both arguments in his *Holy Commonwealth*, even if they were not always compatible. Harrington and Vane were chided for weakening the authority of the civil magistrate and therefore for aiding Rome, but were also themselves denounced for being among the 'Masks' or 'Visors' which the Jesuits take on to avoid detection. In either case, the details of Harrington's scheme are of secondary importance. *A Holy Commonwealth* is as much, and as little, an answer to Harrington as Prynne's *The Sword of Christian Magistracy* was an answer to William Dell. For both men, the importance of their opponents lay, not in what they had written, *but in what they symbolised*: the spirit of anarchy, the destruction of magistracy, the triumph of Popery.

William Dell's sermon, *Right Reformation* of 1646, had provoked Prynne's massive reply. Dell had attacked the orthodox clergy as the last prop of Antichrist and denied the magistrate the power to intervene in spiritual matters. Prynne called such objections a 'scandal and reproach upon Magistrates and their Authority'. He believed that the magistrate must not spare even his closest friends or relatives if they propagate false doctrine: 'he SHAL SURELY KIL THEM (without mercy) and his own hand shal be first upon them to put them to death; and afterwards the hands of all the people, and they shal stone them with stones that they dye.' He even cited precedents for 'corporall and capitall punishment inflicted by Christian Princes and Magistrates against Blasphemous, and execrable Cursers and Swearers'.

Prynne's pamphlet was published in 1647 and re-issued in 1653. At neither date could it be said to have had immediate political implications. It was written in the vacuum between his disenchantment with monarchy in 1643 and his restoration of faith in 1648; it was reprinted at a time when the authority which he recognised as legal was exiled overseas. In other words it was not a blueprint for direct political action; but neither was it an abstract exercise in political theory. At a time when Prynne could not have foreseen the desired transfer of power he was nevertheless hungering after a *discipline*. Against the anarchical implications of Dell's doctrine, Prynne wished to emphasise the totalitarian non-censurability of the magistrate, *any magistrate*: that is why the message continued to have relevance even when it was republished

in 1653 with a hostile régime in power. Dell had argued that outward
punishments cannot reform the beliefs of men. He had used this argument against magistracy, to stress the *futility* of outward compliance.
Oddly enough Hobbes had used the same argument *for* magistracy, to
stress the *utility* of outward compliance: 'as for the inward thought,
and belief of men, which humane Governors can take no notice (for
God only knoweth the heart)'. But to Prynne the dichotomy was arti-
ficial: 'the very body and outward man infect the created soule infused
into it.' Constantine was a useful person to Hobbes, *because he kept
order*; but he was revered by Prynne and Baxter, *because he enforced
discipline.*[174]

Prynne felt the need to defend *the concept behind Constantine's
rule* — even when there was no immediate prospect of a Constantine
enforcing it — at a time when Jesuits and Quakers were impugning it.
Thus in 1653 his position was very similar to that of Baxter, who
wished to uphold the existing magistracy without condoning regicide
or the execution of Christopher Love. Thereafter their paths began to
diverge: most spectacularly over the question of whether ministers
should be paid tithes if they failed to administer the Lord's Supper, but
itself only part of a wider question about the allegiance owed to an ille-
gal government. We have seen how hopes of godliness and fears of
Popery drove Baxter gradually into closer involvement with the Protectorate. We have also seen that no single source provided richer authentication for Baxter's fears of Popery than William Prynne. Baxter at times
betrayed unease about the *acceptability* of the source, not about its
reliability.[175] He accepted from Prynne the reliability of such statements as these: 'Cardinal Richelieu was a promoter of the Rebellion in
Ireland'; Jesuits infiltrated first the episcopacy, and then the Army;
Jesuits worked first through the monarchy and then against it; Quakers
were Jesuits; hundreds of Papists, Friars and Jesuits were at this time
'under the Vizor' of the sects 'playing their part in England'. Yet there
was one important difference. The material from which Baxter made
his points in the 1650s was drawn almost exclusively from Prynne's
writings *between 1643 and 1645.* They marked the low point of
Prynne's relationship with monarchy. The interception of Charles I's
correspondence had been a traumatic blow for a man like Prynne, who
had in an earlier period sincerely sought to defend Charles I from Laudian clericalism. Now he was deprived of excuses: *The Popish Royall
Favourite* was his new bitter description of the man once revered as a
Christian Emperor. The mood did not last. Prynne swung back to the
stance which was more congenial to him, with the perception that the

enemy of Christian Magistracy was no longer Laudian clericalism but Army egalitarianism. He rallied to Charles, sought to win acceptance for reconciliation on the basis of his Isle of Wight concessions, and de-plored Pride's Purge and the regicide. Thereafter he was an unwavering Royalist: he had no truck with the Engagement, Oliver Cromwell or Richard Cromwell. The rightful King was Charles II. He was embarrassed in this later royalism by the material in his pamphlets of 1643 to 1645. Supporters of regicide asked why they *should* trust Charles I's word after Prynne's own revelations, and exposed the inconsistencies in his position in such pamphlets as *Prynne Against Prin*.

Now it was precisely this earlier material which Baxter found so fas-cinating in the 1650s. The paradoxical position was reached that, while Prynne was dabbling in Cavalier plots to restore the monarchy, Baxter was arguing for the need to support the civil magistracy − in part because of those very Jesuit plots which he had learned about in the first place from Prynne. In 1653 both Prynne and Baxter felt the need to defend the *concept* behind Constantine's rule; in 1659 Baxter had found his Constantine *in person* in Richard Cromwell − even if he never saw him, spoke to him, wrote to him or heard from him.[176] That is the difference between *The Sword of Christian Magistracy* and *A Holy Commonwealth*.

It was not surprising that critics of *A Holy Commonwealth* failed to detect a difference of substance between Baxter and Prynne. Both had attacked Harrington and were forever sniffing at Popish Plots in un-likely places. John Rogers, in his *A Christian Concertation*, claimed to be in pursuit of 'the SPIT-FIRE' (Prynne), when he was set upon by 'the HUNTER' (Baxter) who came to the assistance of 'the SPIT-FIRE'. Afterwards Rogers met 'the Fox' (Harrington), not of the same comp-any but at the same employment. Rogers saw Baxter's *Key for Catho-licks* as a second *Gangraena*: breathing the same spirit of intolerance. Baxter had declined from composing 'the SAINTS REST' to planning 'the SAINTS RUINE'. Rogers blamed Prynne's malign influence:

[Prynne] would make us believe (if we would be so besotted) that the Commonwealth is a BASTARD of the Jesuites begetting; (Mr. B. seconds him we need not question) telling us stories of Campanella, Parsons, Watson, etc., and of their designs against King James, and the Nation then; about An.1604 or 1605.

Rogers was concerned with the *real* Popish Plot. He was sceptical of the Jesuits' claims to ubiquity, fuelled by Cromwell's revelation in his speech of 4 September 1654 that 'they have a Consistory and Council that RULES all the Affairs of England', and believed that they exaggerated their own importance in order to deflect Protestants from loyalty to their Commonwealth. This was the Jesuits' master-plot: 'to make us believe that to be their SPAWN, which they never had the least SPERMA of'.[177] In much the same spirit Coleridge would respond in a later age to Baxter's revelations: 'The Pope in his Conclave had about the same influence in Charles's fate as the Pope's eye in a leg of mutton.' The Jesuits' skill was to make men swallow these fantastic fictions while they got on with their *real* plots unmolested. Coleridge, for all his scepticism of a master plan decided at a consistory, believed profoundly that the persecution of Baxter after the Restoration *was* 'part of the Popish scheme of the Cabal'.[178] So too Rogers wanted no slackening in the 'Godly Jealousie' commended by Prynne, since he did not doubt that 'many doubtless are in England under Disguises and Folding-Doors'. But because the Jesuits are more afraid of England as a Commonwealth than as a Kingdom they would be happy to claim the Commonwealth as *their* progeny in order to put gullible Protestants like Prynne and Baxter off the scent. The men who would expose Jesuit treachery — Baxter and Prynne — were themselves therefore their first victims.

Rogers throughout sees Prynne and Baxter as a partnership, 'as between the Womb and the Breasts'. He correctly described Baxter's debt to Prynne: 'let Mr. P. but generate matter, Mr. B. is as ready to generate meat to keep it alive'. But he missed the *point* of the collaboration: that Baxter was using Prynne's material to recruit support for a Commonwealth that was on the brink of becoming 'Holy'. When Rogers attacked the logic of the argument that 'the Jesuits plotted a Commonwealth for England An.1605 therefore a Commonwealth in England was the Jesuits Plot', he was scoring a palpable hit against Prynne, but missing altogether the man who had invested his hopes in Richard Cromwell.

Baxter and Prynne could be bracketed together in their dislike of toleration and liberty of conscience. The Jesuit whom they both loved to quote, Contzen, was quoted tellingly by Rogers against themselves: 'To preserve Popery, that no other religion should be permitted', and Rogers wanted to know therefore whether the destruction of personal freedom was the way to destroy Popery — or the way to introduce it.[179] Baxter's political argument against tolerating Catholicism was accompanied by great magnanimity towards individual Catholics. This was not in itself unusual in seventeenth-century England. Pym had said in his speech of 17 April 1640 that 'we must not looke on a Papist as hee is in himselfe but as hee is in the body of the Church': war against Antichrist on the ideological front was often (although not invariably) compatible with peaceful coexistence at the level of personal relationships.[180] This was not true of Prynne; but it was true of Baxter. Unfairly Rogers seized on Baxter's willingness to cite 'many among the Papists that truly fear God' to suggest that he was more at home with Popery than he would like to have acknowledged. Thus Rogers had it both ways. Baxter's intolerance was denounced as a Popish trait; but his respect for individual Catholics was denounced as Popish fellow-travelling.

But in one respect Rogers' criticism of Baxter was fair and shrewd. If he was misled by Baxter's dependence on Prynne, and by Baxter's own past record of hostility to Cromwell, into assuming that his real wish was for the return to monarchy which Prynne was advocating so shrilly, he was not misled about the hankering after *one sovereign authority* which was at the heart of Baxter's rejection of Harrington. Rogers correctly saw the Baxter of 1658 and 1659 as the unswerving enemy of balance and moderation:

> whose Pinion or Pen is hardened into his own Opinion for the Government of a single person, and recovery of the Kingdome again; and not so for a due and equal temperament of the whole Body, by an even Balance and proportion of the four Elements, and so Aliments of the Politic Body, conducing to the most concinnate and right use of all the Functions in it, as for the Mastery of the One above the other, and all the Rest; which would be the inevitable Ruine of All at last.[181]

'Government of a single Person', rejection of 'an even Balance and proportion of the four Elements', acknowledgement of 'the Mastery of the One above the other, and all the Rest': all these Baxter could, and did, hold without believing that the corollary was a restoration of a *Kingdom*, or that Charles Stuart rather than Richard Cromwell should be that 'single Person'.

Henry Stubbe joined Rogers in an attack upon Baxter's *Holy Commonwealth*. To Stubbe, Baxter was 'a meere Glow-worme in literature, who borrowed his luster from the darknesse of the night, and ignorance of them he converses with'.[182] Much of Stubbe's attack took the traditional snobbish line of the university don confronting the man without a degree. But he made a valid point when he criticised Baxter's failure to distinguish between different schools of thought within English

Catholicism. As Stubbe pointed out, many English Catholics hated Jesuits more than Baxter himself did. But whereas Rogers saw Baxter as a man looking over the water for a return of the Stuarts, Stubbe recognised that Baxter's loyalties were pulling in an opposite direction. Stubbe attacked him as a lackey of the *Cromwellian* Court:

> I know not whose pensioner he is of late become; but any man may see whose projects he venteth: if he be not bribed, I am told he hath been cajolled, and caressed with complements and presents into an esteem for a compliance with those whom he ought to detest no lesse than others. Possibly this is not true; and possibly our young-states-man may be such a novice as to be insensibly drawn in by Court-artifices.

Like Rogers, Stubbe was repelled by Baxter's craving for a single authority. Baxter had said that the Pythagoreans cursed the number '2' because it departed from unity; *a fortiori* democracy was ruled out of court. Stubbe commented: 'Is not this a fine argument for a Theologue? Doth not it overthrow the Trinity, as well as a Common-wealth?' But Stubbe saw that — given Baxter's contempt for the people — government by one person was the obvious answer. Stubbe believed that the multitude is 'not so bad as Mr. B. thinks', and suggested that he would have been most at home in the time of Caligula, when horses were given ministerial office. Stubbe thought that Baxter's learning was cumulative in the way that Strafford's treason had been: a number of deficient facts piled on top of one another constituted a case. Stubbe deplored Baxter's persecuting spirit: 'I am informed that he strook a Quaker openly.' Nor did he think much better of Baxter's reliance upon God's judgement in the form of monster births for Mrs Hutchinson and Mrs Dyer. By the same token, Baxter's bodily infirmities could be seen to be signs of divine displeasure:

> by Hypochondriacall distempers he hath witnessed against the flatulency of his brain; that by the maladies of his spleen and rivers of blood issuing from his nose, he doth wonderfully confound his nose, and sanguinary principles . . . in fine, that the Atrophy of his body is a manifestation of the Sterility of his principles.

Sir Henry Vane had a name that was manna to a punster. 'This Kederminster wit' was how Stubbe described the variations that Baxter rang upon his adversary's name. But why *was* Baxter so hostile to

Vane? Baxter called Vane a 'Hider', but why? As Stubbe said: 'I do not apprehend his reason for it; since Sir H.V. hath never declined to give forth an account of the hope that is in him.' Vane may have been woolly and eclectic; he was not subterranean. But he had to be in order to fit Baxter's stereotype. The Jesuits worked by stealth; their primary aim was to deny the magistrate the power to intervene in spiritual matters. But Vane followed Dell in just such a denial; *ergo* they were Papists who operated by stealth. In defence of Vane, Stubbe pointed out that he had not divested the civil magistrate of spiritual power in order to give it to the Pope. Vane had not needed to go to Italy, and consult Bellarmine or Parsons, to deny the civil magistrate the power of intervening in religion. There were plenty of Scottish and Dutch sources on the Presbyterian side to provide similar arguments in their quarrel with the Erastians. Indeed Stubbe indicated that Baxter could have derived *his* arguments from the Erastian side of that controversy, or even from Catholic, imperial, anti-Papal writings. There was a particular injustice in making regicide the banner of the Vanists, when Vane had been out of sympathy with the regicides: 'If he had not been interested in making the Vanists odious, how come they (who were none at all) to be more Regicides than the late Protector?' How indeed? And had Oliver Cromwell not been an enemy to ministers and to tithes? And had he not been a champion of religious toleration? Why should he escape the stigma of 'Papist'? Prynne had been consistent. He had attacked Cromwell as a Richard III revived. But Baxter's late-found partiality for the Cromwells (father and son), together with his readiness to make 'Vanists' the scapegoats, derived, as Stubbe perceived, from the answer which he gave to the critical question (which Stubbe left to the end of his pamphlet): 'Whether the civil Magistrate hath anything to do in matters of spiritual concernment?'[183] Vane said no; Richard Cromwell might be persuaded to say yes. *A Holy Commonwealth* was Baxter's demonstration to Richard Cromwell how easy it was to say yes.

Baxter never finished *A Holy Commonwealth* because Richard Cromwell's enemies (who included John Owen) had prevented him from saying yes by securing his overthrow. April 1659 is the end of the euphoria. On 25 May John Howe is giving Baxter a grim résumé from the inside of the manoeuvres that destroyed the prospects of a 'Holy Commonwealth'. Howe described the Council in Oliver Cromwell's time as divided in two: one following the Protector in policies to please the nation; the other, mainly Army-dominated, seeking to frustrate the will of the nation in order to secure liberty of conscience. Richard Cromwell had followed in his father's footsteps, and his initial successes threatened the position of the Army grandees. They sought to protect themselves by dissolving Parliament and calling upon 'wild-headed persons of all sorts' to reinforce their ranks. These however infused into the inferior officers a disaffection to government by a single person. This current became so strong that it swept away the restraining powers of the chief officers. Howe wanted Baxter to have no illusions about the men who were now at the top. By May 1659 they were in a strategic position to execute the Popish Plots which had been Baxter's recurrent nightmare:

> for such persons as are now at the head of affaires will blast religion if God prevent not the designe you writ mee of some time since to introduce infidelitie or Popery they have opportunity enough to effect. I know some leading men are not Christians: religion is lost out of England further then as it can creep into corners.[184]

Five days after Howe's letter, William Allen was responding sympathetically to Baxter's efforts to draw Baptists into a union of the godly. At the same time he remonstrated with Baxter for imposing unnecessary barriers by false allegations that Baptists had been regicides. Allen came to Vane's rescue:

> And if by the Vanists, of whom likewise you charge the King's death, you intend a party headed and engaged by Sir Hen. Vane, its thought you doe him a great deale of wrong, because he was so farre from heading and ingaging a party in that work, as that he left the Parlt. whilst they were about it, and dissatisfied; and in the late Parlt. washed his hands of it.[185]

Allen was only repeating in private what Stubbe was saying publicly. After the Restoration Colonel Birch acted as an intermediary between Baxter and Vane, when the question of Vane's attitude to the regicide became literally a matter of life and death. To Ambrose Upton, Baxter maintained in a letter in 1662 that he never had directly accused Vane of a hand in the King's death or that he had been in Italy (although Philip Nye had told Baxter that he had). But Baxter maintained his opposition to the thesis — which he identified with Vane — 'that Liberty for Popery should be woven into our fundamentall constitution'. He added a postscript: 'Conceale Mr, Nyes name.'[186]

'Liberty for Popery' seemed to have been secured with the political defeat of Richard Cromwell. His friend Henry Hickman, writing to him on 20 July, was as gloomy as Howe had been two months earlier. Dr

Whichcote had a story that a grandee overseas had been told of a company that would be sent from Rome to England 'that would turne themselves into all colours, and counterfeit any opinions'. Whichcote had taken the story to Oliver Cromwell. Moreover, Bampfield when Speaker of the House had told Hickman of meeting one 'who had lived long beyond seas' who had 'told him that the city did abound with popish priests'.[187] This is the background to Baxter's hysterical letter to William Mewe, some three weeks later, on 6 August, when he exempts only Hickman from his strictures on Protestant apathy in face of the Popish threat, laments the collapse of the hopes for union with the Baptists, and fears for his life at the hands of the Papists.[188] When he wrote *The Successive Visibility of the Church* in 1660 he had not lost that sense of physical danger or the certainty in ascribing its cause:

> For the last book that I wrote against them (My *Key for Catholickes*) the Parliament-house it self, and all the land did ring of my accusations, and the menaces were so high that my intended ruine was the common talk. And I know their indignation is not abated. My crime is, that their zeal to proselyte me, hath acquainted me with some of their secrets, and let me know what the Jesuits are doing, and how great a party that are masked under the name of Seekers, Familists, etc., they have in the land.[189]

Twelve days after his letter to Mewe, Baxter received from James Stansfield a letter claiming to prove that the King's death had been planned by a council of priests and Jesuits in France under the direction of Mazarin: for Baxter the authentication of the fears he had expressed to Mewe.[190]

On 24 September Hickman was advising Baxter to ignore Stubbe's attack on him: 'Mr. Stubbe hath now shown himselfe to bee Mr. Stubbe'. He informed Baxter that his *Holy Commonwealth* had almost murdered Harrington. The thought that Baxter had quoted Herodotus to make a point about the Roman Army made Harrington laugh so much that medical attention was required.[191] Baxter received more respectful notice from another correspondent three days later, Peter du Moulin, 'a right French Protestant'. He had translated his father's anti-Papal writings at Baxter's request, praised Baxter for his service against the Grotian divines, fulminated against Thorndike, and acknowledged himself as only an Episcopalian because of 'a hereditary dislike of all violent wayes of subjects with their soveraine'. Reformation was needed, but petitions for it should not have been presented 'at our pykes end'.[192]

On 18 October John Tombes, now reconciled with Baxter in the fight for a union of Christians that would include Baptists, wrote to Baxter to ask for details that would help to penetrate the disguise of the Papists and Familists.[193] Almost two weeks later, on 29 October, Tombes reiterated his faith in a godly union and the prevention of the toleration of Popery.[194]

These were not academic questions. From October to December 1659 the Army and a Committee of Safety, which included both Vane and Harrington, ruled England. There was pressure to have a second chamber, or Senate, as a check upon the Commons, the abolition of tithes and liberty of conscience. Baxter's opposition to all three was expressed in his manuscript of 30 November, *An Answer to the Over-turners and New Modelers of the Government about a Senate, Toleration and Tithes.*[195] But his opposition (despite Vane's suspicions) fell short of complicity in Royalist conspiracies. There were good reasons for holding off from the Royalist embrace, as John Wilson expressed them in a letter to Baxter on 28 February 1660. Defending his decision to stay aloof from Booth's Rising, Wilson pointed to some ominous talk that was emanating from the conspirators:

> They gave it out whiles they were amongst us that if they were but successfull against the Parliament they would have about (as they call'd it) with the Presbyterians before they had done; the old grudge is not yet laid aside.

Prophetic words: moreover, Wilson felt that under the Protectorate Presbyterians had 'enjoyed the Maine and principal ends of government' and that Calvin and Paraeus had urged obedience to the *de facto* power.[196]

It was arguments like Wilson's that prompted one anonymous correspondent to write an anxious letter to Baxter in March 1660. He told Baxter that 'our old obligations to CR are in my opinion clearly on us'. The root of all subsequent evils lay in the Army violence of 1647. He was dismissive of the hero of Baxter's *Holy Commonwealth*: 'And as for poore R.P. alas he was but one appendix of his fathers unjust violence.' Sentimentality about the lost leader could debar Baxter from playing an effective role in the Restoration: 'For the Lords sake ingage not in any thing which may hinder you from being the great instrument of union in the Churches.' The correspondent warned Baxter not 'to be a neuter Long' and to become a champion of 'the good old cause'.[197] But Baxter's letter to Thomas Bampfield on 4 April 1660 – only a few weeks before the meeting of the Convention Parliament – shows how impossible it was for Baxter to recapture the euphoria of his *Holy Commonwealth* days. Although he responds to Bampfield's request for a draft of a declaration on religion, his heart is patently not in it. The signature tells all: 'Your very willing but useless servant (in such weather at such a season).'[198] By 13 April, however, Baxter had travelled to London to meet his friend, Lauderdale, released from prison, and who conveyed Charles II's favour and acceptance of him.[199] On the eve of the Restoration, on 30 April, Baxter preached *A Sermon of Repentance*. Perhaps what is remarkable about it is the little that Baxter saw to repent. He was off on his anti-Papal tack once more: 'these masked Juglers have come by night and sown and cherished these Romish tares.' A Papist stops being a Papist when he is loyal to his sovereign; a Protestant stops being a Protestant when he is disloyal, 'for Rom. 13 is part of the Rule of his Religion'. The divisions of the past twenty years were disingenuously swept aside: 'Unhappily there hath been a difference among us, *which is the higher Power*, when those that have their shares in the Sovereignty are divided: But whether we should be subject to the Higher Power is no question with us.' The *fact* of sovereignty was the important issue; *who* exercised it was less important. Similarly the *fact* of discipline was what mattered, not *which* clergymen exercised it:

> The anti-disciplinarian Magistrate I could as resolutely suffer under as the superstitious; it being worse to cast out Discipline, than to erre in the circumstances of it. The question is not, *whether Bishops or no*? but *whether Discipline or none*? *and whether enow to use it*?[200]

All the ingredients of post-Restoration myth-making were there. Baxter had worked with the *de facto* government in order to prevent the collapse of order. He had never confused this *de facto* authority with the *de jure* rights possessed by Charles Stuart. He had let slip some injudicious compliments to Richard Cromwell, but at least he had declined the Engagement Oath to his father. And inasmuch as the address to the son had been over-fulsome, this was the political maladroitness that was to be expected of clergymen when they involved themselves in politics. Like most myth-making, this interpretation was not without a solid factual basis. As a description of Baxter's early involvement in the politics of the Commonwealth it has much to commend it. Even in the last years of the Commonwealth it is faithful to the *letter* of Baxter's writings for the most part; what it betrays is the *spirit*. It contains every-thing of Baxter's *Holy Commonwealth* except the holiness. What it leaves out is the sense of apocalyptic expectation with which Baxter saluted the Protectorate of Richard Cromwell.

We have traced in this chapter the process by which Baxter moved to such a position from an initial grudging recognition at best. There was nothing sudden about the process. It owed much to a simple desire for order and stability, when both seemed threatened by the spread of democratic ideals and the intrigues of Jesuits. It owed much to his involvement in controversies with opponents about predestination, Baptism and admission to the Lord's Supper, which at first seemed to have only a tangential relationship to political allegiances. But it owed most of all to the sense in which Baxter shared in the millenarian excite-ment of the age. This was not at first sight obvious. He made a point of not writing about the Apocalypse. His letter to Bromley in 1654 was a memorable assault on millenarian crankiness. He could not share the certainty of most of his Protestant colleagues that the Pope was the Antichrist. Perhaps this made him more diffident about talking about the Apocalypse than he needed to be. It is certainly interesting that when he does finally in 1684 commit himself publicly to the proposi-tion that the Apocalypse does not mark out Rome as the Antichrist this seems to act as a psychological release. Far from marking the terminus of his interest in the Apocalypse it is the prelude to the period of his most intensive study of the Book of Revelation. While it is true that the intensity of the study brings him no closer to the particular readings of colleagues in this field, like More, Beverley and Mather, it is equally true that they share an adventist faith and an historicist reading of Revelation. The deeper his study, the more Baxter came to respect the apocalyptic tradition of English Protestantism, particularly the writings of his Tudor predecessors.

Baxter had not gained these insights by the end of the Common-wealth period. There were to be several false scents to pursue after the Restoration, as we shall see in the next chapter. Not until 1686 — with his revised views on magistracy and 'National Churches' as the fruit of his prison researches — would Baxter be able to offer a systematic eschatology. And then it was the wrong time: the reign of James II was not the most propitious time to rediscover in a new way the virtues of the Emperor Constantine. But we should not exaggerate the distance between his views in the 1650s and those which he developed in his prison cell in 1686. In an unsystematic way much of the later Baxter was waiting to burst out. His letter to Bromley about the Mad Major is less exposé of irrationalism than an attempt to preserve the reputation of apocalyptic prophecy from those who would discredit it by eccentric interpretation. The discipline which he wants the magistrate — *any magistrate* — to secure, clearly goes beyond the patent need to keep down the rabble to the more ambitious task of distinguishing the precious from the vile; it is the projection of Kidderminster on to a wider canvas. His adventist faith, so clearly present in his *Saints Everlasting Rest*, ensured that he would be responsive to the expectant climate of the age. Whether corresponding with Lewis about founding new universities, or with Durie about developing Church unity, or with Eliot about the extension of missionary work, Baxter was as much a child of the millenarian 1650s as were his opponents, Harrington, Vane and Sterry. And when Baxter developed in 1686 his apocalyptic imperial ideas he did not need to go back to the Emperor Constantine for their embodiment.

There was a model closer at hand: a time in England when Antichrist received a mighty blow and when the precious *were* distinguished from the vile. That time was when England was ruled by the Cromwells. Baxter did not write *A Holy Commonwealth* in order to tell his contemporaries that they were wrong to dream of a more just and pure society. What he was saying, against the peddlers of fantastic visions, was that the dream was already far closer to realisation than they could ever have imagined. Men like Durie and Eliot had shown the way forward: that dream could be consummated by a magistrate who was as respectful of the clergy's *disciplinary* role as he was disrespectful of its *political* role.

Henry More had romanticised the achievements of a Church without a Christian Prince. Like many Anglicans, he also had pretended that the Cromwellian Protectorate had never happened. By 1686 Baxter could draw upon his apocalyptic studies undertaken in prison in order to redress both these injustices. With hindsight he could now bathe Cromwell's Holy Commonwealth in its full apocalyptic splendour:

When Oliver the usurper ruled in England, there was a policie that renounced Popery, and had thousands of Ministers and people that earnestly desired and endeavoured such a concord in Apostolike doctrine as he mentioneth: And yet it seemeth that he [More] is so farre from taking that to be any fall of Antichrist that he taketh it to have bin no Church of England, but a nation in manner unchurcht: for he saith, *that the Church of England was in a maner extinct.*[201]

Notes

1. R.B. Schlatter, *Richard Baxter and Puritan Politics* (New Brunswick, 1957), p. 68.

2. Baxter in N.H. Keeble (ed.), *The Autobiography of Richard Baxter* (Everyman, 1974), p. 47.

3. (DWL) *Baxter Correspondence*, ii, f,269v-270.

4. Quoted in J.I. Packer, 'The Redemption and Restoration of Man in the Thought of Richard Baxter', unpublished D.Phil. Thesis, Oxford, 1954, p. 233: this thesis has some valuable insights into Baxter's doctrinal position.

5. Baxter, *Catholick Theologie* (London, 1675), 1,i, preface; Baxter, *An Account of the Reasons . . .* (London, 1684), p. 27.

6. Baxter, *The Quakers Catechism* (London, 1655), dedicatory epistle; James Nayler, *An Answer to a Book Called The Quakers Catechism* (London, 1655), p. 13.

7. (DWL) *Baxter Correspondence*, i, f.11v.

8. Baxter, *Richard Baxter's Confutation of a Dissertation for the Justification of Infidels* (London, 1654), p. 288.

9. Baxter, *The Scripture-Gospel Defended . . .* (London, 1690), ii, p. 49.

10. J. Bossy, *The English Catholic Community 1570-1850* (London, 1975), p. 395.

11. Samuel Young, *Vindiciae Anti-Baxterianae* (London, 1696), pp. 111-12.

12. Edward Fisher, *The Marrow of Modern Divinity* (London, 1695), dedicatory epistle.

13. See N. Tyacke, 'Puritanism, Arminianism and Counter-Revolution' in C. Russell (ed.), *The Origins of the English Civil War* (London, 1973), pp. 119-44.

14. J.S. Coolidge, *The Pauline Renaissance in England* (Oxford, 1970), pp. 110-11.

15. John Goodwin, *Redemption Redeemed* (London, 1651), p. 94.

16. Blair Worden, *The Rump Parliament* (Cambridge, 1974), p. 122.

17. John Cosin, *Correspondence*, ed. G. Ornsby (Surtees Society, L11), p. 32.

18. Baxter in Matthew Sylvester (ed.), *Reliquiae Baxterianae* (London, 1696), p. 24; William Hazlitt, *Table-Talk* (Oxford, 1901), p. 160. I am grateful to my colleague, Mrs Sybil Oldfield, for this Hazlitt reference. Coleridge responded in a similar way to Hazlitt: see his 'Notes on Baxter's Life of Himself' (1820) in his *Complete Works*, ed. Shedd (New York, 1854), v, pp. 319-20.

19. Baxter, *Plain Scripture Proof . . .* (London, 1653), pp. 137, 148.

20. Coleridge, *Complete Works*, v, p. 324.

21. Christopher Hill, *The World Turned Upside Down* (London, 1972), pp. 186-93.

22. Cf. J.N. Figgis, 'Erastus and Erastianism', *Journal of Theological Studies*, ii (1900) and the fifth chapter of my *Godly Rule* (London, 1969), pp. 106-36.

23. On which, see Baxter, *A Second True Defence of the Meer Nonconformists* (London, 1681), p. 184.

24. (DWL) *Baxter Correspondence*, iv, f. 6v.

25. Baxter, *Plain Scripture Proof*, p. 148.

26. Baxter, *The Reduction of a Digresser . . .* (London, 1654), p. 13.

27. (DWL) *Baxter Correspondence*, i, f.193.

28. Baxter, *Catholick Theologie*, 1, i, pp. 76-7; 1, iii, p. 60.

29. (DWL) *Baxter Correspondence*, v, f.187.

30. Baxter, *Catholick Theologie*, 1, iii, p. 95.

31. Ibid., iii, p. 99.

32. (DWL) *Baxter Correspondence*, v, f.217-217v.
33. Baxter, *Catholick Theologie*, 1, iii, pp. 131, 133.
34. Ibid., 1, iii, p. 60 (a marginal note).
35. Ibid., II, pp. 4-5.
36. Ibid., I, iii, pp. 107-16.
37. Ibid., II, p. 36.
38. Baxter, *Saints Everlasting Rest . . .* (London, 1650), p. 338.
39. Ibid., p. 271.
40. Coleridge, *Complete Works*, v, p. 200.
41. (DWL) *Baxter Treatises*, xiv, f.3-3v.
42. Ibid., xiv, f.4-7v.
43. Ibid., xiv, f.11-12v.
44. 'J.B.', *Kedarminster-Stuff . . .* (London, 1681), p. 16.
45. (DWL) *Baxter Treatises*, xiv, f.57.
46. (DWL) *Baxter Correspondence*, i, f.265-265v.
47. (DWL) *Baxter Correspondence*, vi, f.114-15.
48. (DWL) *Baxter Correspondence*, ii, f.15v-24v. Even so, a couple of years later in his *Plain Scripture Proof*, Baxter would describe Goodwin sympathetically (p. 193) as one 'tempted into a way of Schism, by mens intemperate zeal against his elaborate Treatise of Justification'.
49. (DWL) *Baxter Treatises*, vi, f.56, 56v, 59, 60. Cf. Baxter in Sylvester, *Reliquiae Baxterianae*, i, p. 108 for a characteristic statement of Baxter's diffidence when faced with the superior political judgement of Lawson. Baxter's criticism of Lawson's doctrinal position was similar to his judgement on Amyraut: 'I nowhere speak of his judgment about universal Grace in general, but only about universal Redemption, as approved by me' (*Plain Scripture Proof*, p. 275).
50. (DWL) *Baxter Treatises*, vi, f.60.
51. (DWL) *Baxter Treatises*, vi, f.148v, 149, 154.
52. Baxter, *Aphorismes of Justification . . .* (London, 1649), p. 276.
53. (DWL) *Baxter Correspondence*, iii, f. 266.
54. (DWL) *Baxter Correspondence*, iii, f.272v-273.
55. (DWL) *Baxter Correspondence*, iv, f.179. Not only Oliver Cromwell beseeched in the bowels of Christ: cf. (East Sussex Record Office) *Frewen MSS* 4223 f.475/52v: 'And now, sir, we have done, we intreat you in the bowells of Jesus Christ, just to passe by our weaknesses.'
56. (DWL) *Baxter Correspondence*, vi, f.133.
57. (DWL) *Baxter Correspondence*, iii, f.163-163v.
58. (DWL) *Baxter Correspondence*, i, f.10.
59. (DWL) *Baxter Correspondence*, i, f.11v. The best *critique* of Morley's thesis is: C. Bangs, 'All the Best Bishoprics and Deaneries: The Enigma of Arminian Politics', *Church History*, 42, 1 (1973), pp. 5-16.
60. (DWL) *Baxter Correspondence*, i, f.8v.
61. (DWL) *Baxter Correspondence*, i, f.193.
62. John Crandon, *Mr. Baxter's Aphorismes Exorcized . . .* (London, 1654), dedicatory epistle.
63. Baxter, *Richard Baxter's Confutation of a Dissertation for the Justification of Infidels* (London, 1654), dedicatory epistle, p. 201.
64. (DWL) *Baxter Correspondence*, v, f.189.
65. (DWL) *Baxter Correspondence*, v, f.187.
66. Cf. (DWL) *Baxter Correspondence*, v, f.221, Richard Green: Baxter, 18 September 1658. Green wanted three columns on divinity from Baxter, with two extremes and the truth snugly in the middle.
67. (DWL) *Baxter Correspondence*, v, f.191.
68. (DWL) *Baxter Correspondence*, vi, f.112.

69. (DWL) *Baxter Correspondence*, v, f.187.

70. Baxter, *Confession of his Faith* ... (London, 1655), preface.

71. John Owen, *Vindiciae Evangelicae* (Oxford, 1655), p. 64.

72. Baxter, *Confession of his Faith*, pp. 106, 109, 115, 116, 123, 124. Cf. Baxter, *Apology* ... (London, 1654), dedicatory epistle: 'It is the most Practical Teachers and People in England commonly that are the most Orthodox. I have oft noted many mens Prayers to bee much freer from Libertinism, than their Sermons; and their Sermons than their Writings and Disputes.'

73. Baxter, *Catholick Theologie*, 1, preface. Coleridge's edition, on which he scribbled these comments, is in the British Library.

74. Baxter, *Confession of his Faith*, pp. 123-4.

75. J.B. Torrance, 'Covenant or Contract? A Study of the Theological Background of Worship in Seventeenth-Century Scotland', *Scottish Journal of Theology*, 1 (February 1970), pp. 51-76.

76. Crandon, *Mr. Baxter's Aphorismes Exorcized*, dedicatory epistle.

77. (DWL) *Baxter Correspondence*, vi, f.148.

78. Obadiah Howe, *The Pagan Preacher Silenced* (London, 1655), pp. 9-10.

79. (DWL) *Baxter Correspondence*, i, f.153v.

80. (DWL) *Baxter Correspondence*, i, f.125.

81. Baxter, *Certain Disputations of Right to Sacraments* ... preface.

82. Baxter, *Plain Scripture Proof*, p. 275.

83. Baxter, *The Grotian Religion Discovered* ... (London, 1658), preface.

84. Thomas Pierce, *The New Discoverer Discovered* ... (London, 1659), pp. 55, 83, 84.

85. (DWL) *Baxter Correspondence*, v, f.160.

86. Baxter, *Plain Scripture Proof*, pp. 134, 136, 137.

87. Henry Haggar, *The Foundation of the Font Discovered* (London, 1653), pp. 92-3.

88. John Tombes, *An Antidote* ... (London, 1650), p. 30.

89. Baxter, *Richard Baxter's Admonition to William Eyre* ... (London, 1654), dedicatory epistle. Among the works he attacked in that pamphlet were: William Eyre, *Vindiciae Justificationis Gratuitae* (London, 1653); William Kaye, *Baptism Without Bason* (London, 1653); John Tombes, *Antipaedobaptism* (London, 1652).

90. (DWL) *Baxter Correspondence*, iii, f.143v, 145-6.

91. (DWL) *Baxter Correspondence*, i, f.30. Vaux had written to Baxter on 23 April 1656, praising his writings against Tombes, but querying him on the sufficiency of parents' faith. Baxter's tortuous reply was written on 24 June 1656.

92. Baxter, *Apology*, pp. 106-7.

93. Baxter, *The Reduction of a Digressor*, pp. 90, 13.

94. Baxter, *A Defence of the Principles of Love* ... (London, 1671), pp. 6-7.

95. (DWL) *Baxter Correspondence*, iv, f.281.

96. William Prynne, *A Vindication of Four Serious Questions* ... (London, 1645), pp. 57-8.

97. Coleridge, *Complete Works*, v, p. 339.

98. For a detailed discussion of the reasons for Prynne's change of heart on tithes, and for the significance of the controversy over admission to the Sacrament of the Lord's Supper in general, see the sixth chapter of my *Godly Rule*, pp. 136-58.

99. Baxter, *Certain Disputations of Right to Sacraments*, pp. 433-4, 500, 502.

100. (DWL) *Baxter Correspondence*, i, f.196-7.

101. (DWL) *Baxter Correspondence*, i, f.198, 199, 201v.

102. (DWL) *Baxter Correspondence*, ii, f.293-4; Prynne, *A Vindication of Four Serious Questions*, dedicatory epistle.

103. (DWL) *Baxter Correspondence*, i, f.247, 249.

104. Henry Stubbe, *An Essay in Defence of the Good Old Cause . . .* (London, 1659).

105. John Beverley, *Unio Reformantium . . .* (London, 1659), preface, pp. 2, 22, 36, 40.

106. (DWL) *Baxter Correspondence*, iii, f.138.

107. (DWL) *Baxter Correspondence*, iii, f.196.

108. Benjamin Hanbury, *Historical Memorials* (London, 1844), iii, p. 544: chapter 30, article 8.

109. Blair Worden, *The Rump Parliament* (Cambridge, 1974), pp. 322-5.

110. G.F. Nuttall, *Richard Baxter* (London, 1965), pp. 68-73.

111. A. Gordon, *Heads of English Unitarian History* (London, 1895), p. 65: quoted in Nuttall, *Richard Baxter*, p. 69.

112. Baxter, *Certain Disputations of Right to Sacraments*, p. 500.

113. Baxter, *Gildas Salvianus . . .* (London, 1656), preface.

114. P. Collinson, 'Lectures by Combination: Structures and Characteristics of Church Life in Seventeenth-Century England', *Bulletin of Institute of Historical Research*, XLVIII, 118 (November 1975), pp. 182-213.

115. Baxter, *The Worcestershire Petition to the Parliament for the Ministry of England Defended . . .* (London, 1653), pp. 34-5, 9, 12, 13; R. Culmer, *Lawlesse Tithe Robbers Discovered* (London, 1654), quoted in Margaret James, 'The Political Importance of the Tithes Controversy in the English Revolution, 1640-60', *History*, XXVI (1940), p. 6; Prynne, *A Gospel Plea . . .* (London, 1653), p. 3.

116. Baxter, *Christian Concord . . .* (London, 1653), pp. 1, 2, 31, 36, 45, 46.

117. (DWL) *Baxter Correspondence*, vi, f.127.

118. Baxter, *Confession of his Faith*, preface.

119. Baxter, *Humble Advice . . .* (London, 1655), pp. 3, 4, 5, 7, 8, 10.

120. See Chapter 1.

121. Baxter, *Gildes Salvianus*, dedicatory epistle, preface, p. 46. On 12 April 1655 Samuel Langley had pleaded with Baxter to answer Hammond's 'conceit about Presbytery'. In his reply of 2 August Baxter pleaded the pressure of other controversies, but added this significant tribute: 'Though I know the Learned and Reverend Dr. whom he mentioneth will avoid that reproach wch others comonly use . . . I much revere the Dr. for his Learning, Industry and Sober way, and so have no desire to contend with him' [(DWL) *Baxter Correspondence*, i, f.111.]

122. (DWL) *Baxter Correspondence*, iii, f.3.

123. (DWL) *Baxter Correspondence*, i, f.127.

124. Nuttall, *Richard Baxter*, p. 80.

125. (DWL) *Baxter Correspondence*, iii, f.196, 200.

126. (DWL) *Baxter Correspondence*, i, f.74, 76, 76v, 78, 79v, 87.

127. (DWL) *Baxter Correspondence*, i, f.247, Cf. Baxter's own bitter remarks nearly three months later, on 8 November, to William White about the resurgent vindictiveness of Heylyn, Pierce and other 'Laudians': (DWL) *Baxter Correspondence*, ii, f.45.

128. (DWL *Baxter Correspondence*, iii, f.139.

129. (DWL) *Baxter Correspondence*, iii, f.137, 137v, 138.

130. (DWL) *Baxter Treatises*, vi, f.203.

131. Baxter in Sylvester, *Reliquiae Baxterianae*, i, pp. 97, 103, 104, 198, 199.

132. (DWL) *Baxter Correspondence*, i, f.96, 96v, 97.

133. (DWL) *Baxter Correspondence*, ii, f.320.

134. (DWL) *Baxter Correspondence*, i, f.251-251v.

135. (DWL) *Baxter Correspondence*, iv, f.281. On union with the Baptists see William Allen's letter to Baxter on 29 October 1658: (DWL) *Baxter Correspondence*, i, f.90v. Cf. (BL) Add. MSS.4221, f.96 for Matthew Sylvester's deposition

that Jesuits were waiting on Baxter's death before acting.

136. (DWL) *Baxter Correspondence*, ii, f.15v, 24v.

137. (DWL) *Baxter Correspondence*, iii, f.272-3.

138. (DWL) *Baxter Correspondence*, iv, f.43.

139. (DWL) *Baxter Correspondence*, vi, f.151-2.

140. (DWL) *Baxter Correspondence*, v, f.199-199v.

141. (DWL) *Baxter Correspondence*, v, f.107.

142. (DWL) *Baxter Correspondence*, vi, f.122.

143. N. Penney (ed.), *First Publishers of Truth* (London, 1907), p. 285.

144. E.g. Baxter, *The Quakers Catechism* (London, 1655); *One Sheet Against the Quakers . . ., One Sheet for the Ministry* (London, 1655); *A Second Sheet for the Ministry* (London 1655).

145. (DWL) *Baxter Correspondence*, i, f.53-53v.

146. (DWL) *Baxter Correspondence*, i, f.226-8.

147. (DWL) *Baxter Correspondence*, vi, f.236.

148. (DWL) *Baxter Correspondence*, v, f.156.

149. (DWL) *Baxter Correspondence*, iii, f.119.

150. (DWL) *Baxter Correspondence*, iii, f.115-115v.

151. For which, see Chapter 1.

152. (DWL) *Baxter Correspondence*, iii, f.117-18.

153. Baxter, *Gildas Salvianus*, preface.

154. For details of which, see Chapter 1.

155. Clement Writer, *An Apologetical Narration* . . . (London, 1657), pp. 46-7.

156. (DWL) *Baxter Correspondence*, i, f.230-237v.

157. (DWL) *Baxter Correspondence*, iii, f.200.

158. (DWL) *Baxter Correspondence*, iv, f.102v.

159. (DWL) *Baxter Correspondence*, iii, f.127.

160. (DWL) *Baxter Correspondence*, v, f.5, 9. John Rogers, *A Christian Concertation* (London, 1659), p. 18, blamed Lauderdale for Baxter's spiteful *Key for Catholicks* . . . (London, 1659).

161. (DWL) *Baxter Correspondence*, ii, f.267v-268. But for what Baxter really thought of Heylyn, see his comment to White three weeks later (on 8 November): (DWL) *Baxter Correspondence*, ii, f.45.

162. (DWL) *Baxter Correspondence*, i, f.96-7.

163. Schlatter, *Richard Baxter and Puritan Politics*, pp. 61-6.

164. Baxter, *The Grotian Religion Discovered*, preface, pp. 4, 12, 19, 95, 99, 100, 105, 108.

165. Baxter, *A Key for Catholicks*, dedicatory epistle, pp. 316, 317, 318, 321, 326, 327, 330.

166. Baxter, *A Holy Commonwealth* . . . (London, 1659), preface, pp. 84, 99, 123, 79, 80, 115, 122.

167. Baxter, *A Christian Directory* (London, 1673), p. 736.

168. Baxter, *A Holy Commonwealth*, pp. 346-455, 456-90, 457, 472, 473.

169. I am quoting from the introduction to the edition of Harrington's works, which Professor John Pocock is preparing for the Cambridge University Press. He has kindly allowed me to read the draft manuscript. His concern is with Harrington, not Baxter, but he notes in passing that '*A Holy Commonwealth* is not primarily a debate with Harrington' and that 'the only section which has that character occurs late and contains little beyond a powerful and reiterated conviction that the poor in a lump are bad, and that anyone as anti-clerical as Harrington can be no friend to religion.'

170. (DWL) *Baxter Treatises*, xxii, f.69: omitted from Baxter in Sylvester, *Reliquiae Baxterianae*, i, p. 118.

171. In a review article: *Journal of Ecclesiastical History*, vi, 5 (1955), pp. 77-9.

172. (DWL) *Baxter Treatises*, xxii, f.69: omitted from Sylvester, *Reliquiae Baxterianae*, i, p. 118.

173. For which, see Chapter 2.

174. Prynne, *The Sword of Christian Magistracy* . . . (London 1647), pp. 5, 6, 8, 9, 31, 106; William Dell, *Right Reformation* . . . (London 1646), p. 7; Thomas Hobbes, *Leviathan* (Everyman, London, 1949), p. 254.

175. Baxter, *A Key for Catholicks*, p. 316. Baxter paid tribute to Hunton and Prynne with these words: 'no book more advantaged the Parliament's cause than a Treatise of Monarchy (afterwards published) and Mr. Prins large book of the Sovereign Power of Parliaments wherein he heapeth up Multitude of instances . . . of Parliaments that exercised Soveraign power' (*Reliquiae Baxterianae*, i, p. 41). The tribute reads more gracefully to Prynne by Sylvester's omission of the words, 'right or wrong let others try', from the original manuscript (*Baxter Treatises*, xxii, f.23.)

176. Baxter, *A Defence of the Principles of Love*, p. 142: a typical post-Restoration effort to play down the nature of his involvement with Richard Cromwell.

177. Rogers, *A Christian Concertation*, dedicatory epistle, pp. 15, 27, 34.

178. Coleridge, *Complete Works*, v, pp. 348, 359.

179. Rogers, *A Christian Concertation*, pp. 35, 36, 37, 54, 55.

180. On which, see Keith Lindley, 'The Part Played by the Catholics' in Brian Manning (ed.), *Politics, Religion and the English Civil War* (London, 1973), pp. 127-79.

181. Rogers, *A Christian Concertation*, p. 92.

182. Stubbe, *An Essay in Defence of the Good Old Cause*, preface.

183. Stubbe, *Malice Rebuked* . . . (London, 1659), pp. 15, 17, 18, 19, 37, 38, 43, 44, 45, 49, 54, 55, 57, 59, 60.

184. (DWL) *Baxter Correspondence*, vi, f.235-235v.

185. (DWL) *Baxter Correspondence*, iv, f.187-187v.

186. (DWL) *Baxter Correspondence*, i, f.257.

187. (DWL) *Baxter Correspondence*, iv, f.1.

188. (DWL) *Baxter Correspondence*, iv, f.281.

189. Baxter, *The Successive Visibility of the Church* (London, 1660), p. 26.

190. (DWL) *Baxter Treatises*, iii, f.262.

191. (DWL) *Baxter Correspondence*, v, f.119.

192. (DWL) *Baxter Correspondence*, iv, f.69.

193. (DWL) *Baxter Correspondence*, v, f.136.

194. (DWL) *Baxter Correspondence*, iv, f.175. Cf. Baxter's triumph over the Papist opponent, William Johnson, in 1660 when he is able to show that – despite previous differences over infant baptism – he and Tombes are united in their hatred of Popery: Baxter, *The Successive Visibility of the Church*, p. 190.

195. Schlatter, *Richard Baxter and Puritan Politics*, pp. 125-38.

196. (DWL) *Baxter Correspondence*, i, f.261.

197. (DWL) *Baxter Correspondence*, i, f.210-210v.

198. Schlatter, *Richard Baxter and Puritan Politics*, pp. 139-45.

199. Nuttall, *Richard Baxter*, p. 85.

200. Baxter, *A Sermon of Repentance* . . . (London, 1660), pp. 13, 43, 44, 45.

201. (DWL) *Baxter Treatises*, vii, f.299.

The title of this fourth chapter deliberately echoes that of an important article by Dr Beddard. Entitled 'Vincent Alsop and the Emancipation of Restoration Dissent', it puts forward an interesting thesis about Nonconformity after the Restoration. Dr Beddard believes that the majority of English Puritans were slow to see that their future lay in sectarianism. Presbyterians and Independents, instead of making common cause with Quakers and Anabaptists, continued to pursue the phantom of 'comprehension' with Episcopalians in a National Church. Alsop courageously broke with that tradition in 1687 when he urged his fellow presbyterians to accept James II's Declaration of Indulgence. Dr Beddard says of Alsop: 'As a committed separatist he did not fear the loss of moderate Anglican sympathy — believing in the independence of the gathered church he held no brief for Uniformity, even as a protective dyke against Romanism.' This was a major departure from the historic Nonconformist position:

> Too often debate between the two parties had been vitiated by an unhelpful and at times misleading acknowledgement of common ground. An older generation of contestants, reared in the armchair ethos of Anglo-puritanism, was understandably reluctant to minimise the area of doctrinal agreement. Intellectually they were imprisoned in an increasingly remote and irrelevant past. Their successors were not. They had the future to live for.[1]

The implication of Dr Beddard's article is that Alsop is forward-looking, Baxter imprisoned in a sterile anti-Romanism. In giving this chapter the title 'Baxter and the Non-Emancipation of Restoration Dissent', I seem to be subscribing totally to Dr Beddard's thesis.

This is not so. Dr Beddard has underlined usefully the importance of Alsop. But there are other ways of measuring the emancipation of Restoration Dissent than by the readiness of its leaders to respond to overtures from Papist-inclined sovereigns.

It was more than a suspicion of Popery that informed Baxter's mistrust of 'the independence of the gathered church'. Behind the mistrust of Baxter and many of his colleagues lay a profound commitment to

Protestant imperialism. Anti-Popery was one expression of such a philosophy; but so too was a belief in the historic role of the civil magistrate, in the duty of the elect to bring the reprobate majority into conformity with godly standards, and in a refusal to carry detestation of certain practices in the Established Church to the point of separation from it.

We have seen in earlier chapters the importance of Baxter in articulating such feelings for his fellow Protestants, particularly in the 1650s. There was, however, a growing strain of Independency *within* English Presbyterianism after the Restoration, which meshed ill with the imperial philosophy. Baxter himself blamed the Anglican persecutors for this development: they forced on their victims, whether nominally Presbyterian, Independent or Baptist, a common 'sect' practice, if not theory. And it could be argued that the shift in Restoration Nonconformity represented little more than theory catching up with practice. Indeed a person like Baxter, clinging to his 'church-type' theory while observing 'sect-type' practice, could well seem a rather absurd figure. But Baxter was here being too kind to his fellow Nonconformists. The Clarendon Code did not *create* this problem, although it certainly intensified it. We have seen how, both in the late 1640s and again in the mid-1650s, arguments over the Sacrament of the Lord's Supper threw up critical differences within Protestant Nonconformity, and that these differences only imperfectly followed traditional religious groupings. The greatest exponent of the Independent 'party' line on this controversy was the Scottish Presbyterian, George Gillespie; and it was the attraction of many English Presbyterians to the Independent arguments for unmixed communion which had scandalised such figures as Baillie, Humfrey, Timson, Jeanes and Blake. In this sense Royal intervention — whether inspired by idealism or Popery — in favour of toleration was a side issue. There were impulses at work already pulling Presbyterians, Independents and Baptists in a common 'sect-type' direction. The theory might follow the practice, but it still represented a momentous change within Nonconformity. The emancipation of Restoration Dissent from its imperial roots is a more complex process than reactions to Royal Declarations of Indulgence, and this will be the focus of inquiry in this chapter. We will argue that the critical date in that emancipation is not 1689 but 1704, and that the key contributor to the emancipation is not Vincent Alsop but Edmund Calamy.

This alternative thesis is, at first sight, no more flattering to Baxter. To emancipate Restoration Dissent, we shall see, Calamy would have to revise Baxter. But Calamy did not need to invent new concepts. He transformed Protestant Nonconformity, not by ignoring Baxter or by misunderstanding him, but by developing arguments that had already been advanced by Baxter, *particularly in his writings of the late 1670s and the early 1680s*. Indeed, in that period of his writings, there is evidence to suggest that the development of his views might have led logically to the philosophy that Calamy expressed in 1704. *Baxter might have been the man to emancipate Restoration Dissent*. He did not do so because he went to prison, and there in 1686 he immersed himself more fully than he had ever done before in the Apocalypse. The result was a profound reversal of his thinking of the previous few years: so profound that Calamy could not accommodate these insights into the statement of his own philosophical beliefs in 1704. How the millennium became a barrier to the emancipation of Restoration Dissent will emerge in the study of Baxter's changing ideas after 1660 which now follows.

I think that we can distinguish three distinct phases in Baxter's views on 'National Churches' after the Restoration. Between 1660 and 1676 he is the spokesman, in Dr Beddard's unflattering phrase, of 'the archaic ethos of Anglo-puritanism'. The second phase – roughly between 1676 and 1684 – is the one which Dr Beddard missed, when Baxter turned critic of 'National Churches' and moved his fellow Nonconformists in a sectarian direction. The third phase – between 1684 and 1691 – is when Baxter once more defends 'National Churches', but with arguments strikingly different from those which he employed in his first phase of development.

We will look at each of these phases in turn. The first has been most deeply researched,[2] and from the point of this study may require less documentation than the later two. Immediately after the Restoration Baxter emerged as the champion of Archbishop Usher's model of a 'reduced Episcopacy'. It was the next best thing to a Holy Commonwealth. We saw in the last chapter how Baxter had supported Richard Cromwell's Protectorate for the magisterial authority with which it held down the reprobate majority, whilst the Ministerial Associations had provided the complementary environment in which the godly could flower. The charm to Baxter of Usher's model was that it secured this pastoral discipline, by providing for synods and associations in which parties were consulted about discipline and jurisdiction. Usher's scheme had not been made public until 1655. But in 1641 it had been considered by the House of Commons Committee on Religion, when the idea of a non-Laudian alternative to 'root and branch' exercised great appeal. Usher had revived it during the abortive negotiations with the King in the Isle of Wight in 1648. Usher and Baxter had discussed the scheme together in 1655. It became the basis of the Puritan alternative in 1660-1: a permanent *primus* among fellow bishops, a synod of presbyters associated regularly with bishops in all acts of jurisdiction, and dioceses reduced to the size of counties. For Baxter its basic appeal, at its simplest, was that it secured the pastor the right to exercise discipline in his own parish: for him the yardstick by which all reform proposals were to be measured. It makes sense of what otherwise seems the most perverse of all Baxter's actions after the Restoration: his rejection of the offer of the bishopric of Hereford, together with a polite letter to the Chancellor, suggesting seventeen other likely names for the job. The point was that, in its existing diocesan form, Baxter could not conscientiously participate: he was sceptical of genuine pastoral discipline within such a framework. But he had no doctrinaire objection to Episcopacy itself, and wished to press for reform along Usher's lines, whilst encouraging those who did not share his scruples to commit themselves more directly to service within the existing structure.

Usher's plan was in line with his own Ministerial Associations. Usher wanted to see an association of pastors meeting in every market town, with a president for life *who did not have the pastoral care of more than his own congregation*, and who would not interfere with other pastors in theirs. It was not only Judge Jeffreys who suspected Baxter's good faith in claiming that his objections to conformity would be largely overcome by such a programme. Yet Baxter *was* willing to use the Prayer Book: the famous 'Reformed Liturgy' which he drew up in a fortnight at Savoy was an alternative to it, not a substitute for it.[3] At his ordination (as a deacon in 1638 by Bishop Thornborough) he had subscribed to it and had used it − with certain modifications of his own − at Kidderminster. Nor did he object to re-ordination provided that there was no repudiation of previous ordination: his formula, 'if thou art not already ordained', became the basis of Wilkins's suggestions for comprehension in 1668, and of Tillotson's in 1689. Although Baxter did not wear the surplice, he did not condemn those who did; although he did not *approve* of the sign of the cross in baptism, he was not certain that it *was unlawful*; he opposed kneeling at Communion but did not refuse Communion to those who did; and he approved of organs, choirs and set prayers although not responses.

October 1660 was the critical date for the success of the Usher compromise. The King's Declaration of that month had been preceded in September by Baxter's 'Petition to the King upon our sight of the First Draft of the Declaration'. This had pressed for Usher's model, been amended by certain Presbyterian peers, but was not called by Clarendon for presentation. At the Worcester House meeting of bishops and their critics, the key issue to Baxter was the nature of bishops' consultation of ministers before ordination or confirmation or passing of censures. If ministerial *consent* was necessary this would, in the eyes of many Churchmen, emasculate bishops; if only *advice* were sought, on the other hand, this would not give the protection (which Usher's scheme gave) of the pastor's right to govern his flock. When Clarendon presented a petition for general toleration on behalf of Independents and Baptists, it was Baxter, and not the bishops, who opposed it. But the actual Declaration of 25 October 1660 went further towards meeting Baxter's ideals than these earlier clashes had seemed to indicate. The pastor's consent was ruled as necessary for confirmation and admission to Communion, although not for ordination or Episcopal censures. Baxter's relief was tempered with the suspicion that it was only a temporary expedient: confirmed by the manoeuvres which preceded its defeat in the Commons on 28 November. Dr Bosher is correct in arguing that the defeat of the King's Declaration was more critical for the Restoration Settlement than the happenings at Savoy in 1661.[4] That Conference was the embodiment of the promise in the King's Declaration to consider Prayer Book revision: not at the heart of Baxter's concerns. Indeed the Conference never discussed Usher's proposals, and Baxter was resolute that he and other ministers would not submit to being bishops' curates. They must *govern*; they must have a 'credible profession of faith and obedience' from every communicant (the sticking point in his battles over the Lord's Supper in the 1650s); they must have the power of discipline and excommunication. With Savoy still in session, Parliament appointed a committee to prepare a Bill for the compulsory use of the Prayer Book: the Conference was revealed as a meaningless interlude between the King's Declaration and the Clarendon Code.

The story of Baxter's sufferings under the Clarendon Code is a familiar one. During the time of persecution he never abandoned hopes of some compromise on the lines of Usher's proposals. In 1668 he was working on a 'comprehension' formula with Lord Keeper Bridgman and Bishop Wilkins. It was defeated in the Commons and was followed by the imposition of the second Conventicle Act, and with it Baxter's imprisonment for not taking the Oxford Oath. In 1670 Lauderdale offered Baxter a Scottish bishopric if he would conform. In 1673, after the failure of the Declaration of Indulgence and the imposition of the Test Act, 'comprehension' talks were revived between Baxter and the Earl of Orrery and Bishop Morley. They formed the basis of still later negotiations between Baxter and Tillotson.

Even summarised as baldly as this, Baxter's attitude in the first fif-teen years after the Restoration clearly does seem to fit into Dr Bedd-ard's categorisation. Here is Baxter resolutely refusing to be provoked by Laudian-type persecution into abandoning his faith in the non-sectarian traditions of English Nonconformity. Less easy to fit into this picture are Baxter's parallel negotiations with Independent ministers, led by John Owen. They would seem to show that there were at least occasions when Baxter found the strain upon Nonconformist loyalty intolerable.

There may have been such occasions, but it would be wrong to take Baxter's willingness to confer with Owen and other Independent coll-eagues as a sign that this was so. Certainly for the first fifteen years after the Restoration or so, Baxter is hopeful that Independent minis-ters, as much as non-Laudian Episcopalians, can be brought within the same broad-based 'National Church' as their Presbyterian colleagues. The basis for his hopes was the New England Synod's rejection of sepa-ratism, and of forming gathered churches of baptised persons, in 1662. For Baxter it meant the lifting of the curse of Roger Williams's influ-ence; it meant that New England Independents were reverting to their non-separatist traditions. A happy lead for their colleagues in England! It probably encouraged Baxter to read more flexibility into Owen's position in 1667 than the facts warranted. New England had for Bax-ter, as much as for his fellow English Puritans, a special place in his imagination. Something of that feeling comes over in his correspond-ence with Increase Mather. It is true that, in the 1650s, he would be more likely to value New England as a moral lesson of the dangers of Antinomianism (as in his frequent references to the monsters produced at birth by Mistresses Hutchinson and Dyer.)[5] But earlier aspirations persisted. In an unpublished note in prison in 1686 Baxter supported his point that 'ignorant men talke as in a dreame of things unknown,' with reference to the ill-starred venture of a friend and himself 'about 50 yeares ago', who had decided, on the basis of a map, the exact loca-tion of their emigration to New England. The expedition was called off; the place that they had chanced upon remained, even in 1686, inaccess-ible to New England immigrants. But there was a sense in which the dream of a godly discipline on the New England model remained access-ible to him. He had turned down a bishopric, and supported Usher's proposals, because of his continued concern with an effective discipline. And this discipline could be achieved within a broadly based National Church. English Independents had first to abandon rigid criteria for admitting men to the Lord's Supper, their millenarian fantasies and their strict Calvinist dogma. After 1662 Baxter began to feel more optimistic about all three. The realistic basis for such optimism, and for his parallel hopes for Usher's scheme, would be cruelly questioned by colleagues at the time, who felt that Baxter's great influence was being sadly misdirected. We will study this reaction in some detail now to understand the pressures on Baxter to give an alternative lead to his Nonconformist colleagues: one which he would only adopt in the event as late as 1676 – the second phase of his intellectual development after the Restoration.

The first, non-separatist phase was clouded by unmerited suspicions of his good faith. Civil War and Commonwealth scars had left their mark. His efforts at the Restoration to win acceptance for a reconstruction of Episcopacy on Usher's model were handicapped by the widespread suspicion that his real objections to Episcopacy ran along much more radical lines. He was not a 'root and branch' opponent of Episcopacy, but was often treated as such. That is why there is a certain pathos in reading his correspondence with Cornelius Burges in September 1659 and finding him thrilled at the reassurance, from a London minister at the centre of political controversies in the early 1640s, that he and his colleagues had sought *reform*, not *extirpation*, of the Episcopal order.[6] Baxter had hoped for a sympathetic response to his proposals from an Anglican divine of the stature of Henry Hammond if only he had outlived the Restoration: even as late as 1660 he is writing to Francis Wheeler at Kidderminster, urging him to follow the enlightened lead of a Hammond.[7] We know, however, that what worried Hammond in the Commonwealth – as emerged in his correspondence with Sheldon – was precisely Baxter's crudity in dividing the 'Prelatic clergy' in two: 'One exemplified by Dr. Usher and Dr. Sanderson, the other styled as gross Cassandrian, Grotian Papists'.[8] Now it is true that historically the Puritan critics who distinguished 'moderate' bishops from 'Grotian' colleagues tended to make their High Churchmanship the litmus test of sincerity: those who advocated divine right status for bishops were separating themselves from more moderate colleagues who owned the Royal Supremacy and a *iure humano* status for bishops. On this basis Prynne and Bastwick had constructed their attack upon the Laudians in the 1630s; Henry Parker had developed this theme skilfully in the 1640s; and this was the point at issue in the classic confrontation between Joseph Hall and his 'Smectymnuan' critics. It might have been expected that Baxter, with his respect for the Royal Supremacy and for Tudor bishops, might have also made the Laudians' new-fangled *iure divino* claim for bishops his sticking point. Baxter has, however, some interesting manuscript notes on this question which he wrote in 1684:

> Of the Divine Right of Diocesane Episcopacy, the *Divine Right* was not agreed for or against them, nor is it now. Some took it to be Necessary, *iure divino*, some took it to be most eligible as best but not necessary. Some took it to be only lawfull, and some unlawfull: And to this day the higher sorte (as Dr. Hammond) took it not to be necessary *ad esse*, that a Diocese be any bigger than a Parish or Congregation.[9]

In other words, Baxter was less impressed than were many of his colleagues by the *status* that Episcopalians gave to the office; the critical question was whether the *framework* of their scheme encouraged the exercise of parochial discipline. And on this test Hammond, albeit one of 'the higher sorte', showed up to advantage in comparison with more 'moderate' colleagues. It is a good measure of Baxter's sense of priorities.

The difficulty for Baxter in communicating his priorities was the legacy of mistrust from the Commonwealth period. Formal retractions of dedicatory epistles in his *Holy Commonwealth* could not obliterate from people's minds the knowledge of his previous commitment to the Protectorate. Ralph Josselin, in a diary entry of 19 March 1658, erroneously reporting Baxter's death, could describe him laconically as 'a great pillar to Cromwell and his way'.[10] Less temperately, Thomas Tonkins, in his pamphlet of 1660, *The Rebels Plea*, asked 'by what names are those Ministers of the Nation to be known, that had rather Richard Cromwell should have raigned than King Charls?' With special reference to Baxter he made a distinction between 'paying necessary Tribute' and 'writing fine daintily fine canting Epistles'.[11] Lady Willoughby wrote to Hyde on 20 April 1660 that 'the Presbyterian people thunder against the elections, and Baxter the coryphaeus of Worcestershire is come here for no good.'[12] Over two years later, on 13 August 1662, the Archbishop of York was writing to the Bishop of London in a similar vein about Baxter:

> 'Our Presbyterian Primate' B[axter] arrived the same day. He is dangerously sick. A letter to him (intercepted by Postmaster) from an agent across the ditch was read to writer, but there is little fresh in it, except that Vossius has in the press at Utrecht a treatise against Episcopacy.[13]

Against this background of suspicion, Baxter attempted in his public sermons and writings of 1660 to keep loyal to the *themes* of his Holy Commonwealth, but no longer sustained by belief in their imminent fulfilment.

For Baxter the time for millenarian hopes had passed. He did not now turn to the Book of Revelation to support visions of an imminent Christian magistracy on earth; he did turn to it as an arsenal of anti-Papal judgements. His main concern, in his *Fair Warning* of 1663, was that Papists would, through a Royal Declaration of Indulgence, escape the fate that prophecy had marked for them. But beyond providing useful anti-Catholic fodder, the Book of Revelation had at this stage no special magic for Baxter. Contrast his approach with that of two fellow Protestants who were writing at this same period of time: Samuel Jeake and John Eliot. Jeake, writing to a friend from Rye on 16 December 1663, reflected the Nonconformist gloom of the day – 'our infirmities within us, the divisions amongst us, the darkness of the present night, and sealed up prophecies upon us, when none can tell us how long'. And yet in a letter, soaked with references to Revelation and to the interpretations of Mede and Brightman, there is a characteristically upbeat conclusion: 'it cannot but quicken our cries to heaven, that God would arise, and plead his own cause, and decide the great controversie who are on his side . . . and bring with it the restauration of all things, yea that he would come quickly.'[14] Adventist hopes similarly permeate John Eliot's letter to Baxter on 6 May 1663, in which he expresses his faith in a universal language

> to advance the Kingdom of Jesus Christ, which shall be extended over all the Kingdomes and Nations of the Earth, Rev.11, 15. Not by the personal Presence of Christ, but by putting Power and Rule into the hands of the Godly Learned in all Nations.

Eliot looks forward to the World becoming 'a Divine Colledge', Antichrist overthrown, and the pure distinguished from the vile.[15] Baxter might have said the same in the 1650s, but no such millenarian hopes sustain him at this point. Baxter's reply of 30 November 1663 is admiring but unyielding: he cannot expect the imminent divine government on earth by the saints which Eliot anticipates; he can only counsel faith and patience; he points out resignedly that it is the rich who rule in the world, 'and few rich Men will be Saints'. The Book of Revelation is still welcomed as a source-book for the destruction of Popery, but the positive side is missing: the chiliad hope which sustained both Jeake and Eliot in a period of deep depression for English Protestantism.[16]

To Francis Wheeler, preaching now in Baxter's own beloved Kidderminster, however, he wrote a spirited reply from Acton on 15 May 1666. He rejected Wheeler's accusation that his depressed withdrawal from events implied indifference to the controversies of the time. With some justice he pointed out that attempts to correspond with former parishioners were not likely to be productive when even one innocuous letter to his aged stepmother had been seized by suspicious persecutors. He told Wheeler that he did not know how to respond to his friendly initiative. He had heard from some people of his reputation for integrity, and that he was not one of those who called the Kidderminster godly 'a generation of presbyterian vipers', when there had never been more than two or three Presbyterians in his parish. But he confided to Wheeler the difficulties of sustaining the non-separating Nonconformity which he had set himself as the proper response to the Clarendon Code: 'I am not in love with the deseases or ulcers of any church, but as little with dismembering and dissolving.'

Baxter was, therefore, pleased to hear from Wheeler that there were no sectarians in Kidderminster. Yet he gave Wheeler a candid analysis of the strains now placed upon Nonconformists who opposed the sectarian argument. He found among many of his friends that 'the usage of these times have made a great alteration on their judgments'. Men who were still ready to condemn the Brownists 'yet say, that the case is much altered, and things are not as they were'. Nonconformity could not stand still in six years: if the Episcopal challenge had changed, *so too had the Nonconformist response.*[17]

Baxter was indicating clearly to Wheeler that his own public commitment to support of a visible Church was at variance with the sectarian role that was being forced on him by the Clarendon Code. Thus Thomas Morris's letter to Samuel Jeake on 28 November 1666 has an almost anachronistic air as he wheels out, against a millenarian separatist, Baxter's arguments for a visible Church:

> Would it not be considered (what Mr. Baxter in his Catholick Church sayes) that it unavoidably followes, that then there are no visible Christians now on Earth: for Christians are the Church . . . *You may better Question whether there be any Visible Turks or Jewes in the World? and as well question whether there be any visible men in the world? and how should such be disputed with*? (thus farre Mr. Baxter).

Morris goes on to attack Baptist and Quaker miracle-workers as the triumph of the sectarian spirit. In reply, Jeake writes to Morris on 28 December 1667 that to link salvation with a visible Church is a Papist doctrine:

> Bellarmine and Baxter differ no more than he is the one to annex salvation to a universall or catholike visible church (as he calls it) the other (by yor relation) to a particular Church Or both agree if no Church no Salvation.[18]

Jeake can refute Baxter with the confidence of a man who has found his assurance in Revelation. Without that assurance Baxter was nevertheless (as his correspondence with Wheeler showed) finding himself in greater sympathy with the sectarian argument than either Morris or Jeake realised at this time. This sympathy was more than a reflex response to persecution. Baxter had read Owen's *A Brief Instruction* of 1667 and found in that work two important modifications of Congregational practice: the belief that the whole gathered church has as a society the power to admit into the church, or excommunicate from it; and the belief that the congregation gives the keys at ordination to the church officers. This inspired Baxter to seek a meeting with Owen to effect a union between Presbyterians and Congregationalists.

Talks began in the shadow of the failure of the Wilkins' proposals: a failure which Baxter's friend Manton roundly blamed on Owen in his letter to Baxter of 26 September 1668. The essence of the Wilkins' scheme was that Presbyterians should be comprehended within the Church of England, and Independents tolerated outside. Baxter, Bates and Manton negotiated with Wilkins and Hezekiah Burton; Baxter kept Owen informed about the state of play. Manton felt that it was Owen's efforts, via the Duke of Buckingham, to secure a toleration Bill (excluding Papists) which wrecked the Wilkins' comprehension scheme.[19] Baxter was more inclined to blame the intransigence of the bishops in the House of Lords, and recognised that, with all his faults, Owen was the man whom he had to deal with if talks about unity were to advance. Three major barriers stood in the way of *rapprochement* for Baxter: two temporary, one permanent. The first was that Baxter blamed Owen in large part for the collapse of the Protectorate of Richard Cromwell, and with it his vision of a 'Holy Commonwealth'. Dr Nuttall has established how much Sylvester had to tone down the bitterness of Baxter's manuscript|references|to |Owen|in the published versions| of *Reliquiae Baxterianae*. This was what Baxter thought of Owen's part in the collapse of the Cromwellian Protectorate:

> Dr. Owen and his assistants did the maine work: his high spirit now
> thought the place of Vice Chancellor and Deane of Christs Church to
> be too low: and if the Protector will not do as he would have him,
> he shall be no Protector: he gathered a church at Lieutenant Generall
> Fleetwoods quarters at Wallingford House, consisting of the active
> officers of the Army! (This Church-gathering hath bin the Church-
> scattering project). His parts, and confidence, and busy-bodiness,
> and interest in those men who did give him the opportunity to do
> his exploits; and quite put Hugh Peters beside the chairs (who had
> witt enough to be against the fall of Richard Cromwell, seeing how
> quickly his owne would follow). Here fasting and prayer, with Dr.
> Owen's magisteriall counsell, did soon determine the Case, with the
> proud and giddy headed officers, that Richards Parliament must be
> dissolved, and then he quickly fell himself.[20]

Second, we have seen in the last chapter how Baxter felt that the Owen-
inspired *Declaration of Faith* destroyed his hopes for a *rapprochement*
between Presbyterians, Independents and Baptists by the narrow exclusiveness of the clerical discipline there advocated. Third, there was the
doctrinal division between Owen's emphasis on Free Grace and Baxter's
on Universal Redemption. The first two objections did not prove
insuperable, although they clouded the atmosphere when Baxter began
talks with Owen in 1668. As Baxter put it to Owen, 'that when I
thought of what he had done formerly, I was much afraid lest one that
had been so great a breaker, would not be made an instrument of healing'. The third objection did not surface as a major divisive force during
this period, although the unresolved doctrinal disagreements would
ultimately prove to be the permanent barrier to union. Fifteen months
of consultation ended with Owen's cryptic good wishes to Baxter's
'mathematics'. The doctrinal quarrel, however, did emerge in the post-
Declaration of Indulgence bloom of 1673. Baxter and Owen were two
of six Presbyterian and Congregational lecturers appointed to preach
each Tuesday at Pinner's Hall. As early as 1674 Baxter was arousing
opposition there by his 'Arminian' doctrinal views: a foretaste of the
doctrinal clash of 1694 which ended with the secession of the 'Arminian' Presbyterian lecturers. Thus the 'Happy Union' of 6 April 1691 of
London ministers — by which Independents conceded the right of pastors and elders to ordain and pastors of neighbouring Churches to be
consulted about choosing ministers, and Presbyterians gave up graded

courts and recognised 'gathered' Churches — was to end in a doctrinal schism, with Williams, Howe and Bates attacking the Antinomian tendencies of Independent ministers and withdrawing to Sadler's Hall. But in this earlier stage of negotiations between Presbyterians and Independents, Baxter drew up a series of proposals, upon which Owen commented. Owen's letter to Baxter of 25 January 1669 showed the nature of the gulf which still divided them. Although friendly and conciliatory in tone, Owen worried whether Baxter had been as vigorous against Socinian intrusion into an agreement as he had been against the Papists; more significant still, he disliked Baxter's emphasis on the power of the magistrate to extirpate heresy and error. Baxter, in his reply of 16 February 1669, was unyielding on these points: Socinianism ruled itself out inasmuch as it contradicted Scripture and there was no need for new rules to judge it by; 'the Jealousies and Errors of these times do make it necessary to our Peace, to make some Profession of our Judgment about Magistracy.' But further, he was insistent on the condition that a clear resolve to heal divisions should be owned by all parties. The suspicion, that still held 'Presbyterians and Moderate Episcopal Men' off from joining with Independents, was that they were wedded to the concept of gathered churches of 'all Excommunicate Persons, or Hereticks, or humorous Persons', and to a hostility to parish reformation, as a concession to belief in universal godliness (the nearest that Baxter came to touching on doctrine at this time).

Baxter even referred to an Acton neighbour, 'an honest Scotchman', for information about how *his* nation approved of godliness minus sectarianism. He then broke down for Owen's benefit his neighbour's description of how the discipline worked: twelve Elders in a parish scrutinising the manners of the people, admonishing the culpable, and reporting them to the pastor; the pastor instructing and catechising; a weekly meeting of the people to pray and confer with the pastor; a general examination of the moral state of the parish, in mutual consultation, after every Lord's Day sermon.[21]

If his Acton neighbour were right, Baxter was saying that popular prejudices against Presbyterianism might be misplaced: that there was as real a concern for parish discipline to be found there as among his Ministerial Associations. And this was his real case against Owen's Congregational colleagues: they gave up too easily. One had tried to put a dampener on Eliot's evangelising activities with the comment that 'what shall one, or two, or three in a parish do.' Therein lay the élitist fallacy:

Men first estrange themselves from the poor People whom they should teach with tenderness, and diligence, and then they think their ignorance of the People ground enough to Judge them ignorant, and talk of one or two in a Parish.

Baxter's letter to Owen was thus taking up directly the theme of his letter to Eliot a month previously, in which he had responded with sympathetic outrage at this 'talke of one or two as fit for Church Communion'. In this letter of January 1669 Baxter thrilled at the memory of the Commonwealth Ministerial Associations, in which Episcopalians and Presbyterians collaborated with Independents in an attempt at a real reform of parishioners' morals. The course had been set up and was on the verge of becoming adopted by the nation when in 1659 'confusion buryed all.' And even in the changed situation of the 1660s, when Baxter acknowledged 'it is so dangerous', many came to his home to hear him:

> (But I confesse) I draw them not from the publick assemblies, which is now the mode and mark of sincerity. And (though I goe not to them as I did with my owne charge, yet) I meet occasionally with a very considerable number of them, that I hope will be in heaven.

Baxter blamed 'the separating sort of professours' for the present plight of Nonconformity, and argued that in 1658 and 1659 it was the practical successes of the Ministerial Associations which had won over many men from separatism to a belief in the possibilities of parish discipline, until the political upheavals occurred.[22]

Baxter might profess that he was not intending to draw people from public assemblies, but an indiscreet allusion by one ejected minister to the conventicles that were permitted at Acton led to Baxter's arrest on 12 June 1669 and temporary imprisonment. It was such punitive legislation that marked for John Humfrey the parting of the ways with the old Puritan tradition of obedience to the magistrate. His *A Case of Conscience* in 1669 was inspired by detestation of Samuel Parker's *A Discourse of Ecclesiastical Politie*: he called Parker 'a young Leviathan himself' and argued against Parker that the magistrate could not command what was contrary to 'the Peoples weale'.[23]

This was too much for Baxter. Humfrey was his friend, but Baxter wrote him in 1669 a letter of reproof which showed how deep-rooted was his commitment still to the Protestant traditions of obedience to magistracy. He claimed — as we saw in the last chapter — that his effort to answer Harrington had been a unique lapse from his faith that clergymen should not meddle in politics; that Bilson and Jewel were not teachers of resistance; that Jeremy Taylor and Richard Hooker were the wrong models for the Protestant imperialist; that the King was *universis maior* as well as *singulis*; that it was better to suppress passages which treated the hypothetical possibility that a King might alienate his kingdom; that irritation with the Five Mile Act, however intelligible, was to be deplored if it led men away from respect for magistracy into admiration of populist Anglicans, or Calvinist resisters.[24]

Baxter's refusal to go along with Humfrey's attack on magisterial impositions was costing him the support of some of his admirers. To one of them, Henry Oasland, on 29 June 1670, Baxter wrote a defence of non-separatism. He had seen a letter of Oasland's to Elys in which Oasland had said of Baxter that 'No man hath so lost himselfe.' He wondered how many others Oasland had written to in the same refrain. But, said Baxter, it was the separatist spirit 'that hath bred Ranters, Quakers, Seekers, Infidels' and brought about the collapse of order; it was the separatist spirit which in the past had been successfully opposed by the old English Nonconformists, Ball, Hildersham, Dod, Brightman and Bradshaw. He was irritated at Oasland's praise of Owen as enjoying men's esteem — 'whose esteeme I promote as much as most do', Baxter commented peevishly, with his own negotiations with Owen very much in his mind — and thought that his 'people-pleasing' was as offensive as some conformists' 'prelate-pleasing'. Should men suffer death, he asked, rather than communicate with the present ministries of Bewdley and Kidderminster?[25] Rumours at this time were growing that Baxter was about to make his peace with the Church and win promotion: perhaps Oasland's suspicions were inspired from such a source. Certainly it was in 1670 that Lauderdale was tempting him with a Scottish bishopric. In July 1670 John Rawlet was writing to Baxter of 'many stories of your conformity and preferments, Dean of Rochester, parson of St. Martins and I know not what. A Knight in our parish shewd mee a letter from London very confidently reporting it, but wee soon heard it confuted.' Rawlet noted Baxter's high standing at this point of time with both conformists and Nonconformists.[26] But on 5 August 1670 Joseph Cooper wrote in irritation to Baxter, at his suggestion that ministers should read the printed prayers and sermons of other men, rather than exercise their own gifts. He was not equating *ministerial* spontaneity with that of their *congregations*, who must use the form prescribed by their ministers 'unlesse we mean to turne the teaching Assemblies of Gods people into the Silent Meetings of poore deluded Quakers'. But equally ministers must not stand there in the midst of them, 'like a Dumb Idol', but must exercise their vocational gifts. The contrary view Cooper characterises as 'Levelling'.[27] But Baxter's reply, on 15 August 1670, sounds the same note as his reply five weeks earlier to Oasland: 'its little better to be governed by the populacy than by the prelacy.' Baxter's purpose, as in his letter to Oasland, was to show Cooper the lawfulness of having Communion with a Church that uses a form of prayers, even although it should be imposed. He that can prepare a good sermon in a day with the help of his book is better employed than labouring a week 'to bring forth a Erroneous or barren one of his own only without those helps'. He thinks that Cooper would have to agree that Arminius was better employed reading Calvin to his scholars, instead of his own lectures. This did not make Arminius less of a Minister and hence introduce 'Levelling'. Indeed Baxter claimed: 'I confesse to you I had rather Mr. Dell, Mr. Saltmarsh, Mr. Simpson, Mr. Randall, Dr. Crisp and many another in England had read good bookes than used their talents to preach false doctrine as they did.' Baxter found it '40 and 40 times' harder to learn a sermon of another's without a book, than to preach extempore. There was an old minister who went up and down England preaching, to great applause and laughter. Baxter and another grave divine had both to sit down in the bottom of the pew, 'being not able to forbear', when they heard him in action. But Baxter would still have preferred that he read a sermon 'that would have made sinners weepe, then preacht them into laughter'. Baxter quoted Usher on the greater skills required to teach fundamentals than to make florid orations. There was too much 'people-pleasing' in the advocacy of sectarian solutions to the grave problems of the day.[28] This was the theme of his letter to Eliot on 2 September 1671 in which he voices his concern that 'since Ministers are stript of all by the parliaments, the favour of the people is become their interest'. The most censorious win the most applause: 'the common body of strict professours are strongly addicted to be censorious agt all that are not of their mind.' He particularly deplores, in the more relaxed atmosphere introduced by Charles II, a tendency among ministers to have much more exacting standards for conformity to the Church than for association with the sects: 'And yet because the Quakers suffer with us (who will not any of them owne the scripture or the essentials of Christian faith) we have far more charity for them, than for a pious conformable minister.' This was Baxter's own dilemma:

I that am of the principles of Dod, Cartwright, Hildersham am more censured for sometimes holding communion with such a conformist as Sibs, Preston, Bolton (for such for piety, though of lower parts, we have) than I should be if I had joined with the Quakers.[29]

An understanding with Independency, which found Baxter on the side of the barrier with the Quakers opposed to the conformists, was not the goal towards which he was working in the years between 1668 and 1671. That was the danger: but it is clear in his writings of 1671 how excited he was by a different sort of understanding with the Independents.

In his pamphlet of 1660 (written against the ideas of the Roman Catholic, William Johnson), *The Successive Visibility of the Church*, Baxter had defended the reality of the Protestant 'visible Church'. Yet he had owned up to Johnson the temptation of a very different model: Sulpitius Severus had described how an angel had appeared to St Martin to rescue him from benighted conformity. Baxter acknowledged that the story was unsettling for himself, 'concerning my Communion, the Reader may easily know with whom'. Baxter weighed up the narrative with care. Many ancient writers were credulous. Sulpitius Severus was not, however, one of them. He had received the testimony from St Martin's own mouth. St Martin's miracles had been substantiated by Sulpitius Severus, St Martin's own testimony, and by many other credible witnesses: they were the cause of his canonisation. Baxter concluded: 'And if such History is not to be believed, I will not mention the consequences that will hence follow.'

On the other side a holy man *could* be mistaken 'and take that for an Angels apparition which was but a dream'; St Martin's avoidance of communion with the Bishops might have been appropriate *to his time and place*, without necessarily having relevance to seventeenth-century England; there was danger in making the actions of men – founded 'upon pretense of any Revelations and Miracles' – the arbiter of behaviour against Scripture; his separation was a temporary withdrawal only 'from those individual persons, whom he supposed to be scandalous'. For all these reasons Baxter was able in 1660 to stifle the temptations posed by St Martin.[30] That figure would re-emerge as Baxter's attraction to more radical solutions grew in the 1660s and 1670s.

Baxter's willingness to accommodate both Independents and Baptists in a new Protestant union was put forward by him in a pamphlet of 1671, *A Defence of the Principles of Love*. He related his hopes to the change of mood in New England:

And since their Synods late moderation, I know not many Churches in the world, besides the Waldenses of the Bohemian, Pelonian and Hungarian Government, who are neerer to my own judgment, in Order and Discipline than those in New England are, and none that for Piety I prefer before them.

He knew that some people were cross with him for taking in the Baptists: yet they were not the Munster Anabaptists, but men differing from many of their fellow Protestants on a difficult and abstruse point of doctrine.

The godly, conformists and Nonconformists, should be united with each other, as well as internal parties *within each* among themselves. Nye and Thomas Goodwin had cared for Preston enough to publish his works after he had died. A union which excluded, on the one side, bishops like Grindal, Downame or Hall and, on the other, Nonconformists like Ames, Hildersham, Cartwright and Baynes was valueless. He quoted Dod's gratitude for the Church's sake that some conformed and for Truth's sake that some had not. Baxter particularly disliked the tendency he detected among some of his fellow ministers to shrug off the non-separating tradition of their predecessors with the boast that '*we are grown wiser and have more light than they*! when as in our writings upon the same subjects shew that we are far in that below them'. The path to an understanding with Independency is possible precisely because its leaders *share* that non-separatist tradition: Henry Jacob in the past, Philip Nye in the present. Ames is claimed as a half-Independent, wholly against separation. And most significant:

I need not mention the great moderation of New-England, where their late healing endeavours greatly tend to increase our hopes of reconciliation. (O that the rest of the Churches were as wise and happy!) Whose experience hath possessed them with a deep dislike of the spirit of separation and division.

Baxter went on to defend the Book of Common Prayer against disorderly extempore rhapsodies, to argue against the millenarian crankiness of men like Major Wilkie at Coventry, to protest against Fifth Monarchist and Ranter exploitation of the melancholic, and finally to clear himself of charges of having committed himself totally in the past to Richard Cromwell. Baxter asked to distinguish between the books and the dedications. The *books* were against Popery and English Prelacy: the *dedications* were to the Protector. But Baxter only dedicated them to him because he had heard that he was disposed to peace: 'Nor did I ever see him, speak to him, or write to him else, nor hear from him.' It was necessary to make these protestations to show that a union with Independency was possible once misconceptions had been removed; he even quoted from Bilson that Presbyters were of human, not divine, warrant in order to show that the differences with Independents were even narrower than they had supposed.[31]

He repeated this point in another pamphlet of 1671: that pastoral power is divine, 'being a Power to labour and suffer in patient self-denyal for the Church of Christ and the souls of men', whereas to diminish 'that Secular Church-power' which clergymen (not Bilson) claim to be of divine right, 'is but for Princes to be Princes, whether the Clergie will or no'. The Roman Church's ambition at 'Secular Church-power' must not be confused with ministerial exercise of 'this troublesome ungrateful work of Discipline'. To forgo discipline and concentrate on preaching is the guarantee of a 'sensually pleasant' ministry. The excommunication practised by Presbyters and bishops is not an exercise of the Sword. The more pomp and similarity to the court of a civil magistrate the less Baxter liked it; the true effectiveness of clerical discipline is comparable to the pulpit sermon rather than to lay coercion. Magistrates are to blame who let themselves be the tame executioners of clerical decrees, and thus blur the distinction between true and false ministerial discipline:

> If you say, that Clergy men are to blame that urge them to it, you shall not easily think worse of their so doing, than I do: It is greatly against our wills that the Sword so closely followeth Excommunication.

In arguing against the false clerical discipline Baxter would seem closest to Hobbes and Harrington. But whilst stressing that the minister was more like a physician or a college tutor he added un-Hobbesian riders: that magistrates could not make or unmake the office; that it was of as immediate divine right as the office of magistrate; that the magistrate cannot hinder the ministry. However, if the magistrate acts injuriously, the minister 'must not resist, but patiently suffer for obeying God'.[32]

Baxter could not duck in 1671 the question how far his own practice in the Commonwealth had matched his theory of the relationship between minister and magistrate. In answer to Bagshaw he claimed that he had only ever defended Cromwell's *exercise* of government, not his *right*, although he acknowledged that he had perhaps gone too far in praising even the good done by a usurper 'lest it take off the odium of his usurpation'. His chief regret now was that he had not consulted enough lawyers about Parliament's right to start a Civil War: Hooker, Bilson and other episcopal divines had pushed him too far into populism: 'I was the easilyer drawn to think that Hooker's Political Principles had been commonly received by all.'

It is interesting that in a work which is so defensive and apologetic in tone, Baxter is fierce in refusing to let Bagshaw drive a millenarian wedge between him and the Independent allies he was now seeking. He made the critical distinction between 'those called *Fifth Monarchy Men*' and 'meer Millenaries'. Some of his 'most intimate and honoured friends favour the Millenary Opinion'. Baxter knew 'how commonly it was owned by many of the Ancients'. He asked rhetorically who did not know the name of millenaries like Mede and Twisse, and challenged Bagshaw to document any case when Baxter had tried to expose such men. Bagshaw had claimed that *conversation* with Fifth Monarchy Men, as opposed to the way they were represented in the press, established quietist principles that were similar to his own. Baxter was incredulous. He quoted Leveller writings, the sermons of Vavasour Powell, the activities of the Fifth Monarchy Men whom Cromwell had to suppress, and asked Bagshaw if he thought that 'Venner and his company' held no more than Baxter did. In particular, Erbery, Saltmarsh, Dell and William Sedgwick provided lurid examples of contradictory millenarian visions about the day of the Last Judgement.[33]

Correspondents were urging on Baxter a fuller explanation of his Nonconformity than he had given in reply to Bagshaw. Henry Blake, for instance, wrote to him on 8 July 1672 about a half-an-hour conversation he had held with Baxter's adversary, Hinkley, 'who was pleased to let his passion and prejudice have the reine, while he ran down the aphorismes of justification'. Old scars still bit deep. Hinkley had boasted of Baxter's failure to answer his challenge to explain his position. Blake quoted Baxter's own expressed fear 'of thrusting your head into an oven that is red hott'. He asked Hinkley if 'he would be a skreen to keep you from being scorched'. This fear was a recurrent one with Baxter. Baxter had warned Edward Fowler in a letter of 7 October 1671 against youthful impetuosity and of the 'many wranglers' standing 'at his elbow'.[34] His further rejoinder to Bagshaw in 1672 spoke of Bagshaw's design 'to draw me to talk of those matters over rashly (about Wars and Governments) (which I regret of talking of so much already) that he may catch somewhat for his Malice to make use of to a further end'.[35] But Hinkley had reassured Blake that he would undertake Baxter's indemnity and knew that he could procure it. Therefore Blake begged Baxter for a *full* exposition of his reasons for not conforming, already hinted at in 'your first reply to Bagshaw'.[36]

It was difficult in the face of such pleas for Baxter to remain non-committal. Even in his further reply to Bagshaw, despite the cautionary preamble, Baxter attacked a universal toleration which might bring in Popery, and went on to deal with the *hypothetical* question of an overtly Papist King on the English throne. This was sailing close to the wind, even if Baxter added the reassurance for the imperial Protestant that only a madman (Bilson's one qualification to obedience) would contemplate his own destruction: 'though I know we have the greater security against this, because *Popery is so much against Princes interest, and is the delivering up the Kingdome in part to a foreign power*'.[37]

Richard Taylor wrote a moving letter to Baxter on 10 October 1672 about the dilemma that confronted the loyal Protestant Nonconformist, and appealed to Baxter as umpire. He hated the oaths which the Clarendon Code forced him to take, but should he leave the ministry? Against such a decision were the non-separatist examples of pious men like Sibbes, Dod, Preston, Bolton and Baxter himself. But impelling him out were no less powerful reasons, which Baxter could well sympathise with. The admission of the profane to the Sacrament of the Lord's Supper weighed heavily on his conscience. To exclude, required a painful and laborious accountability 'into the Chancellors Court'. To admit, on the other hand, often inspired the truly religious '(although they may err in this point)' to withdraw from a mixed congregation and make *themselves* the object of the disciplinary process: 'and how should we declare them excommunicate, and in the power and under the dominion of the Devill — without the guilt of sin, whom we account the servants of the Lord?'[38]

It was just this sensitivity to discipline which Baxter found lacking in some of the correspondents who were urging him to conform. Typical was Henry Dodwell, who wrote Baxter a bluff, friendly letter on 14 December 1672. His letter exuded robust common sense. He could not see why Baxter did not conform. After all, Baxter was different from the 'old Puritans' and sectarians: at the Savoy Conference, bishops had intended 'only an Exterior submission, not an Internal Approbation of the Particulars'.[39] The obedience asked was to Hobbes's *Leviathan*, not to the recent updated version by Samuel Parker, which sought to improve on Hobbes by engaging the *souls* of the subject.[40] But this distinction was meaningless to Baxter, who deplored the Familist distinction between the outward and the inward man, whether he encountered it in Hobbes, Saltmarsh or Dell.

In a way, Dodwell was parodying the 'church-type' ideal, to which Baxter had been giving his allegiance. Dodwell was truthfully saying that Baxter was against sectarianism. His overtures to Independency in the previous two or three years had not been contradictory to that principle. Indeed Baxter was building hopes of a *change within Independency* upon the New England Synod of 1662, Owen's pamphlet of 1667, the past of Henry Jacob and the present of Philip Nye, in order that comprehension (on a 'church-type' basis) would be wide enough to include Independents and Baptists as well as moderate Episcopalians and Presbyterians. Emphatically such a resolution did not close the door on pastoral discipline; the reverse. Some variation on the Usher scheme would bring in moderate Episcopalians and ensure parochial discipline; Baxter's Scottish neighbour at Acton had told him how a non-sectarian discipline could work there; Congregational colleagues had collaborated in the past in Ministerial Associations without betraying their principles. If only they would shut up about Free Grace, abandon the chimera of a toleration that would bring in Papists and Quakers, and be less pessimistic about the numbers of godly in a parish!

The trouble was that the 'church-type' ideal was often offered, not as the *instrument* of parochial discipline, but as its *alternative*. This was true of Dodwell's letter, which was asking from Baxter a blanket approval for conformity, and which revealed no sensitivity to the grass-roots problems of pastoral discipline, so memorably set out in Richard Taylor's letter. Dodwell's was the type of letter, in its well-meaning lack of understanding, which suggested that there was something in the very nature of a commitment to diocesan Episcopacy which inevitably militated against godly discipline. This was why Baxter had turned down a bishopric in 1660 and again in 1670: until a substantial concession was won, on the lines of Usher's Model, to securing effective control of discipline at parish level, conformity was untenable. But more: if the 'church-type' ideal could only be defined along Dodwell's lines, perhaps there *was* a case for the alternative 'sect-type' ideal?

Baxter was not ready to ask such questions yet. When he did, he would be taking a momentous step for Restoration Dissent. Such a step is separable from the negotiations with Owen and other Independents between 1668 and 1674, which we have seen to be designed as an accommodation *within the 'church-type' ideal*.

And it is in this sense that Baxter's response to Dodwell on 5 January 1673 has a prophetic significance. Baxter is patently irritated by the incomprehension of the non-participant. What could the don of Trinity College, Dublin, know about the problems that tormented the Richard

Taylors? How easy for *him* to settle on a bland 'church-type' conformity! Baxter's reply was withering:

> I must say, that it is the calamity of Churches, when their Prelates and Pastors are men that never were acquainted with the flocks, that spend one half of their days in Schools and Colledges, and the other in Noblemens or Gentlemens houses, and then talk confidently of the poor people whom they know not, and the *Discipline* which they never tried.[41]

Rather in the way that, only four months later, Baxter would scold Edmund Hough for his arrogance in passing judgement on the origins of the Civil War without having been a participant,[42] he rebuked Dodwell for his unreal sense of detachment:

> Even you whom I honour as a person of extraordinary worth, constrain me by this your Letter to think that I dispute as about war with one that never stormed a Garrison, nor fought a battel; or as about Navigation with one that was never one month at Sea.

Accept the Erastian thesis that no discipline is necessary (apart from the lay use of the sword and the clerical use of preaching) and Baxter could accept Dodwell's complacency with the *status quo*. Discipline is what Dodwell left out; Baxter defined it as 'a personal watch over each member of the flock'.[43]

Francis Fullwood shared Dodwell's conviction that the traditions of English Nonconformity were anti-separatist. Therefore he pleaded with Nonconformists not to make the royal Declaration of Indulgence an excuse for breaking with those traditions. Charles II had acted 'from his own grace and clemency and reasons of State' (including the encouragement of trade): he had not implied that the penal legislation was faulty or that gathered churches had a legitimacy. The anti-separatist arguments of Ball and Baxter were still valid. If Presbyterians now built 'new Synagogues' out of gathered Churches, they would become 'Independent Apes': 'as others are Independents by choice and profession, you will make yourselves so by necessity.'[44] Baxter found Fullwood's interpretation of how Nonconformists should respond to the new situation created by the Declaration of Indulgence disengenuous: 'by notabusing our Liberty, he meaneth, not-using it.' He himself made a distinction between London, 'where it hath ever been usual to go to Neighbours Parish-Churches from their own' and country areas, where

Nonconformists are numerous, on the one hand, when scandal would not be created by separation, and smaller country areas on the other, with fewer Nonconformists, who 'must deny their personal conveniences, rather than hinder a greater good'. The monolith of the 'church-type' was breaking down. Baxter went so far as to say: 'I see not what great hurt it would do any, for Anabaptists, Separatists, etc. that cannot joyn with the Parish-Churches, to have leave to meet among themselves, and worship God together in peace.'[45]

Fullwood and Dodwell were mild advocates of uniformity compared to Samuel Parker. In a letter of 26 February 1673, Robert Middleton reported to Baxter the embarrassment felt by moderate Episcopal divines with the fierce and intemperate language of Parker. But Middleton also took Baxter mildly to task for equating the views of the Church of England with Grotius's. Middleton was, however, interested in reading thoughts of Baxter 'on the subject of conciliation about the Arminian points.[46] This was a subject which Baxter was to develop in full in his *Methodus Theologiae Christianae* of 1681, although only a few months after Middleton's letter, on 12 July 1673. Baxter was telling Alexander Pitcairne about his intention to reconcile 'sober Arminians', and those who hold to the Synod of Dort, with such a project. He acknowledged however that booksellers were far from keen on Latin treatises.[47]

Baxter's views were further refined in correspondence with Edward Eccleston. Writing to him on 2 August 1673, Baxter explained the circumstances in which he had turned down his bishopric in 1660. London Presbyterians had warned Calamy that acceptance would be to his dishonour. No such inhibitions were placed on Baxter and Reynolds, 'having not the same pre-engagements'. He was particularly incensed at the suggestion that, '*how long we blow'd on our offer'd preferments*'. He told the messenger that he was uninterested at the first time of asking, but he wanted to get the response of Worcestershire ministers, who 'rather inclined my acceptance of it, and therefore would have made it no reproach'. Calamy had wanted them to act jointly: in fact Baxter refused the second day after Hyde's offer and Reynolds within a week accepted. Calamy (for a bishopric), Manton and Bates (for deaneries), held out until the King's Declaration had been repulsed in the Commons. Indeed Baxter had written to Hyde that if the King's Declaration had been made into a Law he would have promoted conformity and unity on such terms with all his interest and skill, and that such service would be seen to be disinterested if he had refused office. On the other hand, 'I made no great doubt of it, but that Declaration would quickly dy, and was but for a present jobb.'

But this was the Episcopacy which was offered in the King's Declaration, not the Episcopacy which presided over the Clarendon Code. Therefore Eccleston cannot read conformity to one as a precedent for conformity to the other. Whatever the *name*, as Baxter argued with fellow London ministers at the time, the Declaration altered the *species* of English Episcopacy. And altered it in the way which was crucial to Baxter:

> But this much I well remember; That the power of the Church keyes was much restored to the Parish Pastors: wch was the great change: And so he that before was the sole Bp and Church pastor of many hundred parishes was now (save *de nomine*) but an Archbp; having many hundred Bps or Pastors under him, instead of meere Teachers, without power of the Keyes, wch were before.

This was for Baxter the main attraction. A number of other features flowed from this critical redefinition of Episcopal rule: they were features which Baxter hoped to see incorporated in the reform proposals that he was negotiating with Orrery and Wilkins at this time. The parish pastor consented to the confirmation of all his people and joined in the pastoral discipline of the rural deanery; Archdeacons and Bishops exercised discipline and ordination along with certain of the presbyters; Lay-Chancellors could not excommunicate; suffragan bishops were to be set up under Bishops for the exercise of discipline; whether bishops were *iure humano* or *iure divino* could be left to men's own judgements (his indifference on this question was to be shown later by his manuscript notes on Hammond); no subscription to the Canons of the Church of England would be required; no man was to be constrained to use liturgy, Cross, surplice, kneeling at receiving the Sacrament or bowing at the name of Jesus; no minister was to be forced to refuse to baptise men's children for want of godfathers, or the image of the cross; no reordination was to be required; the subscription about abjuring the Covenant and resistance of the King was not to be required.

Thus Reynolds, in accepting his bishopric, had drawn up in writing his beliefs in *iure humano* Episcopacy and non-arbitrary rule. The terms upon which he accepted office, and upon which Baxter might have accepted office, were not the ones that were now in contention in 1673. Eccleston's invocation of 'the old Episcopall Divines', of Hooker and Sanderson and Stillingfleet's *Irenicum*, is therefore not to the point. Indeed Hooker and Bilson would have been Nonconformists, in Baxter's judgement, 'by our test': and so too 'abundance of Bps and most of the old pious Conformists'. Nonconformists of today are 'not the same men that lived in the daies of our forefathers, nor are obliged by that name to defend their opinions': a striking declaration of independence, which would be the basis of Edmund Calamy's revision of 1704.[48]

Baxter had cause to feel aggrieved with Eccleston, which he outlined on 30 August 1673 in a letter to him. As an unordained young man he had been befriended by Baxter, who had counselled against his being ordained by Presbyters alone, and talked him out of conformity. Baxter then thought highly enough of him that, if he had been allowed a London ministry, Eccleston would have been made his assistant. Later he learned that Eccleston had conformed and been ordained. He was piqued at not being told his reasons by Eccleston himself, but 'it was my judgment and practice never to persuade any man from conformity, unless he constreined me, by asking my advice, lest the Church should be the loser by it.' He broke this practice with Eccleston and felt that, on grounds of special friendship and the difference of thirty years in age, the lapse was venial.[49] Another lapse was when he let his feelings against the unnecessary silencing of the ministers run away with him, as he described in another letter to Eccleston on 6 October.[50]

The largest monument to Baxter's contrition appeared in the same year: his *Christian Directory*. The fourth part was entitled 'Christian Politicks': a development of the theme of his letter to Eccleston, 'how bad it is to catch a distaste of Rulers'. He meant it to stand as a revision of the Political Aphorisms, his 'Holy Commonwealth', which had created so much subsequent trouble for him. Yet he was not recanting the doctrine it proclaimed, 'the Empire of God'. But some of the terms which he then had used had been injudicious; there was need for a treatise which emphasised more powerfully the importance of *obedience*. *Memorandums* to the civil magistrate would replace the *Directions* which he had issued in 1659. The fourteenth Memorandum was the most significant: 'Keep the Sword in his own hand, and trust it not in the hands of Churchmen.' Evil rulers could be rebuked in private when alive or disgraced in history books when they were dead. To dishonour bad rulers while they lived can only excite subjects to rebel: that was why Baxter did not like Humfrey's tone. To weaken magistracy is to enthrone the rabble. Mary Tudor put Protestant martyrs to the stake; there would have been many more 'if she had but turned the rabble loose upon them'. The godly receive more good than hurt from even the most vicious tyrant. The worst of magistrates is better than none. The one limitation on magistracy, raised by Bilson's hypothesis 'if a Prince should go about to subject his Kingdome to a foreign power', is more illusory than real, since to pull one's neck away from the Romish wolf's greedy jaws is a very different thing from theories of resistance. Bilson and Baxter were teachers, not of resistance, but of subjection.[51]

But the more he pursued his differences with Dodwell, not only in 1673 but in later years, the less happy he became with that deference to authority which came so easily to a university man. In his letter of 5 August 1673 Baxter argued that their different educational backgrounds made the crucial separation between them. If Baxter had never been a pastor, and stayed within a college, he might have thought as Dodwell did. Conversely, Dodwell's horizons might have been enlarged by conversation with country people, as Baxter's were. Dodwell's way was to show from old histories that 'some body did so 1400 years ago, or a thousand, in some places of the world, if stories deceive us not; and therefore it may be so now.' Baxter's test, in their particular controversy, was a more pragmatic one: 'whether one Schoolmaster can govern a thousand Schools without any but Monitors under him, and teachers that have no Government' — in the latter case, thinking ruefully of his own vulnerability at Kidderminster as a young pastor, facing the angry rabble who were stoning him for his views on original sin. Blind obedience to such an imperfectly created institution had its own perils: 'And if one at *Muscovy* can get a Courtier to make him a Bishop, he and such others are the Church.'[52] Baxter *wanted* to uphold magistracy. He had said so to Eccleston; every page in the fourth section of his *Christian Directory* echoes those sentiments. But there were practical problems for the Kidderminster parson which the Dublin don could not dream of. It was one thing to defer to the authority of the schoolmaster, with his thousand years of tradition behind him; another, for one who cared about discipline, to accept a structure where the schoolmaster had nominal authority, but where the discipline of individual schools was in the hands of monitors, and of teachers without powers. It was his practical concern with discipline which weakened his theoretical submission to authority.

Owen had wanted Baxter to pursue the logic of his objections to Dodwell: to find his discipline *outside* that National Church which had been found wanting. Perhaps it was his impatience with Baxter's failure to cut the umbilical cord with 'church-type' traditions of deference which led Owen to conclude their attempts at an understanding with the words, 'I am still a well-wisher to these mathematics'. Coleridge thought that it showed 'a very chilling want of open-heartedness on the part of Owen',[53] but there *was* something unreal about negotiations which steered so politely away from the doctrinal issues which had driven such deep wedges between the two ministers in the 1650s. It is possible that, in their negotiations, Baxter found it easier to forgive the man who toppled Richard Cromwell from the Protectorate than Owen did the man who had destroyed Protestant unity of doctrine in 1649. It was not only Hinkley on whom talk of *The Aphorismes of Justification* had disturbing effects. The fact that the newly formed Pinner's Hall Lecture should, as early as 1674, be unsettled by doubts about Baxter's doctrinal orthodoxy boded no good for the attempted union between Presbyterians and Independents. Nor would the promise of Baxter's Latin tome on Free Will be as helpful to ecumenism as Baxter claimed. It was ominous when John Tombes, his enemy when he was against Baptism in the early 1650s and his ally when he was against Popery in the late 1650s, should write a bitter letter to Baxter on 10 August 1670 about the way in which his *Life of Faith* revived old feuds of the 1650s by characterising Calvinist orthodoxy as 'Dominicans' predetermination'.[54] There was a defensive note in Baxter's letter to Dodwell's ally, Sherlock, on 24 December 1673, in which he claimed that 'a few Independents on these points, about free grace, speak not the common sense of the Nonconformists'.[55]

Baxter had hoped that his *Christian Directory* of 1673 would cancel out his *Holy Commonwealth* of 1659. A year later his contrition took another form: reprinting his *Key for Catholicks* of 1659, he replaced his dedicatory epistle to Richard Cromwell with one to the Earl of Lauderdale, and no less effusive. That improbable friendship, cemented by the Earl's translation of French works for Baxter's benefit in the late 1650s, has seemed to show Baxter in a poor light. To Coleridge the twenty guineas it earned him from the Earl was despicable: 'I would as soon have plucked an ingot from the cleft of the Devil's hoof.'[56] In fact he acted out the philosophy of his *Christian Directory*: *public* admiration of the magistrate — 'no Noble Name which I shall prefer'[57] — coupled with stinging *private* censure of his morals: 'the sensualists are hardened by you ... you are not only corrupted but a Corrupter ... sensuality and compliance with sin is your ordinary course.'[58]

The need to respect magisterial authority: the need to correct sin. These two impulses — fused in Baxter's 'Holy Commonwealth' — were in danger of pulling in contrary directions in the mid-1670s. The somewhat desperate formula — by which Lauderdale was honoured in public and rebuked in private — represented Baxter's effort at bringing the two together again. But higher than Lauderdale was Charles II: what was the

Christian subject to make of the magistrate who used his authority to loosen, not tighten, the restraints on Popery?

Baxter's answer was *A Treatise of Self-Denial*, first written in 1660 but published with substantial additions in 1675. His *monitory epistle* warned of the Popish threat, and its source in the false doctrine that magistrates had no right to meddle in matters of religion. There was the yearning for 1659 in his words: 'O what a blessing is a holy self-denying Magistracy to a Nation!' Instead the men in power were for liberty, 'for all that will call it self Religion, even Popery not excepted (nor I think, Infidelity or Mahumetanism)'. This was the cruel test for subjects who prided themselves on their obedience to authority: 'if Great men would set up Popery in the Land by a Toleration, alas, how many ministers think they may be silent, for fear lest the contrivers should call them seditious or turbulent or disobedient.' Meanwhile the need for magisterial discipline was greater than it had ever been. If a house were on fire, the bell is rung, the magistrate feels a call to take action. But not so 'when the fire of Hell is kindling in an Ale-house, that's nothing, but must be left alone.' Excise-farmers are vigilant in detecting clandestine ale-sellers: 'They do not say *I am not bound* to go search after them.' Baxter wanted to see magistrates with the same zeal for sniffing out sin, as the excise-man shows in sniffing out ale. Baxter contrasts the vigour of laws made in the cause of *self* ('Thieves and Traitors must die') and the remissness of Law-givers in the cause of *God*: 'Blasphemy, Malignity and Impiety is not so roughly handled.' The same spirit of self-love is evident in the carping of critics at ministers who took to flight from the plague: 'his loss to the whole Church is more to be regarded than the content or benefit of particular persons.' The spirit of self-love inspires Papist distortion of the Protestant doctrine of Grace. Such critics cavil at the inequality of God's Grace:

> A man that feareth and Loveth God, and an unsanctified man may be both overtaken with the same sin, perhaps a gross one, as Noahs and Davids, and Peters was: and yet this may be a mortal sin in the ungodly; I mean such as proves him in a state of death; and yet not so in the gracious person.'

This is not antinomianism: the Elect may stumble once or twice (as Noah was drunk once in his lifetime) but they do not live by a code of ill-doing. Moreover there is a great difference in the same acts from different hearts: a passionate word from a relative is not the same as that word in the mouth of a sworn enemy.

Is self-denial compatible with property? Baxter believes that it is. Man has not an absolute right to property, but *as a steward* exercises that right on behalf of God. The denial of property would make the exercise of charity impossible. The bowels of compassion must not be closed: 'If we must lay down our lives for the brethren, much more our estates.' Baxter believed that 'Levelling community is abominable' but 'Charitable Community is a Christian duty.' That 'Charitable Community' was found in the primitive Church, where there was no renunciation of property. It is customary to read Baxter's repudiation of Leveller doctrine as the heart of his social teaching, and to treat his injunctions to compassion for the poor as palliatives. Now it is true that Baxter does not believe that property is theft, but it is impossible to read his description of what a 'Charitable Community' meant in the primitive Church without seeing an early vision of the ideal later to be expounded in his *Poor Husbandman's Advocate*:

> And therefore in the Primitive Church there was no forbidding of Propriety; but there was (1) A resignation of all to God, to signifie that they were contented to forsake all for him, and did prefer Christ and the Kingdom of God before all: and (2) There was so great a vigour of true Charity, as that all men voluntarily supplied the wants of the Church and poor, and voluntarily make all things in common that is, *Common by voluntary Communication for use*, though not *common in primary title*: And so no man took any thing as his Own, when God, and his Churches and his Brethrens wants did all for it. O that we had more of that Christian Love that should cause a *Charitable Community* which is the true Mean between the *Monkish Community* and the *selfish tenacious Propriety*!

In such passages Baxter comes closer to the ideal which inspired Tawney to write *Religion and the Rise of Capitalism* than to the phenomenon which Tawney was studying. Egalitarianism was a sin to be avoided, it is true, but compared with the sin of avarice it dwindled into insignificance: 'Levelling hath not destroyed one soul for ten thousand that an inordinate love of Propriety hath destroyed.'[59]

The pathos in the work as a whole comes from the distance between the grandeur of the moral *aims* and the inadequacy of the *means*. The hunger for a godly discipline was as acute as when he wrote his *Holy Commonwealth*. But where was he to find that 'holy self-denying Magistracy'? Not from rulers who, at best, lack the nerve to discipline the ungodly and, at worst, set up Popery under the umbrella of a general toleration. William Penn, writing to Baxter on 8 October 1675, saw that the real case against Baxter's *Holy Commonwealth* was not its revelation of an understanding with Richard Cromwell or sympathy with regicide, but its demonstration of the continuity of Baxter's desire to impose upon the consciences of others. His ideals were unchanging; in 1675 he only lacked the means: 'who writt an holy commonwealth to An usurper to practice, and raise his new Monarchy upon, and that hath preach't up the use of Civill power to restraine Consciences'. Richard Cromwell was Baxter's Joshua, 'that was to lead them to the Holy Land'. Penn was patently worried that, after the Declaration of Indulgence had been quashed, and the Test Act passed, the comprehension initiatives that Baxter was pursuing with sympathetic Churchmen like Tillotson and Stillingfleet[60] would leave Penn's Quakers isolated: 'Richard Baxter and his brethren are for casting us and others to the doggs by a comprehension leaveing us under the Clutches of mercilesse men.'[61] In reply, on 10 October, Baxter claimed to be able to read Penn's mind on religion by his desire for a 'Grotian or Cassandrian concord'. Baxter loved unity, esteemed men like Grotius, Cassander and Erasmus as much as any divine did, and had no desire to be cruel to Papists as individuals. His case against Grotius – as true as when he uncovered the 'Grotian religion' in 1658 – was that he was a Papist in upholding the Council of Trent and Papal primacy 'by the Canons'. Baxter's recently published *Catholick Theologie* aimed at *reconciliation* with Rome on doctrinal matters. Moreover he had been consistent in his scepticism at identifying Papal Rome – as opposed to Heathen Rome – as the Antichrist in Revelation (this was ten years before his *public* testament of his disbelief, in his *Paraphrase on the New Testament*). Some called him Bellarmine Junior for such charity to Popery. Also he had written so many books for the divine right and power of princes, against resistance and separatism, that he enjoyed an international reputation in Germany, Sweden and the United Provinces. He wanted union, but not on 'Grotian' terms which destroyed the power of princes.[62]

These were the lessons which Baxter expounded in his *Catholick Theologie* of 1675. He reviewed, in the light of experience, the significance of what had happened between 1643 and 1675. He isolated three main causes of the unsettled state of the nation. First he put 'Religious Clergie – TYRANNY'. This argument went beyond his customary defence of imperialism from clerical ambitions. *The Emperor Constantine himself could not escape censure*: this was a significant shift in his thinking. Many moderate Papists and more Protestants now agreed that

'Constantine and other Emperors that over-exalted the Clergie, poured out Poyson into the Church'. Second, he deprecated dogmatic zeal: 'it is possible for Christians to live in settled peace and comfort, in respect to their heavenly Felicity, without *a certainty of perseverance and Salvation.*' *Probability* is a good enough antidote to fearfulness: the search for an illusory certainty inspires antinomian excesses on the one hand and melancholia on the other. Third, he attacked an intellectual failure to distinguish between special and universal Grace, and the corresponding failure to distinguish between the inequality of men before God, in His role as *dominus*, and the equality of men before God, in His role as *rector*. Hobbes and Jeremy Taylor, determinist and pelagian, were equally remiss in emphasising only one aspect of God's Nature to the exclusion of the other. God's rectorial licence was 'far from a full permission': an invitation to anarchy. On the contrary, preachers had an overwhelming obligation to set Heaven and Hell before their congregations.[63] But, on the other hand, God in a judicial capacity did not deal unequally with persons, yet as Benefactor or *dominus* He *did* act arbitrarily and unequally: Baxter had argued for the reasonableness of such inequality in his recently republished *Treatise of Self-Denial.*[64] He nevertheless acknowledged the supreme difficulty of routing the determinism of Hobbes, which made every act of the will necessitated by physical premotions; a worse task than reconciling Lutherans and Calvinists. His ideas, taken up by the apostate Jew, Spinoza, had the effect of subverting 'all morality as distinct from physical motion, and consequently of all true Religion'. He acknowledged the seductive appeal of Hobbesian views as an *intellectual* force; fortunately their impact was blunted by their *ethical* inadequacy. The wickedness of Hobbes and Spinoza had discredited their principles; conversely, the goodness of the covenant theologians like Thomas Hooker and Robert Bolton as 'practical Preachers in these practical cases' had been the best defence of the Christian religion. The victories of morality were not to be measured by intellectual conquests. There was an *'objective certainty'* which could be separated from *'subjective certainty'*: 'men may be *uncertain* of that which is certain in it self.' This was a truth which the 'practical preachers' of the 1620s and 1630s had instinctively grasped. The gap between them and Papist casuists was less wide than was commonly supposed. The Papists suffered from the Protestant caricature of their views on merit: Grotius and Cassander were less wedded to salvation through works than their Protestant critics alleged. But could their views be given credence, since Papists were liars? Baxter replied: 'If once you fall upon such Rules as those (as that Accusations against adversaries are to be believed without proof, on one side and not on the other) Gods Rule against receiving evil reports will be cast out.'

And yet it would be quite wrong to see, in such passages, a significant relaxation of Baxter's hostility to Popery. There is an important passage in which Baxter makes clear the distinction he draws, in controversies with Papists, between the topics which 'depend on a Carnal Interest and Mind, and such as do not, but arise from the meer difficulty of the subject'. Questions of Predestination, Free Will, Justification and Merit were placed by Baxter in the second category. That is why he emphasised the intellectual difficulties of confronting Hobbes and praised the good sense of the practical theologians. Baxter's strategy was to dispose of the illusory dividing lines (over Grace, over the identification of the Papacy with Antichrist), not as a preliminary to union with Rome, *but as a preliminary to getting down to the real dividing lines*: 'In the former sort I said our difference is very great, and like to be so; and such are the differences about their Papal power and Church state, their Government, and worship as gathered hereunto.'[65] To these differences he added doctrinal questions 'as that of Purgatory, Indulgences, Auricular Confession abused by them, transubstantiation etc.', but it is striking none the less that Baxter should see the quarrel with Rome as primarily over *church government*. This puts his views on Grotius in perspective, which had already perplexed Middleton when he had written to Baxter two years earlier.[66] Grotius's views on Merit had been misunderstood; he was not wrong to query the identification of Rome with Antichrist. He was personally admirable but politically poisonous: he exalted a foreign jurisdiction and worked for a union between Protestants and Catholics towards that end. Baxter's case against a foreign jurisdiction was rooted in his understanding of history: his imperialism came from Foxe, which in turn came from a reading of the prophetic texts. In an *indirect* sense, therefore, Baxter's rejection of a foreign jurisdiction came from Revelation. But only in an indirect sense: his scepticism of identifying Rome with Antichrist was not only that it was based upon 'a dark text in the Revelations, or Daniel' but upon the supreme difficulty of finding light in *any* passages in Revelation or Daniel. The texts were obscure; the commentators on them disagreed with each other — no wonder Calvin kept out! Baxter did add piously that 'though no doubt but the book of Revelation is a great mercy to the Church, and all men should understand as much of it as they can'[67] — a far cry from the excited mood of 1686 when in prison the secrets of the Apocalypse were opened out to him! And it was then that his objections to a foreign jurisdiction would acquire a new clarity, and that his personal resolution of the constitutional problems would acquire a new form.

Baxter had already made clear in his correspondence with Dodwell and Fullwood that they should not presume too much upon his willingness to conform to authority. The strains which conformity imposed upon tender consciences, like Richard Taylor's, were not to be underrated. If such a conformity were to be exacted to advance a foreign jurisdiction, the case for separatism took on a new dimension. It is interesting that one correspondent, 'T.C.', wrote to Baxter on 3 August 1676 to complain that Baxter was changing his mind. Contrary to previous statements, he was now justifying the withdrawal of men from the Church of England into separate congregations of the faithful: 'No, sir, it lookes like a design, and as few actions can speake, it tells the worlde that tis not religion about wch all this stir is made but pride and interest.'[68] It is certainly of interest that, in his *Naked Popery* of 1677, St Martin, whom Baxter had buried in 1660, not without misgivings,[69] is resurrected as an admired model for separatism. And in the same pamphlet Baxter said – as Calamy would in 1704 – that: 'Nonconformity since 1662 is quite another thing.'[70] In his *Christian Directory* Baxter had argued that tyranny had done less harm than disobedience.[71] He argued the reverse in a letter to Dodwell on 9 July 1677: 'the tyranny of Prelates hath done more hurt than the disobedience of the People towards them.' He quoted his beloved friend, Sir Matthew Hale, on the analogy of the two pikes that devoured the rest of the fish in the fish-pond: 'The Lord forgive the Presbyterians their over-keenness against the Sects, before the Pikes have made an end of them.'[72] Baxter was not seeking now to detach Presbyterians and Independents from the sects in a comprehension but rather to make them recognise their common self-preservative cause *with* the sects. Heylyn's biography of Laud did nothing to lessen Baxter's dread of the episcopal 'pikes'. Alarmed at the plans there revealed for widening the Church doors to Popery, Baxter is to be found in 1678 making a worried additional comment to his *Sacrilegious Desertion of the Holy Ministry Rebuked*: 'seeing a Turke, Heathen or Heretike may be the soveraigne of a Christian nation whether he be therefore the Essentiating head of the nationall Church'.[73]

At the time of the Popish Plot and Exclusion Crisis, deference to a 'National Church' and to the supreme magistrate no longer seemed the highest wisdom. Now, in the dedicatory epistle to his *The Nonconformists Plea for Peace* of 1679, he joins St Martin in renouncing communion with *Ithacius* and *Idacius*, although not going so far as St Martin did in separating from the synods of bishops. The people's right to choose teachers must be defended against the magistrate's will: otherwise all Christian Kingdoms would 'conform to Moscovie when the Prince commandeth it'. Princes might change their religion as often as the moon: were subjects to change with them? *Consent*, not *coercion*, is the basis of Church communion. The power of the magistrate must not be enlarged to the point where 'we must ask leave of Rulers that Christ may be Christ, and souls may be saved; as if the keys of Heaven and Hell were theirs.'

St Martin stood as a symbol of reproach to such dumb obedience. Sulpitius Severus was a reliable source:

> But if it be true, then one of the holiest workers of Miracles since the Apostles, hath assured us, that his separation from communion with these Bishops (tho' cruel to Hereticks, so gross) was confirmed by vision, and by an Angel from Heaven, and he forbidden their communion for the time to come. We again mention this, as not yet having heard any answer to it.

What relevance had the example of St Martin to Restoration Noncon-formity? Only that the Five Mile Act was in preparation while the Plague and the Great Fire were raging:

> At the mention of which the heart of the writer of this trembleth; especially to think how much further the Bishops went in this than the Synod of *Ithacius* and *Idacius* went, from which *Martin* separa-ted to the death by Gods miraculous instruction.

The prelates could no longer get away with beating the 'No Popery' drum to drive Nonconformists into submission to their authority:

> If one Party would bring men to such a pass that they must be hanged, imprisoned, ruined, or worse, unless the favour of the Pap-ists deliver them; and the other Party had rather be saved by Papists, than be hanged or ruined by Protestants, which of them was more to be suspected of Popery?

The choice between sectarian life as a Papist gift and persecution under Muscovy tyranny: this was the Nonconformists' dilemma in 1679. Additions to the pamphlet, 'more particularly of National Churches', showed clearly the drift of Baxter's mind.

There were senses in which the concept of a 'National Church' was unexceptionable. Christians prayed that all nations and kingdoms should become the Kingdoms of Christ; Kings may 'call all their Kingdoms into a holy covenant with God (by lawful means) giving them an example first themselves'; ministerial associations for concord could be called a 'National Church'. But in the common understanding of the term the concept was of a nation of *professed* believers. To the sectarian mind *there* was the rub. Any attempt to scrutinise the worth of the individual communicant led to fragmentation. But the price paid for wholeness was hypocrisy: a price that Baxter had been willing to pay in the past, and would be prepared to do so again after 1686. The wheat and the tares were mixed together. In a 'National Church' an outward profession of holiness was the most that could reasonably be required; inevitably hypocrites exploited this breadth of communion. But in 1679 Baxter did not want to have the hypocrite as the price of a 'National Church'. In desiring a Christian Kingdom the intention of Christians had not been to force all to be baptised or to 'profess themselves Christians, whether they are so or not: for lying will not save men, nor please God; and even the Papists are against this'.

Although God has not made ministers arbitrary judges of men's secret thoughts, the power of the Keys consists in ministers' ability in judging how far an outward profession of holiness corresponds to the working of their mind. Baxter was suggesting that the qualifications for admission to a National Church should not differ from qualifications to the Sacrament of the Lord's Supper. Once a separation of men with an 'inner certainty' had been disclaimed, the alternative was not the promiscuity of common admission: 'If only the seeker be made Judge, it will be a new way of Church-Government, and a bad.' Throughout his critical analysis of the 'National Church' concept Baxter shows a sympathy with the sectarian impulse. He concludes with a denunciation of fanatical enthusiasm, and yet adds:

> serious considerations maketh some of us think, that too little notice is taken of the HOLY GHOST setting Pastors over the flocks, which the Scripture mentioneth ... though none on pretence of the Spirit must reject order or ordination, nor make themselves the sole Judges of their own sufficiency.[74]

Stillingfleet accused Nonconformists like Baxter of betraying earlier principles, in his *The Mischief of Separation* of 1680. In his reply in the same year, Baxter reiterated his points that 'conformity now was quite another thing than it was before, and to us far more intollerable,' that Bilson, Hooker and Usher would have been Nonconformists now, and that Stillingfleet had debased his earlier services to Protestantism. He regretted his own trust in Stillingfleet, which had led him to hope great things from his talks with him and Tillotson. He had urged on his Parliamentary colleagues sympathetic response to healing proposals which emanated from such a source. Stillingfleet for his part had seized on the importance of Baxter's embrace of the St Martin symbol:

> What do such insinuations mean, but that our Bishops are the followers of *Ithacius* and *Idacius* in their cruelty; and they of the good and meek Bishop St. Martin, who refused communion with them on that account? If men entertain such kind thoughts of themselves and such bad thoughts of their Superiors, whatever they plead for, they have no inclination to Peace.[75]

Political circumstances in 1680 made Baxter update some material first written in 1668, and which he now published as *The Second Part of the Nonconformists Plea for Peace*. He had to scotch the rumour 'that our Principles are rebellious' since the revelations of Titus Oates, Prince, Smith, Dugdale and especially Dangerfield were that 'part of the Plot for the destruction of the King and change of Government and Religion' was 'to make King and People believe that the Presbyterians had such a Plot'. In this pamphlet Baxter reiterated the *Christian Directory* arguments, rejected Buchanan and Goodman as seminal influences on Nonconformist political theory, and criticised Richard Hooker and Jeremy Taylor for over-large concessions to populism.[76]

But his reservations, about a 'National Church' and over-reliance on the civil magistrate, remained as strong as ever. In his pamphlet of 1681, *A Search for the English Schismatick*, Baxter had men like Hooker and Bilson in one column as representatives of the 'Old Church of England', whilst Heylyn, Thorndike, Sibthorpe and Mainwaring were chosen as men of the 'New Church of England' on the other. This was a belated recognition of the Parliamentary case against clerical-inspired royal absolutism in the 1630s. Sibthorpe and Mainwaring, the particular targets of attacks in the Commons for their fulsome praise of magistrates who imposed Ship Money, had been ignored by Baxter for fifty years. In the intervening period, if Baxter had wanted to criticise Church of England divines, it would have been Bilson and Hooker for surrendering so much to the people. They were now heroes, representing 'the Old Church of England' with whom the godly *could* conform. Baxter documented the 'strivings of Parliaments since Archbishop Laud's Government against Innovators, Popery and Arbitrary overtopping Law': Hall and Abbott had suspected Laud of Popery, and were themselves opposed to a toleration of Papists. The magistrate's authority was limited: 'yet may they not invade the Pastors office, or peoples rights, nor force men to trust their Souls to the Pastoral Care of unable or untrusty men.' A 'National Church' was allowable if it meant only 'all the Churches of a Nation as under one Prince or as associated for Concord': the term was once more being drained of significance, and very much as Calamy would define it in 1704.[77]

Baxter's *A Treatise of Episcopacy* had been 'meditated' in 1640, written in 1671 and put by, and then reworded as a reply to Dodwell in 1681. It is a pity that we do not have the three stages clearly demarcated: it would be a fascinating insight into the evolution of his ideas. What emerges in the final version are the anti-imperial themes sounded in other writings between 1679 and 1681. First, there is the argument that the rot began with Emperor Constantine, and with his encouragement of a 'swelling and degenerate Prelacy'. There is even doubt on Baxter's part about when to fix the point between the apostolical institution and the height of Popery. Second, he is sceptical about the use of Revelation, not only for identifying Antichrist with Rome but for identifying *bishop* with *angel*: 'I therefore who, because of its obscurity, am apt to be distrustful of almost all Arguments that are fetcht from the dark Prophecies of *Daniel*, or the *Revelations*, am little satisfied with this from the name *Angel*.' Third, whatever doubts Baxter had about a future millennium described in Revelation, he was not impressed by the preterist arguments of men like Hammond, who believed that the major prophecies had been fulfilled in the first century or two of the Church's existence. He said that he would accept Hammond's arguments,

> when I am fallen into so deep a sleep, as to dream, That the famous Coming of Christ, and our gathering together to him (which is a great Article of the Christian Faith) is but Titus his Destruction of Jerusalem; and that the reward promised to all that love his appearing, is meant to all that love the said Destruction of Jerusalem.

Baxter was not prepared to renounce lightly his adventist hopes, which would be rekindled in 1686 with revised thoughts about Revelation. Thus Baxter could offer a fine historicist *critique of* the preterist view in 1681: he poured scorn on the belief 'that the Revelation is made up of such a sense, and that most or much of it, was fulfilled before it was revealed and written, and all the rest fulfilled long ago (about Constantines day) except one Parenthesis, or a few verses in the 20th chapter'. What he could not do – until his revision of 1686 – was to offer *an alternative millennium*. Foxe's idea of a past chiliad, inaugurated by the Emperor Constantine, had been acceptable to him once, in a vague sort of way; it was to revive for him with thrilling clarity as a result of his researches of 1686. But in 1681 the imperial ideal was in shreds. This was how Baxter dismissed Constantine's millennium:

> And that the Resurrection and Thousand Years reign of the Martyrs, is that 1000 years from Constantine's beginning, in which the Bishops had Wealth and Honour, and sate on Thrones, and judged the People in Courts, as our Lay-Chancellors now do; and that the Glory, Wealth and Grandure of Prelates is the Churches Resurrection, Glory and Felicity: And that these happy thousand Years continued 700 years after the rising of Mahomet; and included those 8th, 9th, 10th and 11th Ages which Erasmus and all learned men (even Bellarmine himself) so dolefully bewail.

Fourth, Baxter attacked the very structure of diocesan Episcopacy as making Church discipline impossible. To the objection that 'till Constantines time there was no Christian Magistrate, which made it then needful: But since the case is not the same', Baxter responded with a reference to 'Galaspies *Aaras Rod*, which fully proveth the continued need of discipline'. This is a significant citation: to invoke the name of the man, whom his fellow Scots had accused of making Presbyterianism into an Independent mould, was to show where his sympathies lay in 1681. He even called the present anti-disciplinary Episcopacy 'practically Erastians'. Fifth, Baxter asserted that 'the Magistrates Sword is not the chief strength of true Church discipline.' Never was Baxter's independence of the magistrate more emphatically stated:

> *A natura rei* there is as much of Divine Authority, as much of the power of his Precepts, Prohibitions, Promises and threatnings, as much of Heavenly inducement, as much of the terrors of Hell, as much of internal goodness of holyness, and evil of sins, as much of Soul interest in what the Minister propoundeth for mens conviction, as there is, when it is backt with the Magistrates Sword. And if all these have no force, Christianity must be a dream, and able to do

no good in the world.

Baxter explicitly seeks 'another frame' of discipline, which does not depend on the magistrate's sword, but relies upon *voluntary* participation. He denounces the magistrate's use of the sword against heretics — 'And the case of St. Martin towards Ithacius and Idacius, I have oft enough repeated.' He compares bishops with Druids and deplores their coercive principles, which force men 'to lie and play the Hypocrites'.[78]

It was inevitable, with such ideas dominating his mind in 1681, that another pamphlet which began ostensibly with an attempt to rescue the good name of Lewis du Moulin should end by rebuking him for being 'too zealous for the Magistrates Power in Erastus sense'. He had gone further in this direction than even Stillingfleet in his *Irenicum* had — easier to perceive Stillingfleet's failings now! — and Baxter had tried to persuade him to retract his writings against excommunication. The Papists' ability to don 'divers sorts of Vizors' once more haunted Baxter: 'to him one Court Card signifieth more than many others'. Baxter now paid tribute to the vigilance of the Parliamentary Opposition to Laud's reconciling design, 'described by Doctor Heylin'. Parliament had been engaged in a fight for fifty years against Popish Plots. Grotius's master plot had been taken up by Thorndike: 'Doctor Heylin maketh the syncretism and closure with them in the bosom of the now indulgent Church, to be Arch-Bishop Laud's very laudable designs.' What of the argument that *'there is no reason of separation because of the doctrine of our Church'*? On the contrary, argues Baxter: 'now you have corrupted it . . . there is great cause of Nonconformity.'[79]

There is reason for *Nonconformity*; Baxter cannot quite bring himself to say that there is reason for *separatism*, although he was very near to saying it. *An Apology for the Nonconformists Ministry*, also published in 1681, was less incisively anti-Episcopal, but then most of it had been written between 1668 and 1669. Still, the fact that he should publish it at all, and address it explicitly to the 'moderate' bishops, Compton, Barlow, Croft, Rainbow, Thomas and Lloyd, shows that he had not written off all bishops as Druids. Some 'women and hot-brain'd lads' had indeed wanted to be governed by 'the veriest ignorant sots and drunkards' to legitimise their separation from the Church: an argument which Baxter found repellent. But his pamphlet was a warning to the Barlows and Comptons that their decency was not enough; if pastoral discipline proved impossible under their supervision the Nonconformist ministers would not be deterred, by charges of Brownism and separatism, from doing their duty. This was the analogy which came to his mind:

> If the Law make one in every Parish an Overseer of the poor, and
> forbid all other relief but by that Overseer; and either through the
> number of the poor, or his own disability or negligence, he relieveth
> not one of twenty, or at least so poorly, that twenty, or ten, or two
> to one are in danger of famishing. I will disobey that Law, or relieve
> them as far as I am able, though I go to Goal for it, to be volumin-
> ously railed at as a Schismatick or Rebel.

Baxter was declaring that his vision of a 'Charitable Community'
carried moral imperatives that transcended legal inhibitions on relief to
the poor. Nor was he distinguishing the godly poor from the lazy and
recalcitrant; the moral imperative held:

> Yea, more, if the poor be ideots, foolish, proud and surly, and will
> rather famish than beg relief of their Overseer, I will take my self as
> guilty of their death, if I relieve them not when I am able; and if I
> think their folly to be my excuse, I shall be deceived.[80]

It was characteristic that Baxter should once more see concern to
effect a discipline, and compassion for the poor, *as related impulses*.

On 17 May 1682 John Cheyney wrote an important letter to Baxter, in which he showed how dangerously Baxter had removed away from
belief in a 'National Church' to acceptance of a 'sect-type' thinking.
Baxter had claimed that discipline was incompatible with the diocesan
structure of episcopacy. To Cheyney this erected a false antithesis
between the Churchman and the saint: 'To be a syncere Christian, a
syncere godly man, and a syncere Church-member, so far as my apprehension serves me, are for substance the same, as convertible.' Hypocrites infiltrate the Church of God as tares are mixed with the wheat.
To attempt to distinguish the tares from the wheat is to commit the
separatist fallacy. Baxter had been tempted along that dangerous path
by his mistaken zeal for 'discipline'. Cheyney quoted from Baxter's
*Church-History of the Government of Bishops and their Councils
Abbreviated* his declaration that 'by the diocesane frame true discipline is become impossible and impracticable'. For Cheyney discipline
was simply equated with godliness: where there is true godliness there is
the substance of discipline. Discipline was not then about ministerial
control but about personal ethics. According to Cheyney, Baxter held
the following beliefs:

That there is no such thing as a national Church by divine law under the Gospel; and that when we say, The Church of England, we do either denominate the Church from an accident, or ascribe that to a part which belongs to the whole, or equivocate by corresponding a policy with a community. So that properly and in right speaking there is no such thing as the Church of England: nor can it be told who is the constituted head thereof.[81]

Cheyney was not wrong to see that, as Baxter developed his case against Episcopal opponents like Dodwell and Sherlock, his attack was broadening to a rejection of 'Church-type' thinking. Baxter believed that Dodwell's argument, that there was no true ministry except by ordination going back to the Apostolic Succession, set up 'an Universal human Supreme Government'. He was most uneasy with the deference commended by Dodwell to authority: 'if you really mean so that whatever God commandeth us in Scripture, we must do none of it if the Governors forbid us . . .' 'tis far unlike Bishop Bilsons of subjection, and such others.' Baxter was playing in 1682 his now familiar game: of dividing the old Church of England men like Bilson and Hooker from the new divines, like Dodwell, Sherlock, Heylyn and Thorndike. He estimated in his own diocese some fifty thousand souls needing to be admonished and disciplined. The only Episcopal power which interested Baxter was the ability to administer effective discipline: 'thus personally to convince men, and declare to the Congregation upon proof, the fitness or unfitness of men for their Communion, by penitence or impenitence'. Baxter never forgot the Kidderminster rabble who had stoned him, in his early preaching days, for his views on Original Sin: such would have to be accepted as communicants in Dodwell's National Church.

Dodwell's hunger for totalitarianism made him suspect to Baxter; he wrote of 'Mr. Dodwel's LEVIATHAN or Absolute Destructive Prelacy'. Dodwell had been contemptuous of writings against authority. Baxter now embraced the populism of a Hooker in reply:

Writings are not so contemptible to us in comparison of that which you take *to be all the visible Authority of the Church*. It is your Richard Hooker that saith, that the Law *maketh the King, and giveth and measureth his power*, and that *it's usurpation which obligeth no man's Conscience*, when power is taken, and used which the law never gave.

And the ends to which this totalitarianism were to be put was the most sinister aspect of the new Anglicanism: in the writings of Bramhall, Heylyn, Thorndike and Dodwell Baxter detected the re-awakening of the old Laudian dream of reunion with the French Catholics on the basis of conciliar power rather than Papal supremacy – he noted the way in which they preferred French Catholics to Huguenots.[82]

That is why Baxter dedicated his *The True History of Councils Enlarged and Defended* of 1682 to Protestant Nonconformist ministers, 'who are against our Subjection to a Foreign Jurisdiction'. The Anglicans get an undeserved reputation for anti-Popery because they reject the Italian brand, which would have the Pope rule arbitrarily over Councils, but not the French brand, 'who would have the Pope rule only by the Canons or Church Parliaments, and to be *singulis Maior et universis Minor*'. He was grateful to Beverley (whom he was soon to join in prison), Barrow and Tillotson for alerting him to the new direction of the Catholic threat. He quoted Beverley on the Protestant recognition of councils as instruments of Christian Kingdoms, in which civil and ecclesiastical power were one: this is different from the Laudian cult of councils, which is to be seen – along with the silencing of Protestant ministers and the denial that the Pope is Antichrist – as part of a consistent design at union with Catholicism, mercifully patent in Heylyn's biography of Laud. Once more Baxter cites Hale's analogy of the fish-pond: the two Pikes were 'for ending the Division by reducing all to unity of species'.

The desire for uniformity is now seem as reprehensible: part of the Catholic master plot. But what of its antithesis? Was not the pluralist society equated with anarchy and misrule? Was there not even a convenient text at hand? Thomas Edwards's *Gangraena* was the seminal text for anti-sectarianism: the horror-comic revelation of what England would be like in a society which had allowed a thousand flowers to bloom. It was a text that Baxter had often referred to; which he now revealed that he had in part contributed to. When Baxter deplored the want of discipline, Edwards's *Gangraena* was never far from his consciousness. But in 1682 he urged his readers to take fresh stock of *Gangraena*. Then followed one of his most remarkable revisionist efforts:

The Errours that sprung up were much more tenderly resented then than now. You now have many called Wits and Persons of Quality, who at a Club dispute against the Providence of God, the immortality of the Soul, and a future Life; and there is neither Church-Admonition, Excommunication, nor any great matter made of it, but they are Members of the Church of England, the purest Church in all the world. Whereas in those licentious times, if a Souldier had spoken such a Word, it would have rung out through the Land, and perhaps his Tongue would have been bored with a hot Iron.

The true times of indiscipline were the 1670s and 1680s with a National Church and an absence of ministerial control at parish level, *and not the 1640s when sects reigned supreme*. Edwards' catalogue of vices reflected not the greater wickedness of the actors but the greater sensitivity of the observers. Baxter's explanation of how he came to share, in a minor way, in Edwards's catalogue makes clear how this could be so:

I had a hand in Mr. Edwards Book thus: An Assembly of Ministers after Naseby Fight sent me into the Army to try if I could reduce them. Dayly disputing with them, a few proud self conceited Fellows vented some gross words: At Amersham a few Country Sectaries had set up a Meeting in Dr. Crook's Church, to dispute and deceive the People: A few of Major Bethel's troop (that afterwards turned Levellers and were ruined) joined with them: I met them, and almost all day disputed against them, and shamed them, and they met there no more. I gathered up all the gross words which they uttered, and wrote this in a Letter to Francis Tyton, and after I found them cited in Mr. Edwards *Gangraena*. And whats the absurd Speeches of a few ignorant Souldiers, that are dead with them, to the Heresies and Schisms that these 1000 or 1200 years continue in all the Roman Communion.[83]

Apart from entering into a Covenant with Dell and Saltmarsh, it is hard to imagine a more dramatic *volte-face* by Baxter. The anti-sectarian had played the trump card: Edwards's *Gangraena*. And Baxter had been unmoved. He had, it seemed, turned his back upon the ideal of a 'National Church'. To complete the process of conversion only outward persecution was lacking: this was to be remedied in June 1682.

On 17 June Baxter had written to Mrs Haynes to protest against her rejection of eternal Hell-fire. He assured her that Hell was a reality: 'like the place of Execution and the worst of Earth like Newgate'.[84] Three days later an incident was reported, which was the beginning of a chain of events that would enable Baxter to pursue his analogy with greater familiarity:

20 June 1682 . . . The last Lords day some Constables (took a file of

Souldiers) disturbed Mr. Jenkins, and Mr. Watson in the Citty, and Mr. Baxter and another or two without, but the business was done with great indifferency. Some continued till the Exercise was done without any interruption, and some sunge a Psalme, and so the Officers went away, the armes of very few were taken, very few were apprehended or carryed before any Magistrates, and none I thinke fined or committed to Prison.

Baxter was not to be so fortunate on 20 October when '5 constables, some Beadles and 3 Informers' apprehended him in his own home and seized his goods: 'the Officers staid in his house till Lords day night, and it was expected he should have been sent to Newgate on Monday.'[85] In the event it was not to be until two years later, in November 1684, that he was to be once more apprehended; he was bound over and finally committed to prison in Southwark in February 1685, tried by Jeffreys in May and June of 1685, and imprisoned until 24 November 1686. But he had also fallen foul of Oxford Convocation in July 1683:

> July 19 1683. And now the Toreys tooke the advantage (which they were always ready to doe) to Address for the Prosecuting of the Protestant Dissenters ... Oxford University condemned Baxters Principles Gazette from July 23 to 26 Ann. 1683 ... but let pass Grotius Hooker and Bilson who art far beyond Baxter in placing the Originall of Power in the Populacy; and in the Doctrine of resistance they giving severall instances where the people might take up Arms against their Soveraign and Baxter had in print answered Hookers Arguments for placeing the Originall of Power in the People.[86]

Against such a background of intimidation – and Roger L'Estrange was attacking Baxter as a rebel continually between 1681 and 1687 in his news-sheet *The Observator* – it would not have been surprising if Baxter's commitment to obedience to the civil magistrate and conformity to a National Church – already gravely weakened – would finally snap.

Owen had died in August 1683. An anonymous correspondent wrote to Baxter in March 1684 complaining at his lack of taste in publishing details of private conversations with him after his death. This writer claimed that a refusal to communicate with the diocesan Church was in the best Nonconformist tradition, honoured as much by Baxter as by Owen. He praised Baxter's pastoral services in the Worcestershire Association, his rejection of Blake's open communion and his *Gildas Salvia-nus*: all of which testified to the concern for pastoral discipline which he shared with Owen:

> Mr. B. was very successful in establishing the Divine Right of paro-chiall or Congregationall Churches, restoring to the presbiters the whole of their pastorall Office, and to the exercise of Discipline, in like manner so did the Congregationall Men in the Citty of London and many other places of the kingdome. The Presbyterians indeade attempted the setting Upp a Nationall Church Government on the basis of a Divine Right, but without effect, and since that time the notion has been exploded by most that are of that name.

In the willingness of Baxter and his fellow Presbyterians to reject Blake's promiscuity, and the chimera of a 'National Church', lay real hopes for a union with Independents on the basis of a shared 'sect-type' ideal. There was, said his correspondent, a fundamental incom-patibility between 'the Divine Right of Congregationall Churches' and 'the Divine Right of Diocesane'.[87] Baxter made it clear to the corres-pondent on 1 April 1684 that he had intended no discourtesy to Owen, and would have held back any references to him if the correspondent had written sooner. He was particularly concerned to scotch the allega-tions that, unlike Owen, his role after the Restoration had been one of acquiescence in conformity. He claimed that booksellers would not touch some of the material he had prepared against the persecuting prelates. Moreover he had suffered much: 'Morley and Parker ready to make me a Traytour. The Oxford Convocation have burnt my Holy Commonwealth.'[88] Even so, manuscript material from 1683-4 which has survived shows how concerned Baxter was at this time that poster-ity might judge post-Restoration Nonconformists as having been more passive than they really were.[89] Two points he stressed in explanation of their refusal to make more use of Parliament: 'those that we thought best knew both the Bps and Parlt. told us, that *There was no hope*'; Clarendon had made it clear to them that their refuge was in King, not Parliament. Baxter had this interesting comment:

> I had oft occasion of speech with the Lord Chancellor, Hide, who was not apt to hide his mind, but was I thought an open man: And he plainly made me understand, that he thought that the overvaluing of parlts. had bin the cause of our late warres.

The Cavalier Parliament proved Clarendon correct in his promise that the link between dissent and Parliament would be severed, and that the hopes of Nonconformists would depend on the generous use of the Royal Supremacy:

> And the King had oft attempted wayes of clemencie, wch we never found from the parlt. or Bishops. And we are not so madly out of love with Monarchy, as to be willing rather to be destroyed or land among theives in jailes by a parlt. than saved by a King. He is good to us that doth us good.[90]

That is why, as other unpublished papers from 9 July 1683 show, Baxter was anxious to assure Morley of his rejection of resistance theories. As he drily remarked, 'You need not cite Cooke to prove England a Monarchy. I never doubted of it.' What is more — with a tilt at the 'new' Church of England policy — he believed that the King was not accountable to 'a Pope or Generall Councill, wch is more than every bishop will say'. But non-accountability did not extend, any more than it had with Bilson, to cover madness in a King:

> But if one King had many Kingdomes, some Protestants and some Papists, and he would use the power of his papist Kingdome to destroy his Protestant Kingdome, this would be, as you say, madnesse, but such a Religious madnesse as . . . the Irish would be capable of.[91]

If the choice was between Hooker's writings and Dodwell's (or Morley's) Leviathan, the Irish Rebellion of 1641 showed which was the proper choice for a Protestant subject to make.

Baxter's anonymous critic of March 1684, who had compared Baxter to his disadvantage with Owen, returned to the attack on 20 April. Where Owen had stood out against the Morleys and Dodwells, 'Tom Parkhurst your bookseller' had told this correspondent that Baxter had approved of John Corbet's book in favour of taking the Oxford Oath. In Baxter's reply, of 9 June, he recounted all the sufferings which he had endured since the Restoration, and the scanty recognition which they had won from John Owen and his friends: 'some of your party have printed to the world that I am like to be a Jesuite, or as Mr. Owen insinuated, a Socinian, or at best an Arminian.'[92] Five days later, writing to John Thornton at the Earl of Bedford's home, he expressed his thanks to the Earl as one who *had* recognised his sufferings by sending

him money to alleviate them: 'I do not believe that he and I were ever
in safer state than now, nor in which we had greater cause of thankful-
ness.' The letter, despite a disclaimer, shows interest in Beverley's readings in the Apocalypse:

> I am loath to meddle with secret things, but when I think of Daniel's
> mention of the Ruling Angels of Persia, Judea etc. I am ready to
> entertain Mr. Beverley's notion as possible, that the Superiour
> regions have distinct nations of spirits, and that we shall rejoice and
> be rewarded in the same societies that we did our duties in. But how
> and wer it will be as well if it be not so.[93]

Too much should not be made of a graceful acknowledgement of
patronage. Beverley had been already singled out by Baxter as an astute
critic of 'French' Conciliar Catholicism. It was to be another two years
before prison would draw the two men closer together in correspondence about the millennium. But Baxter had already, in 1684, published
the work which became the pretext for his imprisonment, *A Paraphrase
on the New Testament*. The case for the prosecution was that Baxter
was secretly propagating rebellion when he claimed to be paraphrasing
Scripture; when he spoke of 'devils' he meant clergy of the Church of
England, and when he spoke of 'godly ministers' he meant 'factious
and seditious persons'.[94] The true scandal of the work, on the other
hand, for many of his Protestant colleagues lay in the public repudiation of the identification of Rome with Antichrist. This was what had
shocked opponents like More, and friends like Mather.[95] In his 'postscript' he claimed to have been saying nothing else for 27 years; as we
showed in the first chapter this was a rather disingenuous description
of his engagement with that question over a long period of time. But
there was a truer sense in which he was not offending against Protestant
apocalyptic. He was not merely saying that the Pope was not *the* Antichrist of prophecy; he was saying that he was *an* Antichrist, as an usurper. Seen in the context of his controversies with Dodwell and Thorndike, the work was designed to show that the English nation must not
be subordinated to a foreign jurisdiction:

> Therefore I judg that a Confederacy or Coalition with the Church of
> Rome, in any of these Sins, or in the very form of a Church headed
> by a pretended Universal Head or Soveraign, is to be abhorr'd by all
> sound Christians: And I am glad that this Kingdom is sworn against
> all Foreign Jurisdiction, Civil or Ecclesiastical.

A reference to the deliverance of the Church in Constantine's time anticipated the apocalyptic theme of his writings in prison two years later; even without such reference, his anti-Papal warnings could only have been seen as a concession to Popery by those who measured anti-Popery by a simplistic identification of the Papacy with Antichrist. This was Baxter's worry: too many Protestants had concentrated on a doubtful Scriptural text, and missed the *real* case against Popery. It was more dreadful for Papists to be condemned by 'the known Laws of Christ' than by 'a dark and controverted Prophecy'. And the point is that these 'known Laws of Christ' *were themselves to be found in Revelation*. In rejecting one part of speculation on the millennium Baxter was not rejecting Revelation as a whole: the tentative hypotheses of 1684 would be fleshed out in the researches of 1686.[96]

Baxter's letter to John Faldo, on 25 August 1684, reveals his worry that his arguments against 'the destructive sort of Prelacie' were now being taken up as a simple endorsement of separatism. He had worked for amendments to the liturgy, but no more than 'holy George Herbert', Jewel, Usher, Hall, Downame or Ball, did he think that use of the existing liturgy *dirtied* him.[97] This letter against Faldo was expanded into a pamphlet in the same year, *Whether Parish Congregations Be True Christian Churches*. The pamphlet is notable as a brake on the sectarian enthusiasm inspired by his previous writings. He was aware that Independents were reading into his *A Treatise of Episcopacy* in particular, a condemnation of Episcopacy *per se*, not merely 'prelatical' Episcopacy. They read his arguments as proof that 'by joining with a Parish you can be no part of the national church'. They had grounds for doing so. Now in 1684 Baxter was back-pedalling, seeking to defuse the more inflammatory readings of 'National Churches', and to re-establish the non-separatist traditions of English Nonconformity.

Baxter began his pamphlet by distinguishing two, if not three, meanings of the term 'National Church' — how much he was subconsciously borrowing from Cheyney's earlier reproof to him? — and argued that 'national' did not mean that all persons in the nation belonged to it but that 'the diffused parts of the Nation own it formally in a publick national relation.' There were two senses in which England already *was* a 'National Church': a Christian Kingdom; 'Synodical Agreements for Communion' between many minister's. The third sense was in the subjection of most of the clergy by consent to a superior quthority. Honouring the first two senses, Baxter would allow a submission to diocesan superiority, and would not separate from parish churches which were 'part of a Diocess, but true single Churches'. What Baxter disowned was a 'national Church, headed by one authoritative, pastoral Head'. He claimed, therefore, a consistency in defending the non-separatist traditions of Nonconformity 'not as a rule, but as a corporate example'. This claim is hardly borne out by his writings in the previous few years. Indeed it is clear from the postscript which he added to the pamphlet that he was becoming increasingly aware of the exposed position of English Protestantism, in a historic sense, if commitment to the 'sect-type' ideal were to be carried too far:

> That this opinion must needs make men seekers, who say, that the church was in the wilderness, and lost all true Ministry (and, say they, particular churches and Scripture) after the first (or at most the second) century: and so that for fourteen hundred years Christ had no visible Kingdom on earth: And consequently that we have no wiser answer to the Papist [where was your Church before Luther] than to say that it was *Invisible*; that is, that we cannot prove that there was any such thing on Earth.[98]

Where would Baxter encounter such a view in its most persuasive form? In Henry More's apocalyptic defence of the 'symmetral' virtues of the pre-imperial Church[99]. John Humfrey had encouraged Baxter to extend his paraphrase of the New Testament to Revelation. He had already made public his dissent from More's judgement that the Antichrist found there was Papal Rome. But this gap was not an insurmountable one: More had been coy about the *grounds* for such an identification; rooting it less in the text than in an analysis of the likely characteristics of 'Antichrist'. It is true that the analysis threw up the same conclusion as the straightforward textual approach of orthodox Protestant commentary: that Papal Rome was *the* Antichrist. But Baxter, admiring that approach, would extend it in further researches in prison into the Apocalypse, to offer a modified judgement: that Papal Rome was *an* Antichrist. More significant to Baxter (though not to all of his critics) was the drastic revision, not mere modification, of More's appreciation of the 'symmetral' qualities of the Apostolic Church. For by that date – 1686 – Baxter's ideal of a 'National Church' had acquired its full apocalyptic resonance.

Now the classic objection to a 'National Church', in the conventional understanding of the term, was what Coleridge had noted, in marginalia on Baxter's autobiography: 'when there is Law, there can be no discipline.'[100] In the past few years it had been at the heart of Baxter's own case against conformity: a refusal to accept hypocrisy as the price of unity. Another pamphlet of 1684, *Catholick Communion Defended*, is also an important interim step towards his revisionism in 1686, because it becomes a *defence* of hypocrisy:

> Although it bring in multitudes of Hypocrites, God makes some use for the Church of such: I would ask the Dissenters but two Questions 1. Would you not wish the prosperity of the Church your selves; and that all Power and Laws promoted Godliness and true Reformation? No doubt you wish it: And would not that bring in multitudes of Hypocrites? They are like Vermins and Flies, who swarm most in the warmest seasons.[101]

Baxter was becoming obsessed with the nightmare of fragmentation: from saying that the King is only King of Windsor or Brentford is but a short step to saying that he is not King at all. Similarly the 'Church' must be seen in wider terms than that of the local congregation.

Baxter praised the Independent, Nye,[102] and the Baptist, Tombes, as men who had a grasp of the wider dimension of their religious allegiances. He expanded on their virtues more fully in another pamphlet of 1684:

> Tho' Mr. Tombs wrote for Parish-Communion, few Anabaptists followed him; and tho' Mr. Nye wrote for hearing the Parish-Ministers, few Independents consented: But some of the Ministers took the advantage of the foresaid observance of others, and so brought Separation to pass for a common duty with many: And renewed sufferings made it easier to draw men from the Communion of those that they so much suffered by; following the example of St. Martin, and saying, that persecutors obtruded without their consent, were none of their pastors.

The wheel had turned full circle. St Martin, the admired model in so many of his writings in the previous few years, was now the patron saint of his opponents. Animus against Owen informs almost the entire pamphlet. He figures in the title page as the enemy because of his separatism. The Savoy commitment to Free Grace, which undid Baxter's Commonwealth hopes of a godly union, was *his* doing: 'I asked some yet living, why they consented to these, and did not rather expound the Scripture then deny it? And they said, That it was Dr. O's doing.' Once more his part in toppling Richard Cromwell's Protectorate was deplored. A prudent postscript in which he recognised that Owen mellowed with the years, and praised him as 'a man of rare Parts and worth', looked like what it was: a hasty tribute to the dead, which hardly effaced from memory the serious reservations expressed about him in the rest of the pamphlet.[103]

Yet, from manuscript notes in 1686, Baxter was clearly aware of the dangers to parish discipline in advocating a 'National Church'. He wrote against free admission to the Lord's Supper, which was as much to be avoided as Owen's 'unwarrantable separation'. He wrote of his own practice. He had only cast out three persons, and had called three more to repentance for scandalous sins. The three cast out had been privately warned and publicly prayed for: they hated him as much as ever they had done. One laid hands on Baxter in the churchyard and might have murdered him if he had not been forcibly restrained. Many hundreds of the parish wilfully refused 'to join in Communion or the Sacraments lest they should come under discipline'. To renounce that discipline was not merely to recognise that hypocrites can enter into the Church, but to make 'the Church consist as such of none but grosse hypocrites'. This would be Deism.[104]

Baxter may have been embarrassed by More's praise of him in the same year for his advocacy of 'National Churches' against gathered Churches: 'This is the only remarkable sincere stroke that occurs in all his Notes on the Revelation, so far as I can remember, if he be therein sincere, and heartily contradict his opinions and practises in former times.' We have seen that More was right to salute what was a genuine shift in Baxter's thinking. At the same time — as his notes on open communion make clear — Baxter was not turning his back on his previous hostility to the promiscuity of a Blake. His prison notes a year later would show how this made *his* 'National Church' a different concept from *More's*. The rest of More's pamphlet consists of his criticisms of Baxter for 'this great scepticism touching these holy visions': had he not read Mede? He bracketed Baxter unfairly with Grotius and Hammond, who had also doubted whether the Pope was Antichrist. These were men who had departed from 'the usual Protestant way' out of fright at associations of millenarianism with fanaticism. But their departure was a more fundamental one than Baxter's: as we shall see, in his notes of 1686, Baxter rejected a future millennium, *but not an historicist reading of the prophetic texts*; Grotius and Hammond had adopted a preterist reading which drained all political events, after the first century or two of Church history, of eschatological significance.[105]

His detailed notes in prison in 1686 established his own position. More 'maketh us nonconformists schimaticks and deeply criminall, for not keeping to the patterne of the first four hundred years, when yet no one man can be proved for 800 or 1000 yeares to have expounded the Revelation as he hath done'. Baxter developed (as he had done against Dodwell and Thorndike) his arguments why Nonconformists could not accept that conformity to the persecuting Church of England since the Restoration was compatible with a belief in godly discipline. He might have left his arguments there, but More had thrown down a challenge. He had identified the Church with the 'symmetral' virtues of the Apostolic Church. Baxter could demonstrate the variance of present practice from past tradition, but he did more. He challenged the apocalyptic significance of that past tradition. His own errors he now perceived were two: in his youth he had thought that 'it was half apostasy to question whether Rome now be Babylon and the Pope Antixt'; and he had thought ill of 'Nationall Churches'. He was obliged to expiate both errors. The first he had partly done in his *A Paraphrase on the New Testament*, but this he could now add to; it was the second which involved him in a major restatement of Protestant apocalyptic thought.

Baxter had proof that 'the consistory at Rome' had voted that his anti-Papal writings shall not be answered until he was dead 'or disabled to reply'. More had been contemptuous of such claims and put them down to senility or melancholia. But Baxter knew where he had hurt Papists (and many Anglicans). His exposition of the 'new' design to introduce Popery via the French, not Italian, way, by asserting conciliar supremacy and concord with 'Grotian' English divines, had made not only Papists but many Church of England divines implacably angry against him. They aimed at 'a forreine universall Jurisdiction by a Colledge of Pastors'. But Protestants had the answer to their designs in the Apocalypse: the Book of Revelation revealed that Christ had set up a Christian Empire – 'Wt would any fifth monarchy millenary man desire more at the expected 1000 years then God gave the Church when Christ set up a Christian Empire. I intreat all to think wht more can be hoped for?' Confusions in the Church had come because clergymen had sought to usurp that imperial power by setting up a jurisdiction of their own. They had propagated the lie that Princes cared only for the Body, the Priests for the Soul. Their assault on magistracy (Protestant clergy had followed the Papists) clouded 'the sense of the Revelation'. The constitutional outrages were rooted in an incorrect eschatology.

The true reading of the Apocalypse leads to the exaltation of the civil magistrate. Christian Princes 'are as sacred persons as priests'; Moses was above Aaron; Kings are above Archbishops. Until Princes ruled by the sword, Christian Kingdoms were in their infancy, were merely kept up, until He 'ripened' them into a Christian Empire. The sentimental cult, by which Christianity was assumed to have reached its peak when it was being destroyed, must be abandoned. The cult of the persecuted is the expression of the 'sect ideal'. Baxter answered with robust common sense: 'Why pray we not for persecution but against it?'

The Apocalypse would be easier understood if we had better histories 'of Romane and Christian affairs in those ages'. The majesty of the imperial achievement, the scope of its accomplishments, can only be properly grasped by readers who are aware of the depths to which the Church had sunk before Constantine became Emperor. For it was at that historic point in time that Christ came to 'visibly reigne by Christian Rulers'.[106]

Because Baxter had found in the Apocalypse the justification for Protestant imperialism it was important that this truth should not be discredited by being linked with fallacious arguments, from the same text, that the Pope was Antichrist. The argument — already voiced by More and to be taken up by others — was that Papists would be strengthened by such a concession. But to Baxter this was secondary. The real case against Rome was found in Revelation: to weaken the credibility of the Apocalypse was the most handsome gift that Protestants could make to the advancement of Popery.

Baxter felt the obligation to reconcile the arguments in his *Treatise of Episcopacy* of 1681, at a time when the St Martin separatist ideal had gripped him, with his commitment now to 'a National Church'. He was accused of being a 'contradictor of myselfe'. An anonymous correspondent quoted his admired George Lawson against him with the argument that 'its no prevarication in pleading for a Nationall Church to consider it in the first Notion of it as a Community of Christians in a Nation'; on such a premiss, Nonconformists who subvert it were helping popish designs. This was a restatement of More and Dodwell: vitiated by their indifference to discipline and their acceptance of a foreign jurisdiction.[107] Baxter's answer was that *when Protestants shook off the foreign jurisdiction, and obeyed the Royal Supremacy, the godly discipline would follow.* This was most fully developed in a letter to Boyse. He did acknowledge that a change had taken place in his thinking. He had not in the past fully recognised that National Churches were of divine institution: he had thought that Kings only gave the Church 'in its Ecclesiastick strict notion but an extrinsick accidentall forme'. However in answering Stillingfleet he had said that the name

'church' could be applied with equal force 'to a *Royal Church* as well
as a Sacerdotall'. It was not therefore that he had never in the past
entertained such ideas, but it was reading Beverley 'and my harder study
of the Apocalypse' which had fully converted him. He was now confident that the National Church was, next to the Catholic Church, Christ's
chief intention in establishing His Church — if not the first in His Mind
— and after that 'a family Church'. Overlooking this truth had caused
the errors and divisions of the time; the old Conformists were sounder
on this than present Nonconformists were; Popery is built on the denial
of this truth. The Erastians, like Lewis du Moulin, had not made
enough of the civil magistrate's concern with godly discipline. Papists
had exaggerated the distinction between civil and ecclesiastical for their
own ends. Kings 'are obliged to be sacred persons in exercise, continually to read the Law of God, and to meditate in it day and night'. Of
the imperial ideal Baxter wrote:

> Moses understood it better than Aaron: they are as sacred persons as
> priests: they are Gods anointed, both as Types and officers of Christ:
> they are bound to punish false deceiving prophets and priests, and
> therefore to know where they offend.

Jewel, Bilson and other Tudor conformists had understood that Kings'
power in religion was to be interpreted in Old Testament terms; now
substantially reinforced by the New Testament: 'Almost the whole
book of the Revel. describeth him as punishing the pagan, captivating
Idolatrous Babylon by his sword and setting up his government by a
Christian Empire.' The description of the New Jerusalem and the Last
Judgement proves that Christ's Kingdom contains His sword government: 'All the millenaryes maintaine this Royall Kingdome, except
they be gross selfcontradicters.' The denial of that duty is the true mark
of Antichrist. Protestants who confine kingly government to the Priests
serve Popery and are therefore Anti-Christian. Nothing can so much
diminish Popery as the restoration of 'the ministeriall exercise of Christs
Kingly power by the sword'. Erastus, Selden and Lewis du Moulin had
had it in for the clergy, but that is no reason to reject under the 'Erastian' label their plea for the sanctity of royal power; of which rejection would be to deny 'an essentiall part of Christianity'.[108]

By the end of 1686 Sir John Baber received a letter from Baxter 'to
desire him to use his Interest to get him his liberty, because he thought
his continuance in prison would be his death immediately;[109] on 18
November it was reported that 'Baxter is not yet out, it sticks much

upon his Bonds for his Good behaviour'; on 22 November his old enemy L'Estrange was prohibiting the sale from the Earl of Anglesey's collection of any of Baxter's books or manuscripts; a day later, however, he was discharged from prison on condition of seven years' good behaviour. Residence in London was not interpreted as a breach of good behaviour: he settled in Finsbury as neighbour and assistant to Matthew Sylvester.[110] In a letter to Sir John Baber of 20 October 1687 Baxter confessed he had for 28 years repented of meddling in politics and would not again commit the error of a *Holy Commonwealth*: 'Gentlemen thinke us ministers such fooles in Politicks that they will disdaine to be told by us wt to do.'[111] He took advantage of James II's Declaration of Indulgence of 11 April 1687 to preach regularly, but attempted – not always successfully – to maintain the low profile he had promised Baber, and not to allow his sympathy with William of Orange and alienation from James II to take too active a form.[112]

The difficulties in detaching himself from the cause of the seven defiant bishops are well brought out in the reception of his lecture on bishops on 24 May|1688. Baxter had isolated three reasons for Church divisions. First, there was a failure to distinguish the *ordinary* parts of the Apostolic Office that continue, from the *extraordinary* parts that have ceased. Some people had claimed the ceased apostolic power in order to make new Scripture which passed as God's Word. Others had cried down the ordinary parts which continue, such as the preaching of the gospel, gathering of Churches, and exercise of pastoral discipline. Second, there was a failure to distinguish examples 'of universall standing obligation' from those which are ephemeral and variable 'as they agree with the generall rule of Edification decency and Order'. Third, there was a failure to distinguish between the need to *abolish* corruptions 'that are of humane unlawfull originall' and the need only to *reform* those which 'had a Divine and good Originall'. The case for reforming episcopacy must not, therefore, be made the excuse for a 'root and branch' destruction: 'some argue as if they thought preaching, sacraments, and Gods own Institution must be abolished, because of the abuses and corruptions of them.'

This very mild restatement of his distaste for any rejection of Episcopacy, which went much beyond Usher's 'reduction', was seen by some Episcopalians as a sensational underwriting of the bishops' defiance of James II. Rumours circulated that the petitioning bishops were to go to Baxter to give their 'joynt thanks for that publick attestation that he had given to their proceedings':[113] an hysterical over-valuation of sentiments which would have been platitudinous even in 1641, but had acquired a new status when Nonconformists like Alsop and Lobb were busy reassuring James II that 'Wee could wish your Matie. had a Window in our breasts through which you might discern how our souls imbrace Yor Royall clemency with the highest admiration.'[114] What Baxter thought of such sentiments was to be made clear by him in his writings in 1690 and 1691. On 5 January 1689 when Nonconformist ministers expressed their devotion to William III, 'there were some of eminent note whose age or present infirmities hindered from comeing with them, yet they were concerned in the same gratefull sense of our deliverance'; the King was told that by 'Clergymen of eminent note they meane especially Mr. Baxter and Dr. Bates, who were under such infirmities they could not then waite upon the Prince in person'.[115]

In his last writings Baxter would celebrate the Protestant deliverance by expanding in print his discovery of 'National Churches'. The threat to that celebration lay in a revival of Antinomian doctrine. To his grief, Thomas Beverley — who had put him on the right path about National Churches even before his own prison researches — was an admirer of Dr Crisp's doctrinal deviations. The sermons of Tobias Crisp had been condemned by the Westminster Assembly divines for their Antinomianism; his son, Samuel, republished them in 1689, with a certificate signed by twelve ministers stating that eight additional sermons not previously printed, between 1643 to 1646, were authentic. Baxter protested at Crisp's doctrine in the weekly merchants' lecture at Pinner's Hall, and wrote of his chagrin 'that what seemed these thirty-four years suppressed, now threateneth as a torrent to overthrow the Gospel and Christian Faith'. Howe, one of the twelve signatories, claimed not to have read the sermons and forestalled a further reply from Baxter with the assurance that seven out of the twelve would dissociate themselves from the doctrine. Francis Tallents tried to calm Baxter with the reminder that for twenty years too much had been made of reason and goodness, too little of Christ. The 'Happy Union' of Presbyterians and Congregationalists of April 1691 was hardly robust enough to withstand the doctrinal divisions; Baxter against Crisp became Daniel Williams against Richard Davis; the majority of the Congregationalist United Ministers sided with the position of Crisp and Davis, and attempts by the predominantly Presbyterian United Ministers to stop the secession of their colleagues by a conciliatory document in December 1692 proved abortive. By 1695 the Presbyterians were lecturing at Salter's Hall on the same weekday and hour as their Congregational colleagues were lecturing at Pinner's Hall. The 'Happy Union' foundered on doctrinal schism.[116]

Baxter had perceived this danger as early as 18 May 1690. His letter to Beverley expresses his grief that his friend should have defended Crisp. He had differed from him *with respect* about niceties of millenarian interpretation but the doctrinal divergence could not be condoned:

> But when you come to the extolling of Dr. Crispes Antichristianity as precious light, preparatory to the blessed fall of Antichrist . . . seven years hence, you convinced me that the Love and Reverence of Men, must not draw me to be false to Christ.

He put Crisp's errors in their historic context, and recalled his own efforts to reclaim Cromwell's soldiers in the Civil War. By commending Crisp's 'evangelicall intoxicating errours', Beverley had put himself beyond the pale: 'this cause will endure no indifferency or neutrality: It strikes deeper than the Imagery wch is supposed so early to have turned the Church to Pagan Christianity.'[117] Baxter wrote his *The Scripture-Gospel Defended* in 1690 because of his dismay at 'the sudden reviving of Antinomianism, which seemed almost extinct near Thirty four years'. He claimed that even Owen, before his death, had softened much of the rigidity of his dogma — a rather facile view of negotiations which had largely stayed on 'mathematics', the safer issues of constitutional control. Antinomians like John Bunyan were honest godly men: 'it is the Piety and Strictness of the lives of many of them, which hath drawn many well-meaning ignorant persons to their Errors.'[118] But Bunyan fed on the doctrine which had nourished Coppe.

Baxter had not accepted Beverley's vision of a future millennium any more than he had his dating of the End of the World in 1697. Such differences were trivial compared to their shared adventist faith; they only became serious when linked to the doctrinal error. For it was the combination of Antinomianism and millenarianism which had produced the John of Leydens. There was need to speak out against false millenarian concepts when they buttressed false *doctrinal* concepts:

> the Millennial Opinion I have never been a censorious opposer of, while men kept up Peace and Charity with it . . . But the case lately is altered . . . very many of the Antinomian, and Separating Opinion, that least understand it, lay much of their Religion on it.

Baxter's classic exposition of his revised apocalyptic views, *Of National Churches* in 1691, had been in part dictated by a desire to restore *doctrinal* purity. The fantasy of a future millennium — dear to the new Antinomians – must be destroyed by an understanding of the reality of the past chiliad. Baxter made clear how the separatist illusion fed on the millenarian idea:

> And the Independent Separatists and Anabaptists, for want of under-standing this, as I said before, cry down National Churches with scorn, and run away from National Concord, into endless Divisions and Sects, while at the same time they pray and wait for National Churches in the *Millennium* as the Fifth Monarchy.

Reverence for Church confederacies and for the magistrate's power: these were his antidotes to schism. These were how the Presbyterians in Scotland and Ireland had kept up concord and kept out the sects: 'they maintained National Church Confederacy.' Baxter here made handsome acknowledgement of his error in thinking that 'the Scots way of a National Church Confederacy and General Assemblies was but a sadling the horse for Papal Usurpation to ride upon' – although his Scottish neighbour in Acton had told him different – and he now real-ised that 'National Churches truly stated were Christ's Institution, and the principal way to keep out Popery'.

Where the Presbyterians scored over Erastus, 'an excellent Protestant Physician', was in being in favour of government by Princes but also in refusing to link this with promiscuous communion and indifference to discipline. When he had opposed the 'National Church' of Stillingfleet and Sherlock, he had called the Christian Magistrate 'an Accidental Head', and linked the concept (as they did) with bishops as the 'essen-tiating Head'. The Anglican doctors – led by the betrayer Stillingfleet – had driven Baxter away from the idea of a 'National Church'; its variant, in an Erastian form, was no more acceptable to him. Hence he had been driven closer to a sectarian future; this was when he felt most strongly the force of the St Martin example. The Apocalypse now pushed him back into recognition of the Christian Empire. Confederacy (Presbyterian style) was a viable alternative to diocesan Episcopacy without surrendering to the sects or chaining the magistrate with fetters. Moreover, Stillingfleet and Sherlock had pushed him on the defensive with their charges of *disloyalty* to the magistrate – More did the same with Beaumont – and thus had forced him to argue that the Royal Supremacy was *accidental*. In trying to prove that the civil magistrate had no unlimited claims on the subject's obedience – Dodwell's 'Levia-than' – men easily came to forget that the essence of More's case was *hostility* to the civil magistrate. The exaltation of the pre-imperial

Church, the hostility to Emperor Constantine, the attraction towards conciliar 'foreign jurisdiction' — these features were obscured in the early 1680s by deferential remarks by the Anglican doctors about the powers of the magistrate. It was a paradox that could only emerge for Baxter in his apocalyptic studies of 1686: *the answer to Anglican absolutism was a defence of the Royal Supremacy.*

Kings were not, in Baxter's new dispensation, to take on ministerial functions — 'trying the Faith and Repentance of all that are to be Baptized, Confirmed, Absolved, or Excommunicated' — and this had been the Erastian error. 'By this overdoing they undo': in much the same way as Antinomians abuse God's Grace. Recognition of the Royal Supremacy was, nevertheless, the mark of the National Church, and this was possible under an Anglican *or* Presbyterian government:

> Whether among themselves United as the Scots in General Assemblies, or as in England by Archbishops, Bishops and Convocations, obeying the Laws of Christ, and the just Laws of the King and State that are made for determining needful Circumstances.

Popery did not *essentially* consist in other errors about doctrine or worship, images, praying to saints and angels, masses, relics, Merit, Justification, Free Will, Purgatory, Transubstantiation: these were, at most, 'Integral parts' of Popery *but not essential*: 'The Essence is only the Opinion of *Universal Humane Church Sovereignty, and a Church Universal Unified and formally Constituted thereby.*' Hence the error in dating Popery either from Constantine's exalting of Bishops — in this, critics 'unintentionally and very hurtfully mistake' — or from the beginnings of image-worship or even from the Pope's claim to be Universal Bishop. It was not until the Papacy claimed *Universal Primacy on Earth* that Popery began. When Baxter accused the Pope of being *an* Antichrist, as an usurper, this was what he had in mind. Baxter knew that the greatest disease of a National Church could be complacency about the well-being of the unprivileged:

> Sins of Injustice and Unmercifulness, especially Rich Mens oppression of the Poor, Landlords grinding their Poor tenants, and Judges, Justices and Lawyers unrighteousness in Suits and Judgments, are sins threatened by the Prophets as the forerunners of Destruction.

The poor husbandman's advocate saw indifference to poverty in apocalyptic terms: *prophecy condemned the society which was not founded on compassion*. The National Church and a godly discipline were complementary, not antithetical, concepts. The Restoration Church of England forfeited its status as a National Church, by the cruelty of its persecution, by the failure of its leading apologists to recognise the Royal Supremacy in their quixotic pursuit of union with Rome, and not least by the licence which it condoned or failed to check: 'O what a Torrent of Guilt in the Reign of Charles the Second did from King and Court overflow this Land, by the shameless filth of all uncleanness.'

How far Baxter had turned away from the 'sect-type' ideal is clear in the solution that he offers to the problems of 1691. He quotes Sir Matthew Hale: '*It must be a new Act of Uniformity that must heal the Church*.' This was the non-emancipation of Restoration Dissent: from St Martin to a new Act of Uniformity. He sketched his new Holy Commonwealth, one in which christening by baptism was not made 'an Infant Ceremony' but one where parents were taught to know what was meant by entering their child into a Covenant; one where adults should have their own baptismal Covenant, where parishes should be known to the pastor, where unrighteous Canons should be discarded, where ministers should not impose unnecessary terms, where bishops should ordain in synods, where the scandalous should be kept out of the Sacraments, and where the universities should be purged until there are only 'godly careful Tutors'. Toleration was not an absolute right, but dependent on the will of the law-giver, 'who can difference between Man and Man when the Law cannot'. The programme depended for its implementation on one thing: 'a wise and godly King that must be the principal means to accomplish all this'.[119] Baxter had wound up – via a tortuous route – in 1691, with his 1659 programme. William III had to complete the task begun by Richard Cromwell. The Antinomian still threatened Protestant union. John Owen had destroyed Richard Cromwell; his heirs – the supporters of Dr Crisp – must not destroy William III. The one big difference between the two dates is that, whereas *A Holy Commonwealth* sums up a decade of millenarian hopes, of which it is in part an expression, his faith in magistracy in the later period is more solidly rooted in *personal apocalyptic investigation* – the product of his 1686 prison cell.

John Humfrey did not disapprove of Baxter's search for a National Church, as he made clear to him in a letter of April 1691.[120] Indeed he had suggested in an earlier letter of January 1691 the title, *Of Nationall Churches in order to a Comprehension*, with the words: 'This will make the book sell.'[121] Humfrey shared Baxter's conviction that an Act for a larger constitution of the Church of England must be the business of the Kingdom, 'wch is in Effect a new Act of Uniformity as my Lord Hales said'. But Humfrey believed that it was vital that bishops should be recognised as being of *iure humano* status, not *iure divino*. Humfrey thought that the bishops' claim to divine right sanction was an affront to the Royal Supremacy; Baxter was never too bothered with such niceties. He had made clear in his comments on Hammond that the critical point about bishops was not whether their office was divine or not, but whether or not their office created the framework for ministerial *discipline*. And on that point, Humfrey − the advocate of open communion − and Baxter had already agreed to differ. In his *Union Pursued*, also of 1691, Humfrey hoped that Presbyterians and Independents, who had united with each other, might now unite with the Church of England.[122]

Humfrey and Baxter were not pursuing similar ends. Baxter's search for a 'National Church' did not mean the renunciation of the search for a godly discipline. He wrote a manuscript reply to *Union Pursued* in 1691 in which he made clear his distaste for once more having to oppose his friend. But the issues were still the same ones which had divided them in the 1650s.[123] Baxter pointed out in mitigation that 'I have not bin forward to oppose your old doctrine of common admission to the Sacrament as a Converting Ordnance.' But the promiscuity of free admission had its analogue in a National Church, humanly instituted, into which all must be herded. Humfrey had criticised Baxter for being vague about details, but had he not himself in the past been too prescriptive? Princes 'suspect when a man is over forward and must have vent, that it is not well-digested matter.' Baxter had been too forward with his *Holy Commonwealth* and his epistles to Richard Cromwell, 'though I know of no false doctrine in them'. He would not make that mistake with William III: 'But I will not as you be forward to tell Princes and states uncalled what Nationall Church frame of Government they shall devise themselves, and that in the very essentials of such a Church of so great Consequence.' Humfrey's promiscuity offered a National Church that could take in Papists: a dismal prospect when many Anglicans' craving after a foreign jurisdiction remained unappeased. Indeed Baxter worried that it could be a belated fulfilment of the Grotian dreams of the Pierces and the Thorndikes. Baxter opposed cruelty to individual Papists, but their inclusion in a National Church is unthinkable. But if there are no disciplinary criteria, on what basis *can* Papists be excluded? National Churches, with their *iure humano* bishops, become 'but the creatures of man'. Humfrey always distinguishes *Commonwealth* from *Church*. He makes the fatal mistake of leaving out one word: *Christian*. Baxter goes on: 'A *Christian Commonwealth* that is *No Church* is as grosse a Contradiction, as an *Army* that are no *Soldiours*, or a *Kingdome* that are no *Men*.' Constantine used Heathens under him, it is true, but 'he cannot make uncapable Heterogenalls to be members of one Reformed Church.' Humfrey's talk of Episcopacy, Presbyterianism and Independency shows that he has missed the *point* of a National Church. All three, provided that genuine pastoral discipline is secured, *can* be accommodated within a National Church: 'I would the world had more such Nationall Churches as New England is (If a Province may be called a Nation).' There was nothing in the function of pastoral overseer inimical to Presbyterian or Congregationalist:

> The Government by Councils, and Presbyterian Assemblies, is but each Pastors governing his own flocke by the great hedge and advantage of Commone Consent and Concord of Churches, which is but Brotherly Confederacy. But if those Assemblies appoint any Seniors to have a visiting power to goe to many Churches and take account of their state, and exhort and admonish the junior pastors, without any forcing power of the sword but what the magistrate useth, this is to make the true Diocesane.[124]

Baxter's readiness now to see good in Scottish Presbyterianism was given a cynical gloss by Samuel Young: 'The Scottish Presbytery was condemned when Charles the II had it under his feet, but was approved of again when King William restored it.'[125] This was not fair. Baxter was also ready to see good in Independency which followed the New England model (as he had been when he had praised the 1662 New England Synod earlier). As always for Baxter, the critical test was whether the proposed structure was flexible enough — whether it was Episcopalian, Presbyterian or Independent — to admit a proper pastoral discipline. And if his Scottish neighbour at Acton assured him that the Presbyterian structure allowed for such flexibility, Baxter was prepared to listen. This was the point which Baxter made to Stephen Lobb when they corresponded in September 1691 about the meaning of a 'National Church':

> When presbyteries deny the power of excommunication and absolution to single Pastors and Churches, and appropriate it to Classes, they do as much to nullifie those pastors office as if a Bp. did the same. But neither of them nullifieth it indeed.[126]

'Generall Overseers' were as acceptable to 'Intelligent Independents' as they were to non-doctrinaire Presbyterians. They were compatible with the exercise of personal eminence by such men in the past as Owen, Goodwin and Nye, in their efforts to exclude the unworthy and to stamp out Quakerism, Popery and Socinianism. The pastoral discipline achieved within the framework of a National Church: what was that but what Owen had achieved in Oxford, what the Triers and Ejectors had done in the Commonwealth? There was another model which he did not describe on this occasion, but which was rarely far from his consciousness: the Ministerial Associations which had brought Episcopalians, Presbyterians *and* Congregationalists together in the pursuit of discipline, with the forcing power of the magistrate's sword left to the Cromwells, father and son. Humfrey's 'National Church' offered uniformity minus the Apocalypse. But Baxter had tasted something better in the Commonwealth, and was not ready to settle for anything that fell so woefully short of a 'Holy Commonwealth'.

Thomas Comber was another critic of Baxter's 'National Church' in 1691. Like Humfrey, Comber resented Baxter's insistence on *iure divino* status for his clergymen. This was a threat to the Royal Supremacy. Moreover the real basis for unity between moderate Anglicans, Presbyterians and Independents lay in a modest acceptance of *iure humano* status for bishops.[127] Their thinking was very much in the traditions of late Tudor and early Stuart Protestantism;[128] it was what Calamy *imagined* he was emancipating Dissent from when he launched his great attack on Baxter's 'National Church' in 1704. But they all were missing Baxter's point. His refusal to settle for an inferior warrant for clergymen was because the National Church which he embraced in 1691 was not the shabby compromise which he had himself been rude about on earlier occasions, but the revival of his holy vision of 1659 in a more emphatically apocalyptic form.

This was what Comber dimly perceived. There was a mis-match between the model which Baxter was supposedly advocating and the language in which it was being presented. The 'National Church' had been seen customarily as a restful haven for those who had abandoned visions of holiness; here it was being advocated *as the instrument of their fulfilment*. Comber felt that men had to choose between *peace* and *holiness*. Those who wanted *peace* were drawn to National Churches; those who wanted *holiness* were drawn to sectarian solutions. Calamy in 1704 could assume that the case for a National Church *could only be* argued upon grounds of peace; his argument was that the sectarian solution did not constitute that challenge to peace which his predecessors – with varying degrees of plausibility – had maintained in the past. But if a 'National Church' meant no more than *peace* Baxter would not have been interested. The argument for Baxter was not over whether a 'National Church' secured *peace*, but over whether it secured *holiness*. To Comber this was Baxter's delusion:

> It is *Peace* I perceive you would have, but *Holiness* more; and when the world lyes in wickedness, if you have peace you must be content with so much holiness as can be had. You must not expect that National Churches (Though you will have them *Iure Divino*) should be as Holy, as the select people of your Gathered Congregations.[129]

Comber had a point. At one level Baxter *did* recognise that with a National Church 'you must be content with so much holiness as can be had': the price of uniformity *was* the infiltration of hypocrites. But there was another level at which the majesty of Christian Empire was precisely in its successful separation of the precious from the vile, and in establishing a millenary kingdom beyond the dreams of Fifth Monarchy Men. It was this second level of meaning which Calamy missed.

Edmund Calamy wrote his 'Introduction' to the second part of his *Defence of Moderate Nonconformity* in 1704. Mr Roger Thomas has argued convincingly that its publication was 'an epoch in the evolution of Dissent'.[130] Contemporaries recognised its importance: Presbyterian colleagues stood him a supper in 1704; he won the commendations of Howe and Locke. His opponent Hoadly claimed that the best of the Ejected Ministers would sooner have chosen 'the continuance of the present Establishment than the alteration of it into such a one as is here contrived'.[131] This would have been true of Calamy's grandfather. Would it have been true of Baxter?

It is a question which it is hard to avoid asking, not least because Calamy's revisionism had been prompted by the very task of interpreting Baxter to a later generation of Protestants. Hoadly claimed, naturally enough, that Calamy distorted Baxter and although there would be occasions when Calamy denied the charge, there were other impressive moments of candour, *when he acknowledged the need for Baxter to be updated*. In Thomas's account there is an almost wistful description of Calamy as 'in many ways a typical Baxterian', coupled with a recognition that he had qualities absent from Baxter, notably a catholicity unaffected by anxieties about 'discipline', and a magnanimity 'that was perhaps more faithful to Baxter's genius than Baxter might have been himself'.[132]

It reads almost as if Calamy were Baxter with the bad temper left out. The *real* Baxter was the figure domesticated by the eighteenth century, whom Calamy and Doddridge could enjoy without reliving the *enthusiasms* of seventeenth-century controversy. The Baxter who wrote *The Saints Everlasting Rest* might have been the man himself to have contributed to this 'epoch in the evolution of Dissent', but not the quick-tempered disputant who, ignoring Dr Wallis's cautionary whispers, infallibly rose to the High Church bait at Savoy.[133] The pathos in his career is the gap between magnanimous aim and divisive means. Milton lamented in 1641 the reformation which had not happened in England. Wyclif had given the lead, but it was Hus and Luther who stole the glory from England. A similar might-have-been pervades the story, in many histories of this period, of Baxter's attempts after the Restoration to put Dissent on a new footing.

There is a certain rough justice in such an explanation. But in two ways it distorts. It misses the nearness that Baxter *did* come to Calamy's revisionism. It also, however, misses the final *distance* between Baxter's answers in the 1680s and Calamy's in 1704; a distance, not to be measured in terms of personalities, but in terms of *eschatology*. In the end the difference between even late-seventeenth-century and eighteenth-century Dissent is to be found in the Apocalypse.

Calamy had committed himself to the principle that 'unscriptural Impositions are unwarrantable.' Hoadly countered with the example of Baxter's own practice: his refusal to receive to the Sacrament of the Lord's Supper a gentleman who insisted upon having the Sacrament kneeling and at a distinct time from the rest of the parish. Calamy pointed out, in mitigation, that Baxter did not deny him the liberty of going elsewhere nor even refuse it to him kneeling, if only he gave his reasons for it and submitted to his pastoral discipline. And yet, even if it were true, Baxter's practice did not bind his successors:

> But be that as it will, let some among the Independents, nay let Mr. Baxter himself (as much as I Honour his Memory) do what they will, it still remains a firm Principle, till better disprov'd, that unscriptural Impositions are unwarrantable.

Calamy defended the congregation's right to determine its own practice: 'If any represent this as a meer Independent Scheme, they are at their Liberty.' The basic principle remained that each worshipping Society must determine for itself, and each private Christian must preserve his own discretionary judgement. The individual has no obligation to comply with a determination which clashes with his own judgement. Nor does this rule out 'National Churches', which Calamy understands to be 'but a Confederation of the several particular Churches, which are under one and the same Civil Government, for the joint promoting Purity and Peace, by their acting in Concert'.

More radical still, though, Calamy questions the desirability of 'National Churches'. Better, he argues, for 'each worshipping Congregation in the Land, to manage it self in an entire Independency, than to have a National Church of one sort or another with *Penal Laws*'. Charity weighs more with Calamy than the 'plausible Pleas of Uniformity and Decency'; he believes that the way to Christian Unity is not through a coercive 'pompous Uniformity' but through 'a voluntary Concert of these worshipping Assemblies'. The advantage of breaking out of the 'National Church' straitjacket is that individuals can be excluded from the Sacraments without danger of prosecution, and that Protestants no longer are confronted with the paradox of praying to uphold a Popish Prince on the throne. James II exposed the dangers of theories of non-resistance:

> And if the Prince aim at bringing back Popery, and a Foreign Prince when invited, comes to deliver the Nation from Popery and Slavery, they have nothing to do to make it a part of their Prayers, that *God would be the Defender and Keeper* of their Popish Prince, and *give him the Victory over all his Enemies*, and so Defeat the Designs, of our Deliverer.

Calamy can invoke the pastoral care and catechising commended by Baxter in his *Gildas Salvianus*. He acknowledged that at present Nonconformist ministers fell below that ideal. He was not saying, against Hoadly, that they had achieved perfection. Far from it. There was neglect caused by lack of ministerial help, the distance of habitations and — Calamy acknowledged — 'together with something in Ministers, and also in the People, as makes this Work exceeding difficult after long disuse'. Even so the 'personal Conversation' and 'enquiry' of Nonconformist ministers goes well beyond the promiscuous communion of the Church of England. Separation from such a Church is not irrational or indefensible. It does not follow — and this is the critical break with the anti-separatist tradition of old Nonconformity — that '*the Old Puritans* themselves, had they lived in our times, and found the Church so fix'd in these Corruptions that had been so long complaind of, would not have been for separation as well as we.' Calamy's determination to 'separate from a National Church, whose Bottom is as far as we can judge unscriptural' provoked from Hoadly the outraged comment: 'No Man has loaded it with more Aggravations than Mr. Baxter.' Calamy's answer to this was decisive:

> What, all sorts of Separation, tho' managed with Charity and Moderation? That would be strange, I confess! But 'tis now no new thing for Persons to represent that Good Man as inconsistent with himself, when it seems for their Interest he should be tho't so! However; let him or others have said what they will, it does not follow that a Charitable Separation from a Church of such a Constitution as the National Church of England, and that appears as fix'd in its Corruptions, is a real evil, nay is not strictly defensible. And to apply what has been said by any either in former times, or more lately, against a *Brownisticall Separation*, to those who are well known to separate upon quite difficult Principles, is not fair nor candid.[134]

Hoadly sneered at 'those most irregular and imperfect Churches with which we have chosen to join and unite', but Calamy expressed his readiness indeed to join with 'those of the *Congregational way*' inasmuch as they agreed with Scripture, defended the right of people to choose their own ministers as compatible with Baxter's principles, and joined Locke in refuting the claims of patriarchal authority over children who attain maturity:

> For tho' if my Children, while Minors, should, when *I require them to worship God with me, beg my excuse*, I should refuse it, and use my authority over them; this being a matter which God hath subjected to the Paternal Authority during Minority; yet if when growne up to Years of Understanding, they should *claim a Right to look after themselves*, I must confess I could not gainsay it.

When Hoadly portrayed — on lines familiar to readers of Thomas Edwards and Baxter — a family riven with quarrels when deprived of patriarchal headship, Calamy remarked coolly that it depended upon the family concerned. He asked why must 'the Master of the Family, carry it by Authority over all under his Roof?'[135] Separatism is the logical consequence of the failure of the Church of England to advance; old Nonconformists had condemned the Brownists because they had not abandoned hopes 'of further reformation'. The 'Bartholomew Ejection' marked the end of such hopes: men 'entirely of the Puritan stamp', like

Simeon Ashe and Anthony Burgess, had seen the logic of separatism in the changed situation. Calamy had not given up the cause of the ejected ministers by giving so much to particular congregations: with truth, he invoked the concern for congregational discipline which was at the heart of Usher's scheme. Hoadly's crocodile tears for Calamy's violation of Baxter's principles failed to move him:

> There are not many men in England that I think deserve more general Honour and Esteem. But at the same time shall add, that I have that opinion of him, as to believe, that tho' several of the Extravagances mentioned in that Book deserved to be exposed, yet had he been as sensible at the time of writing it, as he has been since, of the Advantage several Passages in his Book would give to many *to deride serious Religion*, and *the worship of God*, he would have forborn them. And I can safely say, that were I sensible that any Passages of mine would give Advantage to Persons *to deride serious Religion, and the worship of God*, I would discard them, and none should be more free than I to declare against them.[136]

It is important to emphasise that Calamy did not attribute to Baxter statements and meanings which were not already there. What has emerged in this study is the fascinating way in which Baxter does anticipate, particularly between 1676 and 1682, the main thrust of Calamy's argument. This is the period when he is attracted by the example of St Martin, repelled by the claims to submission to magistracy from Anglicans like Dodwell and Sherlock, and haunted by the failure of pastors to exercise a godly discipline over their congregations. This was the time when he too was out of love with National Churches. It is not easy to date the precise moment when he falls *in love with* National Churches. Certainly significant watersheds are his letter to John Faldo of 25 August 1684 and his pamphlet of the same year, *Whether Parish Congregations Be True Christian Churches*. In other words, his revisionism *ante-dates* his prison researches into the Apocalypse, although at that date he had already begun his more intensive study of the Revelation which resulted in his *A Paraphrase on the New Testament*, also published in 1684. What we can say is that it was his prison researches which consolidated impulses that were already present: a faith in Christian magistracy, in National Churches, in submission to authority.

What his close study of the Apocalypse in 1686 did was to show Baxter that, in seeking to obey the magistrate and to honour a National Church, *he was not renouncing his search for a godly discipline*. If the importance of the rule of the Emperor Constantine had only been that he established order and peace, the eschatological significance of the new order of Christian Empire would have been lost. Quite incomprehensible then would have been the terms with which he saluted the beginnings of imperial Christianity: 'O what a change! O what a joyful day!'[137] The ecstasy with which Fifth Monarchists awaited the coming millennium was shared by Baxter, not only because of his adventism but because of his knowledge that in the past men *had* enjoyed a millennial felicity, which only ignorance of history had blinded them to.

Calamy was right to think that the separatism of the Brownists (and of Owen and seventeenth-century Congregationalists) had millenarian overtones, and that the separatism which he was advocating in 1704 was free from such associations. The seventeenth-century separatist might have rejected the Established Church as Antichrist;[138] his eighteenth-century successor rejected the Church simply because it had not produced sufficient reforms. But it was not only Calamy's separatism which was non-apocalyptic; so also was his representation of the rival case for a National Church.

He had made that case indistinguishable from Blake's case for open communion — public decency and peace — and this was as unpalatable to Baxter as it was to Calamy. If the concept of a 'National Church' had only evoked that grey appeal to uniformity, it could not have exercised the appeal that it did upon the imagination of the seventeenth-century Nonconformist. Behind the appeal to 'National Church' lay an appeal to the tradition of Foxe and Jewel; an anti-Papal patriotism, which was rooted in apocalyptic history. The story of Baxter's researches in 1686 is the recovery of that tradition. Although the Anglican doctors were lavish with praise of the civil magistrate, their search for a Grotian union with French Catholics and willingness to surrender England to a 'foreign jurisdiction' could only be countered by a return to Tudor imperial traditions. These imperial traditions gave unbridled authority to the Protestant sovereign. For the Papist sovereign — as Bilson had made clear — on the other hand, the 'madness' of destroying his own imperial authority carried with it its own nemesis. Calamy was wrong then even to associate the concept of a 'National Church' with the problems of the allegiance owed to a Papist King.[139]

In doing so he had missed the moral force that lay behind Baxter's acceptance of 'National Churches'. Baxter had become the poor husbandman's advocate, not because of a wish to turn the world upside down, but because the way in which the poor were treated was the decisive test of the ability of a 'National Church' to carry out its apocalyptic role. In embracing separatism, Calamy consciously rejected the millennialism of the Brownist tradition. What Calamy could not appreciate was the *millennial appeal* to the seventeenth-century mind of *nonseparatism*. There *could be* no emancipation of Restoration Dissent until the case for a National Church had been severed from its apocalyptic connections. That is why Calamy, and not Baxter, was ideally placed to strike the decisive blow for separatism. In asking his colleagues to discard the notion of a 'National Church', Calamy thought that he was challenging sentimentalism, when he was really challenging an eschatology. The effectiveness of that challenge owed much to its innocence.

Notes

1. R.A. Beddard, 'Vincent Alsop and the Emancipation of Restoration Dissent', *Journal of Ecclesiastical History*, XXIV, 2 (1973), pp. 116, 177.

2. Now fully set out and documented in: A.H. Wood, *Church Unity Without Uniformity* (London, 1963), *passim*.

3. Cf. Stephen Mayor, *The Lord's Supper in Early English Dissent* (London, 1972), pp. 135-46.

4. R.S. Bosher, *The Making of the Restoration Settlement* (London, 1951); G.F. Nuttall, *Richard Baxter* (London, 1965), p. 90.

5. (DWL) *Baxter Treatises*, ii, f.18v.

6. (DWL) *Baxter Correspondence*, iii, f.80.

7. (DWL) *Baxter Correspondence*, i, f.95v.

8. (BL) *Harleian MSS 6942*, f. 78.

9. (DWL) *Baxter Treatises*, ii, f.83.

10. Alan Macfarlane (ed.), *The Diary of Ralph Josselin, 1616-1683* (London, 1976), p. 431.

11. Thomas Tonkins, *The Rebels Plea* (London, 1660), p. 45.

12. *Calendar Clarendon State Papers*, 1932, iv, p. 672.

13. Ibid., 1970, v, p. 253.

14. (East Sussex Record Office) *Frewen MSS 4223*, f.475/100.

15. Baxter in Matthew Sylvester (ed.), *Reliquiae Baxterianae* (London, 1696), ii, p. 294.

16. Ibid., ii, p. 297.

17. (DWL) *Baxter Correspondence*, i, f.94, 94v, 95.

18. (East Sussex Record Office) *Frewen MSS 4223*, f.475/104, 105.

19. (DWL) *Baxter Correspondence*, ii, f.273.

20. G.F. Nuttall, 'Richard Baxter's Apology, its occasion and composition', *Journal of Ecclesiastical History*, iv, 1, 1953; pp. 69 *et seq.*, P. Toon, *God's Statesman: The Life and Work of John Owen* (Exeter, 1971), p. 113.

21. P. Toon (ed.), *The Correspondence of John Owen 1616-1683* (London, 1970), pp. 136-45.

22. (DWL) *Baxter Correspondence*, iv, f.6, 6v, 7.

23. John Humfrey, *A Case of Conscience . . .* (London, 1669), pp. 4, 5, 12.

24. (DWL) *Baxter Correspondence*, iii, f.11, 11v, 12, 12v.

25. (DWL) *Baxter Correspondence*, i, f.22, 23v, 25, 26, 26v, 27.

26. (DWL) *Baxter Correspondence*, i, f.68v.

27. (DWL) *Baxter Correspondence*, iii, f.223v, 224.

28. (DWL) *Baxter Correspondence*, iii, f.228v, 231, 231v, 232, 236.

29. (DWL) *Baxter Correspondence*, i, f.59.

30. Baxter, *The Successive Visibility of the Church* . . . (London, 1660), p. 317.

31. Baxter, *A Defence of the Principles of Love* . . . (London, 1671), i, pp. 6, 7, 14, 17, 18, 36, 55, 56, 58; ii, pp. 4, 55, 58, 59, 60, 142, 153.

32. Baxter, *The Difference Between the Power of Magistrates and Church – Pastors and the Roman Kingdom and Magistracy* (London, 1671), pp. 16, 18, 19, 21.

33. Baxter, *A Second Admonition to Mr. Edward Bagshaw* (London, 1671), pp. 46, 47, 52, 55, 56, 60, 61, 68, 69.

34. (DWL) *Baxter Correspondence*, iv, f.36.

35. Baxter, *The Church Told of Mr. Ed. Bagshaw's Scandals* (London, 1672), p. 11.

36. (DWL) *Baxter Correspondence*, i, f.108-108v.

37. Baxter, *The Church Told of Mr. Ed. Bagshaw's Scandals*, pp. 33-4.

38. (DWL) *Baxter Correspondence*, iv, f.37-37v.

39. Baxter, *An Answer to Mr. Dodwell and Dr. Sherlocke* . . . (London, 1682), p. 74.

40. The fifth chapter of Samuel Parker's *A Discourse of Ecclesiastical Politie* (London, 1670) was a refutation of Hobbes's *Leviathan* for its failure to demand more of the subject than an *outward* conformity to the magistrate's authority. See W. Lamont and S. Oldfield (eds.), *Politics, Religion and Literature in the Seventeenth Century* (London, 1975), p. 199.

41. Baxter, *An Answer to Mr. Dodwell and Dr. Sherlocke*, p. 76.

42. (DWL) *Baxter Correspondence*, i. f.70.

43. Baxter, *An Answer to Mr. Dodwell and Dr. Sherlocke*, pp. 76-7.

44. Framcis Fullwood, *Toleration Not to be Abused* (London, 1672), pp. 8, 9, 13, 16, 20.

45. Baxter, *Sacrilegious Desertion of the Holy Ministry Rebuked* (London, 1673), pp. 3, 21, 22, 23.

46. (DWL) *Baxter Correspondence*, v, f.146v.

47. (DWL) *Baxter Correspondence*, i, f.185.

48. (DWL) *Baxter Correspondence*, ii, f.217v, 218, 218v, 219.

49. (DWL) *Baxter Correspondence*, ii, f.210.

50. (DWL) *Baxter Correspondence*, ii, f.211.

51. Baxter, *The Christian Directory* (London, 1673), pp. 722, 725, 727, 733, 745.

52. Baxter, *An Answer to Mr. Dodwell and Dr. Sherlocke*, pp. 93-4.

53. S.T. Coleridge, *Complete Works*, ed. Shedd (New York, 1854), v, p. 355.

54. (DWL) *Baxter Correspondence*, i, f.106.

55. Baxter, *An Answer to Mr. Dodwell and Dr. Sherlocke*, p. 172.

56. Coleridge, *Complete Works*, v, p. 357.

57. Baxter, *Full and Easie Satisfaction* . . . (London, 1674), dedicatory epistle.

58. (BL) *Additional MSS 32,094*, f.263.

59. Baxter, *A Treatise of Self-Denial* (London, 1675), monitory epistle, pp. 42, 45, 46, 332, 333.

60. (DWL) *Morrice Entering Book P*, f.359-60.

61. (DWL) *Baxter Correspondence*, ii, f.111v-112.

62. (DWL) *Baxter Correspondence*, vi, f.186.

63. Baxter, *Catholick Theologie* (London, 1675), I, i, preface; iii, pp. 60, 95.

64. See Baxter, *Treatise of Self-Denial*, p. 91.

65. Baxter, *Catholick Theologie*, II, pp. 4, 5, 155, 199, 280, 283.
66. (DWL) *Baxter Correspondence*, v, f.146v.
67. Baxter, *Catholick Theologie*, II, p. 293.
68. (DWL) *Baxter Correspondence*, v, f.272-3.
69. Baxter, *The Successive Visibility of the Church*, pp. 376-7.
70. Baxter, *Naked Popery* (London, 1677), pp. 108-9, 33.
71. Baxter, *The Christian Directory*, p. 736.
72. Baxter, *An Answer to Mr. Dodwell and Dr. Sherlocke*, pp. 117-18.
73. (DWL) *Baxter Treatises*, vi, f.305-7v: additional comments on his *Sacrilegious Desertion of the Holy Ministry Rebuked* (London, 1672).
74. Baxter, *The Nonconformists Plea for Peace . . .* (London, 1679), dedicatory epistle, pp. 90, 91, 110, 115, 239, 245, 246, 250, 251, 299, 300, 301, 310.
75. Baxter, *Richard Baxter's Answer to Dr. Stillingfleet's Charge of Separation* (London, 1680), preface, pp. 53, 56, 94. Cf. Baxter, *A Moral Prognostication* (London, 1680), p. 21: 'If they will go as far as Martin (in *Sulpitius Severus*) to avoid all Communion with *Ithacius* and *Idacius* and the Councils of Bishops, that prosecuted the Priscillianists to the scandal of Godlinesse it self: yet not for their sakes to avoid all others, that never consented to it.'
76. Baxter, *The Second Part of the Nonconformists Plea for Peace* (London, 1680), preface, pp. 64, 130, 167, 174.
77. Baxter, *A Search for the English Schismatick* (London, 1681), postscript, pp. 9, 30, 31.
78. Baxter, *A Treatise of Episcopacy* (London, 1681), pp. 19, 27, 69, 83, 212, 213, 188, 190, 191, 198, 221, 195.
79. Baxter, *A Second True Defence of the Meer Nonconformists . . .* (London, 1681), pp. 183-91, 18, 38, 70. Glanvill was another fallen Anglican idol to join Stillingfleet in Baxter's reappraisals in this pamphlet: see Jackson Cope, *Joseph Glanvill, Anglican Apologist* (St Louis, 1956), p. 9.
80. Baxter, *An Apology for the Nonconformists Ministry* (London, 1681), pp. 8, 47, 48.
81. (DWL) *Baxter Correspondence*, vi, f.219-f.229v.
82. Baxter, *An Answer to Mr. Dodwell and Dr. Sherlocke*, pp. 54, 61, 78, 84. It is interesting to note that Tillotson bracketed Dodwell and Baxter together, in temperament if not in politics: (BL) *Additional MSS.4236*, f.102v.
83. Baxter, *The True History of Councils Enlarged and Defended* (London, 1682), dedicatory epistle, preface, pp. 18, 19, 88, 187, 189, 190.
84. (DWL) *Baxter Correspondence*, iv, f.283v.
85. (DWL) *Morrice Entering Book P.*, f.337-f.340.
86. (DWL) *Morrice Entering Book Q.*, f.80.
87. (DWL) *Baxter Correspondence*, vi, f.244; ii, f.95-f.101.
88. (BL) *Egerton MSS 2570*, f.124-f.124v.
89. (DWL) *Baxter Correspondence*, v, f.240v.
90. (DWL) *Baxter Treatises*, i, f.323v.
91. (BL) *Egerton MSS 2570*, f.117.
92. (DWL) *Baxter Correspondence*, ii, f.83-f.92; f.93-f.94.
93. (Bodleian Library) *Rawlinson Letters* 109, f.8.
94. (DWL) *Morrice Entering Book P.*, f.515-f.516.
95. For which, see Chapter 1.
96. Baxter, *A Paraphrase on the New Testament* (London, 1684), no pagination.
97. (DWL) *Baxter Treatises*, vii, f.238.
98. Baxter, *Whether Parish Congregations Be True Christian Churches* (London, 1684), p. 27.
99. For which, see Chapter 1.

100. (BL) *Additional MSS 32,568*, f.9.

101. Baxter, *Catholick Communion Defended* (London, 1684), pp. 12, 15, 17.

102. Cf. Edward Pierce's commendation of Nye's non-separatist lead to Independents, in a letter to Baxter on 23 December 1687: (BL) *Egerton MSS 2570*, f.128.

103. Baxter, *An Account of the Reasons Why the Twelve Arguments Said to be Dr. John Owen's Change not my Judgment about Communion with Parish-Churches* (London, 1684), pp. 6, 8, 27. The pamphlet is not in A.G. Matthews's *The Works of Richard Baxter: an Annotated List*, reproduced in G.F. Nuttall, *Richard Baxter* (London, 1965), Appendix.

104. (DWL) *Baxter Treatises*, i, f.37v-f.40.

105. 'Phillicrines Parrhesiastes', *Some Cursory Reflexions Impartially Made Upon Mr. Richard Baxter His Way of Writing Notes* (London, 1685), pp. 7, 18, 20.

106. (DWL) *Baxter Treatises*, vii, f.295, f.297, f.299v, f.300v.

107. (DWL) *Baxter Correspondence*, v., f.201-f.203.

108. (DWL) *Baxter Correspondence*, ii, f.11-f.12v.

109. (DWL) *Morrice Entering Book P.*, f.639.

110. (DWL) *Morrice Entering Book Q.*, f.11, f.14, f.16.

111. (DWL) *Baxter Correspondence*, i, f.110.

112. E.g. on 30 April 1687: 'On Thursday last . . . there was an Address presented (about ten a clock) to his Matie . . . Mr. Baxter, Dr. Bates and severall others I am most acquainted with have not been consulted in this matter. Mr. Baxter said he was bound to the Good behaviour, he concerned not himselfe in this office of Addressing': (DWL) *Morrice Entering Book Q*, f.112.

113. (DWL) *Morrice Entering Book Q.*, f.262, f.265.

114. (DWL) *Morrice Entering Book Q.*, f.115.

115. (DWL) *Morrice Entering Book Q.*, f.411.

116. See P. Toon, *Puritans and Calvinism* (Pennsylvania, 1973), pp. 85-105.

117. (DWL) *Baxter Treatises*, vii, f.48v, f.45v.

118. Baxter, *The Scripture-Gospel Defended* . . . (London, 1690), i, preface; ii, p. 49.

119. Baxter, *Of National Churches* (London, 1691), pp. 13, 5, 12, 49, 41, 53, 70, 68.

120. (DWL) *Baxter Correspondence*, v, f.138.

121. (DWL) *Baxter Correspondence*, i, f.72.

122. John Humfrey, *Union Pursued* . . . (London, 1691), p. 2.

123. For which, see Chapter 3.

124. (DWL) *Baxter Treatises*, vi, 'A Political Primer for Nationall Church-makers', f.296, f.296v, f.299v, f.301, f.302.

125. Samuel Young, *Vindiciae Anti-Baxterianae* (London, 1696), p. 83.

126. (DWL) *Baxter Treatises*, vi, f.318v.

127. Thomas Comber, *Union Pursued, in a Letter to Mr. Baxter, Concerning his late book Of National Churches* (London, 1691), pp. 12-13.

128. See my *Godly Rule* (London, 1969), pp. 28-52.

129. Comber, *Union Pursued*, pp. 12-13.

130. Roger Thomas, 'Presbyterians in Transition' in C.G. Bolam, Jeremy Goring, H.C. Short, Roger Thomas (eds.), *The English Presbyterians* (London, 1968), p. 128.

131. Ibid., p. 129.

132. Ibid., p. 127.

133. Cf. A.H. Wood, *Church Unity Without Uniformity* (London, 1963), p. 149.

134. Edmund Calamy, *A Defence of Moderate Nonconformity* (London,

1704), ii, pp. 64, 65, 86, 87, 89, 90; (London, 1705), iii, pp. 99, 100, 102, 109, 111, 112.

135. Ibid., iii, pp. 172-3. Cf. Gordon Schochet, *Patriarchalism in Political Thought: the Authoritarian Family and Political Speculation and Attitudes especially in Seventeenth-Century England* (New York, 1975), pp. 244-68 for Locke's *critique* of patriarchal reasoning, which anticipates Calamy's argument against Hoadly.

136. Ibid., iii, pp. 180, 181, 183, 298, 299, 383.

137. Baxter, *The Glorious Kingdom of Christ* (London, 1691), p. 7.

138. P. Toon, *God's Statesman* (Exeter, 1971), p. 136, argued that for John Owen, at least, the Church of England had too many 'marks of the beast' to be an acceptable 'National Church'.

139. Calamy, *A Defence of Moderate Nonconformity*, iii, p. 100.

5 CONCLUSION: PROTESTANT IMPERIALISM AND THE ENGLISH REVOLUTION

On 11 August 1661 one Jonathan Jenner found himself staying at an inn next door to the famous Richard Baxter. Too shy to approach the great man — he admitted to 'a melancholy disposition' — he wrote down twelve questions on fundamental theological points, including a request for a proof of the immortality of the soul. He pronounced himself ready to wait upon an answer until '10 of the Clock tomorrow night.' Baxter's reply, also dated 11 August 'neer ten a clock at night', opened with the not unreasonable supposition that Jenner must be

> a very quick and unwearyed person, though I know you not, proportioning your expectations to your parts, in that you expect a considerable volume to be written by a man not free from infirmities or busyness between nine of the clock (when I received yours) and that time, after a journey yesterday and preaching today.

The scratchy tone, the obsession with his health: these are authentic Baxter touches. But so too is the important fact that this passage is a preamble to action, not an excuse for inaction: 'I have but one half houre that is consistence with the necessary care of my health I can bestow on you, and that you shall have as far as it will goe.' Then follows a wonderfully patient, sensitive resolution of Jenner's queries.[1] One correspondent, Thomas Seale, writing to Baxter in 1680, compared him to Robert Bolton in the patience with which he dealt with correspondents, even from overseas.[2] Even an enemy, George Ashwell, writing to him in 1658 in a letter which compared him to Martin Marprelate in the reckless violence of his language, could not hold back this awed tribute:

> But that you should returne so large answere to it in lesse than three dayes (especially the intermediate Day being the Sunday, wherein, I presume, you were taken up with the publick service of the Lord, whose name it beares) is a far greater marvaile to mee. You have deservedly the repute of a Person very at your Pen. But this, I thinke, exceeds all that ever you did before.[3]

It is important to realise how lightly this book has touched upon a career of such outstanding range and depth of interests. There are three ways in which this study has drastically limited itself. It has not been a biography, although it has drawn fully upon his private letters and papers. It has focussed on four themes only: his apocalyptic studies of 1686, his explanations of the origins of the Civil War, his identification of the Protectorate with a Holy Commonwealth, and his leadership of Nonconformity after the Restoration. Most serious of all has been its *conceptual* limitation: the choice — explained in the Introduction — to opt for the 'horizontal' approach rather than the 'vertical' one. What this study has done is to emphasise the qualities which bound Baxter to his contemporaries, rather than those which set him apart. Yet it was the latter which won him the stature he commanded in his lifetime, and which have continued to inspire later generations. Wesley, Doddridge, Bishop Wilson, Spurgeon, Isaac Watts, Wilberforce and Whitefield are just some of the names, plucked almost at random by one writer, whose lives were transformed by the life and teachings of Baxter.[4] There is a real sense in which Baxter is a man for all seasons. And it is in that sense that a 'horizontal' study which flattens Baxter into the anti-Catholic mould of his time misses the important insights into his life; which is why Professor Collinson has argued that a 'vertical' study is more likely in the end to get it right. We do not lack good 'vertical' studies of Baxter: Powicke and Nuttall are the outstanding exponents of that genre. The case against the 'horizontal' approach is not the one which Baxter himself made: 'We are all like Pictures that must not be looked on too near. They that come near us find more faults and badness in us than others at a distance know.'[5] It is true that the 'vertical' approach can flatter, by drawing at a distance upon the qualities which Baxter had in common with the Doddridges and Wesleys, and by failing to emphasise more immediate disagreeable personal traits. But this is not true of a very good 'vertical' study like Nuttall's, which can hold the 'faults and badness' in a sensitive balance with the enduring virtues. Moreover, the 'horizontal' approach itself does not necessarily have the reductionist overtones which Baxter supposed; on the contrary, a study of his private correspondence often corrects the public image of the unforgiving polemicist. As we come nearer to Baxter, the man who comforts Mrs Gell out of her fears of the dark pushes into the background the man who trades Billingsgate language with John Tombes.

There is, however, another sense in which the 'horizontal' might be said to diminish: it reduces Baxter's stature as a classical authority. This point would be least telling of all to Baxter. His wife '(and some others) thought I had done better to have written fewer Books, and to have done those few better',[6] but he had made clear his philosophy on another occasion:

> And though for the Matter it is as necessary to the greatest, yet it is for the Vulgar principally that I publish it; and had rather it might be numbred with those Bookes that are carryed up and downe the Country from doore to doore in Pedlers Packs, than with those that lye on Booksellers Stalls, or are set up in the Libraries of learned Divines.[7]

It is true that a classical work, like *The Saints Everlasting Rest*, which moved inexorably into the libraries of learned divines almost from the time when he wrote it,[8] gains little from a 'horizontal' approach, and that it is the minor controversial works – among which even his *Holy Commonwealth* might be included – which gain most from an increased understanding of the context in which they are written.

The most serious objection, however, against the 'horizontal' approach remains: Baxter and Prynne become brothers under the skin. They were both remarkable seventeenth-century Puritans; they shared a respect for magistracy, Elizabethan bishops, John Foxe and the Emperor Constantine, and shared an obsession with Popish Plots. This study has emphasised their affinities in every chapter. And this is where the 'horizontal' approach seems most crude and insensitive as an analytical tool. Doddridge and Wesley would not be turning to *Prynne* for great insights. Remarkably for the age in which he lived and the distinction and courage of his career, Prynne repelled any sort of biographical interest in his lifetime, and for many generations after. Contemporaries and succeeding generations, in other words, were fully aware of the world of difference between the nasty obsessionalism of a Prynne (who disrupted Pepys's dinner table with his insistence on regaling the company with salacious tales from ancient manuscripts of lewd nuns[9]), and the charity of a Baxter to individual Catholics, which had alarmed such diverse figures as Lauderdale and Henry Bartlett by the breadth of its magnanimity. Second in Samuel Young's satirical Baxterian Ten Commandments was this proposition: 'That you always Think, Speak and Write favourably of those Good Christians and Brethren in the Church of Rome'.[10] Baxter's friend, John Humfrey, praised him for being one 'that can like a truth from a Bellarmine or Arminius, as from a Calvin or Melanchthon'. Almost immediately Humfrey checked himself: 'I should not therefore have mentioned Arminius there as I did, because it looks like a glancing at you, even for that I say I like in you.'[11] Clearly Humfrey was sincere in his respect for the breadth of sympathy of his friend. To say that Baxter and Prynne were alike in their enmity to Rome is possibly to make the least important point about them.

But that is not to deny that there is an important sense in which their two very different temperaments converge. Vertical studies are better on the differences than on the similarities. A horizontal study, like this present one, has concentrated on the similarities in the belief that this is one way to re-enter the mental world of the seventeenth-century English Puritan. It was easier to fit Prynne than Baxter, at first sight, into the revision of that mental world which I offered in *Godly Rule*. Prynne made few direct allusions to prophecy, it is true, but at least his pamphlets were studded with references to Foxe, Jewel, Brightman, Constantine, Elizabeth and the Marian martyrs.[12] As such they could be accommodated within that one continuous Protestant apocalyptic tradition which I described in *Godly Rule*. Not so Baxter. Such intimations were present in some writings, as we have seen. But one difference between them seemed insurmountable initially. That was Baxter's conscious decision to set himself against the received Protestant wisdom on one important apocalyptic point: the identity of Antichrist with Rome. His reservations on that issue had been expressed as early as 1654, although they did not surface publicly until 1684. We have seen that his later researches strengthened, not weakened, that scepticism. Since he also had boasted on numerous occasions of his lack of interest in millenarian ideas there seemed every excuse for ignoring Baxter in any general study of the Apocalypse in seventeenth-century England. When Dr Capp, for instance, discussed the extent of millenarian ideas among ministers publishing three or more works between 1640 and 1653 he produced a huge list of authors showing millenarian ideas. The list ran to 77 names: an effective rejoinder to old-fashioned authorities who had thought in terms of a 'lunatic fringe' interest.[13] Even so, Baxter figures on the much shorter list (of 34, to be precise) of 'authors not showing millenarian ideas'. How then did this man come to feel so involved with the Apocalypse in 1686? For reasons not so far removed, I would find, from those which made Prynne a 'root and branch' man in 1641.

There was one more formidable barrier to a re-creation of Baxter. This was the problem of the two Baxters. Baxter's old enemy, Roger L'Estrange, had composed a pamphlet successfully on the basis of a dialogue between 'Richard' and 'Baxter'.[14] This was a cheap debating trick, but it did have a wider validity. Edmund Calamy and Matthew

Sylvester were both to produce versions of Baxter's autobiography, and each had claims to be the authentic interpreter of Baxter. Calamy, stressing Charles I's warrant to the Earl of Antrim, showed why Parliament was driven to self-preservation action, and later revamped Baxter to justify separatism. Samuel Young was thrilled by the Antrim revelations, but was dismayed at Sylvester's edition of Baxter's autobiography, with its heavy emphasis on Tory non-resistance, and the non-separatist traditions of English Nonconformity. Who was cheating, Calamy or Sylvester? Both were. Calamy was the honest rogue — admitting to leaving out, and putting in, matters which suited him; refusing to be over-solemn about the status of Baxter's pronouncements. Sylvester was ostensibly more scrupulous, but perhaps ultimately the more misleading. His omissions were few, but they were at decisive points. The omissions in Sylvester's published text of some of Baxter's statements in his manuscript conceal the extent to which Baxter saw the Civil War as a war against Popery, and Harrington's *Oceana* as a Popish treatise. But in another sense *neither was cheating*. As Calamy pointed out, he did not invent the Antrim story; he got it from Baxter. And his revision of English Nonconformity leaned heavily upon Baxter's own writings between 1677 and 1682. But, equally, Sylvester did not manufacture Baxter's 'Toryism': the heavy emphasis on non-resistance and non-separatism was to be found throughout Baxter's writings. How to reconcile Calamy and Sylvester, Richard and Baxter? The 'horizontal' approach helps to provide access to both.

The two seem furthest apart in explaining the origins of the Civil War. L'Estrange was not slow to exploit the difference: 'Richard says, the War began about Religion. Baxter says, it began about matters of Law.'[15] Stillingfleet was on the same scent. How could Baxter reconcile his case against the bishops with his often repeated assertion that 'the War was not founded in Theological differences but Law-differences'? Stillingfleet's question then seemed unanswerable: 'and how then did the Bishops begin it?'[16]

Now it is quite true that Baxter was attracted by Lawson's reductionist interpretation, 'Religion is but pretended,'[17] although it is equally true that, at the end of his life, he was at equal pains to emphasise the limitations of such explanations. Writing after the Restoration, however, that legal niceties were 'thought improper for Divines', he was happy to follow Lawson's lead and draw as the moral, from the outbreak of the Civil War, the proposition that clergymen should keep out of politics.[18] This had several advantages. It excused his own lapse in writing his *Holy Commonwealth*; although his recantation of that work was always studiedly vague. The memory of Laudian clergymen meddling in affairs of state was unhappily revived in their successors – the Sheldon, the Morleys and the Gunnings. Nearer at hand a more fatal example was John Owen's part in toppling Richard Cromwell, although for obvious political reasons he could say less about that than he would have liked to have done. But, over and above these considerations, a simple fact of principle lay behind his endorsement of this thesis: there *was* a real sense in which he believed that the Civil War had nothing to do with religion.

He best expressed this view in a pamphlet in 1681. The important distinction he then makes is between *Finis* and *Fundamentum*. He denies that the question at issue is, *'What were the final Motives of the War?'* Therefore it is irrelevant for critics to challenge ideas which he had expressed in his *Saints Everlasting Rest*, when he *was* talking about such matters. But to decide whether or not the Civil War were lawful, the issue is 'the Controversie of the warranting Cause and Foundation'. As he explains:

> The *Bonum Publicatum*, and the *Gospel* and *Religion*, and *Mens Salvations*, are the *great moveing ends and Reasons* for a lawful *War*. But it is not these *Ends* that will serve to prove a *War* lawful? Could that be the *Cause* or *Controversie* which they were both agreed in? Did not the King profess to be for *Religion, Liberty* etc. as well as they . . . The *Finis* and the *Fundamentum* are not the same. I there talkt of the *Finis* and *Motives*, I now speak of the *Fundamentum* and *Controversie*, which is well known to be, whether the *King* or *Parliament* then had the power of the *Militia* . . . I know no Theological Controversie therein.[19]

Baxter's statement after the Glorious Revolution about the *inadequacy* of Lawson-type analyses[20] is not as contradictory of earlier positions as it appears: it is a continuation of earlier interests expressed in *The Saints Everlasting Rest* in the problems of motives or *Finis*, as a corrective to a total preoccupation with the questions which Lawson had legitimately raised over *Fundamentum*.

The advantage of this distinction was to protect the office of magistracy, which was a genuine concern for him and his fellow Protestants. He took very seriously indeed Parliament's early protestations not to be opposing the office of the Crown. When religion intruded into this dispute over the militia it did so illegitimately. It did so first, in the populist theory of Richard Hooker, with its unnecessary emphasis on the supremacy of law and the limitations of magistracy. Baxter is to be acquitted of disingenuousness here; Hooker was not a simple stick with which to beat Anglicans, and to tell them that it was *their* war. This was certainly how Baxter often used Hooker, but it is clear from his private papers the depth of his revulsion throughout his life from teachings which tacitly exalted the popular will above the sovereign. (The exception was the period between 1675 and 1682, when Hooker's 'laws' were a valuable counter against the oppressive absolutism argued by the Dodwells and Sherlocks.) As imperialists, Baxter and Prynne were not interested in the orthodox constitutional arguments against unlimited monarchy. Baxter said of the civil dispute that 'at the heart I little regarded it'; apart from his treatise on Ship Money, published in 1641, Prynne had nothing to say on the great constitutional divisions in his writings between 1628 and 1641. Neither of them even referred to Mainwaring and Sibthorpe, the Anglican upholders of absolute monarchy; although, again, Baxter did so belatedly only in that period of his life when 'Dodwell's Leviathan' haunted his imagination. Prynne even doctored the record of the trial against Laud to make it appear as a case against a man who had undermined the Royal Supremacy, rather than one who had puffed it up far too high.[21]

After Hooker, Knox. Religion again intruded illegitimately into the *Fundamentum* when King-killing resistance theories were taken up on the Parliamentary side with the dubious sanction of Geneva. The popularity of such ideas cast an indelible stain upon the justice of the good old cause. Baxter fought such ideas with all the vigour he could sustain. Things had taken a decisive turn for the worse as early as 1643, when the Civil War became 'a War for Religion'; uglier still when sectarian chaplains in Cromwell's regiments spread egalitarian and determinist ideas.

But if religion were to be kept out of *Fundamentum*, it could not be kept out of *Finis*. Men *were* moved to arms by a self-preservative principle: the Irish Rebellion was the intended prelude to the conquest of England by Irish Papists. This belief was no more inimical to the Crown than was the constitutional argument. The King was in need of rescue, not only from evil counsellors who advised him to impose Ship Money, but equally from his Papist would-be captors. It was not until 1643 that Prynne saw Charles I as an *accomplice*, rather than the *dupe*, of Papist designs. Charles's own guilt could not be ignored once his private correspondence with Papists had been intercepted. Charles was now *The Popish Royall Favourite*. In his *Third Defence of the Cause of Peace* Baxter acknowledged the profound effect made on him by Prynne's revelations in that work of a history of Crown/Papist collaboration; in his own *Holy Commonwealth* and *A Key for Catholicks*, references to Prynne's allegations abound. But the link between the King and Irish Papist rebels remained circumstantial. That was the importance of the Antrim commission: it authenticated the link between them. When Baxter came to write up his explanation of the Civil War after the Restoration he concentrated on the *Fundamentum* rather than the *Finis*, although to a much lesser extent than the Everyman edition of his autobiography — and even Sylvester's edition, we now see — would have led us to suppose. The Antrim story was in the air, however, and Baxter would not let it alone. He was not the only Protestant to do so: we have seen from Carte's papers how this topic continued to fascinate men into the eighteenth century.[22] Above all in 1679 the political sensitivity of the story was evident. Borlase's researches into the Irish rebellion were subject to the censorship of Roger L'Estrange; L'Estrange's note of 20 February 1679 emphasises the need to clear the King of complicity in the Irish Rebellion. Among the papers in Borlase's manuscripts, which were not finally included in his published account of the Irish Rebellion, is the copy of Charles II's pardon to the Earl of Antrim of 12 August 1663, with its ambiguous acknowledgement of the service rendered to 'our Royale father'.[23] What L'Estrange did to Borlase in 1679, Sylvester would do to Baxter in 1696: the Antrim story was better suppressed.

The issues which it raised, however, were different in kind from those raised by Hooker or the Calvinist resistance theorists. The Antrim story was an important substantiation of the Popish Plot which had first driven men into the streets: it touched upon men's motives, and in this sense religion was legitimately part of the *Finis*. Moreover, even if the Antrim story were true, and were subsequently *proved* to be true, it did not challenge the authority of the magistracy in the way that Anglican populism or Calvinist rebellion did. This was because of the imperial loophole: Bilson, Grotius and Barclay recognised that a King who went mad, invaded his own realm, and subordinated his imperial authority to the Pope, ceased to have authority over his subjects. This was a sensible *extension* of the imperial principle rather than a contradiction of it; that is why Baxter hailed Bilson as the supreme teacher of *obedience*. That was why Baxter was worried at the way in which his friend, John Humfrey, subtly mis-stated the Nonconformist position. He was using Bilson as if he were an authority for resistance rather than obedience. Corbet and Humfrey were very close to Baxter on these matters. Baxter wrote of the oath never to take up arms against any persons commissioned by the King: 'What if a bold limited Expositor will here come in, and say [Except King John deliver up the Kingdom to the Pope; or except the King's Commissioners through the Officers would be so contradictory] or such Exceptions as Wil Barclay and Grotius made?'[24] Corbet showed how Grotius and Barclay did not advance arguments which ruled out such oaths: 'are not properly Restrictions laid upon the tenet, but Explanations of its meaning, that their Readers may not mistake some for delinquents against it, who indeed are not such according to this Judgement.'[25] Humfrey explicitly argued against the seventeenth proposition of the Oxford Convocation Decree of 21 July 1683, condemning the view that 'an Oath Obligeth not in the sense of the Imposer, but the Taker': 'Put the Case then that a Prince should go about to Destroy his whole People, which is a Case put by Grotius from Barclay, as inconsistent with ruling them.' Such a Prince would be a madman, but King John had been prepared to alien-ate his Kingdom: 'What if a Prince would raise an Army out of one of his Dominion that were Papists, and bring it into another of them that are Protestants.'[26] All three were arguing in a similar vein. They wished to show how an oath of non-resistance did not rule out the exceptional cases allowed for by Bilson, Grotius and Barclay. Baxter, Humfrey and Corbet were bracketed together by an anonymous correspondent for their bad faith in doing so.[27] But this is not quite correct. Baxter puts the exception in the mouth of an unnamed 'bold limited Expositor'; Corbet denies that it is, properly understood, an exception at all; only Humfrey states the exception in his own person, to show why an oath cannot *oblige* in the sense of the imposer. Even Humfrey qualifies his remarks with the further point that 'these are Cases may be supposed; not that I imagine any such in good earnest ever like to be.' But he still inches that fatal step further forward towards resistance, which Baxter and Corbet refused to take. It was that same impetuosity in Humfrey which had led Baxter earlier to rebuke him for distorting Bilson's subtle balancing act, and for going the populist way of a Hooker or Jeremy Taylor.

These wafer-thin distinctions were necessary in a discussion of *Finis*, if Protestant imperialism were not to become a euphemism for godly rebellion. As Baxter put it: 'rebellion is so heynous a sin, that we have 100 times more reason to cry it down . . . than to tell the people when they may resist.'[28] When Baxter wrote up his account of the origins of the Civil War he was too honest to ignore the *Finis*; he could not discuss men's motives at the time without acknowledging the overwhelming terror of a Popish Plot. With or without the Antrim revelations, such discussion – as we have seen in the second chapter – inevitably threw up questions about the right of resistance, in a way which discussion of the *Fundamentum* did not (unless, in that case, religion were illegitimately intruded into it).

Baxter's analysis of the Civil War has been praised for the wrong reasons. For almost the only time in his writing life Baxter produced catalogues of the constitutional conflicts between King and Parliament before the Civil War. They have little value. He was not interested himself in these civil matters, and this showed in the writing. There are serious confusions about the sequence and dating of events: the Etcetera Oath, the formation of the National Covenant and the Ship Money case, and the origins of the First Bishops' War, for example.[29] He produced a sociological analysis of the forces on either side, but his friend John Corbet had anticipated most of his findings in his book on Gloucester, published as early as 1645.[30] Corbet — of whom Baxter once said, 'we were of one Mind and Heart, our agreement is no wonder,'[31] and on another occasion that 'in forty years (I remember not that ever we differed once)'[32] — also gives a sketchy account of the *Fundamentum*, but is unambiguous about the *Finis*:

> Therefore when the fire kindled and fomented by Jesuited Papists and their adherents, was blowne up into a flame, and the heads of two Parties appeared within the Realme, the City of Gloucester determined not to stand Neutrall in action.[33]

The most recent authority on histories of the English Civil War has emphasised the hiatus between the Restoration and the Glorious Revolution of books critical of the monarchy.[34] Baxter deserves praise for not suppressing sentiments after the Restoration which were similar to Corbet's in 1645, *but at a time when these had become dangerous to voice*. Sylvester suppressed the most provocative of them, it is true, but enough survived to provide an arsenal for Calamy's Whiggery. It was not only fear of political reprisals which encouraged caution; the sincerity of Baxter's own respect for magistracy worked in the same direction. And yet, even so, Baxter did not forget the fear of Popery as the principal motivation of the Civil War; he wrote it up in his autobiographical manuscripts, but it also surfaced in his published works after the Restoration. It would re-emerge as the vindication of *two* Revolutions in his writings in 1691.

Conrad Russell has criticised the traditional view of the political and constitutional disputes of the early seventeenth century, in which they are seen as a trial of strength between two developing institutions —

Crown and Parliament — only to be resolved by the coming of the Civil War.[35] That tradition was early in its formation and, even after the Restoration, Baxter's explanation of the Civil War was written partly under its influence. The civil controversies may not have interested him, but no conscientious effort to explain how the Civil War had come about could ignore the *Fundamentum*. Baxter's trite summary of the constitutional disputes assumes greater prominence in Sylvester's edition than it does in the original manuscript of Baxter thanks to Sylvester's deletions, but the *Finis* is still given major status. Only in the Everyman edition, which pares the discussion of *Finis* to the bone, does the Civil War appear, as *par excellence*, a crisis of the constitution. By a nice touch of irony, the abbreviated Everyman edition of Baxter — containing Baxter's assertion that, by 1643, the Civil War was *transformed* into a 'war for Religion' (he is speaking of the *Fundamentum*, not the *Finis*) — becomes in time the classic source for the view that the English Civil War *was not, in its origins, a war about religion at all*.

Only when we restore religion to its central position as the mover of men can we understand Baxter's ambivalence about the execution of the King. There seems at first to be no ambiguity. Baxter never condoned regicide. Leslie was wrong when he said that 'this rare Baxter did canonise those as Saints who brought him to the Block.'[36] Baxter did nothing of the sort, and in fact it swiftly becomes apparent that Leslie was only reviving the old *canard* that Pym and Hampden were among the saints whom Baxter looked forward to meeting in Heaven in his *Saints Everlasting Rest*. Stillingfleet went still further: 'Who hath said more to justifie not the War onely, but the Death of the Royal Martyr ... Would not this man have made a better Solliciter against the Royal Martyr, then Cooke?'[37] But he, too, could draw on no direct evidence of Baxter's approval of the execution; only that his *Holy Commonwealth* and *A Key for Catholicks* had portrayed Charles I as the Grotian instrument, who was richly deserving of his final punishment. But Baxter's revulsion from the regicide was genuine. He deplored it as the logical end of the populist theories and justifications of resistance which had come to disfigure the Parliamentary cause. He deplored it even more as a Popish triumph; which is why he, Prynne, Morice, Peter du Moulin and other imperial Protestants attached so much weight to the rumour that Henrietta Maria's Confessor had waved his sword in jubilation as the King died. But the King's culpability — not even in 1659 as a flat Papist, but as a Grotian fellow-traveller — drained the event of pathos at a personal level.[38] The origins of the Civil War and its resolution had for Baxter a symmetry: Papists first used, and then destroyed, their Royal Favourite.

The regicide became, for Baxter, a part of a wider quarrel: with the sectaries who had infiltrated Cromwell's Army. The critical importance of his first published work, his *Aphorismes of Justification* of 1649, was to elevate this political quarrel to a theological level: Antinomianism begat Coppe; a false view of God's Grace underlay the excesses of the sects. Baxter was not the first Puritan critic of Free Grace in the 1640s; John Goodwin was there first, and he hit harder. Baxter's novelty lay in the way in which he bypassed a generation of stale polemics against the Laudians, and went back for his theology to the Synod of Dort and to a modified version of the 'hypothetical universalism' of Davenant, Cameron and Amyraut.

One of the most sustained attacks on Baxter's theology is Thomas Edwards's *Baxterianism Barefaced* of 1699. He recites Herbert Palmer's character of a Christian in Paradoxes, 'who was an antient worthy Presbyterian Puritan, and yet an abhorrer of Baxterianism, which is another Paradox amongst some, tho' not all of them'. First of Palmer's 85 Paradoxes, quoted approvingly by Edwards, was this: 'A Christian is one who believes things which his Reason cannot comprehend.'[39] No formulation could have seemed more empty to Baxter. Like his friend Glanvill, Baxter saw Roman Catholic fideism and sectaries' determinism as *related* enemies. Samuel Young quoted the verdict of one divine on Baxter: 'That he would die a Thomas Aquinas, distinguish and distinguish till he had distinguish'd all into nothing'.[40] Baxter *was* on the side of Aquinas against the fideists; it was as Aquinas's pupil that Baxter reassured Mrs Gell that, in this life, 'Grace itselfe doth usually worke accordinge to the way of nature.'[41] John Owen was swift to accuse Baxter of 'Socinianism' for the emphasis he gave to rational inquiry. Sylvester, Manton and Bates were among the co-signatories with Baxter of the very important work of 1676, *The Judgment of Non-conformists, of the Interest of Reason, in Matters of Religion*, in which accusations of 'Socinianism' did not deflect them from a collective affirmation of the primacy of reason.[42] L.I. Bredvold has brilliantly captured the intellectual milieu of John Dryden, in which Catholicism was making headway at the Restoration by virtue of its fideism, while on the opposite flank Owen and his Independent colleagues were extolling the arbitrary nature of God's Grace.[43] Jackson Cope has shown how Glanvill was drawn to Baxter precisely by his commitment to rational investigation of 'providences'.[44] Their correspondence together about witches, ghosts and apparitions shows the lengths to which they went to satisfy themselves that such occurrences met the strict canons of rational inquiry.[45] Henry More's investigation of apparitions belonged to the same school of rationalism, and was welcomed as such by Baxter. The perils in entering such fields were notorious: they attracted the quacks and the manic depressives. But the rewards were comparably high. As Baxter wrote to John Lewis: 'I am glad L. Coll. Bowen believes there are witches for then sure he believes there is a God, Angells, Devills or some Spirittes, which I heare he did not before.'[46] To protect themselves from the fanatics, ministers had a special responsiblity to set up watchdog committees to investigate 'occurrences': this is clear in the correspondence between Baxter and his colleagues, White, Poole and Mather.[47] This extract from another letter of Baxter to John Lewis in 1657 conveys the authentic flavour of a Baxter investigation, in this case into the mystery of strange lights:

> I pray you returne my hearty thanks to Mr. Davis for his great paines in the matter of the Lights. I have communicated his papers to divers ministers, and they commonly aske me these Questions 1. Whether people use to tell of those Candles, when the persons are liveing, or only after their death (ordinarily) 2. Whether they do not pass by many that are seene, where no such death ensues, and mention only those that are followed with a corps . . . I remember once 6 or 7 of my friends, Gentlemen of Quality, having visited me overnight and invited me to meet them (three miles off at the sea side in Devonshire) the next day, they told me that as they went there in a storme for a miles ridinge, their horses eares were on fire, and their rods ends, and they could feele no hurt they toucht them. I heare also of a place where the horses breath in the night time hath such a fire, at their mouths frequently. Its comonest near the sea. I perceive you only see many of the candles in the house, but not going to the graves.[48]

Was rational inquiry to stop short of an investigation of the strange 'signs' and 'providences' in Daniel and Revelation? More believed not: his exposition of the Apocalypse was an *extension* of his interest in apparitions. He claimed that it was 'diametrically opposite' to an 'Enthusiastick Phrensie', and accused Baxter of being one of those 'affected Rationalists, who pretend that Prophecies, especially those of Daniel and the Apocalypse, are utterly unintelligible'.[49] This stung Baxter on the raw: he did *not* believe the Apocalypse to be unintelligible, but was wary of the men who normally claimed that they had understood it. As Baxter's letter to Bromley of 1654 had made clear, it was men like the Mad Major who were attracted to such studies.[50] And in a pamphlet a year later he was warning against any encouragement to 'one that hath a strong melancholly, opinionated or diabolically deluded fancy to conclude that they are justified by Revelation'. The highest which he himself could come to was 'experience of strange unusual incomes of Light suddenly, when I least expected it'. But Baxter dampened even this vision, since he discovered that invariably 'it is only a Revelation of Conclusions from Premises, shewing me suddenly the name of things which I observed not, or sought after before in vain'.[51] But 'incomes of Light' could come when reading Revelation as they could come when studying apparitions: More was wrong to suppose that Baxter had closed the door on either investigation. It was as fellow members of a rationalist club that Baxter and Mather would discuss the collation of 'providences' and the meaning of the Apocalypse in the 1680s; Baxter's scepticism of a *future* millennium, and the identity of Antichrist, did not − for Mather − bar Baxter from membership. The club was rejected by conformist and sectarian. Edward Bagshaw warned against Baxter's 'Itch of anxious Enquiry', which led inevitably to atheism. Baxter, on the other hand, believed that more men, like Lieutenant-Colonel Bowen, would be led through inquiry about witches into acceptance of God. That was the difference between them. Bagshaw remonstrated with him: 'to reconcile Religion to Natural Reason? to bring down the Things of God into the understanding of Man; which is in effect to say you do not believe them to be *Tremendous Mysteries*'.[52] From the opposite flank, Thomas Edwards, writing in 1699, wished that Presbyterians had been as tough with Baxter as Owen had been with his fellow Independent, John Goodwin. Baxter's errors, Edwards concluded regretfully, were not 'the offspring of his Dotage': they were of a piece with his earlier arguments against Owen.[53] This unhealed doctrinal rift between Baxter and Owen mocked the 'mathematics' of negotiations for union between Presbyterians and Independents in the 1670s.[54]

Cromwell was initially rejected by Baxter as the man who sponsored the Antinomian wild men − the Saltmarshes, Dells and Peters. Baxter refused to take the Engagement Oath to the Commonwealth. The cumulative process of withdrawal from this position is easy to miss, especially as Baxter himself was not anxious to spell out that process in detail in memoirs which were after all composed after the Restoration. Even a recent intelligent commentator has missed the full force of the change:

Baxter realises that there was an apparent contradiction between his

disaffection to the Protectorate of Oliver Cromwell and the benefits
he and godliness in general received from it, but for him his moral
obligation to uphold the legitimate monarchy justified his disaffection and he gives no sign in the *Reliquiae Baxterianae* of repenting of
it.[55]

It is not in the *Reliquiae Baxterianae* that one would expect to find
such repentance; it is his private papers and correspondence which give
the lie to that judgement. Sir Francis Nethersole, for one, found that
appeals to uphold the legitimate monarch by the end of the Commonwealth period cut little ice with Baxter.[56] Not all contemporaries had
access to Baxter's correspondence, but there was no mistaking the
enthusiasm for the régime in his *Holy Commonwealth* and *A Key for
Catholicks*; that is to say, in the texts themselves, and not merely — as
Baxter would have it — in their fulsome dedicatory epistles. Contemporaries did not miss their significance: their accusations pursued Baxter throughout the post-Restoration period. But even the most hostile
critics missed their *full* significance. Stillingfleet begins promisingly, it is
true, with the claim that for Baxter 'Oliver is as David, and his Son
Richard as Solomon.' But he does not pursue the theme. The accusation dribbles away into a charge of peevishness: 'The plain truth is, he
was neither for Oliver nor Richard, but so far only as to hinder the
return of his Majesty and the Church to their lawful and ancient
Rites.'[57] The comment fairly reflects the prosecution case against
Baxter after the Restoration. He was seen as the type of the Puritan
fanatic who had begun the Civil War.[58] Stories of his killing a man in
cold blood and snatching a medal from a dying soldier's chest were
circulated with venomous glee. *A Holy Commonwealth* was ransacked
for material which could be used for his discomfiture, in much the same
way as his *Paraphrase on the New Testament* would be used against him
later. But there is no evidence that his critics had gauged the depth of
his emotional investment in the Commonwealth régime. Baxter wrote
to an anonymous correspondent about his retraction of *A Holy Commonwealth*, with oblique self-satisfaction, in 1684: 'Sr. are you acquainted with all my reasons for its retraction and why I quickly wisht I
had never wrote it.'[59] We know his *public* reasons for regret; clergymen
should not meddle in politics; he had unwittingly wounded monarchy.
We know now also his *real* reasons for regret, written in his manuscript
autobiography and excised from the published edition by Matthew
Sylvester: that he had shown the Army officers, and their sectarian
friends, the need for a pre-emptive strike if Richard Cromwell's *Holy*

Commonwealth were not to become an enduring constitutional reality.[60]

We have traced in his correspondence[61] the stages by which he was seduced, beginning with a negative wish to hold Popery at bay, and culminating in a positive expectation of a New Jerusalem. The magistrate's sword would maintain order; clerical discipline would separate the precious from the vile. Baxter was a child of the times in having his millennial dreams. These dreams were not derived from a specific study of the prophetic texts, but they were part of the common eschatological assumptions of that time; drawn upon by himself and others, as they collated 'providences', formed ministerial associations, planned new universities and organised missions overseas. They differed from the millennial dreams of the Fifth Monarchists because they *were not merely dreams*; rooted in rationality, they awaited immediate practical fulfilment by a reforming government. When Baxter did make his detailed study of prophetic texts in 1686, he could base his argument for a past chiliad on men's ignorance of the blessings of the past. He meant the distant past: he showed the achievements of the first Christian Empire under Constantine. But he also drew upon the more recent past to describe the Protectorate as the time of 'the fall of Antichrist'.[62]

The collapse of Richard Cromwell's Protectorate was a traumatic blow for Baxter. For the next twenty years, in the period of persecution and disappointment, he drew upon a quieter imperial comfort. He did not look to Charles II to inaugurate a millennial rule, but he still believed that imperial authority must be upheld. Relief from persecution was not to be won at the price of toleration alongside Papists and Quakers; Nonconformists must submit to detested legislation, and John Humfrey was quite wrong to appeal to the authority of Bishop Bilson for defiance of the Five Mile Act. Even Nero must be obeyed: Bilson's qualification of obedience to a ruler was not his unbridled tyranny, but his insane self-destructiveness. The formula seemed bleak, and there were other men than Humfrey to argue that Baxter was far too timid. But Baxter was a reformist, not a revolutionary; his main hopes for relief rested upon 'comprehension' plans, based on Usher's model of a 'reduced' Episcopacy, to be negotiated with sympathetic Anglicans like Tillotson and Wilkins. Even talks with Owen and Independent ministers were conducted on the same premisses: there was to be no break with the tradition of a 'National Church'; no concession to separatism; no truck with Papists or Quakers.

It is not easy to document precisely when Baxter changed, but it is clear that by the late 1670s a remarkable transformation was occurring. As early as 3 August 1676 one correspondent was accusing Baxter of

changing his mind, and of becoming a convert to the arguments that
Nonconformists should withdraw into separate congregations of the
faithful and abandon the *chimera* of a National Church.[63] These certainly became the themes of his published writings between 1679 and
1682. His *Treatise of Episcopacy* of 1681 is a good specimen from this
period: denying that the magistrate's sword is the chief strength of
Church discipline, quoting the anti-Erastian Gillespie on the need for
ministerial power, ridiculing the claims of Constantine's Christian
Empire, arguing that National Churches breed hypocrites and holding
up for admiration the separatist model of St Martin.[64] Or, as he put it
pithily in another work in the same year, 'I am more for Martin's spirit
than the Ithacian Bishops.'[65]

Why did he change? One explanation offered by Dr MacGillivray is
that there is no reason to suppose that he did. On this view, the lapse
of the Licensing Act in 1679, and the crises of the Popish Plot and
succession struggle, left the government unable to supervise the press
as effectively as before.[66] Baxter himself said that 'the act restraining
the Press being expired, I published a Book that lay by me to open the
case of Nonconformity.'[67] The *Treatise of Episcopacy* supports this
argument: according to Baxter it was planned as early as 1640, partly
written in 1671 and then put in cold storage until 1681, when it could
be revised and published. The relaxation of censorship permitted the
airing of separatist views.

One can accept that the political climate in the late 1670s and early
1680s had a liberating effect, without finding this explanation wholly
satisfactory. It is clear from Baxter's private correspondence that his
public voice in the 1660s was not at variance with his own convictions.
It is true, of course, that his letters were subject to censorship, particularly when Venner's uprising threw the government into a panic. Baxter
wrote of that period to Thomas Beavans on 16 August 1669:

> I wrote but one to my Mother when she was there, at the time of
> Venner's uprising. And though there was nothing in it but exhorta-
> tions to heavenlynesse, and invectives agt. that insurrection, it was
> taken at Kidderminster and carryed to the Bishop and Lord Chan-
> cellour to London, in hope to have hanged me for ... treason, till
> the Lord Chancellour sent the Lord Windsor to bring it me to my
> Lodgings as innocent.[68]

But it is difficult to believe that Baxter's letters throughout this period
were composed with a potential censor in mind; when he ticks Humfrey

off for his impetuosity it is for his breach of imperial principles rather than of security regulations.[69] In the last chapter I offered an evolutionary explanation, based upon a detailed study of the letters themselves. It is not merely wisdom by hindsight to detect a growing disenchantment in Baxter with the non-separatist formula which he had advocated in the early 1660s. The basic point of irritation was the low dividends which the Nonconformists had earned by this investment in self-denial. It was the point that Calamy was to hammer at with telling effect in 1704 to justify a break with the whole tradition of non-separatism. Nonconformists had reason to follow non-separatism when reformist hopes were high: but by 1704 what victories could be chalked up to asceticism? For a man like Baxter who cared so passionately about effective ministerial discipline the complacency of an Anglican don like Dodwell was intolerable. But there was a more serious point still. Many of the bishops *were* complacent, vindictive and proud. But the Episcopal order – and this was his comfort at the darkest moments – was not itself irredeemable: Tillotson and Wilkins could be set against Morley and Gunning. Heylyn's biography of Laud, published in 1668, dispelled such optimism. What disturbed Baxter – and this became a recurrent theme in his writings in the 1670s and 1680s – was its revelation of a coherent plot to bring Anglican and Catholic together in a closer union, based upon a repudiation of Papal headship and a recognition of the supremacy of conciliar jurisdiction.

The choice of title for Heylyn's biography, *Cyprianus Anglicus*, was itself significant: Laud had referred admiringly to the third-century martyr/saint as one who held 'no great opinion of the Roman infallibility'. Here was the basis for union: not the 'Italian' way, with its emphasis on Papal primacy, but the 'French' way, with its emphasis on conciliar power. Heylyn was probably less the confidant of Laud's designs than Baxter supposed,[70] but he conjured up for Baxter the convincing nightmare of a planned drive towards a foreign jurisdiction. Baxter had a sensitive nose for conspiracies: particularly when they were concocted for the benefit of Roman Catholicism. In 1658 he had discovered the 'Grotian Religion'; Hammond had confided to Sheldon his dislike of Baxter's characterisation of a number of bishops as 'Grotian' at that period.[71] Yet Laud had, in general, not loomed large in Baxter's writings as the weaver of conspiracies. He had written too little to touch Baxter's polemical nerve; his Arminianism was less offensive to the author of *Aphorismes of Justification* than it was to Baxter's fellow Puritans. *But Heylyn spoke for Laud*: this assumption – warranted or not – inspired Baxter's attacks in the 1670s upon Dodwell, Thorndike,

L'Estrange, Saywell and Stillingfleet. He described Heylyn to Stillingfleet in such terms as 'your Perversest Champion' and 'Your Goliath'.[72]

With the recognition of the Laudian Plot, sectarianism lost its dubi-
ety. The 'Muscovy' tyranny advocated by Dodwell was recognised and
deplored by Baxter as an instrument of the Grotian design. He quoted
Hale — again and again — for the story of the two 'pikes' devouring the
sects. Belatedly he recognised the importance of the Parliamentary
struggles in the 1620s and 1630s against royalist absolutism. Hooker's
populism became the Protestant shield, not the Papist knife. Sibthorpe
and Mainwaring were condemned for their encouragement of Kings to
trample upon the laws. St Martin was right: separatism from such
corrupt bishops was now a logical imperative for English Protestants.
Had Baxter died in 1682, Calamy's revisionism of 1704 would have
seemed its natural sequel. John Rastrick's *An Account of the Nonconformity*, published in 1705, is a moving testament by one minister of
how his gradual disenchantment with conformity over the years gave
way to an acceptance of separatism in 1679 on reading Baxter's *The
Nonconformists Plea for Peace*, and later his *Treatise of Episcopacy*.[73]
And that is why Hoadly's outrage at Calamy's violation of Baxter's non-
separatist principles fails to carry conviction.[74]

But Baxter did not die in 1682. Instead, John Humfrey encouraged
him in the task of paraphrasing the New Testament. This led him to the
Book of Revelation, and ultimately to the scandalous public assertion
that the Pope was not Antichrist. But for Baxter this conclusion was
not in itself of great moment: the Pope was not *the* Antichrist of
prophecy, but *an* Antichrist, inasmuch as he was a usurper. What he
learned from reading Revelation more closely was the incompatibility
of such an usurper *with a Protestant National Church*:

> Therefore I judge that a Confederacy or Coalition with the Church
> of Rome, in any of these Sins, or in the very form of a Church
> headed by a pretended Universal Head or Soveraign, is to be abhorred
> by all sound Christians: And I am glad that this Kingdom is sworn
> against all Foreign Jurisdiction, Civil or Ecclesiastical; tho'
> Union and Concorn with all Foreign Churches must be as far kept as
> we are able, not partaking of their Sins.[75]

'Not partaking of their Sins': that was the vital point of difference between Durie and Heylyn, Eliot and Grotius. In the prophetic texts, Baxter was discovering the answer to the Anglican divines' 'revolt to a
foreign jurisdiction'. That answer only became fully formulated in the

course of his apocalyptic researches in prison.

The answer was an unexpected one. Anglicans – with their 'Grotian' designs for union with Rome – were exalting magistracy, exhorting subjects to passive obedience, and dragooning dissenters into their National Church. We have seen how, in retaliation, Baxter was being driven into a separatist position, even to the point of identifying with the villains of Thomas Edwards's *Gangraena*.[76] What could ostensibly be more gratifying to his Anglican opponents than for Baxter in prison to proclaim the 'Grotian' thesis that Rome was not Antichrist, that magistracy must be exalted, that subjects must obey, and that no separatism from the National Church could be countenanced? No wonder that he should ask his literary executors to conceal the material if he were right, and to burn it if he were wrong. Jonathan Southwell seemed to be aware of the gravity of this threat when he wrote in these terms to Baxter on 24 June 1691: 'pray sir! let me entreat you to bestow your manuscript disputations on me, sure you cannot be so unkind as to burn them or any of your manuscripts, if you would not have any of them published.'[77] By then the danger had passed. Baxter was by then publishing his mature thoughts on National Churches, his rejection of a 'foreign Jurisdiction' and his answer to Beverley's millenarian speculations. Baxter's 'National Church' had, in truth, no relationship to the concept in the minds of his Anglican critics. Henry More thought that Baxter's commendation of National Churches, and rejection of gathered Churches, was 'the onely remarkable sincere Stroke that occurs in all his Notes on the Revelation', and noted how it 'heartily contradicted his Opinions and Practices in former times'.[78] More was responding only to Baxter's published *Paraphrase on the New Testament*: how much more he would have made of the *unpublished* material if he had been given the chance!

But it was not only his enemies who misunderstood his idea of a 'National Church'. So did his friends. Even John Humfrey, who had inspired him to begin his Scriptural search, and who was a believer in the concept of a 'National Church', misunderstood what Baxter meant by the term. Comber was nearer to the mark, when he perceived that Baxter was hoping to combine *order* with *discipline. Discipline* had not the same primacy for Humfrey as it had for Baxter: he was an advocate of common admission, and the National Church which he championed was that grey concept which Calamy had found inadequate in his later defence of separatism. There was nothing grey about Baxter's National Church; the illusion behind it, in Comber's perception, was that the discipline exercised over individual congregations could be transferred to a national canvas. But this was not illusory. Only ignorance of history, in Baxter's eyes, deprived men of the insight into the achievements of past societies. Everything that the Fifth Monarchists craved for had been fulfilled in Constantine's time:

> It is a far more glorious Christian Monarchy which Christ by Constantine set up, than most of the Millenarians give any probability of ... The knowledge of what hath been long ago would have prevented many mens expectation of the same.[79]

And when he wrote his pamphlet of 1691, *Against the Revolt to a Foreign Jurisdiction*, he recognised that his exposition of Revelation had offended many, but remained impenitent: John Foxe, with his 'Divine Revelation', was 'much to be regarded'.[80]

It was Foxe's belief in a past millennium, inaugurated by the first Christian Emperor, Constantine, which Baxter defended in his researches in 1686. The Christian Empire continued 'truly Christian, though faulty, for at least 600, if not 1290 yeares after Christ'.[81] The transition to Papal primacy was hard to document, although it probably began with Hildebrand. References in the prophetic texts to Christ's Coming are cryptic. It could mean His Coming to destroy Jerusalem by the Roman Armies, or His Coming to put down the Pagan Empire and to reign by Christian Emperors, or His Coming to reign a thousand years before the Day of Judgement, or His Coming to the Final Judgement. Baxter thought that it was certain both that Christ came by the Roman armies to destroy Jerusalem and that He reigned by Christian Princes; 'very probable at least' that a thousand years before the end 'he will head a sabbatisme of Holynes'; and certain again that 'he will finally judge all the world.' The *worst* opinion that Baxter encountered was that which identified the beginning of Antichrist with Constantine and the Christian Empire. He himself had 'nothing against the millenary hope', but queried whether the 'Kingdom of God', which he hoped for, would be confined to the space of a thousand years. Mather would correct him on that point subsequently: the thousand years is only 'the morning of that great day' foretold in Revelation. Brightman and More were rejected as 'fanatike and cabbalisticall', but he had no personal axe to grind against More, whom he had only ever met once. More wanted to know what he had against the Church of England 'that never did me wrong'; they had done him wrong — quite apart from personal slights — in propagating false 'Grotian' ideas about a foreign jurisdiction. His secret communications in prison with Beverley had helped to form his judgement. He admired More's technique — 'the easyest and ready method' — of describing the qualities of an Antichrist, before finding whether Rome fitted the measurements.[82] This was what made More cross with Baxter: 'in allowing that such things are found in the Papacy that may well furnish out an Antichrist', but still refusing to make the critical identification.[83] Baxter also liked More's 'copious confutation of Grotius and Hammond', but since he did not share their preterism, his case was unaffected.

His quarrel with More was that he dated the rise of Antichrist so close to the beginnings of the Christian Empire: a view which, if true, would shake Baxter's 'hopes in Christ'. His own two sins in the past had been 'in thinking that it was halfe apostasy to question whether Rome now be Babylon and the Pope Antixt' and in thinking ill of National Churches. He now saw that to cloud the glory of Christian Empire is to pervert 'the sense of the Revelation'. National Churches are 'the forme of Government that Christ expressly offered the Jews'.[84]

Comber was wrong, therefore, to see Baxter's vision of a 'National Church' as a fantasy. It was grounded in a systematic exposition of the prophetic texts. When he wrote *Of National Churches* in 1691 he singled out the 'Sins of Injustice and Unmercifulness, especially Rich Mens oppression of the Poor, Landlords grinding their Poor Tenants' as the vices which destroyed their very essence.[85] *The Poor Husbandman's Advocate*, published posthumously as his last work, was in its way also an advocacy of a National Church. It was this apocalyptic dimension of the non-separatist case which Calamy never grasped, as we shall see when we look at this work more closely.

Written by Baxter two months before his death in December 1691, *The Poor Husbandman's Advocate* shows the tenacity with which he held to the ideal of a Commonwealth that would be truly *Holy*. It is not an egalitarian tract. He refers (twice) to Levelling doctrine, only to declare his distance from it. Commonwealths — whether those described in 1659 or 1691 — are in their essence anti-democratic; he never felt that his earlier work had received its proper due, as a defence of monarchy and as an exposure of Harrington's error in relating *Commonwealth* to *democracy*. The poor are the cause of their own suffering; God afflicts them for their sins. Employers' self-interest is appealed to: impoverishing the peasant is to impoverish the land. If the French peasant wore cloth instead of canvas, leather instead of wooden shoes, this would be good news for the cloth trade and shoemakers. Property confers not absolute rights but those of stewardship. The gentry who reduced their rents by a third and paid for the education of the children of the poor could prosper in health on a more reasonable diet and succeed in business too. Baxter quoted a London man who lived by selling rags and glass bottles. He not only found work for the many poor 'tho' he had not five shillings to set up' but paid for the teaching of about thirty poor children: accused by his friends of excessive charity, he answered that 'the more he giveth the more he thriveth.' And that was why Baxter's friend Thomas Gouge could write a book for charity entitled *The Way to Grow Rich*. Finally Baxter has little faith in appeals to the conscience of the rich: 'The Great Dog will not be moved by argument or oratory to give up his bone or carrion, nor to let the little dogs partake with him'; the poor husbandman must, therefore, rely upon *self-discipline*.

But once the limitations of the analysis are accepted, what Baxter achieved within these limitations in describing the misfortunes of the poor is a marvellously feeling document. The solutions may be footling and trite; the diagnosis is angry and compassionate. Should Romanism prevail, the restoration of monasteries and church lands would be a Judgement on Protestants, as the Great Fire was, for their iniquity in creating a community lacking in charity. Men enjoy labour which is 'great, and circular or endless'; the bodies of the poor are 'allmost in constant wearyness and their minds in constant carre or trouble'. They are so poor that they have no time to read the Bible or join in family prayer. Their labours are so exhausting that they are fit, not to read or pray, but only to sleep. Baxter is moved to pity when he sees them asleep at his sermon or at prayer. This is a better education than Popish canons to keep men from the Scriptures. Worldlings bleed their poor tenants in order to leave fortunes for their own children and make their chances of salvation as likely 'as a camel going thro' the eye of a needle'. Lawyers and doctors exploit the poor; although no physician, Baxter had shown how it was possible 'for every ingenious Minister to become the parish physician for the poore (when they have not better)'. Did his teaching smack of Leveller and Quaker doctrine? Baxter refused to be alarmed by the comparison. And what of the objection that the rich were weighed down with taxes? Baxter gave such argument short shrift: 'Who should pay money but those that have it? and who should pay dearer for the publike safety than they that have most to lose?' The taxpayers' lament stemmed from a profound lack of imagination. When they surrendered some money, others on land and sea were surrendering their lives: 'While you sit warme at home out of feare and danger, they are night and day in suffering and perill.' And what of the argument that, to cry up a Commonwealth is to cry down a monarchy? The contrary is true: 'you cry downe the King when you cry downe a Commonwealth.' A squint of the soul produces politics of error:

> The Ignoramuses seem not to know that the common welfare is so essentially the *Terminus* of the Policie, that to exclude it is to dissolve all the Policie, Kingdom and State. Had you been bred as Selden and Hale and such men of study were, or as statesmen are bred in France, Holland and Germany, you would better know what a Commonwealth is.

The Antinomian error haunted Baxter as vividly in the last two months of his life as it had in 1649 when he wrote his first pamphlet, *The Aphorismes of Justification*. Even the names of the enemy had not changed. Saltmarsh still mocked Baxter with his views on Free Grace; Tobias Crisp had died in 1643 and yet his ideas lived on through the mediation of his son, to wreck Baxter's comradeship with Beverley and the hopes for 'Happy Union' with fellow Congregationalists:

> any of the Libertine Generation should infect you, that know not how to *exalt Christ* and extoll *Free Grace* without crying down Christ's Kingly Government and Lawes, and our obedience and its motives, and say, as Crispe, that nothing that we do will do us any good, nor must we look to be ever the better for it, because Christ hath done all for us, and we did it for him; nor will any sin do us any harm because it is Christ's sin that hath taken it on him and not ours, or as *Saltmarsh*, that *Christ hath repented and believed* for us.[86]

No wonder that Samuel Young should try to refute the *canard* that, two days before his death, Baxter affirmed that Dr Crisp was an ortho-dox man, and equally that his literary executors Daniel Williams and Matthew Sylvester should put into context his dying words, *No works, I will leave out works, if he grant me the other!* They wrote of his genu-ine humility about the value of his own works, which was *life-long*. Questioned on the night before his death, he had reaffirmed the doc-trine in his writings of the previous 42 years 'and after a little Pause, with his Eyes lifted up to Heaven, he cryed, *Lord, pity, pity, the Ignor-ance of this poor City*.'[87]

There thus remained for Baxter a connection between Antinomian-ism and the pursuit of profit. And yet Sylvester and Williams, who produced a posthumous edition of his *Protestant Religion Truely Stated and Justified* in 1697, with a careful preface to scotch rumours that he had lost his doctrinal purity, showed no similar zeal to preserve his *Poor Husbandman's Advocate*. The latter tract was also posthumously published, but not until 1926 by F.J. Powicke, who believed that Sylvester and Williams had deliberately suppressed it because they were embarrassed by its social radicalism.

This point is important because, primarily through the writings of Weber and Tawney, Baxter has been seen as the apologist for capitalism. Yet neither Weber nor Tawney had access to Baxter's last social treatise. Max Weber's pioneering essay on the relationship between the Protestant Ethic and the spirit of capitalism had been published as early as 1904. The Holland Memorial Lectures, which were the basis of R.H. Tawney's *critique* of Weber, were given by him in 1922. If *The Poor Husbandman's Advocate* had been accessible earlier than 1926, would knowledge of that work have transformed their views of Baxter?

Let us be clear what their views were. They were more subtle and complex than a simple-minded rejection of a Christian who condoned the profit motive. Both recognised in Baxter a man torn between contradictory impulses: a figure belonging to tragedy, not melodrama.

To Weber, Baxter towered above other writers on Puritan ethics, 'both because of his eminently practical and realistic attitude, and, at the same time, because of the universal recognition accorded to his works, which have gone through many new editions and translations'. Weber made full allowance for the fact that Baxter went further than Calvin in condemnation of the acquisitive principle, but argued the *irrelevance* of Baxter's 'anti-mammonistic doctrines' as a check to the advance of economic rationalism. The welcome which Baxter gave to 'the fundamentally ascetic rational motives' was more important from the point of view of Weber's general thesis than were his suspicion of the rich and his concern for the poor. Weber had not regarded the 'anti-mammonistic' sentiments of leading Calvinistic divines as insincere or unimportant. *Subjectively* Baxter deplored the consequences of the ethic which *objectively* he had advanced, by his emphasis upon the vices of wasting time, luxury and indolence, and upon the virtues of following a specific calling, asceticism and rational organisation of behaviour. In this sense Baxter replayed in the seventeenth century some of the self-contradictions of Calvin himself in the sixteenth century, and which indeed lie at the heart of the Protestant Ethic. If Baxter went beyond Calvin in his welcome to business, this was not because he had less traditionalist scruples than had his predecessor – he had *more*, as Weber himself recognised – but because, by the later date, 'a specifically bourgeois economic ethic had grown up.' By his realism and practicality, Baxter was ideally placed to emphasise the positive points which his congregations wanted to hear; they could reject – often at an unconscious level – the less permissive aspects of the teaching.[88]

Tawney did not find this picture wholly convincing. He believed that Weber had overlooked Calvinist 'discipline'. Although Weber's thesis did not presume in either preacher or preached a necessary collusion *at a conscious level* in a process of deception, it did presume a shift of priorities in emphasis, which was all the more deadly for its being unintended, and indeed often for its being unrecognised. Tawney's historical investigation of England in this period produced a modified thesis, which did allow for shifts in emphasis at different stages in the evolution of casuistry but which, nevertheless, found the most striking change between the sixteenth and seventeenth centuries in the will, and the capacity, of Protestant clergy and laity to *enforce the sanctions* against the economic appetites which they went on deploring. It is no accident that Tawney should discuss Baxter's social teachings in his *Religion and the Rise of Capitalism* in a section under the heading 'A Godly Discipline versus the Religion of Trade'.

Tawney is as quick as Weber to emphasise Baxter's conservatism. Baxter stands in the line of medieval schoolmen: from Aquinas through St Antonius to Baxter. And there lies the poignancy of Baxter's *Christian Directory*: expelled from the world of fact – the Barebone's Parliament represented the last gasp of the theocratic ideal in practical politics – the notion that commerce and business should be subjected to the same controls as the world of politics *could* only now survive in the world of ideas. Baxter's *Christian Directory* is a touching restatement of the medieval *Summae* in a modern dress. But its irrelevance is not because Baxter has embraced fantasy – Tawney, on the contrary, repeatedly praises Baxter's sensitivity to the realities of his age – but because his practical, sensible proposals could no longer be backed by a credible discipline, Calvin's Geneva could only ever be reproduced imperfectly in England – this was the point of Tawney's historical survey which took in the Edwardian Commonwealth preachers, the Elizabethan *classes*, the Laudian counter-revolution, the Westminster Assembly, the New Model Army, the Parliament of the Saints – and these stuttering attempts at theocracy had finally lapsed into the great post-Restoration silence. *Pace* Weber, the change was not within Puritanism itself – 'in reality, the same ingredients were present throughout, but they were mixed in changing proportions, and exposed to different temperatures at different times' – but in the political and economic developments which had prepared 'a congenial environment for their growth'. Tawney believed that 'the rules of Christian morality elaborated by Baxter were subtle and sincere'; if they were also toothless, this was because 'the attempt to crystallize social morality in an objective discipline was possible only in a theocracy.'[89]

How far then would Weber and Tawney have modified their general interpretation of Baxter if they had access to his last unpublished treatise? The answer probably is: not much. That is, if one judges by its reception in R.B. Schlatter's monograph, *The Social Ideas of Religious Leaders 1660-1688.* When Powicke reprinted the treatise he pointed to one puzzling feature. Baxter had patently *expected* that the work would be published. The work *must* have been known to both Matthew Sylvester and Daniel Williams. They had collaborated in preparing for the press another of Baxter's posthumous manuscripts. Why not *The Poor Husbandman's Advocate*? Powicke had thought that its sentiments were 'too radical' and the author 'too frank or fierce' in expressing them. Certainly Weber and Tawney might have been impressed by the continuity of Baxter's social concern – *The Poor Husbandman's Advocate* was written in 1691, nearly twenty years after his *Christian Directory* was published – and by the vehemence of its expression. But no profound modification of their picture was required; they had allowed for the sincerity of his compassion, only perhaps had miscalculated its depth. The difference was one of degree, not kind.

This is very much how Dr Schlatter domesticates Baxter. He uses *The Poor Husbandman's Advocate* extensively in his analysis of the social teachings of the religious leaders after the Restoration. He describes it as 'one of the few important works of social criticism written by a divine of the period' and even, a few pages further on, as 'one of the great pamphlets of the seventeenth century'. But its greatness and its importance are not to be measured by the profundity of the analysis or by the ingenuity of the solution. What impresses, rather, is the honesty of the reporting and the compassion of the reporter. Ultimately Baxter's remedy for distress is to abate rents, even up to a third, and to encourage farmers to learn about true religion by giving them books, teachers and personal instruction. And in this sense Baxter is part of the bankruptcy of the age. In his conclusion Dr Schlatter emphasised four ways in which post-Restoration divines, including even Baxter, colluded with capitalism. First, effective social control would have to be organised by the state, but such control had been tried and it had failed. Second, whatever the state should or should not do was thought to be exempt from clerical control in theory and practice: 'Policy was a matter for the Government to decide by itself. Progressives as well as sinners resented clerical shackles. "I purposely forbear", said Baxter "to meddle with the sins of magistrates" '. Third, criticism was inhibited by ignorance. Without Marxist insight into the structure of society Baxter was condemned — like his friend Tillotson — to a mechanistic view of wickedness cancelling out wickedness and to an uncritical acquiescence in the money-making of his godly friends, like Foley and Ashurst. Fourth, the material prosperity of the Restoration period blunted the edge of social criticism.[90]

I would argue that only the third of the four points genuinely limits the importance of Baxter's social criticism. And on that point Baxter himself had been consistent: he was not an egalitarian, he looked for no drastic alteration to the structure of society, he abhorred Levellers. It is also true — as we have seen — that he would look on Levelling as less of a sin than the unbridled pursuit of profit, but this does not alter the fact that his criticisms are written within the confines of the political theory of 'possessive individualism'.[91] Within those confines, however, he pursued his *critique* of conventional practice to a greater extent than Dr Schlatter appears to recognise. He was not reconciled by the material advances *for some* after the Restoration, nor did he shrink from endorsing a more interventionist role for the state. The crucial point is Dr Schlatter's second — where significantly he quotes Baxter's repudiation of interference with the sins of magistrates — with its assumption that Churchmen should stay out of politics. For this is the heart of Dr Schlatter's thesis: that after the Restoration the clergymen had lost their faith to intervene in matters of state. Most clergymen lacked the desire to intervene; but even when, like Baxter, they had the desire, *they no longer had the will*. Dr Schlatter's first appendix is significant in this respect. He discusses the contribution which clergymen made to the concept of a just war. He points out that Baxter is one of only three divines after the Restoration to make such a contribution, but that this is vitiated in the end by his deference to civil authority:

> But in the end Baxter's distinctions were of little use, for he said that it was usually the case that the subject could not determine whether the war was unlawful or not. And whether they ought to obey the command of governors when the case was doubtful he declined to say, on the grounds that government did not tolerate such meddling by divines.[92]

Both of the testaments to political passivity quoted by Dr Schlatter are from Baxter's *Christian Directory*. That work provided the great arsenal for Tawney's and Weber's quotations from Baxter. How far is it representative of Baxter's thought?

It is certainly representative of one aspect of Baxter's thought, but it is an aspect which is grossly over-emphasised in that particular work. There can be no question that Baxter genuinely deplored the way in which clergymen meddled in politics. But to this sincere conviction was added an awareness of the extent to which he had compromised himself by his *Holy Commonwealth*. He had cheerfully acknowledged that his *Christian Directory* was written partly to cancel out the effects of his *Holy Commonwealth*. His emphasis in the later work on the folly of clergymen giving 'Directions' to magistrates could be read — and was intended by him to be read — as an apology for his involvement with Richard Cromwell in 1659. This emphasis was no doubt agreeable to the general mood of the time — and in this sense both Tawney and Dr Schlatter were right to see it as a representative tract — but as the final statement *of Baxter's own philosophy* it leaves much to be desired. It is written in the aftermath of his disappointment at the collapse of a 'Holy Commonwealth', and before the recrudescence of his apocalyptic vision of a National Church in 1686. *A Christian Directory* comes near in its praise of clerical non-involvement — although even here Baxter defends clerical 'Memorandums', if not 'Directions', to the civil magistrate — to the *laissez-faire* mentality of the eighteenth century. Tawney (with admiring nods to the stubborn resilience with which Baxter defended some traditionalist principles) was forever trying to judge him in that direction. On such a view his *Christian Directory* is a testament of transition: interesting, because it catches Baxter in the process of shedding the theocratic dreams of his 'Holy Commonwealth' days, and not quite coming to terms (although he tries) with a world

in which commerce is carried on by the East India Company in distant markets, trade is universally conducted on credit, the iron manufacture is a large-scale industry demanding abundant supplies of capital and offering a profitable opening to the judicious investor, and the relations of landlords and tenants have been thrown into confusion by the fire of London.[93]

It is not easy to accommodate Baxter's apocalyptic researches of 1686 into this picture, except perhaps as a caprice of old age. But these researches are no nine-day wonder, as we have already shown,[94] and the insights there painfully won are not discarded in his writings of 1690 and 1691. The tone *then* is certainly not one of diffidence; no apologies for clergymen meddling in politics at that date. Rather the contrary truth is proudly asserted: that politicians *need* clergymen to tell them what is right and what is wrong. That pride is linked with confidence in the coming realisation of a Christian Commonwealth. The way in which the poor are treated in such a society will be the test of its apocalyptic claims.

That is the context in which Baxter offers his last treatise of 1691. It makes a difference to how we are to regard Baxter's professions of compassion for the poor. One way is to discount them as humbug. That was the way to be followed by industrial employers in later ages, who would ignore the warnings in his sermons, but who would extract from them the residual comforts to economic individualism. That was not how Weber, Tawney and Dr Schlatter read Baxter. They all took seriously the checks which he sought to impose on economic licence. If these checks ultimately were indecisive, this was not because Baxter had not sincerely intended that they *would* be decisive. The failure lay at a deeper level than personal will: in the evolution of a rival ethic (Weber); in the erosion of faith in a godly discipline (Tawney). In following and developing Tawney's argument, Dr Schlatter took over Tawney's reliance on *A Christian Directory* as the authentic expression of Baxter's political philosophy. *The Poor Husbandman's Advocate* could be accommodated within this analysis by treating the seventh and last chapter as the climax of the work:

> Although he used the most persuasive arguments, seasoned with pitiless denunciation, Baxter had little hope that his reforms would ever take place ... Consequently, the last chapter of the treatise was directed to the poor farmers themselves, instructing them to reform in order that they might deserve better treatment, and schooling them in the virtues of contentment and resignation.[95]

That is one way of reading the treatise, which I personally find unconvincing. It is a hard thing to prove or disprove. I see the seventh chapter as an epilogue, written from a very practical recognition that reformation would not come overnight. In the interim the poor husbandmen need not themselves be passive:

> Because the knowledge of the wickednes of the world perswades me that it is not the most of Rich Landlords that all this will prevail with, yea that there is little hope that they will so much as read it,

I will speake to you for yourselves: And if you will not be persuaded to do good to yourselves you are unworthy of clemency or helpe from others.[96]

But this is not the *point* of the treatise. Self-discipline *earns the right to* 'helpe from others', rather than serves as an alternative programme in its own right. In the same way, when Baxter was most endlessly fertile in propounding new constitutions in the 1650s, he was equally tireless in emphasising the need for electors — *and* elected — to work at improving their *personal* ethical standards. When Powicke speculated on the reasons for Sylvester's repression of the treatise he thought that its sentiments were too radical. Pointing out that 'on more than one former occasion Baxter had brought trouble to himself by the blunt assertion of unpopular views, political and social as well as religious', Powicke compared *The Poor Husbandman's Advocate* with his *Holy Commonwealth*.[97] I think that the comparison is a good one: as much for its millennial hopes as for its 'radicalism'. It is interesting that in the section which immediately precedes the seventh chapter, Baxter feels the need to restate his definition of 'Common Wealth'. A Commonwealth is not Levelling or Democracy, but neither is it the subjugation of slaves: 'The Ignoramuses seem not to know that the common welfare is so essentially the *Terminus* of the Policie, that to exclude it is to dissolve all the Policie, Kingdom and State.'[98] Far from having 'little hope that his reforms would ever take place', as Dr Schlatter argued, Baxter had every reason to cherish such hopes. From the time that Constantine became Emperor there had been societies in the past where 'the common welfare' had been jealously regarded; only ignorance of history prevented the millenaries of his day from giving proper recognition to such achievements. Nor were such achievements confined to a remote past. They had happened in England under the Protectorate of Richard Cromwell. Baxter's own practice at Kidderminster, his own Worcestershire Association of Ministers, had pointed the way. In 1691 Baxter was reconverted to the virtues of 'National Churches'; his apocalyptic faith in their triumph was expressed in other writings of his at the time. Such faith was compatible with the recognition that rich landlords were not likely to take immediate remedial action on their own behalf; such inaction did not excuse a corresponding passivity in their husbandmen. The test of a National Church, a Holy Commonwealth, was not some impossible Utopian requirement, but simply whether it provided, for 'the common welfare', that same care and discipline which a minister exercised over his flock in a properly run congregation. Baxter was nearer to the Welfare State than he was to the acquisitive society. If Tawney gave him less than his due, it was not because he ignored the compassion in Baxter's views (in which he correctly saw an Aquinas-like assertion of traditional morals) but because he read in his *Christian Directory* a more pronounced repudiation of the search for 'godly discipline' than was in fact the case. For Tawney, theocracy had been expelled from *the world of fact* with the end of the Barebone's Parliament; it survived, *but only in the world of ideas*, in the *Christian Directory*. In that sense the passivity before the magistrate, the failure to link the proposals with specific institutions or persons – Charles II was no Constantine! – were as significant as the proposals themselves. But for Baxter, theocracy had been expelled *in the world of fact* with the fall of Richard Cromwell's Protectorate and not with the end of the Barebone's Parliament; that whole period between 1653 and 1659 is, for Baxter, the working out of the theocratic ideal in the world of fact *and* in the world of ideas. By the time that Baxter's *Christian Directory* is published in 1673, fact and ideas were pulling in opposite directions, as Tawney correctly argued; and this is what gives the work its poignancy. Tawney's mistake was to treat 1673 as if it represented the final chapter in Baxter's evolution; one in which he had come – however reluctantly and fitfully – to accept the permissive code of a new age. This hypothesis does not allow for the remarkable restirring of millennial expectations in the last ten years of his life. Old dreams of the 1650s – from collating testimonies of 'Providences' and ghosts to founding a Christian Commonwealth with a godly discipline – were now revived with renewed vigour (and more solid scriptural foundation). *The Poor Husbandman's Advocate* belongs to this phase of Baxter's development, and is no tired rehash of his *Christian Directory*.

Once earlier, in 1658, a correspondent had tried to link concern for the poor with the separatist cause. Thomas Lamb had once been an Independent follower of John Goodwin. He had been won to Baptism, but was now wavering back to his earlier allegiance. And yet, as he explained to Baxter, on 16 September 1658, he had qualms:

I should leave the Poor, and go among the Rich, that minded more the adorning of the outward Man than the glorious Gospel of Church ordinarily; whereas my Spirit is much set against gay Apparel and following of Fashions; not but that Mr. Goodwin's Church is as sober as most, I think as any, But the Truth is, it is a sin in my Apprehension (at least) that few are sufficiently sensible of.

In his reply of 29 September 1658 Baxter made clear that his concept of non-separation was also non-separation from the problems of the poor:

> What! a Physician fly because his Patients are sick! O that we had no sorer Diseases to encounter, than fine Cloaths! If you were with me, I could tell you quickly where to find Forty Families of humble, godly Christians, that are as bare, and Poor as you would wish, and need as much as you can give them or procure them; that scarce lose a Day's Work by Sickness, but the Church must maintain them. And I could send you to Sixty Families that are as poor, and yet so ignorant as more to need your spiritual Help. When they have sat by me to be instructed in my Chamber, they sometimes leave the Lice so plentifull that we are stored with them for a competent space of time. Never keep in a Separated Church to avoid Riches and fine Cloaths, and for fear lest you cannot meet with the Poor. I warrant you a Cure of that Melancholy Fear in most places in England.[99]

Lamb's mistake was a critical one. He assumed that godly discipline, and concern for the poor, were only possible outside a National Church, when the truth was precisely the opposite. It was only *within* a National Church that a true godly discipline could be established.

And that was what was wrong with the advocacy of 'open communion' put forward by his opponents in the debates over the Lord's Supper in the 1650s. Calamy could see its tawdriness, and responded by a retreat into sectarianism. But Baxter had learned from his study of the Apocalypse that to dream of a separation of the precious from the vile was no fantasy, nor need it be confined to one parish. It had happened when Constantine began the Christian Empire; it had happened in Kidderminster in the 1650s, but it had not stopped at congregation level. Through the Worcestershire Association a godly discipline had spread into all parts of England, until the political changes had destroyed the reformers' hopes. But a New Jerusalem could still be built in England. He died with that hope, embodied in *The Poor Husbandman's Advocate*.

Baxter hated Levellers and Diggers. He did not believe in democracy. He thought that property was stewardship, not theft. He appealed to owners' enlightened self-interest. He did not want the world turned upside down. He wanted the poor to exercise self-restraint. Some of the wealthiest godly were among his closest friends. A Birmingham button manufacturer in 1790 made his works prescribed reading for his ungodly working force.[100] And yet rapacious landlords – as much as Grotian bishops and Papist Kings – were judged in the end by this test: by whether or not they perverted the sense of Revelation. Humfrey's advocacy of mixed communion, Lawson's analysis of the constitutional breakdown, Owen's arguments for separatism – all touched genuine chords in Baxter, and yet were ultimately found wanting. None of these solutions was capable of satisfying apocalyptic yearnings, as National Churches and magistracy would do for him after he had completed his studies in prophecy of 1686. Baxter sincerely believed that his *Holy Commonwealth* was a contribution against democracy, but opponents were right to detect something deeply subversive of the existing values of society in that strange work. They pursued the wrong issues to attack. They accused him of favouring resistance theories and populist solutions: both of which he hated. The work was subversive at a deeper level: in holding out to men a vision of a better society as a standard by which to pass judgement on the existing structure. Baxter could condemn the Fifth Monarchists' seductive dreams of a Golden Age.[101] *His* dreams were different: embodied in existing organs of state and involving no cataclysmic change of direction. He taught submission, obedience to the civil magistrate, non-separation from the Established Church. Like many of his fellow Protestants who were touched by apocalyptic longings, and who themselves rejected crude millenarian fanaticism, he imagined that he stood for a simple stability and the maintenance of the *status quo*. This self-image is no more a travesty than that projected by later historians, who discarded Puritans' professions of loyalty to existing institutions as insincere, and who proved adept at reading into their qualifications and reservations in the 1620s and 1630s a logical preparation for the 'revolution of the saints' in the 1640s and 1650s.[102] The more we study in depth men like Prynne and Baxter, *the less easy it is to accept either their self-evaluation or that made of them by later historians*. The closer we come to the point of connection between magistracy and the Apocalypse,[103] the nearer we come to the heart of the English Revolution. The formulation, however, remains elusive: the English apocalyptic Protestant was no more an embryonic Munster radical than he was a simple defender of traditional values. Baxter's 'Holy Commonwealth' of 1659 and 'National Church' of 1691 have nothing in common with Gerrard Winstanley's communal experiment, except at one important level. *Both men derived from the Apocalypse the standards by which to measure their own society*. This is perhaps the point at which the analogy between the seventeenth-century Puritan and the Victorian Nonconformist breaks down. Macaulay's description of the seventeenth-century Puritan going through the world, 'like Sir Artegal's iron man Talus with his flail, crushing and trampling down oppressors, mingling with human beings, but having neither part nor lot in human infirmities', draws us closer to the truth.[104] It is not quite the truth about Baxter: the man who declaimed so feelingly, 'Oh my Head, Oh my Stomach, Oh my sides, or Oh my bowels'[105] *did* have his part or lot in human infirmities, but Macaulay's image conveys something of the restiveness and apartness of the man who has found his truth in prophecy. Baxter has customarily been identified with the Protestant Ethic, but it was as its apocalyptic critic that he wrote his last work on behalf of poor husbandmen, and left this final disturbing question for all self-pitying taxpayers: 'You think that this doctrine savours of the Levellers or Quakers. What would you have done if you had lived when the Spirit of Love made the Christians sell all that they had and live in common?'[106]

Notes

1. (DWL) *Baxter Correspondence*, i, f.3-5.
2. (DWL) *Baxter Correspondence*, i, f.243.
3. (DWL) *Baxter Correspondence*, ii, f.102-102v.
4. Sidney H. Rooy, *The Theology of Missions in the Puritan Tradition* (Delft, 1965), p. 70.
5. Baxter, *A Breviate of the Life of Margaret . . .* (London, 1681), p. 97.
6. Ibid., p. 73.
7. Baxter, *True Christianity . . .* (London, 1655), dedicatory epistle.
8. (DWL) *Baxter Treatises*, iv, f.276v.
9. Samuel Pepys, *Diary*, ed. R. Latham and W. Matthews, (London, 1970), iii. p. 93.
10. Samuel Young, *Vindiciae Anti-Baxterianae* (London, 1696), epilogue.
11. (DWL) *Baxter Correspondence*, f.196v.
12. See my *Marginal Prynne* (London, 1963), pp. 59-84.
13. B.S. Capp, *The Fifth Monarchy Men* (London, 1972), pp. 46-9.
14. Roger L'Estrange, *The Casuist Uncased* (London, 1680).
15. Ibid., p. 79.
16. Edward Stillingfleet, *The Unreasonableness of Separation: The Second Part* (London, 1682), p. 2.
17. George Lawson, *An Examination . . .* (London, 1657), p. 32.
18. (DWL) *Baxter Treatises*, iii, f.111.
19. Baxter, *A Third Defence of the Cause of Peace* (London, 1681), p. 88.
20. (DWL) *Baxter Treatises*, vi, f.284-5.
21. For which, see my *Marginal Prynne*, pp. 119-48.
22. For the Carte correspondence, see Chapter 2.
23. (BL) *Stowe MSS* 82, f.1, f.325, f.326. See Appendix for details.
24. Baxter, *A Third Defence of the Cause of Peace*, pp. 92-3.
25. John Corbet, *An Enquiry into the Oath Required of Nonconformists by an Act made at Oxford* (London, 1682), p. 5.
26. John Humfrey, *The Third Step of a Nonconformist* (London, 1684),

pp. 16-17.

27. (DWL) *Baxter Correspondence*, vi, f.245.

28. (DWL) *Baxter Treatises*, vi, f.293.

29. Royce MacGillivray, *Restoration Historians and the English Civil War* (The Hague, 1974), pp. 153-4, has some telling criticisms of Baxter as an historian of the Civil War.

30. John Corbet, *An Historical Relation of the Military Government of Gloucester* (London, 1645).

31. In a foreword to John Corbet, *An Account Given of the Principles and Practices of Several Nonconformists* (London, 1682).

32. Baxter, *A Sermon Preached at the Funeral of . . . Mr. John Corbet . . .* (London, 1680), p. 27.

33. Corbet, *An Historical Relation*, p. 7.

34. MacGillivray, *Restoration Historians, passim.*

35. Conrad Russell, 'Parliamentary History in Perspective, 1604-29', *History*, 61, 201 (1976), pp. 1-27. Similar objections to conventional readings of the prelude to Civil War are to be found in my article, 'The English Revolution: Sunbeams and Lumps of Clay', *Encounter*, XLII, 5 (May 1974), pp. 66-72.

36. Charles Leslie, *A Case of Present Concern* (London, 1702), p. 9.

37. Stillingfleet, *The Unreasonableness of Separation*, pp.14, 27.

38. My judgement has been supported by another recent author: 'For all the disapproval of the execution, Baxter provides no grounds in the *Reliquiae Baxterianae* for believing that he ever experienced the shock many Royalists professed to feel at the deed' (MacGillivray, *Restoration Historians*, p. 161).

39. Thomas Edwards, *Baxterianism Barefaced* (London, 1699), p. 408.

40. Young, *Vindiciae Baxterianae*, p. 86.

41. (DWL) *Baxter Correspondence*, v, f.217.

42. Baxter *et al., The Judgment of Non-conformists, of the Interest of Reason in Matters of Religion* (London, 1676), *passim.*

43. L.I. Bredvold, *The Intellectual Milieu of John Dryden* (Michigan, 1956), especially pp. 73-129.

44. Jackson Cope, *Joseph Glanvill: Anglican Apologist* (St Louis, 1956), pp. 7, 9, 13, 15, 50, 51, 62. Cf. Boyle's tribute to Baxter: 'there are divers things that speak you to be none of those narrow-sould-divines, that by too much suspecting natural philosophy tempt too many of its votaries to suspect Theology': (BL) *Additional MSS 4229*, f.142.

45. (DWL) *Baxter Correspondence*, i, f.170; ii, f.138.

46. (DWL) *Baxter Correspondence*, i, f.130.

47. For which, see Chapter 1.

48. (DWL) *Baxter Correspondence*, i, f.127.

49. Henry More, *Paralipromena Prophetica* (London, 1685), pp.iii, xvii.

50. For which, see Chapter 1.

51. Baxter, *Confession of His Faith . . .* (London, 1655), p. 214.

52. Edward Bagshaw, *A Review and Conclusion of the Antidote . . .* (London, 1671), p. 11.

53. Edwards, *Baxterianism Barefaced*, pp. 411, 412.

54. For which, see Chapter 4.

55. MacGillivray, *Restoration Historians*, p. 163. For a similar misreading of Baxter in the Commonwealth, see J.H. Franklin, *John Locke and the Theory of Sovereignty*, (Cambridge, 1978) p. 58.

56. (DWL) *Baxter Correspondence*, vi, f.236.

57. Stillingfleet, *The Unreasonableness of Separation*, pp. 52, 89.

58. E.g. Bagshaw, *A Review and Conclusion of the Antidote*, p. 4: 'Oh poor deluded People of England! How have thy Preachers, thy Baxters . . . caused thee

to erre, and swallowed up the way of thy Parliaments?'

59. (DWL) *Baxter Correspondence*, ii, f.94.

60. (DWL) *Baxter Treatises*, xxii, f.69.

61. In Chapter 3.

62. (DWL) *Baxter Treatises*, vii, f.299.

63. (DWL) *Baxter Correspondence*, v, f.222-3.

64. Baxter, *A Treatise of Episcopacy* . . . (London, 1681), pp. 212, 213, 188, 83, 195, 198.

65. Baxter, *A Third Defence of the Cause of Peace*, pp. 111-12.

66. MacGillivray, *Restoration Historians*, p. 2.

67. Baxter in Matthew Sylvester (ed.), *Reliquiae Baxterianae* (London, 1696), iii, p. 187.

68. (DWL) *Baxter Correspondence*, iv, f.63.

69. (DWL) *Baxter Correspondence*, iii, f.12v.

70. See MacGillivray, *Restoration Historians*, pp. 31-2, for an interesting discussion of the Laud/Heylyn connection.

71. (BL) *Harleian MSS 6942*, f.78.

72. Baxter, *A Third Defence of the Cause of Peace*, pp. 74, 71.

73. John Rastrick, *An Account of the Nonconformity* (London, 1705), p. 18.

74. Benjamin Hoadly, *A Defence of the Reasonableness of Conformity* . . . (London, 1705), p. 77.

75. Baxter, *A Paraphrase on the New Testament* . . . (London, 1684), no pagination.

76. Baxter, *The True History of Councils Enlarged and Defended* (London, 1682), p. 190.

77. (DWL) *Baxter Correspondence*, iii, f.237.

78. 'Phillicrines Parrhesiastes', *Some Cursory Reflexions Impartially Made Upon Mr. Richard Baxter His Way of Writing Notes* (London, 1685), p. 7.

79. Baxter, *The Glorious Kingdom of Christ* . . . (London, 1691), p. 10.

80. Baxter, *Against the Revolt to a Foreign Jurisdiction* (London, 1691), p. 102.

81. (DWL) *Baxter Treatises*, vi, f.354.

82. (DWL) *Baxter Treatises*, vii. f.249v, 254, 277, 296, 295.

83. 'Phillicrines Parrhesiastes', p. 14.

84. (DWL) *Baxter Treatises*, f.295, 296, 308v, 300v.

85. Baxter, *Of National Churches* . . . (London, 1691), p. 53.

86. F.J. Powicke (ed.), *The Reverend Richard Baxter's Last Treatise* (Manchester, 1926), pp. 20, 21, 23, 30, 34, 37, 38, 42, 48, 51, 52, 53, 56.

87. Samuel Young, *A New-Years Gift for the Antinomians* (London, 1699), p. 5; Baxter, *The Protestant Religion Truely Stated and Justified* (London, 1697), preface by Daniel Williams and Matthew Sylvester.

88. Max Weber, *The Protestant Ethic and the Spirit of Capitalism* (London, 1930), pp. 155, 156, 157, 259. Cf. also H.M. Robertson, *Aspects of the Rise of Economic Individualism* (Cambridge, 1933), p. 21; M.J. Kitch, *Capitalism and the Reformation* (London, 1967), pp. 178-80; and John Dunn, *The Political Thought of John Locke* (Cambridge, 1969), pp. 206-13, for a trenchant criticism of the Weberian approach to Locke.

89. R.H. Tawney, *Religion and the Rise of Capitalism* (London, 1926), pp. 211-6.

90. R.B. Schlatter, *The Social Ideas of Religious Leaders 1660-1688* (New York, 1971), pp. 74, 75, 76, 224.

91. For which see C.B. Macpherson, *The Political Theory of Possessive Individualism* (Oxford, 1962), *passim*.

92. Schlatter, *Social Ideas*, p. 230.

93. Tawney, *Religion and the Rise of Capitalism*, p. 220.

94. See Chapter 1.

95. Schlatter, *Social Ideas*, p. 75.

96. Powicke, *Baxter's Last Treatise*, p. 56.

97. Ibid., p. 14.

98. Ibid., p. 53.

99. Baxter in Sylvester, *Reliquiae Baxterianae*, Appendix, pp. 59, 63.

100. Douglas Reid, 'The Decline of Saint Monday 1766-1876', *Past and Present*, 71 (1976), pp. 76-102.

101. E.g. N.H. Keeble (ed.), *The Autobiography of Richard Baxter* (Everyman, 1974), p. 122.

102. Cf. M. Walzer, *The Revolution of the Saints . . .* (London, 1966) and his 'Puritanism as a Revolutionary Ideology', *History and Theory*, III, 1963-4, pp. 63-72.

103. I tried to show the complexity of that connection – with particular reference to Robert Bolton – in my article, 'Puritanism as history and historiography: some further thoughts', *Past and Present*, 44 (August 1969), pp. 139-40.

104. Lord Macaulay, *Critical and Historical Essays* (London, 1898), 1, pp. 52-3.

105. Baxter, *The Saints Everlasting Rest* (London, 1650), p. 117.

106. Powicke, *Baxter's Last Treatise*, p. 48. Cf. Christopher Hill, *The World Turned Upside Down* (London, 1972), p. 266, for the customary identification of Baxter with the Protestant Ethic.

A NOTE ON SOURCES

(A) Printed

It would be a work of supererogation to list all the printed sources — primary and secondary — consulted in the course of this study, since full references are given in the footnotes (which follow each chapter) to individual works. Dr Nuttall has appended to his biography of Baxter a complete list of Baxter's writings, itself based upon *The Works of Richard Baxter: an Annotated List*, compiled by A.G. Matthews, revised from *Congregational Historical Society Transactions* XI (1932).

(B) Unprinted

It might, however, be helpful to list some of the main unprinted primary sources which have been consulted. Roger Thomas has compiled a catalogue of the *Baxter Treatises* (Dr Williams's Library, Occasional Paper No. 8, 1959) whilst Baxter's correspondence has been expertly calendared by Dr Nuttall.
Occasional Paper No.8, 1959) whilst Baxter's correspondence has been expertly calendared by Dr Nuttall.

British Library

Additional MSS 4,221 (Matthew Sylvester's deposition)
Additional MSS 4,229 (Boyle: Baxter, 1665)
Additional MSS 32,094 (Baxter's rebuke to Lauderdale)
Additional MSS 32,568 (Coleridge's notes on Baxter)
Additional MSS 54,224 (Baxter against Crandon in 1654)
Additional MSS 22,548
Sloane MSS 1008,1015 (Borlase and the Irish Rebellion)
Stowe MSS 82
Egerton MSS 2,570 (Baxter against Danvers, 1676; Baxter against Morley, 1683)
Egerton MSS 2,882 (the charges against Baxter for his *Paraphrase on the New Testament*)
Harleian MSS 6,648 (Mede and the Apocalypse)
Harleian MSS 6,621 (Baxter's directions to a young Divinity student)
Harleian MSS 6,942 (Hammond/Sheldon correspondence)
Harley/Portland Loan 29/73/2 and 3 (Baxter, Beverley and Harley on

interpreting the Apocalypse, 1690/1)

Bodleian Library, Oxford

Carte MSS 255 (Carte and the Irish Rebellion)
Rawlinson MSS 51 (Baxter: Wharton)
Rawlinson MSS 109 (Baxter: Thornton)
Tanner MSS 52 (Baxter: Jacombe)

Dr Williams's Library

Baxter Correspondence Volumes 1-6
Baxter Treatises Volumes 17, 13-16, 18-22
    [N.B. Volume 8 now forms part of *(British Library) Egerton MSS 2570*, a photostat of which is included as Volume 22 of *Baxter Treatises*].
MSS 90 Henry 90.5.1 (Henry correspondnece)
Morrice MSS M XII (Catalogue of Baxter's Library)
Morrice Entering Book P (Baxter's trial before Jeffreys and Oxford Convocation charges against him in 1683)
Morrice Entering Book Q (Baxter's release from prison and subsequent activities)

East Sussex Record Office

Frewen MSS 4,223 (Jeake correspondence)
Frewen MSS D677 (Allin/Frith correspondence)

My thanks are due to the archivists in all these establishments but a particular appreciation should be recorded for the courtesy and kindness given to me by the librarians at Dr Williams's Library where I spent so many hours among the Baxter archives. A final word of heartfelt thanks to Mrs Margaret Paine, MBE, for her skilful typing of my manuscript.

Allestree, Richard (1619-81) Provost of Eton and one-time fellow scholar with Baxter at his village school in Donnington. He became the recipient of Baxter's confidences on his reasons for supporting Parliament in the Civil War.

Alsop, Vincent (d.1703) Presbyterian minister who shared Baxter's dislike for Bishop Sherlocke, but disagreed with him over the correct Protestant response to James II's offers of Indulgence.

Bilson, Thomas (1547-1616) Bishop of Winchester and the inspiration behind Baxter's advocacy of 'Protestant imperialism'.

Blake, Thomas (1597-1657) Puritan minister who became identified as one of Baxter's leading opponents in the 1650s for his views on baptism and admission of communicants to the Sacrament of the Lord's Supper.

Boyse, Joseph (1660-1728) Presbyterian minister who became the recipient of Baxter's changed views about 'National Churches' following his millenarian studies in the 1680s.

Brightman, Thomas (1562-1607) Great commentator on the Apocalypse, whom Baxter had hoped to meet in Heaven (along with Pym and Hampden) in his *Saints Everlasting Rest*, but whose views on prophecy were markedly different from his own.

Burges, Cornelius (1589-1665) Puritan opponent of the Covenant and regicide: he reassured Baxter of the reformist, not revolutionary, nature of Puritanism in the 1640s.

Calamy, Edmund (1600-66) Like Baxter, a Puritan who turned down the offer of a bishopric at the Restoration; Baxter thought of him as a natural minister to scrutinise 'collections' of 'providences', because of his experience in authenticating cases of witchcraft.

Calamy, Edmund (1671-1732) Grandson of the ejected Puritan and producer of a revised edition of Baxter's autobiography; has some claim to be regarded as the emancipator of post-Restoration Dissent.

Comber, Thomas (1645-99) Dean of Durham and a shrewd critic of Baxter's inconsistencies in arguing in 1691 for an apocalyptic 'National Church'.

Corbet, John (1620-80) One of Baxter's closest friends. His analysis of the outbreak of Civil War in his native Gloucester has some interesting parallels with Baxter's own account.

Cressener, Drue (1638-1718) Interpreter of the Apocalypse: successful in prophesying the Glorious Revolution but not in changing Baxter's mind about Antichrist.

Cressy, Hugh (1605-74) Roman Catholic apologist: challenged Baxter to substantiate some of his extreme statements against Popery.

Crisp, Tobias (1600-43) Antinomian champion: the reprinting of his sermons by his son was the cause of the collapse of hopes for reunion between Presbyterians and Independents, in Baxter's view. More particularly they drove a wedge between Baxter and his millenarian prison companion, Thomas Beverley.

Davenant, John (1576-1641) Bishop of Salisbury, who had worked out at the Synod of Dort his doctrinal compromise of 'hypothetical universalism', which was to influence profoundly Baxter's own response to the divisions of doctrine within Protestantism.

Dodwell, Henry (1641-1711) University don and non-juror: seen by Baxter as a key figure in the 'new' Anglicanism of the late 1670s.

Durie, John (1596-1680) Indefatigable collaborator with Baxter on schemes for Church unity.

Du Moulin, Lewis (1606-80) Camden Professor of Ancient History at Oxford, and a Nonconformist controversialist. Cared more for Parliament, and less for ministers, than Baxter did, but in other respects their 'imperial' philosophies were very similar.

Du Moulin, Peter (1601-84) Lewis's conforming older brother and chaplain to Charles II in 1660, but identified with many of the causes associated with his brother and Baxter.

Eliot, John (1604-90) Admired by Baxter as the missionary who converted Red Indians, and as the minister who bore witness against the Antinomian Mrs Hutchinson.

Faldo, John (1633-90) Nonconformist opponent of the Quakers and a correspondent with Baxter on the Apocalypse and National Churches.

Fisher, Edward (1627-55) Author of the *Marrow of Modern Divinity*: recognised by Baxter, and indeed by all his contemporaries, as the single most powerful statement of the doctrine of unconditional grace.

Foxe, John (1516-87) His *Acts and Monuments* reinterpreted the Apocalypse as the working out of Christian imperialism: his amillennial historicism was adopted by Baxter for most of his life, but not given a full eschatological exposition until his prison researches of 1686.

Gillespie, George (1613-48) Scottish anti-Erastian: his development of the argument against common admission to the Lord's Supper influenced many fellow Presbyterians in a sectarian direction.

Glanvill, Joseph (1636-80) Admired Baxter for his views on witchcraft, apparitions and the place of reason in religion, but their paths ultimately diverged.

Goodwin, John (1594-1665) The Arminian of the Left, who went further than Baxter would go in opposition to the prevalent Calvinist orthodoxies.

Hammond, Henry (1605-60) Chaplain to Charles I, whose uncompromising High Churchmanship and preterist eschatology would seem to have marked him out as an enemy of Baxter. This was not so, however: in his concern for parochial discipline Baxter recognised a kindred spirit, and lamented his death at the Restoration.

Harrington, James (1611-77) Baxter wrote his *Holy Commonwealth* against Harrington's *Oceana*, which he disliked as much for its anticlericalism as for its approval of democracy – and, more quaintly still, for its 'Popery'!

Heylyn, Peter (1600-62) His posthumous biography of Laud, *Cyprianus Anglicus*, published in 1668, was seen by Baxter – perhaps too readily? – as the revelation of a coherent 'Grotian' master plan.

Hickman, Henry (d.1692) Nonconformist minister who converted Baxter's wife by his preaching and who seemed – in the dark days after the fall of Richard Cromwell – Baxter's one ally in what he saw as a Promethean stand against the forces of Popery.

Hill, Thomas (d.1653) Master of Trinity College, Cambridge, whom Baxter sought to interest in ecumenism and book-burning (he wanted to see Hobbes's *Leviathan* proscribed).

Hoadly, Benjamin (1676-1761) Opposed Calamy's arguments for separation from the Established Church by appealing to the traditions of Baxter.

Hooker, Richard (1554-1600) Baxter admired his moderation, but not his populist principles, which had inspired men erroneously to take up arms against their King.

Jewel, John (1522-71) With Foxe, the great formative influence upon Baxter and his seventeenth-century Protestant imperialist colleagues.

Maitland, John, second Earl and first Duke of Lauderdale (1616-82) Baxter's unlikely friend and patron. Unpublished correspondence reveals the relationship to be less discreditable to Baxter than is commonly supposed.

Lawson, George (d.1678) A divine whose judgement Baxter respected greatly on religious doctrine and political theory. Quoted many times publicly with approval for an explanation of the origins of the Civil War which played down religion – but note the important qualifications to that endorsement in Baxter's last unpublished writings.

Mainwaring, Roger (1590-1653) Bishop of St David's, who outstripped all his Anglican colleagues in defending the absolutism of monarchy: a crime which neither Baxter nor Prynne took as seriously as many Parliamentarians did.

Mather, Increase (1639-1723) President of Harvard College. Did not share Baxter's views on a past millennium or the identity of Antichrist, but did think that his apocalyptic researches and studies of 'providences' should be published, and successfully overcame Baxter's initial diffidence.

Mede, Joseph (1586-1638) The Newton of the Apocalypse, whose achievement was to 'synchronise' the various signs and symbols in the prophetic texts.

More, Henry (1614-87) Cambridge Platonist, with an idiosyncratic method of proving that the Pope is Antichrist. Baxter liked the method — as he liked More's investigations of the supernatural — but he did not like the conclusion. This disagreement — along with his friend, John Humfrey's encouragement of him to write a paraphrase of the New Testament — must be regarded as the stimulus to Baxter's apocalyptic researches in 1686.

Morrice, Sir William (1602-76) Secretary of State at the Restoration and an influential advocate in the critical debates on the Lord's Supper in the 1650s.

Morley, George (1597-1684) Bishop of Winchester, but in Baxter's eyes an unworthy successor to Bilson.

Nayler, James (1617-60) Quaker, condemned by the Protectorate Parliament for blasphemy: for Baxter — and for others — convincing proof of the identification of Quakers with Ranters.

Nye, Philip (1596-1672) Independent minister, whom Baxter identified with non-separatist views and with less stringent requirements for communicants to the Lord's Supper than those favoured by John Owen.

Oasland, Henry (1625-1703) Ejected minister of Bewdley and admired friend of Baxter. Urged Baxter to clarify his views on civil magistracy, and thus may have been partly responsible for his *Holy Commonwealth*.

Owen, John (1616-83) Foremost Independent spokesman: despite efforts at accommodation with Baxter after the Restoration, old Interregnum scars were never properly healed.

Penn, William (1644-1718) Quaker supporter of James II's Declaration of Indulgence; had clashed earlier with Baxter over his alternative 'comprehension' schemes, which excluded Quakers.

Pierce, Thomas (1622-91) Bad-tempered Anglican scholar who grossly caricatured Baxter's views: one important reason for Baxter's discomfort at the restoration of Episcopacy in 1660.

Poole, Matthew (1624-79) Erudite biblical commentator, and enthusiastic collaborator with Baxter in proposed schemes for collating records of strange occurrences in the Commonwealth period.

Prynne, William (1600-69) Baxter's ally in exposure of Popish Plots, attacks on Quakers and defence of magistracy: important differences, however, emerged between them in debates over the Sacrament of the Lord's Supper in the 1650s.

Rogers, John (1627-65) Fifth Monarchist critic of Baxter's *Holy Commonwealth*, but who largely missed its point.

Saltmarsh, John (d.1647) Antinomian Army chaplain. Revulsion from his ideas inspired Baxter's first published work, *The Aphorismes of Justification*, and he was still singled out by Baxter as the principal enemy in his last unpublished treatise, *The Poor Husbandman's Advocate*.

Sterry, Peter (d.1672) Cromwell's chaplain and, in Baxter's eyes, a Hobbes in pretty clothes: inspired Baxter to his most eloquent attack on determinism.

Stillingfleet, Edward (1635-99) Bishop of Worcester and, more spectacularly even than Joseph Glanvill, Baxter's fallen idol. Admired for his earlier irenicism, he became Baxter's enemy in the debates on separatism in the late 1670s.

Sylvester, Matthew (1636-1708) Baxter's friend and disciple; published *Reliquiae Baxterianae*, a less obviously tendentious edition of Baxter's memoirs than the later version edited by Calamy but perhaps even more misleading.

Tillotson, John (1630-94) Archbishop of Canterbury and, for both Prynne and Baxter, finest proof that hopes of 'comprehension' on the basis of imperial Protestantism were not illusory or quixotic.

Tombes, John (1603-76) Baptist minister at Bewdley, who had some rough exchanges with Baxter. But they were prepared to sink differences in the face of a Papist revival.

Usher, James (1581-1656) Archbishop of Armagh, who influenced profoundly Baxter's thoughts on Episcopal organisation, prophecy and universal redemption.

Vane, Sir Henry (1613-62) Butt of many punning attacks by Baxter, who linked him with Harrington as Jesuit agents who were bent on the destruction of Richard Cromwell's 'Holy Commonwealth'.

APPENDIX: LUDLOW AND THE ANTRIM PARDON

This study has demonstrated Richard Baxter's concern, both about the claim of the Earl of Antrim that he had the backing of Charles I for his actions in the Irish Rebellion, beginning in 1641, and about Charles II's recognition of the strength of that claim in his subsequent pardon of the Earl after the Restoration. For nearly twenty years after the Restoration the story circulated in clandestine form, surfacing only in such a scurrilous pamphlet as *Murder Will Out*. When Edmund Borlase attempted to document the allegation we saw that Sir Roger L'Estrange intervened to prevent the publication of what was seen in 1679 as inflammatory material. The original Borlase manuscript shows how thoroughly L'Estrange did his job: for the most notable deletions see (BL) *Stowe Mss* 82, f.1, 10, 14, 30, 127, 128, 131, 326. The wording of the Antrim pardon was less than felicitous. In Borlase's original manuscript readers would have learned from the pardon – had L'Estrange not intervened – how 'severall private messages' which Charles II had had from 'our Royall father, and Royall mother' about Antrim's good faith meant that the Earl's ostensibly friendly relations with the Irish rebels had, in fact, all along been consonant with 'letters, instructions and directions' from Charles I. This was bad enough but worse followed. Borlase had the testimony of Dr Robert Maxwell that Sir Phelim O'Neill's actions in 1641 were contingent upon his assurance of support from Antrim. Thus the circumstantial link between Charles I and the leader of the Irish Catholic Rebellion had been provided by Antrim.

Since the main research for this study was completed there has been an important historical discovery: the recovery of sections of the original manuscript of Ludlow's memoirs from Warwick Castle. This exciting development has been ably described by A.B. Worden in his long introduction to part of the manuscript material which he has published under the title, *A Voyce from the Watch Tower* (Camden, Fourth Series, Volume 21, 1978). Ludlow's interest in Antrim was well known before, but it is now possible to see this interest documented in full. Thus we can see Ludlow's observation: 'The Earle of Antrim, though an Irish papist, was seized the same tyme that Argyle was, and sent to the Tower; but on different grounds, the one for the service he had done against popery and prelacy and the other for having sayd that the Irish had authority from the late King for what they did' (ibid., p. 179).

More revealing for our purpose is a section from Ludlow's manuscript which Dr Worden did not print:

> The Earle of Antrim who was committed to the Tower of London about two yeares since (as it was said for counterfeyting the great Seales of England in 1641 in order to the carrying of the Irish Rebellion, and for affirming that they had the late King's authority for the rising) being sent into Ireland a close prysoner under pretense of being to be tryed for his life there, for high Treason, is now not only at Liberty, but restored to his Seate in the House of Lords.
>
> (Bodleian Library *Ms.Eng.hist*, c.487, f.939)

And a little later in the manuscript:

> But though Parliament and people are ready to brake forth into a flame, and the Reports of risings there, and seisures of Garrisons come into England, and forraigne partes also, yet are provocations increased daily, most Irish being judged Innocent, and the Earle of Antrim though proved to be in the first yeares Rebellion is ordered to be released by a Letter of Charles Steward himselfe, who is now growne to that hight of Impudence, that he stickes not to owne his father to have authorized that bloody Rebellion Publishing in a Proclamation [these last four words were struck out and altered to: 'Printing in a letter'] for the vindication of the said Earle of Antrim, that he had not done any thing for which he had not Warrant and Authority from the King his father though it was but too well knowne that he had his heade and hands deepely and early Engaged in the contrivance and carrying on of that bloody designe.
>
> (Ibid., f.958)

Although Ludlow and Baxter were poles apart politically, conventional wisdom hitherto has been that they converged in one important sphere. The secular tone of Ludlow's *Memoirs* matched Baxter's recognition of the priority of constitutional issues in the origins of the Civil War. Neither judgement can now be supported by the evidence. Baxter had no Toland to rewrite his memoirs, though he had a Sylvester to leave some things out. The net effect was similar: the millennial interests of both men have been seriously underrated by later historians. This book offers nothing so sensational as the 'new' Ludlow which Dr Worden has presented to us, but its revision of the conventional view of Baxter complements Dr Worden's findings in some respects. Ironically the two political opponents now converge, not in their secular tone, but in their absence of it: in their millennial commitment. Ludlow's remark – a few pages earlier than the first quotation from Dr Worden's edition cited above – that 'though Charles Steward was not the Anti-Christ spoken of by the Apostle, yet was he one of the kinges that gave his power to the Beast' (*A Voyce from the Watch Tower*, p. 144) would have been impossible for the 'old' Ludlow to have uttered or the 'old' Baxter to have comprehended, and yet would have seemed to the 'new' Baxter, which has been presented in this study, a logical preamble to the discussion of the Antrim commission which followed shortly. And it is in fact significant that Ludlow's discussion of the provocation offered to Protestants by Antrim's release from imprisonment and rehabilitation is preceded by an attack on Baxter's own arch-enemy Bishop Morley. Ludlow claims that 'the rest of the diocessans take a measure by him in what they have to doo' (*Bodleian Library Ms Eng. hist. c.487*, f.938). Fear of Popery and interest in the Apocalypse brought the two opponents closer together than has commonly been supposed: Antrim's pardon provided that link.

INDEX

INDEX OF REFERENCES TO BAXTER'S WRITINGS